Lecture Notes in Computer Science 4677

Commenced Publication in 1973
Founding and Former Series Editors:
Gerhard Goos, Juris Hartmanis, and Jan van Leeuwen

T0224431

Alessandro Aldini   Roberto Gorrieri (Eds.)

Foundations
of Security Analysis
and Design IV

FOSAD 2006/2007 Tutorial Lectures

 Springer

Volume Editors

Alessandro Aldini
Università degli Studi di Urbino "Carlo Bo"
Istituto di Scienze e Tecnologie dell'Informazione
Piazza della Repubblica 13, 61029 Urbino, Italy
E-mail: aldini@sti.uniurb.it

Roberto Gorrieri
Università degli Studi di Bologna
Dipartimento di Scienze dell'Informazione
Mura Anteo Zamboni 7, 40127 Bologna, Italy
E-mail: gorrieri@cs.unibo.it

Library of Congress Control Number: 2007933834

CR Subject Classification (1998): D.4.6, C.2, K.6.5, K.4, D.3, F.3, E.3

LNCS Sublibrary: SL 4 – Security and Cryptology

ISSN   0302-9743
ISBN-10   3-540-74809-1 Springer Berlin Heidelberg New York
ISBN-13   978-3-540-74809-0 Springer Berlin Heidelberg New York

Springer is a part of Springer Science+Business Media

springer.com

© Springer-Verlag Berlin Heidelberg 2007
Printed in Germany

Typesetting: Camera-ready by author, data conversion by Scientific Publishing Services, Chennai, India
Printed on acid-free paper   SPIN: 12119967   06/3180   5 4 3 2 1 0

International School on Foundations of Security Analysis and Design

The last decade has witnessed a widespread shifting of real-life and usual practice operations, which are moving from the real-world scenario toward the Internet world, as shown for instance by the success of electronic payments and Internet banking. At the same time, this fast-growing interest toward the new technologies is open to criticism whenever it is not accompanied with an adequate development of the security machinery, as shown in the past by malfunctions in electronic voting and shopping systems.

The critical aspect of security of computer systems is dealt with by an increasing number of academic and industrial research groups, scientific conferences and events. The "International School on Foundations of Security Analysis and Design" (FOSAD, for short) has been one of the foremost events established with the objective of disseminating knowledge in this critical area and favoring the study of foundations for the analysis and the design of security aspects. FOSAD is mainly addressed to young scientists and graduate students at their initial approaches to the field, but also to researchers aiming at establishing novel scientific collaborations and scientists coming from less-favored and non-leading countries in this field.

FOSAD is held annually at the Residential Centre of Bertinoro, Italy, in the fascinating scenario of a former convent and episcopal fortress that has been transformed into a modern conference facility with computing services and Internet access. The first edition of FOSAD was held in 2000, and since then another six editions (including the present one in September 2007) followed, by attracting about 350 participants and 70 leading scientists of the computer security community worldwide. The Web site of the FOSAD series is available at http://www.sti.uniurb.it/events/fosad/.

The present volume gathers a collection of tutorial lectures from FOSAD 2006 and FOSAD 2007. In the past, three volumes published in the Springer LNCS series were dedicated to FOSAD: LNCS 2171 for FOSAD 2000, LNCS 2946 for FOSAD 2001 and 2002, and LNCS 3655 for FOSAD 2004 and 2005. The contributions to this volume, which range from formal methods to software and critical infrastructures security and from identity-based cryptography to trust and reputation systems, are detailed as follows.

The opening paper by Martín Abadi is an introduction to the design and analysis of security protocols. The author presents the principles of protocol design and of a formalism for protocol analysis. Massimo Bartoletti, Pierpaolo Degano, Gian Luigi Ferrari, and Roberto Zunino present a formal framework for designing and composing secure services. The authors show how to employ a core functional calculus for services and a graphical design language in order to correctly plan secure service orchestrations. Daniel Le Métayer provides an overview of the best industrial practices in IT security analysis. In particular, the paper presents recent research results in the area of formal foundations and powerful tools for security analysis. The contribution by Úlfar Erlingsson outlines the general issues of low-level software security. Concrete details of low-level attacks and defenses are given in the case of C and C++ software compiled into machine code. Fabio Martinelli and Paolo Mori describe a solution to improve the Java native security support. Two examples of the application of the proposed solution, with history-based monitoring of the application behavior, are given in the case of grid computing and mobile devices. The purpose of the chapter by Javier Lopez, Cristina Alcaraz, and Rodrigo Roman is to review and discuss critical information infrastructures, and show how to protect their functionalities and performance against attacks. As an example, the chapter also discusses the role of wireless sensor networks technology in the protection of these infrastructures. The paper by Liqun Chen is a survey in the area of asymmetric key cryptographic methodologies for identity-based cryptography. Audun Jøsang gives an overview of the background, current status, and future trend of trust and reputation systems. In the following chapter, Marcin Czenko, Sandro Etalle, Dongyi Li, and William H. Winsborough present the trust management approach to access control in distributed systems. In particular, they focus on the RT family of role-based trust management languages. Chris Mitchell and Eimear Gallery report on the trusted computing technology for the next-generation mobile devices.

We would like to thank all the institutions that have promoted and founded this school and, in particular, the IFIP Working Group 1.7 on "Theoretical Foundations of Security Analysis and Design," which was established to promote research and education in security-related issues. FOSAD 2007 was sponsored by CNR-IIT, Università di Bologna, and the EU project ARTIST2, and was supported by EATCS-IT, EEF, and ERCIM Working Group on Security and Trust Management. Finally, we also wish to thank the entire staff of the University Residential Centre of Bertinoro for the organizational and administrative support.

July 2007

Alessandro Aldini
Roberto Gorrieri

Table of Contents

Foundations of Security Analysis and Design

Security Protocols: Principles and Calculi

Tutorial Notes

Martín Abadi

Microsoft Research
and
University of California, Santa Cruz

Abstract. This paper is a basic introduction to some of the main themes in the design and analysis of security protocols. It includes a brief explanation of the principles of protocol design and of a formalism for protocol analysis. It is intended as a written counterpart to a tutorial given at the 2006 International School on Foundations of Security Analysis and Design.

1 Introduction

Over the last 30 years, work on security protocols has led to a number of ideas and techniques for protocol design, to a number of protocol implementations, and also to many attacks. Gradually, it has also led to mature techniques for analyzing protocols, and to an understanding of how to develop more robust protocols that address a range of security concerns.

These notes are based on a tutorial on security protocols given at the 2006 International School on Foundations of Security Analysis and Design. The tutorial was an introduction to the following topics:

- security protocols (informally),
- some design principles,
- a formal calculus for protocol analysis: the applied pi calculus,
- automated proof methods and tools, such as ProVerif.

The slides from the tutorial are available on-line [1]. These notes are essentially a summary of the material presented there. They do not aim to provide a balanced survey of the entire field, nor to explain some of its advanced points, which are covered well in research papers. Instead, the notes aim to introduce the basics of security protocols and the applied pi calculus. They may help readers who are starting to study the subject, and may offer some perspectives that would perhaps interest others.

The next section is a general description of security protocols. Section 3 gives an example, informally. Section 4 explains a few principles for the design of protocols. Section 5 is an introduction to informal and formal protocol analysis. Sections 6 and 7 present the applied pi calculus and the ProVerif tool, respectively. Section 8 revisits the example of Section 3. Section 9 concludes by discussing some further work.

A. Aldini and R. Gorrieri (Eds.): FOSAD 2006/2007, LNCS 4677, pp. 1–23, 2007.

2 Security Protocols

Security protocols are concerned with properties such as integrity and secrecy. Primary examples are protocols that establish communication channels with authenticity and confidentiality properties—in other words, communication channels that protect the integrity and secrecy of the data sent between the intended protocol participants. Other examples include protocols for commerce and for electronic voting.

This section describes security protocols in a little more detail. It introduces a protocol due to Needham and Schroeder, which serves as a running example in the rest of these notes.

2.1 Cryptography

In distributed systems, security protocols invariably employ some cryptography [65], so they are sometimes called cryptographic protocols. We call them security protocols in order to emphasize ends over means, and also in order to include some exchanges in which cryptography is not needed or not prominent. For the purposes of these notes, only very simple cryptography is needed.

We focus on symmetric cryptosystems (such as DES and AES). In these, when two principals communicate, they share a key that they use for encryption and for decryption. Therefore, symmetric cryptosystems are also called shared-key cryptosystems. When integrity is required, as it often is, a shared key also serves for producing and for checking message authentication codes (MACs). A MAC is basically a signature, with the limitation that only the principals that know the corresponding shared key can check it, and that any of these principals could produce it. So, although any principal that knows the shared key could convince itself that some other principal has produced a given MAC, it may not be able to convince a judge or some other third party.

In SSL [46] and other practical protocols, multiple shared keys are often associated with each communication channel. For instance, for each point-to-point connection, we may have two shared keys for encryption, one for communication in each direction, and two for MACs, again one per direction. However, these four keys may all be derived from a shared master key. Furthermore, protocols often rely on both symmetric cryptosystems and asymmetric cryptosystems (such as RSA). While we may not explicitly discuss them, many of these variants do fall within the scope of the methods presented in these notes.

As in many informal protocol descriptions, below we assume that the encryption function provides not only secrecy but also authenticity. In other words, we proceed as though the encryption function includes a built-in MAC.

2.2 Other Machinery

There is more to the mechanics of protocols than cryptography. Moreover, protocols exist and should be understood in the context of other security machinery, such as auditing and access control.

Protocols often include timestamps or other proofs of freshness. They may also include sequence numbers for ordering messages. At a lower level, practical protocols also include key identifiers (so that the recipient of an encrypted message knows which key to try), message padding, and facilities for message compression, for instance.

Furthermore, protocols often rely on trusted third parties. These trusted third parties may function as certification authorities, as trusted time servers, and in other roles. Trust is not absolute, nor always appropriate—so protocols often aim to eliminate trusted third parties or to limit the trust placed in them.

2.3 Authentication Protocols

In systems based on the access-control model of security [58], authorization relies on authentication, and protocols that establish communication channels with authenticity and confidentiality properties are often called authentication protocols. There are many such protocols. They typically involve two principals (hosts, users, or services) that wish to communicate, and some trusted third parties. In particular, the two principals may be a client and a server, and the purpose of the channel may be to convey requests and responses between them.

Despite these commonalities, there are also a number of differences across authentication protocols; no single authentication protocol will be suitable for all systems. For performance, designers consider communication, storage, and cryptographic costs, and sometimes trade between them. The choice of cryptographic algorithms is influenced by these cost considerations, and also by matters of convenience and law. In addition, systems rely on synchronized clocks to different extents.

At a higher level, no single authentication protocol will be suitable for all purposes. Protocols vary in their assumptions, in particular with respect to trusted third parties. They also vary in their objectives:

- Some protocols achieve mutual authentication; others achieve only one-way authentication, and in some cases guarantee the anonymity of one of the parties (typically the client).
- Data secrecy is sometimes optional.
- A few protocols include protection against denial-of-service attacks. This protection aims to ensure that protocol participants cannot be easily burdened with many costly cryptographic operations and other expensive work.
- Going beyond the basic security properties, some protocols aim to ensure non-repudiation (so participants cannot later deny some or all of their actions), for instance. A few protocols aim to support plausible deniability, which is roughly the opposite of non-repudiation.

3 An Example

We describe a protocol due to Needham and Schroeder as an example. The protocol is the first from their seminal paper on authentication [74]; it relies on a symmetric cryptosystem. Throughout, we refer to this protocol as the Needham-Schroeder protocol, because of its importance and because we do not consider other protocols by the same authors.

The Needham-Schroeder protocol is one of the classics in this field. It has served as the basis for the Kerberos system [68, 56] and much other subsequent work. Many of its ingredients occur in other protocols, including many recent ones. Recent protocols, however, typically have more moving parts—more modes, options, and layers.

3.1 Model

Needham and Schroeder set out the following informal model:

> We assume that an intruder can interpose a computer in all communication paths, and thus can alter or copy parts of messages, replay messages, or emit false material.
>
> We also assume that each principal has a secure environment in which to compute, such as is provided by a personal computer or would be by a secure shared operating system.

The first assumption is common across the field, and is probably even more reasonable now than it was when it was first formulated. The second assumption is also common, but unfortunately it is often somewhat questionable because of the widespread software failures that viruses and worms exploit.

3.2 The Protocol

In this protocol, A and B are two principals that wish to establish a secure communication session. An authentication server S is a trusted intermediary.

Initially the principals A and B share K_{AS} and K_{BS} with S, respectively. The goal of the protocol is to establish a session key K_{AB} for A and B.

In the course of the protocol, A and B invent the nonces N_A and N_B, respectively. Nonces are quantities generated for the purpose of being fresh. In particular, A can reason that any message that includes N_A was manufactured after N_A's invention; so A can conclude that any such message belongs in the current protocol session, and is not a replay from a previous session. The use of nonces dispenses with the requirement of a single network clock; nonces are still prevalent today, in protocols such as SSL and IKE [46, 53].

Figure 1 depicts the message exchange. Here, we write $\{X\}_K$ for an encryption of the plaintext X under the key K, and X, Y for the concatenation of X and Y (with markers, as needed, in order to avoid ambiguities).

Only A contacts the server S, in Message 1. This message includes N_A. Upon receipt of this message, S generates K_{AB}, which becomes the session key between A and B. In Message 2, S provides this session key to A, under K_{AS}. This message includes A's nonce, as a proof of freshness. Message 2 also includes a certificate (or a "ticket", in Kerberos parlance) under K_{BS} that conveys the session key and A's identity to B. Message 3 transmits this certificate from A to B. After decrypting Message 3 and obtaining the session key, B carries out a handshake with A, in Messages 4 and 5. The use of $N_B - 1$ in Message 5 is somewhat arbitrary; almost any function of N_B would do as long as B can distinguish this message from its own Message 4.

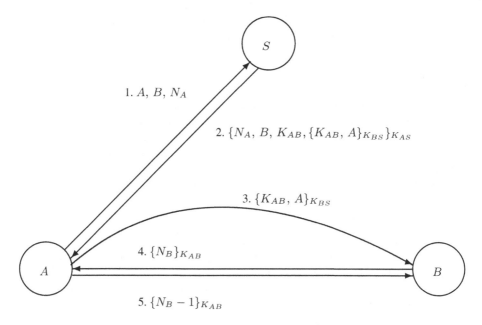

Fig. 1. The Needham-Schroeder protocol

3.3 A Limitation

As Denning and Sacco observed [41], this protocol has a serious limitation:

- Suppose that an attacker has a log of the messages exchanged during a protocol run.
- Suppose further that, long after a run, the attacker may discover the session key K_{AB} somehow—for instance, through a long brute-force attack or as a result of the careless exposure of old key material.
- The attacker may then replay Message 3 to B. Unless B remembers K_{AB} or has some external indication of the attack, B is not able to distinguish the replay from a legitimate, new instance of Message 3.
- The attacker may then conduct a handshake with B. Although B uses a fresh nonce for this handshake, the attacker is able to produce a corresponding response because it knows K_{AB}.
- Subsequently, the attacker may continue to communicate with B under K_{AB}, impersonating A.

In order to address this limitation, one may try to make K_{AB} strong, and to change K_{BS} often, thus limiting the window of vulnerability. One may however prefer to use an improved protocol, in which B and S interact directly (as Needham and Schroeder suggested [75]), or in which messages include timestamps (as Denning and Sacco proposed, and as done in Kerberos).

As this example illustrates, most security protocols have subtleties and flaws. Many of these have to do with cryptography, but many of these do not have to do with the details of cryptographic algorithms. For design, implementation, and analysis, a fairly abstract view of cryptography is often practical.

4 Principles of Protocol Design

While protocol design often proceeds informally, it need not be entirely driven by trial and error. Some general principles can guide the creation and understanding of protocols (e.g., [9,14,79,15]). Such principles serve to simplify protocols and to avoid many mistakes. They also serve to simplify informal reasoning about protocols and their formal analysis [76,28].

In this section we explain some of these principles, with reference to our example.

4.1 Explicit Messages

In the early logics of authentication, an informal process of idealization turned loose protocol narrations into formulas that expressed the perceived intended meanings of messages [37]. Over time, it was noticed that many attacks were identified in the course of this informal process—even more than during the later formal proofs. More broadly, it was noticed that many attacks appeared because of gaps between the actual contents of messages and their intended meanings. This realization and much experience led to the following principle [9]:

> Every message should say what it means: the interpretation of the message should depend only on its content.

In other words, the meaning of the message should not depend on implicit information that is presumed clear from context. Such presumptions are often unreliable in the presence of attackers that do not play by the rules.

As an important special case of this principle, it follows:

> If the identity of a principal is important for the meaning of a message, it is prudent to mention the principal's name explicitly in the message.

For instance, Message 2 of the Needham-Schroeder protocol consists of the ciphertext $\{N_A, B, K_{AB}, \{K_{AB}, A\}_{K_{BS}}\}_{K_{AS}}$. The first three fields N_A, B, K_{AB} of the plaintext message are intended as a statement to A that K_{AB} is a good key for a session with B sometime after the generation of N_A. The name A is implicit, and can be deduced from K_{AS}. Making it explicit would not be costly, and it would lead to a more robust protocol—allowing, for instance, the possibility that the key K_{AS} would be a key for a node with multiple users $(A_1, A_2, \ldots)$. On the other hand, the name B is and must be explicit. Omitting it enables an attack, as follows.

- Suppose that an attacker C intercepts Message 1, replaces B with C, and sends the modified message to S.
- In response, Message 2 includes $\{K_{AC}, A\}_{K_{CS}}$, where K_{CS} is known to C, rather than $\{K_{AB}, A\}_{K_{BS}}$. However, A cannot detect this substitution: A can check its nonce N_A, and obtains K_{AC} and this certificate, but the certificate is opaque to A. The subscript C in K_{AC} is merely a meta-notation; nothing in the key itself indicates that it is shared with C rather than with B.

- Suppose further that C intercepts Message 3 in which A forwards $\{K_{AC}, A\}_{K_{CS}}$ to B. Then C obtains K_{AC} and can conduct a handshake with A, in B's place.
- Subsequently, C may continue to communicate with A under K_{AC}, impersonating B.

Many successful attacks against published protocols resemble this one, and stem from the omission of some names.

Similarly, Message 3 of the Needham-Schroeder protocol consists of the ciphertext $\{K_{AB}, A\}_{K_{BS}}$. To B, this message should mean that K_{AB} is a good key for a session with A. Again, one of the names (B in this case) is implicit, while the other (A) is explicit and is needed in order to thwart an attack. (The attack is left as an easy exercise for the reader.) Remarkably, the meaning of this message does not specify at which time K_{AB} is a good key. While the handshake has something to do with timeliness, the exact significance of $\{N_B\}_{K_{AB}}$ and $\{N_B - 1\}_{K_{AB}}$ is a little unclear. Denning and Sacco exploited these shortcomings in their attack.

Often, the meanings of messages pertain to the goodness of keys. As Needham noted, years later, much progress can be made without further elaboration on what is a good key [73]:

> The statement that a key was "good" for certain communication bundles up all sorts of useful notions—that it was made by a careful agent, had not been scattered about, had sufficient variety, and so forth.

Still, if several kinds of good keys are possible (from different cryptosystems, or with different parameters), then messages should be explicit on which kind is intended.

4.2 Explicit Design

Cryptography is a powerful tool, but a proper understanding of its guarantees, nuances, and limitations is required for its effective use in protocols. Accordingly, the next principle concerns the use of cryptography, rather than the specifics of particular cryptographic algorithms [9].

> Be clear as to why encryption is being done.
> Encryption is not synonymous with security.

In protocols, encryption and other cryptographic functions are used for a variety of purposes.

- Encryption is sometimes used for confidentiality. For example, in Message 2, encryption protects the secrecy of K_{AB}.
- Encryption is sometimes used in order to guarantee authenticity. For example, A may reason that Message 2 is an authentic message from S because of the encryption.
- Encryption sometime serves for proving the presence of a principal or the possession of a secret. Message 5 exemplifies this use.
- Encryption may also serve for binding together the parts of a message. In Message 2, the double encryption may be said to serve this purpose. However, in this example, rewriting the message to $\{N_A, B, K_{AB}\}_{K_{AS}}, \{K_{AB}, A\}_{K_{BS}}$ would work

just as well. Double encryption is not double security—and indeed sometimes it is a source of confusion and insecurity, as in the Woo-Lam protocol [9, 82, 81].
– Encryption is sometimes used in random-number generation, in defining MACs, and in other cryptographic tasks. It is generally best to leave those uses for the lower-level constructions of cryptographic primitives, outside the scope of protocol design.

While the principle above refers to encryption, it also applies to other cryptographic functions. More generally, it is desirable that not only messages but also the protocol design be explicit [14]:

Robust security is about explicitness; one must be explicit about any properties which can be used to attack a public key primitive, such as multiplicative homomorphism, as well as the usual security properties such as naming, typing, freshness, the starting assumptions and what one is trying to achieve.

5   Analysis

The development of methods for describing and analyzing security protocols seems to have started in the early 1980s (e.g., [30, 83, 42, 40, 66, 55]). The field matured considerably in the 1990s. Some of the methods rely on rigorous but informal frameworks, sometimes supporting sophisticated complexity-theoretic definitions and arguments (e.g., [30, 47, 83, 19]). Others rely on formalisms specially tailored for this task (e.g., [37, 80]). Yet others are based on temporal logics, process algebras such as CSP and the pi calculus, and other standard formalisms, sometimes in the context of various theorem-proving tools, such as Isabelle (e.g., [52, 78, 8, 61, 76, 64]). The next section presents the applied pi calculus as an example of this line of work.

Overall, the use of these methods has increased our confidence in some protocols. It has also resulted in the discovery of many protocol limitations and flaws, and in a better understanding of how to design secure protocols.

Many of these methods describe a protocol as a program, written in a programming notation, or as the corresponding set of executions. In addition to the expected principals, this model of the protocol should include an attacker. The attacker has various standard capabilities:

– it may participate in some protocol runs;
– it may know certain data in advance;
– it may intercept messages on some or all communication paths;
– it may inject any messages that it can produce.

The last of these is the most problematic: in order to obtain a realistic model, we should consider non-deterministic attackers, which may for example produce keys and nonces, but without such luck that they always guess the keys on which the security of the protocol depends.

One approach to this problem consists in defining the attacker as some sort of probabilistic program that is subject to complexity bounds. For instance, the attacker may be a probabilistic polynomial-time Turing machine. Such a machine is not able to explore an exponentially large space of possible values for secret keys. This approach can be quite successful in providing a detailed, convincing model of the attacker. Unfortunately, it can be relatively hard to use.

Going back to early work on decision procedures by Dolev and Yao [42], formal methods adopt a simpler solution. They arrange that non-deterministic choice of a key or a nonce always yields a fresh value (much like object allocation in object-oriented languages always returns a fresh address). In this respect, keys and nonces are not ordinary bitstrings. Accordingly, cryptographic operations are treated formally (that is, symbolically). Some assumptions commonly underly these formal methods. For instance, for symmetric encryption, we often find the following assumptions:

- Given K, anyone can compute $\{M\}_K$ from M.
- Conversely, given K, anyone can compute M from $\{M\}_K$.
- $\{M\}_K$ cannot be produced by anyone who does not know M and K.
- M cannot be derived from $\{M\}_K$ by anyone who does not know K (and K cannot be derived from $\{M\}_K$).
- An attempt to decrypt $\{M\}_K$ with an incorrect key K' will result in an evident failure.

Here, M, K, and $\{M\}_K$ represent formal expressions. The first assumption says that anyone with the expressions K and M can obtain the expression $\{M\}_K$; the operation applied is a symbolic abstraction of encryption, rather than a concrete encryption operation on bitstrings. Similarly, the second assumption corresponds to a symbolic abstraction of decryption, and the fifth assumption to a related symbolic check. The third and the fourth assumptions are reflected in the absence of any operations for encrypting or decrypting without the corresponding key.

Despite their somewhat simplistic treatment of cryptography, formal methods are often quite effective, in part because, as noted above, a fairly abstract view of cryptography often suffices in the design, implementation, and analysis of protocols. Formal methods enable relatively simple reasoning, and also benefit from substantial work on proof methods and from extensive tool support.

The simplistic treatment of cryptography does imply inaccuracies, possibly mistakes. The separation of keys and nonces from ordinary data implies that attackers cannot do arbitrary manipulations on keys and nonces. For instance, attackers may not be allowed to do bitwise shifts on keys, if that is not represented as a symbolic operation somehow. Thus, attacks that rely on shifts are excluded by the model, rather than by proofs.

A recent research effort aims to bridge the gap between complexity-theoretic methods and formal methods. It aims to provide rigorous justifications for abstract treatments of cryptography, while still enabling relatively easy formal proofs. For instance, a formal treatment of encryption is sound with respect to a lower-level computational model based on complexity-theoretic assumptions [10]. The formal treatment is simple but fairly typical, with symbolic cryptographic operations. In the computational model, on the other hand, keys and all other cryptographic data are bitstrings, and adversaries have access to the full low-level vocabulary of algorithms on bitstrings. Despite these additional capabilities of the adversaries, the secrecy assertions that can be proved formally are also valid in the lower-level model, not absolutely but with high probability and against adversaries of reasonable computational power. Further research in this area addresses richer classes of systems and additional cryptographic functions (e.g., [16,67,59,60,39]). Further research also considers how to do automatic proofs in a computational model, starting from formal protocol descriptions but with semantics and proof principles from the complexity-theoretic literature (e.g., [26,29]).

6   The Applied Pi Calculus

This section introduces the applied pi calculus [6], focusing on its syntax and its informal semantics. Section 7 describes ProVerif, a tool for the applied pi calculus; Section 8 gives an example of the use of the applied pi calculus.

6.1   Security Protocols in the Pi Calculus

The pi calculus is a minimal language for describing systems of processes that communicate on named channels, with facilities for dynamic creation of new channels [70,69]. We use it here without defining it formally; some definitions appear below, in the context of the applied pi calculus. As usual, we write $\bar{c}\langle\ldots\rangle$ for a message emission and $c(\ldots)$ for a message reception, "." for sequential prefixing, "|" for parallel composition, and "ν" for name restriction. Equations like $A = \ldots$, $B = \ldots$, and $P = \ldots$ are definitions outside the pi calculus: the operator "=" is not part of the calculus itself.

At an abstract level, the pi calculus is sufficient for describing a wide range of systems, including security protocols. For instance, we may describe an abstract version of a trivial one-message protocol as follows:

$$A = \bar{c}\langle V \rangle$$
$$B = c(x).\bar{d}\langle\rangle$$
$$P = (\nu c)(A \mid B)$$

Here, A is a process that sends the message V on the channel c, and B is a process that receives a message on the channel c (with x as the argument variable to be bound to the message), then signals completion by sending an empty message on the channel d. Finally, P is the entire protocol, which consists of the parallel composition of A and B with a restriction on the channel c so that only A and B can access c.

The attacker, left implicit in the definitions of this example, is the context. It may be instantiated to an arbitrary expression Q of the pi calculus, and put in parallel with P, as in $P \mid Q$.

This process representation of the protocol has properties that we may interpret as security properties. In particular, in any context, P is equivalent to a variant P' that sends V' in place of V, for any other message V'. Indeed, P and P' are so trivial that they are equivalent to $\bar{d}\langle\rangle$. Thinking of the context as an attacker, we may say that this property expresses the secrecy of the message V from the attacker.

In more complicated examples, the security properties are less obvious, but they can still be formulated and established (or refuted) using the standard notations and proof techniques of the pi calculus. In particular, the formulations rely on universal quantification over all possible attackers, which are treated as contexts in the pi calculus. This treatment of attackers is both convenient and generally useful.

6.2   The Applied Pi Calculus

As in the small example above, the pi-calculus representations of protocols often model secure channels as primitive, without showing their possible cryptographic implementations. In practice, the channel c of the example may be implemented using a public channel plus a key K shared by A and B. Sending on c requires encryption under K, and receiving on c requires decryption with K. Additional precautions are necessary, for instance in order to prevent replay attacks. None of this implementation detail is exposed in the pi-calculus definitions.

Moreover, even with the abstraction from keys to channels, some protocols are hard to express. The separation of encryption from communication (an important aspect of the work of Needham and Schroeder) can be particularly problematic. For instance, Message 2 of the Needham-Schroeder protocol, from S to A, includes $\{K_{AB}, A\}_{K_{BS}}$, to be forwarded to B. This message component might be modeled as a direct message from S to B on a secure channel—but such a model seems rather indirect, and might not be sound.

One approach to addressing this difficulty consists in developing encodings of encryption in the pi calculus [8, 17]. While this approach may be both viable and interesting, it amounts to a substantial detour.

Another approach to addressing this difficulty relies on extensions of the pi calculus with formal cryptographic operations, such as the spi calculus [8] and the applied pi calculus. The applied pi calculus is essentially the pi calculus plus function symbols that can be used for expressing data structures and cryptographic operations. The spi calculus can be seen as a fragment that focuses on a particular choice of function symbols. In both cases, the function symbols enable finer protocol descriptions. These descriptions may show how a secure channel is implemented with encryption, or how one key is computed from another key. Next we introduce the syntax and the informal semantics of the applied pi calculus.

We start with a sort of variables (such as x and y) and a sort of names (such as n). We use meta-variables u and v to range over both names and variables. We also start with a set of function symbols, such as f, encrypt, and pair. These function symbols have arities and types, which we generally omit in this presentation. In addition to arities and types, the function symbols come with an equational theory (that is, with an equivalence relation on terms with certain closure properties). For instance, for binary function symbols senc and sdec, we may have the usual equation:

$$\mathsf{sdec}(\mathsf{senc}(x, y), y) = x$$

If in addition we have a binary function symbol scheck and a constant symbol ok, we may have the additional equation:

$$\mathsf{scheck}(\mathsf{senc}(x, y), y) = \mathsf{ok}$$

Intuitively, senc and sdec stand for symmetric encryption and decryption, while scheck provides the possibility of checking that a ciphertext is under a given symmetric key.

The set of terms is defined by the grammar:

$U, V ::=$	terms
$c, d, n, s, K, N, \ldots$	name
$x, y, K, \ldots$	variable
$f(U_1, \ldots, U_l)$	function application

where f ranges over the function symbols and $U_1, \ldots, U_l$ match the arity and type of f. Terms are intended to represent messages and other data items manipulated in protocols.

The set of processes is defined by the grammar:

$P, Q, R ::=$	processes
nil	null process
$P \mid Q$	parallel composition
$!P$	replication
$(\nu n)P$	name restriction ("new")
$if\ U = V\ then\ P\ else\ Q$	conditional
$u(x_1, \ldots, x_n).P$	message input
$\overline{u}\langle V_1, \ldots, V_n \rangle.P$	message output

Informally, the semantics of these processes is as follows:

- The null process nil does nothing.
- $P \mid Q$ is the parallel composition of P and Q.
- The replication $!P$ behaves as an infinite number of copies of P running in parallel.
- The process $(\nu n)P$ generates a new name n then behaves as P. The name n is bound, and subject to renaming.

   The use of ν is not limited to generating new channel names. We often use ν more broadly, as a generator of unguessable values. In some cases, those values may serve as nonces or as keys. In others, those values may serve as seeds, and various transformations may be applied for deriving keys from seeds.
- The conditional construct $if\ U = V\ then\ P\ else\ Q$ is standard. Here, $U = V$ represents equality in the equational theory, not strict syntactic identity. We abbreviate it $if\ U = V\ then\ P$ when Q is nil.
- The input process $u(x_1, \ldots, x_n).P$ is ready to input a message with n components from channel u, then to run P with the actual message components replaced for the formal parameters x_1, ..., x_n. We may omit P when it is nil. The variables $x_1, \ldots, x_n$ are bound, and subject to renaming.
- The output process $\overline{u}\langle V_1, \ldots, V_n \rangle.P$ is ready to output a message with n components V_1, ..., V_n on channel u, then to run P. Again, we may omit P when it is nil.

Processes are intended to represent the components of a protocol, but they may also represent attackers, users, or other entities that interact with the protocol.

As an abbreviation, we may also write $let\ x = U\ in\ P$. It can be defined as $(\nu c)(\overline{c}\langle U \rangle \mid c(x).P)$, where c is a name that does not occur in U or in P.

As these definitions indicate, the applied pi calculus is rather abstract. It allows us to omit many details of cryptography and communication. On the other hand, both cryptography and communication are represented in the applied pi calculus. We can describe every message, under what circumstances it is sent, how it is checked upon receipt, and what actions it triggers.

Research on the spi calculus and the applied pi calculus includes the development of formal semantics, the study of equivalences and type systems, the invention of decision procedures for particular problems, the definition of logics, other work on proof techniques and tools, and various applications (e.g., [34, 5, 2, 18, 36, 35, 43, 44, 49, 50, 54]). Research on related formalisms touches on many of these topics as well (e.g., [45, 13, 12, 77, 38]). We discuss only a fraction of this work in the present notes, and refer the reader to the research literature for further material on these topics.

7 ProVerif

A variety of methods for protocol analysis rely at least in part on tool support. They are effective on abstract but detailed models of important protocols. Many of them employ elaborate proof techniques—some general, some specific to this area.

Since the work of Dolev and Yao, there has been much research on special decision procedures. In recent years, these have been most successful for finite-state systems (e.g., [18]). Since the mid 1990s, general-purpose model-checking techniques have also been applied in this area (e.g., [62, 71]). Again, they are usually most effective for finite-state systems. There has also been research on proofs with semi-automatic proof assistants (e.g., [76, 33]). These proofs can require a fair amount of expert human guidance. On the other hand, they can produce sophisticated theorems and attacks, even for infinite-state systems.

Several other approaches rely on programming-language techniques, such as typing, control-flow analysis, and abstract interpretation (e.g., [72, 31, 2]). These techniques are often incomplete but useful in examples and (relatively) easy to use. It turns out that some of these techniques are equivalent, at least in theory [32, 2]. We give a brief description of ProVerif [23, 24, 25, 27], as an important example of this line of work.

ProVerif is an automatic checker for the applied pi calculus. It features a somewhat modified input syntax, in which function symbols are categorized as constructors and destructors. Pairing and encryption are typical examples of constructors, while projection operations and decryption are examples of destructors.

Internally, ProVerif translates from the applied pi calculus to Horn clauses, and thus represents protocols as logic programs. For example, if a process sends the name A on channel c when it receives the name B on channel d, then the Horn clauses that represent the protocol will imply

$$mess(d, B) \rightarrow mess(c, A)$$

where $mess$ is a predicate that indicates the possible presence of a message on a channel. Some of the Horn clauses deal with communication and with cryptography (not specifically to a protocol). For example, we may have:

$$attacker(x) \wedge attacker(y) \rightarrow mess(x, y)$$
$$attacker(x) \wedge attacker(y) \rightarrow attacker(\mathsf{senc}(x, y))$$

where $attacker$ is a predicates that characterizes the knowledge of an attacker.

ProVerif then applies automated analysis techniques based on resolution to these Horn clauses. It contains proof methods for certain classes of properties. These include secrecy and authenticity properties. In particular, the secrecy of a name s may be formulated in terms of whether or not $attacker(s)$ is provable.

ProVerif has been effective on a wide range of examples. For instance, it can treat the Needham-Schroeder protocol without much difficulty, using definitions similar to those presented in Section 8. More advanced examples include a protocol for certified email [3], the JFK protocol [11] for keying for IP security [4], some password-based protocols [27], some electronic-voting protocols [57], and several web-services protocols [63, 20]. ProVerif seems to be fairly accessible to new users. Remarkably, it has also served as a powerful basis for sophisticated tools for analyzing web-services protocols [22].

ProVerif proofs typically take seconds or minutes, though longer proofs are possible too. ProVerif guarantees termination only in certain cases [28]. Manual arguments are sometimes combined with automatic proofs.

8   An Example, Revisited

As an example, we write the Needham-Schroeder protocol in the applied pi calculus.

An analysis of this example may be done by hand, using a variety of proof techniques for the applied pi calculus that go beyond the scope of these notes. An analysis may also be done automatically with ProVerif, as mentioned above.

8.1   Preliminaries

We assume that e is a public channel on which all principals may communicate. Therefore, we do not restrict the scope of e with the ν operator. We do not represent the details of addressing and routing. In our formulation of the code, it is possible for a principal to receive a message intended for some other principal, and for the processing to get stuck. It is straightforward to do better. We choose this simplistic model because the details of addressing are mostly orthogonal to the primary security concerns in this protocol. In other protocols, the details of addressing may be more important, for instance if one is interested in hiding the identities of the principals that communicate, in order to obtain privacy guarantees (e.g., [7]).

We use the following function symbols:

- We use constant symbols A, B, ... for principal names.
- We also use the function symbols introduced above for symmetric cryptography (senc, sdec, scheck, and ok).
- We use two unary function symbols that we write in postfix notation, as -1 and $+1$, with the equation $(x - 1) + 1 = x$.

  While this equation may not seem surprising, it is worth noting that it is not essential to writing the processes that represent the protocol. We introduce it because we wish to emphasize that anyone (including an attacker) can invert the -1 function. Without this equation, -1 might appear to be a one-way function, so one might wrongly expect that it would be impossible to recover N_A from $N_A - 1$.

Similarly we could add other equations, such as $(x + 1) - 1 = x$. We return to the subject of choosing equations in Section 8.4.

- We also assume tupling and the corresponding projection operations. We write $(U_1, \ldots, U_n)$ for the tuple of $U_1, \ldots, U_n$, for any n, and write p_i for the projection function that retrieves U_i, for $i = 1..n$, with the equation $\mathsf{p}_i((x_1, \ldots, x_n)) = x_i$.
- Finally, we introduce a binary function symbol skeygen. We use skeygen to map a master key and a principal name to a symmetric key. Relying on this mapping, the server S needs to remember only a master key K_S, and can recover K_{AS} by computing $\mathsf{skeygen}(K_S, A)$ and K_{BS} by computing $\mathsf{skeygen}(K_S, B)$.

Thus, we model a practical, modern strategy for reducing storage requirements at S. An alternative set of definitions might encode a table of shared keys at S.

8.2 A First Version

As an initial attempt, we may model the messages in the protocol rather directly. We write a process for each of A, B, and S, then combine them.

The code for A includes a top-level definition of K_{AS} (formally introduced as a variable, not a name). We do not model more realistic details of how A may obtain K_{AS}. We write the code for A in terms of auxiliary processes A_1, A_2, ... Basically, A_i represents A at Message i of a protocol execution. For instance, A_1 generates N_A, then sends A, B, N_A on e, then proceeds to A_2. In turn, A_2 receives a message x, checks that it is a ciphertext under the expected key, decrypts it, extracts four components from the plaintext, and checks that N_A is the first component and B the second, then proceeds to A_3; a failure in any of the verifications causes the processing to stop. Each of these auxiliary processes may have free names and variables bound in previous processes; for instance N_A is bound in A_1 and used in A_2.

$$A = let\ K_{AS} = \mathsf{skeygen}(K_S, A)\ in\ A_1$$
$$A_1 = (\nu N_A)\overline{e}\langle A, B, N_A \rangle.A_2$$
$$A_2 = e(x).if\ \mathsf{scheck}(x, K_{AS}) = \mathsf{ok}\ then$$
$$\qquad let\ x' = \mathsf{sdec}(x, K_{AS})\ in$$
$$\qquad let\ x_1 = \mathsf{p}_1(x')\ in$$
$$\qquad let\ x_2 = \mathsf{p}_2(x')\ in$$
$$\qquad let\ x_3 = \mathsf{p}_3(x')\ in$$
$$\qquad let\ x_4 = \mathsf{p}_4(x')\ in$$
$$\qquad if\ x_1 = N_A\ then$$
$$\qquad if\ x_2 = B\ then\ A_3$$
$$A_3 = \overline{e}\langle x_4 \rangle.A_4$$
$$A_4 = e(x_5).if\ \mathsf{scheck}(x_5, x_3) = \mathsf{ok}\ then\ A_5$$
$$A_5 = \overline{e}\langle \mathsf{senc}((\mathsf{sdec}(x_5, x_3) - 1), x_3) \rangle$$

Similarly, we write the code for S as follows:

$$S = S_1$$
$$S_1 = e(x_1, x_2, x_3).S_2$$
$$S_2 = (\nu K)let\ x' = \mathsf{senc}((K, x_1), \mathsf{skeygen}(K_S, x_2))\ in$$
$$\qquad \overline{e}\langle \mathsf{senc}((x_3, x_2, K, x'), \mathsf{skeygen}(K_S, x_1)) \rangle$$

Here the key K stands for the new symmetric key for communication between clients (named K_{AB} above for clients A and B).

Finally, we write the code for B as follows:

$$B = let \ K_{BS} = \text{skeygen}(K_S, B) \ in \ B_3$$
$$B_3 = e(x).if \ \text{scheck}(x, K_{BS}) = \text{ok} \ then$$
$$let \ x' = \text{sdec}(x, K_{BS}) \ in$$
$$let \ x_1 = \text{p}_1(x') \ in$$
$$let \ x_2 = \text{p}_2(x') \ in \ B_4$$
$$B_4 = (\nu N_B)\overline{e}\langle \text{senc}(N_B, x_1)\rangle.B_5$$
$$B_5 = e(y).if \ \text{scheck}(y, x_1) = \text{ok} \ then$$
$$if \ \text{sdec}(y, x_1) - 1 = N_B - 1 \ then \ nil$$

We assemble the pieces so as to represent a system with A, B, and S:

$$P = (\nu K_S)(A \mid B \mid S)$$

8.3 A Second Version

The first version of the code is not entirely satisfactory in several respects.

– A appears to initiate a session with B spontaneously, and communication stops entirely after a shared key is established. For instance, B checks the last message, but stops independently of whether the check succeeds.

  A more complete model of the protocol would show that A initiates a session because of some event. This event may for example come from a process R_A that represents an application that uses the protocol at A. Upon completion of a successful exchange, the resulting key may be provided to the application. (Alternatively, the protocol could include its own layer for encrypted data communications, like SSL's record layer.) Similarly, upon completion of a successful exchange, the resulting key and the identity of the other endpoint could be passed to a process R_B at B, which may check the identity against an access-control policy. Thereafter, R_A and R_B may use the session key; they should never use the master key K_S.

– If the possibility of session-key compromise is important, as indicated by Denning and Sacco, then it should be modeled. For instance, upon completion of a successful exchange, the session key may be broadcast. An analysis of the protocol without such an addition would not detect the possibility of an attack that relies on the compromise of old session keys.

  In a model with user processes R_A and R_B, we may simply consider the possibility that one of these processes leaks old session keys.

– A should not be limited to initiating one session, and the identity of the principals A and B should not be fixed. Rather, each principal may engage in the protocol in the role of A or B, or even in both roles simultaneously, multiple times.

  Therefore, the code for these roles should use, as a parameter, the claimed name of the principal that is running the code. In addition, the code should be replicated.

We arrive at the following variant of our definitions for A:

$$A(x_A) = (\nu c)(\nu d)(R_A \mid let\ K_{AS} = \text{skeygen}(K_S, x_A)\ in\ !c(x_B).A_1)$$
$$A_1 = (\nu N_A)\overline{e}\langle x_A, x_B, N_A\rangle.A_2$$
$$A_2 = \text{as above, except for the last line, which becomes}$$
$$if\ x_2 = x_B\ then\ A_3$$
$$A_3 = \text{as above}$$
$$A_4 = \text{as above}$$
$$A_5 = \overline{e}\langle\text{senc}((\text{sdec}(x_5, x_3) - 1), x_3)\rangle.\overline{d}\langle x_3, x_B\rangle$$

Here the variables x_A and x_B represent A's and B's names, respectively. Channels c and d are for communication between R_A and the rest of the code. Channel c conveys the identity of the other endpoint; channel d returns this identity and a session key; R_A may then use the session key, and perhaps leak it. A replication indicates that an unbounded number of sessions may be initiated.

Similarly, we revise the code for B as follows:

$$B(x_B) = (\nu d)(R_B \mid let\ K_{BS} = \text{skeygen}(K_S, x_B)\ in\ !B_3)$$
$$B_3 = \text{as above}$$
$$B_4 = \text{as above}$$
$$B_5 = e(y).if\ \text{scheck}(y, x_1) = \text{ok}\ then$$
$$if\ \text{sdec}(y, x_1) - 1 = N_B - 1\ then\ \overline{d}\langle x_1, x_2\rangle$$

As in the code for A, channel d conveys the session key and the identity of the other endpoint. Again, a replication indicates that an unbounded number of sessions may be initiated.

In S, only an extra replication is needed:

$$S = !S_1$$
$$S_1 = \text{as above}$$
$$S_2 = \text{as above}$$

Suppose that we wish to represent a system with client principals named $C_1, \ldots, C_n$, all of them able to play the roles of A and B, and all of them with the same application code for each for the roles. The corresponding assembly is:

$$P = (\nu K_S)(A(C_1) \mid B(C_1) \mid \ldots \mid A(C_n) \mid B(C_n) \mid S)$$

Many variants and elaborations are possible. For instance, some of the checks may safely be removed from the code. Since the applied pi calculus is essentially a programming language, protocol models are enormously malleable. However, complex models are rarely profitable—the point of diminishing returns is reached fairly quickly in the analysis of most protocols.

8.4 Discussion

As in the pi calculus, scoping can be the basis of security properties for processes in the applied pi calculus. Moreover, attackers can be treated as contexts for processes. In our example, the scoping on K_S reflects that it cannot be used by attackers. Principals other than S use K_S only as prescribed in their code, which is given explicitly as part of the process P above.

On the other hand, the added expressiveness of the applied pi calculus enables writing detailed examples, such as this one. Not only we can represent cryptographic operations, but we need not commit to a particular cryptosystem: we can introduce new function symbols and equations as needed. The awareness of such extensibility is far from new: it appears already in Merritt's dissertation [66, page 60]. This extensibility can be a cause of concerns about soundness. Indeed, we may want to have a method for deciding whether a given set of rules captures "enough" properties of an underlying cryptosystem. At present, the most attractive approach to this problem consists in developing complexity-theoretic foundations for formal methods.

The applied pi calculus also gives rise to the possibility that a process may reveal a term that contains a fresh name s without revealing s itself. For instance, in our example, the process reveals an encryption of a session key, by sending this encryption on the public channel e, without necessarily disclosing the session key. This possibility does not arise in the pure pi calculus, where each name is either completely private to a process or completely known to its context. Technically, this possibility is a significant source of complications in reasoning about security in the applied pi calculus. These complications should not be too surprising, however: they reflect the difficulty of reasoning about security protocols.

9   Outlook

The development of new security protocols remains active. As mentioned in Section 3, recent protocols typically have many moving parts—many modes, options, and layers. Their complexity can be a source of serious concerns. Moreover, from time to time, security protocols are used in new contexts, in which their assumptions may not hold exactly. We may therefore conjecture that understanding how to design and analyze security protocols will remain important in the coming years. What new research will be necessary and most fruitful remains open to debate.

The applied pi calculus and its relatives are idealized programming languages. As formal analysis matures, it becomes applicable to more practical programming languages, at least for protocol code written in a stylized manner [51, 21, 48]. For such code, it is possible to translate to the applied pi calculus—more specifically to the dialect understood by ProVerif—and to obtain automatic proofs. We may expect that these stylistic requirements will be relaxed over time. We may also expect that general-purpose static analysis techniques (not specifically developed for security) will be helpful in this progress. Moreover, in light of some of the research described in Section 5, we may expect to obtain not only formal but also complexity-theoretic security results. With this further development, formalisms may ultimately be externally visible neither in protocol descriptions (which would be in ordinary programming languages) nor in security guarantees.

Acknowledgments

These notes are largely based on joint work with Bruno Blanchet, Mike Burrows, Cédric Fournet, Andy Gordon, and Roger Needham. Bruno Blanchet, Cédric Fournet, and Andy Gordon commented on a draft of these notes. I am grateful to all of them.

I am also grateful to the organizers of the 2006 International School on Foundations of Security Analysis and Design for inviting me to lecture and then for the encouragement to write these notes.

This work was partly supported by the National Science Foundation under Grants CCR-0208800 and CCF-0524078.

References

1. Abadi, M.: Security protocols: Principles and calculi. Lectures at 6th International School on Foundations of Security Analysis and Design, (September 2006), Slides at http://www.sti.uniurb.it/events/fosad06/papers/Abadi-fosad06.pdf
2. Abadi, M., Blanchet, B.: Analyzing security protocols with secrecy types and logic programs. Journal of the ACM 52(1), 102–146 (2005)
3. Abadi, M., Blanchet, B.: Computer-assisted verification of a protocol for certified email. Science of Computer Programming 58(1-2), 3–27 (2005)
4. Abadi, M., Blanchet, B., Fournet, C.: Just Fast Keying in the pi calculus. ACM Transactions on Information and System Security (to appear, 2007)
5. Abadi, M., Cortier, V.: Deciding knowledge in security protocols under equational theories. Theoretical Computer Science 367(1-2), 2–32 (2006)
6. Abadi, M., Fournet, C.: Mobile values, new names, and secure communication. In: 28th ACM Symposium on Principles of Programming Languages (POPL'01), pp. 104–115 (January 2001)
7. Abadi, M., Fournet, C.: Private authentication. Theoretical Computer Science 322(3), 427–476 (2004)
8. Abadi, M., Gordon, A.D.: A calculus for cryptographic protocols: The spi calculus. Information and Computation 148(1), 1–70 (1998) (An extended version appeared as Digital Equipment Corporation Systems Research Center report No. 149, January 1998)
9. Abadi, M., Needham, R.: Prudent engineering practice for cryptographic protocols. IEEE Transactions on Software Engineering 22(1), 6–15 (1996)
10. Abadi, M., Rogaway, P.: Reconciling two views of cryptography (The computational soundness of formal encryption). Journal of Cryptology 15(2), 103–127 (2002)
11. Aiello, W., Bellovin, S.M., Blaze, M., Canetti, R., Ioannidis, J., Keromytis, A.D., Reingold, O.: Just Fast Keying: Key agreement in a hostile internet. ACM Transactions on Information and System Security 7(2), 242–273 (2004)
12. Amadio, R., Lugiez, D.: On the reachability problem in cryptographic protocols. In: Palamidessi, C. (ed.) CONCUR 2000. LNCS, vol. 1877, pp. 380–395. Springer, Heidelberg (2000)
13. Amadio, R., Prasad, S.: The game of the name in cryptographic tables. In: Thiagarajan, P.S., Yap, R.H.C. (eds.) ASIAN 1999. LNCS, vol. 1742, pp. 15–27. Springer, Heidelberg (1999)
14. Anderson, R., Needham, R.: Robustness principles for public key protocols. In: Coppersmith, D. (ed.) CRYPTO 1995. LNCS, vol. 963, pp. 236–247. Springer, Heidelberg (1995)
15. Aura, T.: Strategies against replay attacks. In: 10th IEEE Computer Security Foundations Workshop, pp. 59–68 (1997)

16. Backes, M., Pfitzmann, B., Waidner, M.: A composable cryptographic library with nested operations. In: 10th ACM conference on Computer and Communications security (CCS'03), pp. 220–230 (October 2003)
17. Baldamus, M., Parrow, J., Victor, B.: Spi calculus translated to pi-calculus preserving maytests. In: 19th Annual IEEE Symposium on Logic in Computer Science (LICS'04), pp. 22–31 (July 2004)
18. Baudet, M.: Sécurité des protocoles cryptographiques: aspects logiques et calculatoires. PhD thesis, Ecole Normale Supérieure de Cachan (2007)
19. Bellare, M., Rogaway, P.: Entity authentication and key distribution. In: Stinson, D.R. (ed.) CRYPTO 1993. LNCS, vol. 773, pp. 232–249. Springer, Heidelberg (1994)
20. Bhargavan, K., Fournet, C., Gordon, A.D.: Verifying policy-based security for web services. In: ACM Conference on Computer and Communications Security (CCS'04), pp. 268–277 (October 2004)
21. Bhargavan, K., Fournet, C., Gordon, A.D.: Verified reference implementations of WS-security protocols. In: Bravetti, M., Núñez, M., Zavattaro, G. (eds.) WS-FM 2006. LNCS, vol. 4184, pp. 88–106. Springer, Heidelberg (2006)
22. Bhargavan, K., Fournet, C., Gordon, A.D., Pucella, R.: TulaFale: A security tool for web services. In: de Boer, F.S., Bonsangue, M.M., Graf, S., de Roever, W.-P. (eds.) FMCO 2003. LNCS, vol. 3188, pp. 197–222. Springer, Heidelberg (2004)
23. Blanchet, B.: An efficient cryptographic protocol verifier based on Prolog rules. In: 14th IEEE Computer Security Foundations Workshop, pp. 82–96 (June 2001)
24. Blanchet, B.: From secrecy to authenticity in security protocols. In: Hermenegildo, M.V., Puebla, G. (eds.) SAS 2002. LNCS, vol. 2477, pp. 342–359. Springer, Heidelberg (2002)
25. Blanchet, B.: Automatic proof of strong secrecy for security protocols. In: 2004 IEEE Symposium on Security and Privacy, pp. 86–100 (May 2004)
26. Blanchet, B.: A computationally sound mechanized prover for security protocols. In: 2006 IEEE Symposium on Security and Privacy, pp. 140–154 (May 2006)
27. Blanchet, B., Abadi, M., Fournet, C.: Automated verification of selected equivalences for security protocols. Journal of Logic and Algebraic Programming (to appear, 2007)
28. Blanchet, B., Podelski, A.: Verification of cryptographic protocols: Tagging enforces termination. In: Gordon, A.D. (ed.) Foundations of Software Science and Computation Structures: 6th International Conference, FOSSACS 2003, Held as Part of the Joint European Conferences on Theory and Practice of Software, ETAPS 2003, Warsaw, Poland, April 7-11, 2003. LNCS, vol. 2620, pp. 136–152. Springer, Heidelberg (2003)
29. Blanchet, B., Pointcheval, D.: Automated security proofs with sequences of games. In: Dwork, C. (ed.) CRYPTO 2006. LNCS, vol. 4117, pp. 537–554. Springer, Heidelberg (2006)
30. Blum, M., Micali, S.: How to generate cryptographically strong sequences of pseudo random bits. In: 23rd Annual Symposium on Foundations of Computer Science (FOCS 82), pp. 112–117 (1982)
31. Bodei, C., Degano, P., Nielson, F., Nielson, H.: Flow logic for Dolev-Yao secrecy in cryptographic processes. Future Generation Computer Systems 18(6), 747–756 (2002)
32. Bodei, C.: Security Issues in Process Calculi. PhD thesis, Università di Pisa (January 2000)
33. Bolignano, D.: Towards a mechanization of cryptographic protocol verification. In: Grumberg, O. (ed.) CAV 1997. LNCS, vol. 1254, pp. 131–142. Springer, Heidelberg (1997)
34. Boreale, M., De Nicola, R., Pugliese, R.: Proof techniques for cryptographic processes. SIAM J. Comput. 31(3), 947–986 (2001)
35. Borgström, J., Briais, S., Nestmann, U.: Symbolic bisimulation in the spi calculus. In: Gardner, P., Yoshida, N. (eds.) CONCUR 2004. LNCS, vol. 3170, pp. 161–176. Springer, Heidelberg (2004)
36. Borgström, J., Nestmann, U.: On bisimulations for the spi calculus. In: Kirchner, H., Ringeissen, C. (eds.) AMAST 2002. LNCS, vol. 2422, pp. 287–303. Springer, Heidelberg (2002)

37. Burrows, M., Abadi, M., Needham, R.: A logic of authentication. Proceedings of the Royal Society of London A 426, 233–271 (1989) (A preliminary version appeared as Digital Equipment Corporation Systems Research Center report No. 39, February 1989)
38. Datta, A., Derek, A., Mitchell, J.C., Pavlovic, D.: A derivation system and compositional logic for security protocols. Journal of Computer Security 13(3), 423–482 (2005)
39. Datta, A., Derek, A., Mitchell, J.C., Roy, A.: Protocol composition logic (PCL). Electronic Notes in Theoretical Computer Science 172(1), 311–358 (2007)
40. DeMillo, R.A., Lynch, N.A., Merritt, M.: Cryptographic protocols. In: 14th Annual ACM Symposium on Theory of Computing, pp. 383–400 (1982)
41. Denning, D.E., Sacco, G.M.: Timestamps in key distribution protocols. Communications of the ACM 24(7), 533–535 (1981)
42. Dolev, D., Yao, A.C.: On the security of public key protocols. IEEE Transactions on Information Theory IT-29(12), 198–208 (1983)
43. Durante, L., Sisto, R., Valenzano, A.: A state-exploration technique for spi-calculus testing-equivalence verification. In: Formal Techniques for Distributed System Development, FORTE/PSTV. IFIP Conference Proceedings, vol. 183, pp. 155–170. Kluwer, Dordrecht (2000)
44. Durante, L., Sisto, R., Valenzano, A.: Automatic testing equivalence verification of spi calculus specifications. ACM Transactions on Software Engineering and Methodology 12(2), 222–284 (2003)
45. Focardi, R., Gorrieri, R.: The compositional security checker: A tool for the verification of information flow security properties. IEEE Transactions on Software Engineering 23(9), 550–571 (1997)
46. Freier, A.O., Karlton, P., Kocher, P.C.: The SSL protocol: Version 3.0 (November 1996), http://www.mozilla.org/projects/security/pki/nss/ssl/draft302.txt
47. Goldwasser, S., Micali, S.: Probabilistic encryption. Journal of Computer and System Sciences 28, 270–299 (1984)
48. Gordon, A.D.: Provable implementations of security protocols. In: 21st Annual IEEE Symposium on Logic in Computer Science (LICS'06), pp. 345–346 (2006)
49. Gordon, A.D., Jeffrey, A.: Authenticity by typing for security protocols. In: 14th IEEE Computer Security Foundations Workshop, pp. 145–159 (June 2001)
50. Gordon, A.D., Jeffrey, A.: Types and effects for asymmetric cryptographic protocols. In: 15th IEEE Computer Security Foundations Workshop, pp. 77–91 (June 2002)
51. Goubault-Larrecq, J., Parrennes, F.: Cryptographic protocol analysis on real C code. In: Cousot, R. (ed.) VMCAI 2005. LNCS, vol. 3385, pp. 363–379. Springer, Heidelberg (2005)
52. Gray III, J.W., Ip, K.F.E., Lui, K.-S.: Provable security for cryptographic protocols—exact analysis and engineering applications. In: 10th IEEE Computer Security Foundations Workshop, pp. 45–58 (1997)
53. Harkins, D., Carrel, D.: RFC 2409: The Internet Key Exchange (IKE) (November 1998), http://www.ietf.org/rfc/rfc2409.txt
54. Hüttel, H.: Deciding framed bisimilarity. In: 4th International Workshop on Verification of Infinite-State Systems (INFINITY'02), pp. 1–20 (August 2002)
55. Kemmerer, R.A., Meadows, C., Millen, J.K.: Three systems for cryptographic protocol analysis. Journal of Cryptology 7(2), 79–130 (1994)
56. Kohl, J., Neuman, C.: RFC 1510: The Kerberos network authentication service (v5) (September 1993), ftp://ftp.isi.edu/in-notes/rfc1510.txt
57. Kremer, S., Ryan, M.D.: Analysis of an electronic voting protocol in the applied pi calculus. In: Sagiv, M. (ed.) ESOP 2005. LNCS, vol. 3444, pp. 186–200. Springer, Heidelberg (2005)

58. Lampson, B.W.: Protection. In: 5th Princeton Conference on Information Sciences and Systems, pp. 437–443 (1971)

59. Laud, P.: Symmetric encryption in automatic analyses for confidentiality against active adversaries. In: 2004 IEEE Symposium on Security and Privacy, pp. 71–85 (May 2004)

60. Laud, P.: Secrecy types for a simulatable cryptographic library. In: 12th ACM Conference on Computer and Communications Security (CCS'05), pp. 26–35 (November 2005)

61. Lincoln, P., Mitchell, J., Mitchell, M., Scedrov, A.: A probabilistic poly-time framework for protocol analysis. In: 5th ACM Conference on Computer and Communications Security (CCS'98), pp. 112–121 (1998)

62. Lowe, G.: Breaking and fixing the Needham-Schroeder public-key protocol using FDR. In: Margaria, T., Steffen, B. (eds.) TACAS 1996. LNCS, vol. 1055, pp. 147–166. Springer, Heidelberg (1996)

63. Lux, K.D., May, M.J., Bhattad, N.L., Gunter, C.A.: WSEmail: Secure internet messaging based on web services. In: ICWS '05: Proceedings of the IEEE International Conference on Web Services, pp. 75–82 (2005)

64. Lynch, N.: I/O automaton models and proofs for shared-key communication systems. In: 12th IEEE Computer Security Foundations Workshop, pp. 14–29 (1999)

65. Menezes, A.J., van Oorschot, P.C., Vanstone, S.A.: Handbook of Applied Cryptography. CRC Press, Boca Raton (1996)

66. Merritt, M.J.: Cryptographic Protocols. PhD thesis, Georgia Institute of Technology (February 1983)

67. Micciancio, D., Warinschi, B.: Soundness of formal encryption in the presence of active adversaries. In: Naor, M. (ed.) TCC 2004. LNCS, vol. 2951, pp. 133–151. Springer, Heidelberg (2004)

68. Miller, S.P., Neuman, B.C., Schiller, J.I., Saltzer, J.H.: Kerberos authentication and authorization system, Project Athena technical plan, section E.2.1. Technical report. MIT, Cambridge (1987)

69. Milner, R.: Communicating and Mobile Systems: the π-Calculus. Cambridge University Press, Cambridge (1999)

70. Milner, R., Parrow, J., Walker, D.: A calculus of mobile processes, parts I and II. Information and Computation, 100, 1–40, 41–77 (1992)

71. Mitchell, J.C., Shmatikov, V., Stern, U.: Finite-state analysis of SSL 3.0. In: 7th USENIX Security Symposium, pp. 201–216 (January 1998)

72. Monniaux, D.: Abstracting cryptographic protocols with tree automata. Science of Computer Programming 47(2-3), 177–202 (2003)

73. Needham, R.M.: Logic and over-simplification. In: 13th Annual IEEE Symposium on Logic in Computer Science, pp. 2–3 (1998)

74. Needham, R.M., Schroeder, M.D.: Using encryption for authentication in large networks of computers. Communications of the ACM 21(12), 993–999 (1978)

75. Needham, R.M., Schroeder, M.D.: Authentication revisited. Operating Systems Review 21(1), 7 (1987)

76. Paulson, L.C.: The inductive approach to verifying cryptographic protocols. Journal of Computer Security 6(1-2), 85–128 (1998)

77. Ramanathan, A., Mitchell, J., Scedrov, A., Teague, V.: Probabilistic bisimulation and equivalence for security analysis of network protocols. In: Walukiewicz, I. (ed.) FOSSACS 2004. LNCS, vol. 2987, pp. 468–483. Springer, Heidelberg (2004)

78. Schneider, S.: Security properties and CSP. In: 1996 IEEE Symposium on Security and Privacy, pp. 174–187 (1996)

79. Syverson, P.: Limitations on design principles for public key protocols. In: 1996 IEEE Symposium on Security and Privacy, pp. 62–73 (1996)

80. Thayer Fábrega, F.J., Herzog, J.C., Guttman, J.D.: Strand spaces: Why is a security protocol correct? In: 1998 IEEE Symposium on Security and Privacy, pp. 160–171 (May 1998)
81. Woo, T.Y.C., Lam, S.S.: Authentication for distributed systems. Computer 25(1), 39–52 (1992)
82. Woo, T.Y.C., Lam, S.S.: A lesson on authentication protocol design. Operating Systems Review 28(3), 24–37 (1994)
83. Yao, A.C.: Theory and applications of trapdoor functions. In: 23rd Annual Symposium on Foundations of Computer Science (FOCS 82), pp. 80–91 (1982)

Secure Service Orchestration

Massimo Bartoletti, Pierpaolo Degano, Gian Luigi Ferrari, and Roberto Zunino

Dipartimento di Informatica, Università di Pisa

Abstract. We present a framework for designing and composing services in a secure manner. Services can enforce security policies locally, and can invoke other services in a "call-by-contract" fashion. This mechanism offers a significant set of opportunities, each driving secure ways to compose services. We discuss how to correctly plan service orchestrations in some relevant classes of services and security properties. To this aim, we propose both a core functional calculus for services and a graphical design language. The core calculus is called λ^{req} [10]. It features primitives for selecting and invoking services that respect given behavioural requirements. Critical code can be enclosed in security framings, with a possibly nested, local scope. These framings enforce safety properties on execution histories. A type and effect system over-approximates the actual run-time behaviour of services. Effects include the actions with possible security concerns, as well as information about which services may be selected at run-time. A verification step on these effects allows for detecting the viable plans that drive the selection of those services that match the security requirements on demand.

1 Introduction

The Web service protocol stack (WSDL, UDDI, SOAP, WSBPEL) offers basic support for the development of service-oriented architectures, including facilities to publish, discover and orchestrate services. Although this has been extremely valuable to highlight the key innovative features of the service-oriented approach, experience has singled out several limiting factors of the service protocol stack, mainly because of the purely "syntactic" nature of standards. This has lead to the idea of extending the stack with higher level, "semantic" functionalities. For instance, the design and exploitation of service ontologies is a first attempt to address these concerns.

A challenging issue of the service approach is how to *orchestrate* existing services into more complex ones, by properly selecting and configuring services so to guarantee that their composition enjoys some desirable properties. These properties may involve *functional* aspects, speaking about the goals attained by a service, and also *non-functional* aspects, like e.g. security, availability, performance, transactionality, quality of service, etc. [45].

In this paper we describe a semantics-based framework to model and orchestrate services in the presence of both functional and non-functional constraints, with a special concern for security properties. The formal foundation of our work

A. Aldini and R. Gorrieri (Eds.): FOSAD 2006/2007, LNCS 4677, pp. 24–74, 2007.

is λ^{req} [10,6], a core calculus for securely orchestrating services. The λ^{req} calculus extends the λ-calculus with primitive constructs to describe and invoke services in a *call-by-contract* fashion. Services are modelled as functions with side effects. These side effects represent the action of accessing security-critical resources, and they are logged into *histories*. A run-time security monitor may inspect histories, and forbids those executions that would violate the prescribed policies.

Unlike standard discovery mechanisms that match syntactic signatures only, ours also implements a matchmaking algorithm based on service behaviour. This algorithm exploits static analysis techniques to resolve the call-by-contract involved in a service orchestration. The published interface of a service takes the form of an annotated type, which represents both the signature of the service (i.e. its input-output information) and a suitable semantic abstraction of the service behaviour. In our call-by-contract selection, the client is required to know neither the service name nor its location. Operationally, the service registry is searched for a service with a functional type (the service signature) matching the request type; also, the semantic abstraction must respect the non-functional constraints imposed by the request. Our orchestration machinery constructs a *plan* for the execution of services, e.g. a binding between requests and service locations, guaranteeing that the properties on demand are always satisfied.

We envisage the impact of our approach on the service protocol stack as follows. First, it requires extending services description languages: besides the standard WSDL attributes, service description should include semantic information about service behaviour. Moreover, the call-by-contract invocation mechanism adds a further layer to the standard service protocol stack: the *planning* layer. This layer provides the orchestrator with the plans guaranteeing that the orchestrated services always respect the required properties. Hence, before starting the execution of the orchestration, the orchestrator engines collects the relevant service plans by inquiring the planning layer. These plans enable the orchestration engine to resolve all the requests in the initiator service, as well as those in the invoked services.

1.1   Service Interfaces and Contracts

In our approach, the published interface of a service is an annotated functional type, of the form $\tau_1 \xrightarrow{H} \tau_2$. When supplied with an argument of type τ_1, the service evaluates to an object of type τ_2. The annotation H is a *history expression*, a sort of context-free grammar that abstractly describes the possible run-time histories of the service. Thus, H will be exploited to guide the selection of those services that respect the requested properties about security or other non-functional aspects. Since service interfaces are crucial in the implementation of the call-by-contract primitive, they have to be *certified* by a trusted party, which guarantees that the abstract behaviour is a sound over-approximation of the actual service behaviour. For instance, service interfaces can be mechanically inferred through a type and effect system, as shown in Section 8.

A *contract* φ is a regular property of execution histories. We express contracts as languages accepted by finite state automata. Although in this paper we mainly focus on security policies, in the general case contracts can be arbitrary safety properties (e.g. resource usage constraints [7]).

To select a service matching a given contract φ, and with functional type $\tau_1 \to \tau_2$, a client issues a request of the form $\texttt{req}\,(\tau_1 \xrightarrow{\varphi} \tau_2)$. The call-by-contract mechanism ensures that the selected service, with interface $\tau_1 \xrightarrow{H} \tau_2$, will always respect the contract φ, i.e. that all the histories represented by H are recognized by the automaton defining φ.

Since service interactions may be complex, it might be the case that a local choice for a service is not secure in a broader, "global" context. For instance, choosing a low-security e-mail provider might prevent you from using a home-banking service that exchanges confidential data through e-mail. In this case, you should have planned the selection of the e-mail and bank services so to ensure their compatibility. To cope with this kind of issues, we define a static machinery that determines the *viable plans* for selecting services that respect all the contracts, both locally and globally. A plan resolves a call-by-contract into a standard service call, and it is formalized as a mapping from requests to services.

1.2   Planning Service Composition

Our planning technique acts as a *trusted orchestrator* of services. It provides a client with the viable plans guaranteeing that the invoked services always respect the required properties. Thus, in our framework the only trusted entity is the orchestrator, and neither clients nor services need to be such. In particular, the orchestrator infers functional and behavioural types of each service. Also, it is responsible for certifying the service code, for publishing its interface, and for guaranteeing that services will not arbitrarily change their code on the fly: when this happens, services need to be certified again. When an application is injected in the network, the orchestrator provides it with a viable plan (if any), constructed by composing and analysing the certified interfaces of the available services. The trustworthiness of the orchestrator relies upon formal grounds, i.e. the soundness of our type and effect system, and the correctness of the static analysis and model-checking technique that infers viable plans.

As said above, finding viable plans is not a trivial task, because the effect of selecting a given service for a request is not always confined to the execution of that service. Since each service selection may affect the *whole* execution, we cannot simply devise a viable plan by selecting services that satisfy the constraints imposed by the requests, only. We have then devised a two-stage construction for extracting viable plans from a history expression. Let H be the history expression inferred for a client. A first transformation of H, called linearization, lifts all the service choices to the top-level of H. This isolates from H the possible plans, that will be considered one by one in the second stage: model-checking for validity. Projecting the history expression H on a given plan π gives rise to another history expression H', where all the service choices have been resolved according to π. Validity of H' guarantees that the chosen plan π will drive executions that never go wrong at run-time (thus run-time security monitoring becomes unneeded). To verify the validity of H', we first smoothly transform it into a Basic Process Algebra. We then model-check this Basic Process Algebra with a finite state automaton, specially tailored to recognize validity. The correctness of all these steps (type safety, linearization, model-checking) has been formally proved in [6].

1.3 Contributions

We briefly summarize the key features of our approach.

1. *Taxonomy of security aspects.* We discussed some design choices that affect security in Web Services. These choices address rather general properties of systems: whether services maintain a state across invocations or not, whether they trust each other or not, whether they can pass back and forth mobile code, and whether different threads may share part of their state or not. Each of these choices deeply impacts the expressivity of the enforceable security properties, and the compositionality of planning techniques.
2. *Design Methodology.* We introduced a formal modelling language for designing secure services. Our graphical formalism resembles UML activity diagrams, and it is used to describe the workflow of services. Besides the usual workflow operators, we can express activities subject to security constraints. The awareness of security from the early stages of development will foster security through all the following phases of software production. Diagrams have a formal operational semantics, that specifies the dynamic behaviour of services. Also, they can be statically analysed, to infer the contracts satisfied by a service. Our design methodology allows for a fine-grained characterization of the design choices that affect security (see Section 2). We support our approach with the help of some case study scenarios. The design of UML profiles is currently under development.
3. *Planning and recovering strategies.* We identified several cases where designers need to take a decision before proceeding with the execution. For instance, when a planned service disappears unexpectedly, one can choose to replan, so to adapt to the new network configuration. Depending on the boundary conditions and on past experience, one can choose among different tactics. We comment on the feasibility, advantages and costs of each of them.
4. *Core calculus for services.* We extended the λ-calculus with primitives for selecting and invoking services that respect given security requirements. Service invocation is implemented in a call-by-contract fashion, i.e. you choose a service for its (certified) behaviour, not for its name. Security policies are arbitrary safety properties on execution histories. A key point is that our policies are applied within a given scope, so we called them *local policies*. They are more general than traditional global policies. Instead of having a single, large, monolithic policy, simple requirements on security can be naturally composed. Also, local policies are better than local checks. Programmers are not required to foresee the exact program points where security violations may occur.
5. *Planning secure orchestration.* We defined a three-step static analysis that makes secure orchestration feasible. An abstraction of the program behaviour

is first extracted, through a type and effect system. This abstract behaviour is a history expression that over-approximates the possible run-time histories of all the services involved in an orchestration. The second and third steps put this history expression in a special form, and then model-checks it to construct a correct orchestrator that securely coordinates the running services. Studying the output of the model-checker may highlight design flaws, suggesting how to revise the call-by-contract and the security policies. All the above is completely mechanizable, and we have implemented a prototype to support our methodology. The fact that the tool is based on firm theoretical grounds (i.e. λ^{req} type inference and verifier) positively impacts the reliability to our approach.

The paper is organized as follows. In Section 2 we introduce a taxonomy of security aspects in service-oriented applications. Sections 3, 4 and 5 present our design methodology. In particular, Section 3 introduces our design notation and the operational semantics of diagrams; Section 4 presents service contracts, and outlines how they can be automatically inferred; Section 5 illustrates how to select services under the call-by-contract assumption, and discusses some planning and recovering strategies. A car repair scenario for secure service composition is presented in Section 6. Sections 7, 8 and 9 formally introduce the calculus λ^{req} and the planning machinery. Specifically, Sections 7 formalizes the syntax and the operational semantics of λ^{req} ; Section 8 gives semantics to history expressions, defines a type and effect system for λ^{req} , and states its type safety; Section 9 shows our model-checking technique for planning. We conclude the paper with some remarks (Section 11) about the expected impact of our proposal. Portions of this paper have appeared in [10,6].

2   A Taxonomy of Security Aspects in Web Services

Service composition heavily depends on which information about a service is made public, on how to choose those services that match the user's requirements, and on their actual run-time behaviour. Security makes service composition even harder. Services may be offered by different providers, which only partially trust each other. On the one hand, providers have to guarantee that the delivered service respects a given security policy, in any interaction with the operational environment, and regardless of who actually called the service. On the other hand, clients may want to protect their sensitive data from the services invoked.

In the *history-based* approach to security, the run-time permissions depend on a suitable abstraction of the history of all the pieces of code (possibly partially) executed so far. This approach has been receiving major attention, at both levels of foundations [3,27,43] and of language design/implementation [1,24].

The observations of security-relevant activities, e.g. opening socket connections, reading and writing files, accessing memory critical regions, are called *events*. Sequences of events are called *histories*. The class of policies we are concerned with is that of *safety* properties of histories, i.e. properties that are expressible through finite state automata. The typical run-time mechanisms for enforcing history-based policies are *reference monitors*, which observe program executions and abort them whenever about to violate the given policy. Reference monitors enforce exactly the class of safety properties [41].

Since histories are the main ingredient of our security model, our taxonomy speaks about how histories are handled and manipulated by services. We focus on the following aspects.

Stateless / Stateful Services

A stateless service does not preserve its state (i.e. its history) across distinct invocations. Instead, a stateful service keeps the histories of all the past invocations. Stateful services allow for more expressive security policies, e.g. they can bound the number of invocations on a per-client basis.

Local / Global Histories

Local histories only record the events generated by a service locally on its site. Instead, a global history may span over multiple services. Local histories are the most prudent choice when services do not trust other services, in particular the histories they generate. In this case, a service only trusts its own history — but it cannot constrain the past history of its callers, e.g. to prevent that its client has visited a malicious site. Global histories instead require some trust relation among services: if a service A trusts B, then the history of A may comprise that of B, and so A may check policies on the behaviour of B.

First Order / Higher Order Requests

A request type $\tau \xrightarrow{\varphi} \tau'$ is first order when both τ and τ' are base types (*Int*, *Bool*, etc.). Instead, if τ or τ' are functional types, the request is higher order. In particular, if the parameter (of type τ) is a function, then the client passes some code to be possibly executed by the requested service. Symmetrically, if τ' is a function type, then the service returns back some code to the caller. Mobility of code impacts the way histories are generated, and demands for particular mechanisms to enforce security on the site where the code is run. A typical protection mechanism is *sandboxing*, that consists in wrapping code within an execution monitor that enforce a given security policy. When there is no mobile code, more efficient mechanisms can be devised, e.g. local checks on security-critical operations.

Dependent / Independent Threads

In a network of services, several threads may run concurrently and compete for services. Independent threads keep histories separated, while dependent threads may share part of their histories. Therefore, dependent threads may influence each other when using the same service, while independent threads cannot. For instance, consider a one-shot service that can be invoked only one time. If threads are independent, the one-shot service has no way to enforce single use. It can only check that no thread uses it more than once, because each thread keeps its own history. Dependent threads are necessary to correctly implement the one-shot service.

3 Designing Secure Services

The basic entity in our design formalism is that of *services*. A service is represented as a box containing its code. The four corners of the box are decorated with information about the service interface and behaviour. The label $\ell : \tau$ indicates the *location* ℓ where the service is made available, and its certified published *interface* τ (discussed later on in Section 4). The other labels instead are used to represent the state of a service at run-time.

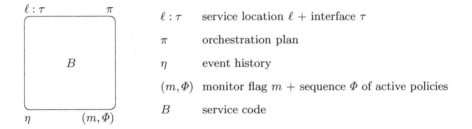

$\ell : \tau$	service location ℓ + interface τ
π	orchestration plan
η	event history
(m, Φ)	monitor flag m + sequence Φ of active policies
B	service code

Fig. 1. Execution state of a service

The label $\eta = \alpha_1 \cdots \alpha_k$ is an abstraction of the service execution *history*. In particular, we are concerned with the sequence of security-relevant events α_i happened sometimes in the past, in the spirit of history-based security [1]. The label (m, Φ) is a pair, where the first element is a flag m representing the on/off status of the execution monitor, and the second element is the sequence $\varphi_1 \cdots \varphi_k$ of active *security policies*. When the flag is on, the monitor checks that the service history η adheres to the policy φ_i (written $\eta \models \varphi_i$) for each $i \in 1..k$. Security policies are modelled as regular properties of event histories, i.e. properties that are recognizable by a Finite State Automaton. Since our design notation does not depend on the logic chosen for expressing regular properties of histories, we shall not fix any logic here. However, in our examples (e.g. Fig. 9 in Section 6) we find convenient to describe policies through the *template usage automata* of [7].

The block B inside the box is an abstraction of the service code. Formally, it is a special control flow graph [40] with nodes modelling activities, blocks enclosing sets of nodes, and arrows modelling intra-procedural flow.

Nodes can be of two kinds, i.e. *events* or *requests*. Events $\alpha, \beta, \ldots$ abstract from some security-critical operation. An event can possibly be parametrized, e.g. $\alpha_w(foo)$ for writing the file *foo*, $sgn(\ell)$ for a certificate signed by ℓ, etc. A service request takes the form $\mathbf{req}_r\tau$. The label r uniquely identifies the request in a network, and the request type τ is defined as:

$$\tau \ ::= \ b \ | \ \tau \xrightarrow{\varphi} \tau$$

where b is a base type (*Int*, *Bool*, ...). The annotation φ on the arrow is the query pattern (or *"contract"*) to be matched by the invoked service. For instance, the request type $\tau \xrightarrow{\varphi} \tau'$ matches services with functional type $\tau \to \tau'$, and whose behaviour respects the policy φ.

Blocks can be of two kinds: *security blocks* $\varphi[B]$ enforce the policy φ on B, i.e. the history must respect φ at each step of the evaluation of B; *planning blocks* $\{B\}$ construct a plan for the execution of B (see Section 9 for a discussion on some planning strategies). Blocks can be nested, and they determine the scope of policies (hence called *local* policies [5]) and of planning.

The label π is the *plan* used for resolving future service choices. Plans may come in several different shapes [9], but here we focus on a very simple form of plans, mapping each request to a single service. A plan formalises how a call-by-contract $\mathbf{req}_r\tau$ is transformed into a call-by-name, and takes the form of a function from request identifiers r to service locations ℓ. Definition 1 gives the syntax of plans.

Definition 1. Syntax of plans

$\pi, \pi' ::=$	0	empty	
	$r[\ell]$	service choice	
	$r[?]$	unresolved choice	
	$\pi \mid \pi'$	composition	

The plan 0 is empty; the plan $r[\ell]$ associates the service published at site ℓ with the request labelled r. The plan $r[?]$ models an unresolved choice for the request r: we call a plan *complete* when it has no unresolved choices. Composition $\mid$ on plans is associative, commutative and idempotent, and its identity is the empty plan 0. We require plans to have a single choice for each request, i.e. $r[\ell] \mid r[\ell']$ implies $\ell = \ell'$.

Note that in this design language, we do not render all the features of λ^{req} (see Section 7). In particular, we neglect variables, conditionals, higher-order functions, and parameter passing. However, we feel free to use these features in the examples, because their treatment can be directly inherited from λ^{req}.

3.1 Graph Semantics

We formally define the behaviour of services through a graph rewriting semantics [4]. In this section, we resort to an *oracle* that provides the initiator of a computation with a viable plan. The oracle guarantees that the overall execution satisfies all the contracts and the security policies on demand, unless services become unavailable. In the following sections, we will discuss a static machinery that will enable us to correctly implement the oracle, guaranteeing that an expression will never go wrong. We will also show some strategies to adopt when services disappear unexpectedly.

The semantics is defined through graph rewriting. The graph semantics for the case of dependent threads is depicted in Fig. 2 and in Fig. 5. We shall briefly discuss the case of independent threads in Section 3.2. All the remaining axes in the taxonomy are covered by our semantics; in particular, Fig. 3 defines the behaviour of requests and returns according to the possible choices in the taxonomy.

An overlined block $\overline{B}$ means that the first node in B is going to be executed; similarly, an underlined block $\underline{B}$ means that the last node in B has just been executed. A service with a slashed box (rule FAIL) is unavailable, i.e. either is down, unreachable or removed from the directory.

We now briefly discuss the graph rewritings in Fig. 2.

– The evaluation of an event α (rule Ev) consists in appending α to the current history. It is also required that the new history obeys all the policies φ in Φ (denoted $\eta\alpha \models \Phi$), if the execution monitor is on.
– The rule SEQ says that, after a block B has been evaluated, the next instruction is chosen non-deterministically among the blocks intra-procedurally connected with B. Note that branching is a special case of SEQ, where the block B is a conditional or a switch.
– Entering a security block $\varphi[B]$ results in appending the policy φ to the sequence of active policies. Leaving $\varphi[B]$ removes φ from the sequence. In both cases, as soon as a history is found not to respect φ, the evaluation gets stuck, to model a security exception (for simplicity, we do not model here exceptions and exception handling. Extending our formalism in this direction would require to define how to compensate from aborted computations, e.g. like in Sagas [28,20]).
– A request $\mathtt{req}_r\tau$ under a plan $r[\ell'] \mid \pi$ looks for the service at site ℓ'. If the service is available (rule REQ), then the client establishes a session with that service (dashed arrow), and waits until it returns. Note that the meaning of the labels η' and Φ' is left undefined in Fig. 2, since it depends on the choice made on the security aspects discussed in Section 2. The actual values for the undefined labels are shown in Fig. 3. In particular, the initial history of the invoked service is: (i) empty, if the service is stateless with local history; (ii) the invoker history, if the service has a global history; (iii) the service past history, if the service is stateful, with local history.
– Returning from a request (rule RET) requires suitably updating the history of the caller service, according to chosen axes in the taxonomy. The actual values for η'' are defined in Fig. 3.

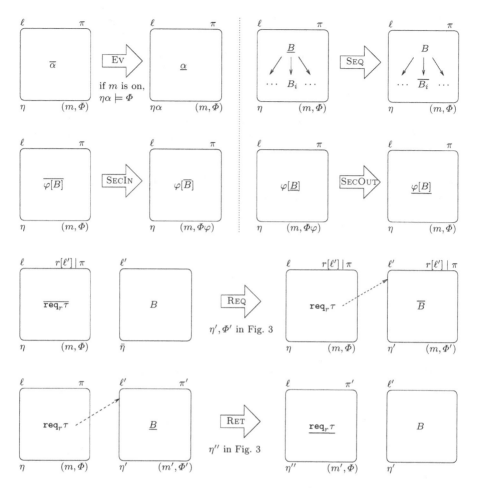

Fig. 2. Semantics of services: events, branches, policies, requests and returns

	Stateless services		Stateful services	
	Local histories	Global histories	Local histories	Global histories
REQ	$\eta' = \varepsilon$ $\Phi' = \varepsilon$	$\eta' = \eta$ $\Phi' = \Phi$	$\eta' = \bar{\eta}$ $\Phi' = \varepsilon$	$\eta' = \eta$ $\Phi' = \Phi$
RET	$\eta'' = \eta$	$\eta'' = \eta$	$\eta'' = \eta$	$\eta'' = \eta'$

Fig. 3. Histories and policies in four cases of the taxonomy

The cases FAIL, PLG IN and PLG OUT are defined in Fig. 5, and they have many possible choices. When no service is available for a request (e.g. because the plan is incomplete, or because the planned service is down), or when you have to construct a plan for a block, the execution may proceed according to one of the strategies discussed in Section 5.

A plan is *viable* when it drives no stuck computations. Under a viable plan, a service can always proceed its execution without attempting to violate some security policy, and it will always manage to resolve each request.

3.2   Semantics of Independent Threads

To model independent threads, each service must keep separate histories of all the initiators. Therefore, histories take the form $\ell_I : \eta, \{\ell_j : \eta_j\}$, where the first item represents the current thread (initiated at site ℓ_I) and its history η, while $\{\ell_j : \eta_j\}$ is the set of the histories associated with the other threads. The rule depicted in Fig. 4 for the case REQ shows that (stateful) services must maintain all the histories of the various threads. The actual value of η' is defined as in Fig. 3. The rule RET is dealt with similarly.

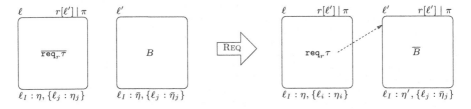

Fig. 4. Maintaining separate histories in the case of independent threads

4   Service Contracts

A service is plugged into a network by publishing it at a site ℓ, together with its interface τ. We assume that each site publishes a single service, and that interfaces are certified, e.g. they are inferred by the type and effect system defined in Section 8. Also, we assume that services cannot invoke each other circularly, since this is quite unusual in the SOC scenario. The functional types are annotated with *history expressions* H that over-approximate the possible run-time histories. When a service with interface $\tau \xrightarrow{H} \tau'$ is run, it will generate one of the histories denoted by H. Note that we overload the symbol τ to range over both service types and request types $\tau \xrightarrow{\varphi} \tau'$. The syntax of types and history expressions is summarized in Definition 2.

History expressions are a sort of context-free grammars. They include the empty history ε, events α, and $H \cdot H'$ that represents sequentialization of code, $H + H'$ for conditionals and branching, security blocks $\varphi[H]$, recursion $\mu h.H$ (where μ binds the occurrences of the variable h in H), localization $\ell : H$, and planned selection $\{\pi_1 \rhd H_1 \cdots \pi_k \rhd H_k\}$.

A history expression represents a set of histories η, possibly carrying security annotations in the form $\varphi[\eta]$. We formally define the semantics of history expressions in Section 8.1; here we just give some intuition. The semantics of $H \cdot H'$ (denoted by $[\![H \cdot H']\!]$) is the set of histories $\eta\eta'$ such that $\eta \in [\![H]\!]$ and $\eta' \in [\![H']\!]$.

Definition 2. Service interfaces: types and history expressions

τ, τ'	$::=$		types
	b		base type
	$\tau \xrightarrow{H} \tau'$		annotated function
H, H'	$::=$		history expressions
	ε		empty
	h		variable
	α		access event
	$H \cdot H'$		sequence
	$H + H'$		choice
	$\varphi[H]$		security block
	$\mu h.H$		recursion
	$\ell : H$		localization
	$\{\pi_1 \rhd H_1 \cdots \pi_k \rhd H_k\}$		planned selection

The semantics of $H + H'$ comprises the histories η such that $\eta \in \llbracket H \rrbracket \cup \llbracket H' \rrbracket$. The last three constructs (recursion, localization and planned selection) will benefit of some extra explanation.

- The semantics of a recursion $\mu h.\, H$ is the usual fixed point construction. For instance, the semantics of $\mu h.\, (\gamma + \alpha \cdot h \cdot \beta)$ consists of all the histories $\alpha^n \gamma \beta^n$, for $n \geq 0$ (i.e. γ, $\alpha \gamma \beta$, $\alpha\alpha\gamma\beta\beta$, ...).
- The construct $\ell : H$ localizes the behaviour H to the site ℓ. For instance, $\ell : \alpha \cdot (\ell' : \alpha') \cdot \beta$ denotes two histories: $\alpha\beta$ occurring at location ℓ, and α' occurring at location ℓ'.
- A planned selection abstracts from the behaviour of service requests. Given a plan π, a planned selection $\{\pi_1 \rhd H_1 \cdots \pi_k \rhd H_k\}$ chooses those H_i such that π includes π_i. For instance, the history expression $H = \{r[\ell_1] \rhd H_1, r[\ell_2] \rhd H_2\}$ is associated with a request $\mathtt{req}_r\tau$ that can be resolved into either ℓ_1 or ℓ_2. The histories denoted by H depend on the given plan π: if π chooses ℓ_1 (resp. ℓ_2) for r, then H denotes one of the histories represented by H_1 (resp. H_2). If π does not choose either ℓ_1 or ℓ_2, then H denotes no histories.

Typing judgments have the form $H \vdash B : \tau$. This means that the service with code B has type τ, and has execution histories included in the semantics of the effect H. Note that only the initiators of a computation may have $H \neq \varepsilon$; all the other services have typing judgments of the form $\varepsilon \vdash B : b \xrightarrow{H'} b'$. Typing judgments for our diagrams can be directly derived from those of the λ^{req} calculus (see Section 8.3).

In Section 8.4 we will state two fundamental results about our type and effect system. First, it correctly over-approximates the actual run-time histories. Second, it enjoys the following type safety property. We say that an effect H is *valid* under a plan π when the histories denoted by H, under the plan π, never violate the security policies in H. Type safety ensures that, if (statically) a service B is well-typed and its effect is valid under a plan π, then (dynamically) the plan π is viable for B, i.e. it only drives safe computations.

In Section 9 we will present a model-checking technique to verify the validity of history expressions, and to extract the viable plans.

5 Service Selection

We now consider the problem of choosing the appropriate service for a block of requests. While one might defer service selection as long as possible, thus only performing it when executing a request, it is usually advantageous to decide how to resolve requests in advance, i.e. to build a plan. This is because "early planning" can provide better guarantees than late service selection. For instance, consider a block with two consecutive requests r_1 and r_2. It might be that, if we choose to resolve r_1 with a particular service ℓ_1, later on we will not be able to find safe choices for r_2. In this case we get stuck, and we must somehow escape from this dead-end, possibly with some expensive compensation (e.g. cancelling a reservation). Early planning, instead, can spot this kind of problem and try to find a better way, typically by considering also r_2 when taking a choice for r_1.

More in detail, when we build a complete viable plan π for a block B, we ensure that B can be securely executed, and we will never get stuck unless a service mentioned in π becomes unavailable. Furthermore, we will need no dynamic checks while executing B, and thus the execution monitor can be kept off, so improving the overall performance. This is a consequence of the type safety result for λ^{req}, formally proved in [6]. When we cannot find a complete viable plan, we could fall back to using an incomplete plan with unresolved requests $r[?]$. In this case, we get a weaker guarantee than the one above, namely that we will not get stuck until an unresolved request must actually be executed.

The rule PLN IN in Fig. 5 defines the semantics for constructing plans. The actual values for the labels π', m' and Φ' are defined in Fig. 7. To provide graceful degradation in our model, the FAIL rule considers the unfortunate case of executing a request r when either (i) r is still unresolved in the plan, or (ii) r is resolved with an unavailable service. Therefore, we will look for a way to continue the execution, possibly repairing the plan as shown in Fig. 6. The rules DOWN and UP say that a service may become unavailable, and then available again. We assume that transitions from available to unavailable state (and viceversa) can only happen when a service is not fulfilling a request.

Several strategies for constructing or repairing a plan are possible, and we discuss some of them below. Note that no strategy is always better than the others, since each of them has advantages and disadvantages, as we will point out. The choice of a given strategy depends on many factors, some of which lie outside of our formal model (e.g. availability of services, cost of dynamic checking, etc.).

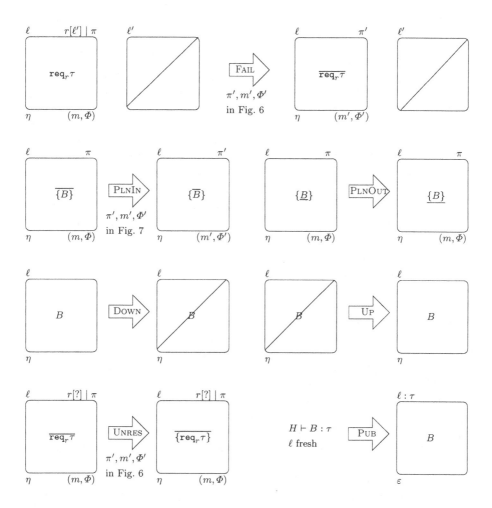

Fig. 5. Semantics of services: failing, planning and becoming up/down

We devise four main classes of strategies:

Greyfriars Bobby.[1] Follow loyally a former plan. If a service becomes unavailable, just wait until it comes back again. This strategy is always safe, although it might obviously block the execution for an arbitrarily long time — possibly forever.

---

[1] In 1858, a man named John Gray was buried in old Greyfriars Churchyard. For fourteen years the dead man's faithful dog kept constant watch and guard over the grave until his own death in 1872. The famous Skye Terrier, Greyfriars Bobby was so devoted to his master John Gray, even in death, that for fourteen years Bobby lay on the grave only leaving for food.

Patch. Try to reuse as much as possible the current plan. Replace the unavailable services with available ones, possibly newly discovered. The new services must be verified for compatibility with the rest of the plan.

Sandbox. Try to proceed with the execution monitor turned on. The new plan only respects a weak form of compatibility on types ignoring the effect H, but it does not guarantee that contracts and security policies are always respected. Turning on the execution monitor ensures that there will not be security violations, but execution might get stuck later on, because of attempted insecure actions.

Replan. Try to reconstruct the whole plan, possibly exploiting newly discovered services. If a viable plan is found, then you may proceed running with the execution monitor turned off. A complete plan guarantees that contracts and security policies will be always respected, provided than none of the services mentioned in the plan disappear.

In Fig. 6, we describe the effects of these strategies in the context of the FAIL rule. There, we also make precise the recovered plan π' and the labels m' and Φ' appearing in the rule. For the "Greyfiars Bobby" strategy, we patiently wait for the service to reappear; on timeout, we will try another strategy. The Patch strategy mends the current plan with a local fix. Note that the Patch strategy is not always safe: in the general case, it is impossible to change just the way to resolve the failing request r and have a new safe plan. We shall return on this issue later on. However, as the figure shows, in some cases this is indeed possible, provided that we check the new choice for resolving r, to ensure the plan is valid again. The Replan strategy is safe when a suitable plan is found, but it could involve statically re-analysing a large portion of the system. When all else fails, it is possible to run a service under a Sandbox, hoping that we will not get stuck.

From now onwards, we use the following abbreviations for the various alternatives described in Section 2: stateless (1) / stateful (ω), local (L) / global (G), first order (F) / higher-order (H), dependent (D) / independent (I). For instance, the case IFL1 in the figure is the one about independent threads, first order requests, local histories, and stateless services.

In Fig. 7 we list the strategies for the rule PLN IN, describing how to build a plan for a block B. Note that, when we construct a new plan π' we already have a plan $\pi \mid \pi_B$, where π_B only plans the requests inside B. We can then reuse the available information in π and π_B to build π'. The former plan $\pi \mid \pi_B$ can be non-empty when using nested planning blocks, so reusing parts from it is indeed possible. Since we can reuse the old plan, the strategies are exactly the same of those for the FAIL case.

The "Greyfriars Bobby" strategy waits for *all* the services mentioned in the old plan to be available at planning time. This is because it might be wise not to start the block, if we know that we will likely get stuck later. Instead, if some services keep on being unavailable, we should rather consider the other strategies.

Strategy	State update	Case	Condition
Greyfriars Bobby	$\dfrac{\pi}{\varPhi}$	all	The current plan π has a choice for r
Patch	$\dfrac{\pi \mid r[\ell_i]}{\varPhi}$	IFL1	$\varphi[H_i]$ is valid
		IFLω	$\varphi[H_i]$ is valid, and $\ell_i \notin \pi$
		IFG1	$\eta\varphi[H_i]$ is valid
		DFL1	$\varphi[H_i]$ is valid
Sandbox	$\dfrac{\pi \mid r[\ell_i]}{(on, \varPhi\varphi)}$	all	The service ℓ_i has type $\tau \to \tau'$
Replan	$\dfrac{\pi'}{(off, \varPhi\varphi)}$	all	The new plan π' has a choice for r

Fig. 6. Failure handling strategies for a request $\texttt{req}_r \tau \xrightarrow{\varphi} \tau'$

As for the FAIL rule, the Patch strategy is not always safe, but we can still give some conditions that guarantee the safety of the plan update, which is local to the block B. The Replan strategy, instead, can change the whole plan, even for the requests outside B. If possible, we should always find a complete plan. When this is not the case, we might proceed with some unresolved requests $r[?]$, deferring them to the FAIL rule. As a last resort, when no viable plan can be found, or when we deem Replan to be too expensive, we can adopt the Sandbox strategy that turns on the execution monitor.

We now show a situation where the Patch strategy is not safe. We consider the case IFLω case (independent threads, first order requests, local histories, stateful services). The initiator service, in the middle of Fig. 8, performs two requests r_1 and r_2 in sequence. The two requests have the same contract, and thus they can be resolved with the stateful services ℓ_1 and ℓ_2. The service at ℓ_2 performs an event α, within a security block φ. If φ allows only a single α, we

Strategy	State update	Case	Condition
Greyfriars Bobby	$\dfrac{\pi \mid \pi_B}{\varPhi}$	all	The plan π_B has a choice for all r_i
Patch	$\dfrac{\pi \mid r_i[\ell_i] \mid \cdots}{\varPhi}$	IFL1	$\varphi[H_i]$ is valid, for all i
		IFLω	$\varphi_i[H_i]$ are valid, ℓ_i are distinct, and all $\ell_i \notin \pi$
		IFG1	$\eta_i\varphi_i[H_i]$ are valid, for all i
		DFL1	$\varphi_i[H_i]$ are valid, for all i
Sandbox	$\dfrac{\pi \mid r_i[\ell_i] \mid \cdots}{(on, \varPhi\varphi)}$	all	The services ℓ_i have type $\tau_i \to \tau_i'$
Replan	$\dfrac{\pi'}{(off, \varPhi\varphi)}$	all	ηH valid under π', where η is the current history, and H approximates the future behaviour (may need to refine the analysis)

Fig. 7. Planning strategies for a block B involving requests $\texttt{req}_{r_i} \tau_i \xrightarrow{\varphi_i} \tau_i'$

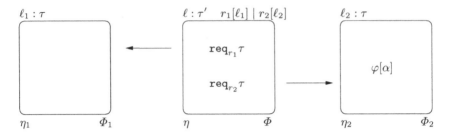

Fig. 8. An unsafe use of the Patch strategy

should be careful and invoke the (stateful) service ℓ_2 at most once. The current plan $\pi = r_1[\ell_1] \mid r_2[\ell_2]$ is safe, since it invokes ℓ_2 exactly once.

Now, consider what happens if the service ℓ_1 becomes unavailable. The FAIL rule is triggered: if we apply Patch and replace the current plan with $r_1[\ell_2] \mid r_2[\ell_2]$, then this patched plan is *not* viable. Indeed, the new plan invokes ℓ_2 twice, so violating φ. The safety condition in Fig. 6 is false, because $\ell_2 \in \pi$: therefore, this dangerous patch is correctly avoided.

6   A Car Repair Scenario

To illustrate some of the features and design facilities made available by our framework, we consider a car repair scenario, where a car may break and then request assistance from a tow-truck and a garage.

In this scenario, we assume a car equipped with a diagnostic system that continuously reports on the status of the vehicle. When the car experiences some major failure (e.g. engine overheating, exhausted battery, flat tyres) the in-car emergency service is invoked to select the appropriate tow-truck and garage services. The selection may take into account some driver personalized policies, and other constraints, e.g. the tow-truck should be close enough to reach both the location where the car is stuck and the chosen garage.

The main focus here is not on the structure of the overall system architecture, rather on how to design the workflow of the service orchestration, taking into account the specific driver policies and the service contracts on demand.

The system is composed of three kinds of services: the CAR-EMERGENCY service, that tries to arrange for a car tow-trucking and repair, the TOW-TRUCK service, that picks the damaged car to a garage, and the GARAGE service, that repairs the car. We assume that all the involved services trust each other's history, and so we assume a shared global history, with independent threads. We also design all the services to be stateful, so that, e.g. the driver can personalize the choice of garages, according to past experiences.

We start by modelling the CAR-EMERGENCY service, i.e. the in-vehicle service that handles the car fault. This service is invoked by the embedded diagnosis system, each time a fault is reported. The actual kind of fault, and the geographic

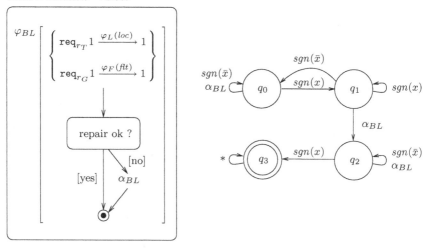

Fig. 9. The CAR-EMERGENCY service and the black-listing policy φ_{BL}

location where the car is stuck, are passed as parameters — named *flt* and *loc*. The diagram of the CAR-EMERGENCY service is displayed on the left-hand side of Fig. 9.

The outer policy φ_{BL} (black-list) has the role of enforcing a sort of "quality of service" constraint. The CAR-EMERGENCY service records in its history the list of all the garages used in past repair requests. When the selected garage ℓ_G completes repairing a car, it appends to the history its own signature $sgn(\ell_G)$. When the user is not satisfied with the quality (or the bill!) of the garage, the garage is black-listed (event α_{BL}). The policy φ_{BL} ensures that a black-listed garage (marked by a signature $sgn(\ell_G)$ followed by a black-listing tag α_{BL}) cannot be selected for future emergencies. The black-listing policy φ_{BL} is formally defined by the *template usage automaton* [7] in Fig. 9, right-hand side. Note that some labels in φ_{BL} are parametric: $sgn(x)$ and $sgn(\bar{x})$ stands respectively for "the signature of garage x" and "a signature of any garage different from x", where x can be replaced by an arbitrary garage identifier. If, starting from the state q_0, a garage signature $sgn(x)$ is immediately followed by a black-listing tag α_{BL}, then you reach the state q_2. From q_2, an attempt to generate again $sgn(x)$ will result in a transition to the non-accepting sink state q_3. For instance, the history $sgn(\ell_1)sgn(\ell_2)\alpha_{BL}\cdots sgn(\ell_2)$ violates the policy φ_{BL}.

The crucial part of the design is the planning block. It contains two requests: r_T (for the tow-truck) and r_G (for the garage), to be planned together. The contract $\varphi_L(loc)$ requires that the tow-truck is able to serve the location *loc* where the car is broken down. The contract $\varphi_F(flt)$ selects the garages that can repair the kind of faults *flt*.

The planning block has the role of determining the orchestration plan for both the requests. In this case, it makes little sense to continue executing with

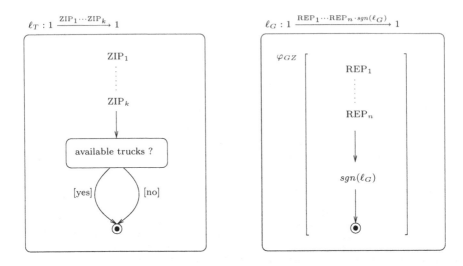

Fig. 10. The TOW-TRUCK (left) and GARAGE (right) services

an incomplete plan or with sandboxing: you should perhaps look for a car rental service, if either the tow-truck or the garage are unavailable. Therefore, a meaningful planning strategy is trying to find a couple of services matching both r_T and r_G, and wait until both the services are available.

The diagram of the TOW-TRUCK service is displayed in Fig. 10, on the left. The service will first expose the list of geographic locations $ZIP_1, \ldots, ZIP_k$ it can reach. Each zip code ZIP_i is modelled as an event. The contract $\varphi_T(loc)$ imposed by the CAR-EMERGENCY service ensures that the location loc is covered by the truck service. Formally, $\varphi_T(loc)$ checks if the zip code loc is contained in the interface of the tow-truck service (we omit the automaton for $\varphi_T(loc)$ here). Then, the TOW-TRUCK may perform some internal activities (irrelevant in our model), possibly invoking other internal services. The exposed interface is of the form $1 \xrightarrow{ZIP_1 \cdots ZIP_k} 1$, where 1 is the void type.

The GARAGE service (Fig. 10, right) exposes the kinds of faults $REP_1, \ldots,$ REP_n the garage can repair, e.g. tyres, engine, etc. The request contract $\varphi_G(flt)$ ensures that the garage can repair the kind of fault flt experienced by the car. The GARAGE service may perform some internal bookkeeping activities to handle the request (not shown in the figure), possibly using internal services from its local repository. After the car repair has been completed, the garage ℓ_G signs a receipt, through the event $sgn(\ell_G)$. This signature can be used by the CAR-EMERGENCY service to implement its black-listing policy.

The GARAGE service exploits the policy φ_{GZ} (for Garage-Zip) to ensure that the tow-truck can reach the garage address. If the garage is located in the area identified by ZIP_G, the policy φ_{GZ} checks that the tow-truck has exposed the event ZIP_G among the locations it can reach. When both the contract $\varphi_T(loc)$ and the policy φ_{GZ} are satisfied, we have the guarantee that the tow-truck can pick the car and deposit it at the garage.

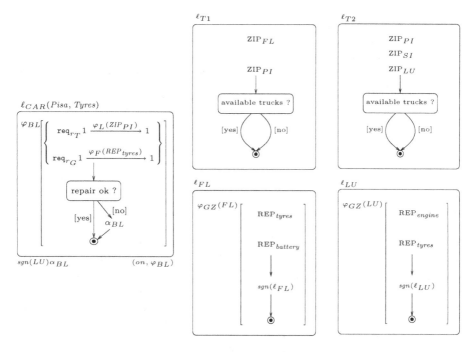

Fig. 11. The CAR-EMERGENCY client (ℓ_{CAR}), two tow-truck services (ℓ_{T1}, ℓ_{T2}), and two garages (ℓ_{FL}, ℓ_{LU})

In Fig. 11, we show a system composed by one car ℓ_{CAR}, two TOW-TRUCK services ℓ_{T1} and ℓ_{T2}, and two GARAGE services ℓ_{FL} and ℓ_{LU}. The car has experienced a flat tyres accident in Pisa (ZIP_{PI}), and it has black-listed the garage in Lucca, as recorded in the history $sgn(LU)\,\alpha_{BL}$. The tow-truck service ℓ_{T1} can reach Florence and Pisa, while ℓ_{T2} covers three zones: Pisa, Siena and Lucca. The garage ℓ_{FL} is located in Florence, and it can repair tyres and batteries; the garage ℓ_{LU} is in Lucca, and repairs engines and tyres.

We now discuss all the possible orchestrations:

- the plan $r_T[\ell_{T1}] \mid r_G[\ell_{LU}]$ is not viable, because it violates the policy $\varphi_{GZ}(LU)$. Indeed, the tow-truck can serve Florence and Pisa, but the garage is located in Lucca.
- similarly, the plan $r_T[\ell_{T2}] \mid r_G[\ell_{FL}]$ violates $\varphi_{GZ}(FL)$.
- the plan $r_T[\ell_{T2}] \mid r_G[\ell_{LU}]$ is not viable, because it violates the black-listing policy φ_{BL}. Indeed, it would give rise to a history $sgn(LU)\,\alpha_{BL} \cdots sgn(LU)$, not accepted by the automaton in Fig. 9.
- finally, the plan $r_T[\ell_{T1}] \mid r_G[\ell_{FL}]$ is viable. The tow-truck can reach both the car, located in Pisa, and the garage in Florence, which is not black-listed.

7 A Core Calculus for Services

In this Section we describe λ^{req} , a core calculus for secure service orchestration. The version of λ^{req} we present here has stateless services, local histories, higher-order requests, and independent threads. We first define the syntax of services and the *stand-alone* operational semantics, i.e. the behaviour of a service in isolation. We then define the syntax and operational semantics of networks.

7.1 Services

A service is modelled as an expression in a λ-calculus enriched with primitives for security and service requests. Security-relevant operations (i.e. the events) are rendered as side-effects in the calculus. Roughly speaking, λ^{req} services e implement the specification of blocks B in the graphical notation (Section 3). Note that λ^{req} augments the features of the design language with recursion (instead of loops), parameter passing and higher-order functions.

The abstract syntax of services follows. To enhance readability, our calculus comprises conditional expressions and named abstractions (the variable z in $e' = \lambda_z x. e$ stands for e' itself within e, so allowing for explicit recursion). We assume as given the language for guards in conditionals, and we omit its definition here.

Definition 3. Syntax of services

e, e' ::=	x	variable
	α	access event
	$\text{if } b \text{ then } e \text{ else } e$	conditional
	$\lambda_z x. e$	abstraction
	$e\, e'$	application
	$\varphi[e]$	safety framing
	$\{e\}$	planning
	$\text{req}_r \tau$	service request
	$\text{wait}\, \ell$	wait reply
	N/A	unavailable

The values v of our calculus are the variables, the abstractions, and the requests. We write $*$ for a distinguished value, and $\lambda. e$ for $\lambda x. e$, for x not free in e. The following abbreviation is standard: $e; e' = (\lambda. e')\, e$. Without loss of generality, we assume that framings include at least one event, possibly dummy.

The stand-alone evaluation of a service is much alike the call-by-value semantics of the λ-calculus; additionally, it enforces all the policies within their framings. Since here services are considered in isolation, the semantics of requests is deferred to Section 7.2. The configurations are triples η, m, e. A transition $\eta, m, e \rightarrow \eta', m', e'$ means that, starting from a history η and a monitor flag m, the service e evolves to e', extends η to η', and sets the flag to m'. We assume as given a total function $\mathcal{B}$ that evaluates the guards in conditionals.

Definition 4. Service semantics (stand-alone)

$\eta, m, (\lambda_z x.\, e)v \rightarrow \eta, m, e\{v/x, \lambda_z x.\, e/z\}$

$\eta, m, \alpha \rightarrow \eta\alpha, m, *$

$\eta, m, \text{if } b \text{ then } e_{tt} \text{ else } e_{ff} \rightarrow \eta, m, e_{\mathcal{B}(b)}$

$\eta, m, \mathcal{C}(e) \rightarrow \eta', m', \mathcal{C}(e') \quad$ if $\eta, m, e \rightarrow \eta', m', e'$ and $m' = \textit{off} \vee \eta' \models \Phi(\mathcal{C})$

$\eta, m, \mathcal{C}(\varphi[v]) \rightarrow \eta, m, \mathcal{C}(v) \quad$ if $m = \textit{off} \vee \eta \models \varphi$

where $\mathcal{C}$ is an *evaluation context*, of the following form:

$$\mathcal{C} \quad ::= \quad \bullet \mid \mathcal{C}\, e \mid v\, \mathcal{C} \mid \varphi[\mathcal{C}]$$

and $\Phi(\mathcal{C})$ is the set of *active policies* of $\mathcal{C}$, defined as follows:

$$\Phi(\mathcal{C}\, e) = \Phi(v\, \mathcal{C}) = \Phi(\mathcal{C}) \qquad \Phi(\varphi[\mathcal{C}]) = \{\varphi\} \cup \Phi(\mathcal{C})$$

The first rule implements β-reduction. Notice that the whole function body $\lambda_z x.\, e$ replaces the self variable z after the substitution, so giving an explicit copy-rule semantics to recursive functions. The evaluation of an event α consists in appending α to the current history, and producing the no-operation value $*$. A conditional if b then e_{tt} else e_{ff} evaluates to e_{tt} (resp. e_{ff}) if b evaluates to true (resp. false). The form of contexts implies call-by-value evaluation; as usual, functions are not reduced within their bodies. To evaluate a redex enclosed in a set of active policies $\Phi(\mathcal{C})$, the extended history η' must obey each $\varphi \in \Phi(\mathcal{C})$, when the execution monitor is on. A value can leave the scope of a framing φ if the current history satisfies φ. When the monitor is on and the history is found not to respect an active policy φ, the evaluation gets stuck.

7.2   Networks

A service e is plugged into a network by publishing it at a site ℓ, together with its interface τ. Hereafter, $\ell\langle e : \tau\rangle$ denotes such a *published service*. Labels ℓ can be seen as Uniform Resource Identifiers, and they are only known by the orchestrator. We assume that each site publishes a single service, and that interfaces are certified, i.e. they are inferred by the type system in Sect. 8.3. Recall that services cannot invoke each other circularly. A *client* is a special published service $\ell\langle e : unit\rangle$. As we will see, this special form prevents anyone from invoking a client. A *network* is a set of clients and published services.

The *state* of a published service $\ell\langle e : \tau\rangle$ is denoted by:

$$\ell\langle e : \tau\rangle : \pi \triangleright \eta, m, e'$$

where π is the plan used by the current instantiation of the service, η is the history generated so far, m is the monitor flag, and e' models the code in execution. When unambiguous, we simply write ℓ for $\ell\langle e : \tau \rangle$ in states.

The syntax and the operational semantics of networks follows; the operator $\|$ is associative and commutative. Given a network $\{\ell_i\langle e_i : \tau_i\rangle\}_{i \in 1..k}$, a *network configuration* N has the form:

$$\ell_1 : \pi_1 \rhd \eta_1, m_1, e'_1 \parallel \cdots \parallel \ell_k : \pi_k \rhd \eta_k, m_k, e'_k$$

abbreviated as $\{\ell_i : \pi_i \rhd \eta_i, m_i, e'_i\}_{i \in 1..k}$. To trigger a computation of the network, we need to single out a set of *initiators*, and fix the plans π_i for each of them. We associate the empty plan to the other services. Then, for all $i \in 1..k$, the initial configuration has $\eta_i = \varepsilon$, $m_i = \mathit{off}$, and $e'_i = *$ if ℓ_i is a service, while $e'_i = e_i$ if ℓ_i is an initiator.

We now discuss the semantic rules of networks in Definition 5. A transition of a stand-alone service is localized at site ℓ (rule STA), regardless of a plan π. The rule NET specifies the asynchronous behaviour of the network: a transition of a sub-network becomes a transition of the whole network. Rule PUB inserts a new service in the network, by publishing its interface τ, certified by the type and effect system. The rules DOWN/UP make an idle service unavailable/available. The rules REQ and RET model successful requests and replies. A request r, resolved by the current plan with the service ℓ', can be served if the service is available, i.e. it is in the state $\ell' : 0 \rhd \varepsilon, *$. In this case, a new activation of the service starts: e is applied to the received argument v, under the plan π', received as well from the invoker. The special event σ signals that the service has started. The invoker waits until ℓ' has produced a value. When this happens, the service becomes idle again. Since we follow here the *stateless* approach, we clear the history of a service at each activation (indeed, statefullness could be easily obtained by maintaining the history η' at ℓ' in the last rule). Rule UNRES triggers the construction of a new plan, in case of an unresolved choice. The rules PLN and FAIL exploit the planning/failing strategies to obtain a plan in case of a planned expression $\{e\}$ and of a chosen service which has become unavailable. The actual implementations of the auxiliary functions *plan* and *fail* may vary; in Section 8.5, we shall show a simple case that mixes replan and sandboxing.

Note that each service has a single instance in network configurations. We could easily model replication of services, by creating a new instance for each request. Note also that a network evolves by interleaving the activities of its components, which only synchronize when competing for the same service. It is straightforward to derive a truly concurrent semantics from the above one, e.g. using C/E Petri nets.

8   Static Semantics

In this Section we define a static analysis for our core calculus. The analysis takes the form of a type and effect system [29,39,44] where the effects, called

Definition 5. Network semantics

$[\textsc{Sta}]$
$$\frac{\eta, m, e \rightarrow \eta', m', e'}{\ell : \pi \rhd \eta, m, e \rightarrow \ell : \pi \rhd \eta', m', e'}$$

$[\textsc{Net}]$
$$\frac{N_1 \rightarrow N_1'}{N_1 \parallel N_2 \rightarrow N_1' \parallel N_2}$$

$[\textsc{Pub}]$ $\quad N \rightarrow N \parallel \ell\langle e : \tau \rangle : 0 \rhd \varepsilon, f\!f, * \quad$ if ℓ fresh and $\vdash_\ell e : \tau$

$[\textsc{Down}]$ $\quad \ell\langle e : \tau \rangle : 0 \rhd \varepsilon, m, * \rightarrow \ell\langle e : \tau \rangle : 0 \rhd \varepsilon, m, \mathsf{N/A}$

$[\textsc{Up}]$ $\quad \ell\langle e : \tau \rangle : 0 \rhd \varepsilon, m, \mathsf{N/A} \rightarrow \ell\langle e : \tau \rangle : 0 \rhd \varepsilon, m, *$

$[\textsc{Req}]$ $\quad \ell : (r[\ell'] \mid \pi) \rhd \eta, m, \mathcal{C}(\mathbf{req}_r \rho\, v) \parallel \ell'\langle e : \tau \rangle : 0 \rhd \varepsilon, m', * \rightarrow$
$\qquad \ell : (r[\ell'] \mid \pi) \rhd \eta, m, \mathcal{C}(\mathbf{wait}\,\ell') \parallel \ell'\langle e : \tau \rangle : (r[\ell'] \mid \pi) \rhd \sigma, m, e\, v$

$[\textsc{Ret}]$ $\quad \ell : \pi \rhd \eta, m, \mathbf{wait}\,\ell' \parallel \ell' : \pi' \rhd \eta', m', v \rightarrow$
$\qquad \ell : \pi \rhd \eta, m', v \parallel \ell' : 0 \rhd \varepsilon, m', *$

$[\textsc{Unres}]$ $\quad \ell : (r[?] \mid \pi) \rhd \eta, m, \mathcal{C}(\mathbf{req}_r \rho\, v) \rightarrow \ell : (r[?] \mid \pi) \rhd \eta, m, \mathcal{C}(\{\mathbf{req}_r \rho\, v\})$

$[\textsc{Pln}]$ $\quad \ell : \pi \rhd \eta, m, \{e\} \rightarrow \ell : \pi' \rhd \eta, m', e \quad$ if $(\pi', m') = plan(\pi, m, e)$

$[\textsc{Fail}]$ $\quad \ell : (r[\ell'] \mid \pi) \rhd \eta, m, \mathcal{C}(\mathbf{req}_r \rho\, v) \parallel \ell'\langle e : \tau \rangle : 0 \rhd \varepsilon, m'', \mathsf{N/A} \rightarrow$
$\qquad \ell : \pi' \rhd \eta, m', \mathcal{C}(\mathbf{req}_r \rho\, v) \parallel \ell'\langle e : \tau \rangle : 0 \rhd \varepsilon, m'', \mathsf{N/A}$
$$\text{if } (\pi', m') = fail(r[\ell'] \mid \pi, m, \mathbf{req}_r \rho)$$

history expressions, represent all the possible behaviour of services, while the types extend those of the λ-calculus.

In Section 8.1 we formally give semantics to history expressions, introduced in Section 4. In Section 8.2 we define *validity* of history expressions: roughly, a history expression is valid when the histories it represents do not violate any security constraint. In Section 8.3 we introduce our type and effect system, and in Section 8.4 we establish type safety.

8.1 History Expressions

The *denotational semantics* of a history expression is a set, written $(\ell_i : \mathcal{H}_i)_{i \in I}$. The intended meaning is that the behaviour of the service at location ℓ_i is approximated by the set of histories $\mathcal{H}_i$ (I is a finite set of indexes). Technically, $\mathcal{H}$ belongs to the lifted cpo of sets of histories [47], ordered by (lifted) set inclusion $\subseteq_\perp$ (where $\perp \subseteq_\perp \mathcal{H}$ for all $\mathcal{H}$, and $\mathcal{H} \subseteq_\perp \mathcal{H}'$ whenever $\mathcal{H} \subseteq \mathcal{H}'$). The least upper bound between two elements of the cpo is standard set union $\cup$, assuming that $\perp \cup \mathcal{H} = \mathcal{H}$. The set of events is enriched with *framing events* of the form $[_\varphi,]_\varphi$,

Definition 6. Semantics of history expressions

$$\langle\!\langle H \rangle\!\rangle^\pi = \{\, \ell : \{\, \langle\!\langle \eta \rangle\!\rangle \mid \eta \in \mathcal{H}\,\} \mid \ell : \mathcal{H} \in [\![H]\!]^\pi_\emptyset \,\}$$

$$\text{where } \langle\!\langle \eta \rangle\!\rangle = \begin{cases} \eta & \text{if } \sigma \notin \eta \\ \langle\!\langle \eta_0 \rangle\!\rangle \cup \langle\!\langle \eta_1 \rangle\!\rangle & \text{if } \eta = \eta_0\, \sigma\, \eta_1 \end{cases}$$

$$[\![\varepsilon]\!]^\pi_\theta = (?:\{\varepsilon\}) \quad [\![\alpha]\!]^\pi_\theta = (?:\{\alpha\}) \quad [\![\ell : H]\!]^\pi_\theta = [\![H]\!]^\pi_\theta \{\ell/?\}$$

$$[\![\varphi[H]]\!]^\pi_\theta = \varphi[[\![H]\!]^\pi_\theta] \qquad [\![H \cdot H']\!]^\pi_\theta = [\![H]\!]^\pi_\theta \odot [\![H']\!]^\pi_\theta$$

$$[\![h]\!]^\pi_\theta = \theta(h) \qquad [\![H + H']\!]^\pi_\theta = [\![H]\!]^\pi_\theta \oplus [\![H']\!]^\pi_\theta$$

$$[\![\mu h.H]\!]^\pi_\theta = \bigcup_{n>0} f^n(\{\ell_i : \{!\}\}_i) \quad \text{where } f(X) = [\![H]\!]^\pi_{\theta\{X/h\}}$$

$$[\![\{\pi_1 \triangleright H_1 \cdots \pi_k \triangleright H_k\}]\!]^\pi_\rho = \bigoplus_{i \in 1..k} [\![\{\pi_i \triangleright H_i\}]\!]^\pi_\rho$$

$$[\![\{0 \triangleright H\}]\!]^\pi_\rho = [\![H]\!]^\pi_\rho \qquad [\![\{\pi_0 \mid \pi_1 \triangleright H\}]\!]^\pi_\rho = [\![\{\pi_0 \triangleright H\}]\!]^\pi_\rho \oplus [\![\{\pi_1 \triangleright H\}]\!]^\pi_\rho$$

$$[\![\{r[\ell] \triangleright H\}]\!]^\pi_\rho = \begin{cases} [\![H]\!]^\pi_\rho & \text{if } \pi = r[\ell] \mid \pi' \\ (?:\bot) & \text{otherwise} \end{cases}$$

that denote the opening and closing of a framing $\varphi[\cdots]$. For example, the history $\eta = \alpha[_\varphi \alpha']_\varphi$ represents a computation that (i) generates an event α, (ii) enters the scope of φ, (iii) generates α' within the scope of φ, and (iv) leaves the scope of φ. Also, a history may end with the *truncation marker* ! (bang). The history $\eta!$ represents a prefix of a possibly non-terminating computation that generates the sequence of events η. We assume that histories are indistinguishable after truncation, i.e. $\eta!$ followed by η' equals to $\eta!$. For notational convenience, we feel free to omit curly braces when writing singleton sets, and we write $\varphi[\mathcal{H}]$ for $\{\, [_\varphi \eta]_\varphi \mid \eta \in \mathcal{H}\,\}$.

The *stateless* semantics $\langle\!\langle H \rangle\!\rangle^\pi$ of a closed history expression H depends on the given evaluation plan π, and is defined in two steps. In the first, we define the *stateful* semantics $[\![H]\!]^\pi_\theta$ (in an environment θ binding variables), i.e. a semantics in which services keep track of the histories generated by all the past invocations. A simple transformation then yields $\langle\!\langle H \rangle\!\rangle^\pi$, in which each invocation is instead independent of the previous ones, i.e. it always starts with the empty history.

We first comment on the rules for $[\![H]\!]^\pi_\theta$. The meaning of an event α is the pair $(?:\{\alpha\})$, where ? is dummy and will be bound to the relevant location. The rule for localizing H at ℓ records the actual binding: the current location ℓ replaces "?". The semantics of a sequence $H \cdot H'$ is a suitable concatenation of

Definition 7. Auxiliary operators $\odot$ and $\oplus$

$$\{\ell_i : \mathcal{H}_i\}_I \odot (? : \bot) = (? : \bot) = (? : \bot) \odot \{\ell_i : \mathcal{H}_i\}_I$$

$$\{\ell_i : \mathcal{H}_i\}_I \oplus (? : \bot) = (? : \bot) = (? : \bot) \oplus \{\ell_i : \mathcal{H}_i\}_I$$

$$\{\ell_i : \mathcal{H}_i\}_I \odot \{\ell_j : \mathcal{H}'_j\}_J = \{\ell_i : \mathcal{H}_i\mathcal{H}'_i\}_{I \cap J} \cup \{\ell_i : \mathcal{H}_i\}_{I \setminus J} \cup \{\ell_j : \mathcal{H}'_j\}_{J \setminus I}$$

$$\{\ell_i : \mathcal{H}_i\}_I \oplus \{\ell_j : \mathcal{H}'_j\}_J = \{\ell_i : \mathcal{H}_i \cup \mathcal{H}'_i\}_{I \cap J} \cup \{\ell_i : \mathcal{H}_i \cup \{\varepsilon\}\}_{I \setminus J} \cup \{\ell_j : \mathcal{H}'_j \cup \{\varepsilon\}\}_{J \setminus I}$$

the histories denoted by H and H' site by site (the operator $\odot$ is defined below). Similarly for the semantics of choices $H + H'$, that joins the histories site by site through the operator $\oplus$. The semantics of $\mu h. H$ is the least fixed point of the operator f above, computed in the cpo obtained by coalesced sum of the cpos of sets of histories $\mathcal{H}$. The semantics of a planned selection $\{\pi_i \rhd H_i\}_{i \in I}$ under a plan π is the sum of the semantics of those H_i such that π resolves π_i.

The sequentialization $\odot$ of $(\ell_i : \mathcal{H}_i)_{i \in I}$ and $(\ell_j : \mathcal{H}'_j)_{j \in J}$ comprises $\ell_i : \mathcal{H}_i\mathcal{H}'_j$ for all $i = j$ (i.e. $\ell_i : \{\eta\eta' \mid \eta \in \mathcal{H}_i, \eta' \in \mathcal{H}'_i\}$), and it also comprises $\ell_i : \mathcal{H}_i$ and $\ell_j : \mathcal{H}'_j$ for all $i \notin J$ and $j \notin I$. As an example, $(\ell_0 : \{\alpha_0\}, \ell_1 : \{\alpha_1, \beta_1\}) \odot (\ell_1 : \{\gamma_1\}, \ell_2 : \{\alpha_2\}) = (\ell_0 : \{\alpha_0\}, \ell_1 : \{\alpha_1\gamma_1, \beta_1\gamma_1\}, \ell_2 : \{\alpha_2\})$. The choice operator $\oplus$ is pretty the same, except that union replaces language concatenation. For example, $(\ell_0 : \{\alpha_0\}) \oplus (\ell_0 : \{\beta_0\}, \ell_1 : \{\beta_1\}) = (\ell_0 : \{\alpha_0, \beta_0\}, \ell_1 : \{\beta_1\})$. Note that both $\odot$ and $\oplus$ are strict.

Example 1. Consider the history expression:

$$H = \ell_0 : \alpha_0 \cdot \{r[\ell_1] \rhd \ell_1 : \sigma \cdot \alpha_1, r[\ell_2] \rhd \ell_2 : \sigma \cdot \alpha_2\} \cdot \beta_0$$

The stateful semantics of H under plan $\pi = r[\ell_1]$ is:

$$[\![\alpha_0 \cdot \{r[\ell_1] \rhd \ell_1 : \sigma \cdot \alpha_1, r[\ell_2] \rhd \ell_2 : \sigma \cdot \alpha_2\} \cdot \beta_0]\!]^\pi \{\ell_0/?\}$$
$$= \big((? : \{\alpha_0\}) \odot [\![\{r[\ell_1] \rhd \ell_1 : \sigma \cdot \alpha_1, r[\ell_2] \rhd \ell_2 : \sigma \cdot \alpha_2\}]\!]^\pi$$
$$\odot (? : \{\beta_0\})\big)\{\ell_0/?\}$$
$$= \big((? : \{\alpha_0\}) \odot [\![\ell_1 : \sigma \cdot \alpha_1]\!]^\pi \odot (? : \{\beta_0\})\big)\{\ell_0/?\}$$
$$= \big((? : \{\alpha_0\}) \odot (\ell_1 : \{\sigma\alpha_1\}) \odot (? : \{\beta_0\})\big)\{\ell_0/?\}$$
$$= (? : \{\alpha_0\beta_0\}, \ell_1 : \{\sigma\alpha_1\})\{\ell_0/?\}$$
$$= (\ell_0 : \{\alpha_0\beta_0\}, \ell_1 : \{\sigma\alpha_1\})$$

In this case, the stateless semantics just removes the event σ, i.e.:

$$\langle\!\langle H \rangle\!\rangle^\pi = (\ell_0 : \{\alpha_0\beta_0\}, \ell_1 : \{\alpha_1\}) \qquad\qquad \square$$

Example 2. Consider the history expression:

$$H = \ell_0 : (\mu h. \beta_0 + \alpha_0 \cdot \{r[\ell_1] \rhd \ell_1 : \sigma \cdot \alpha_1\} \cdot h)$$

This represents a service ℓ_0 that recursively generates α_0 and raises a request r (which can be served by ℓ_1 only). Let $\pi = r[\ell_1]$. Then:

$$\begin{aligned}
\llbracket H \rrbracket^\pi &= \llbracket \ell_0 : \mu h. \beta_0 + \alpha_0 \cdot \{r[\ell_1] \triangleright \ell_1 : \sigma \cdot \alpha_1\} \cdot h \rrbracket^\pi \\
&= \llbracket \mu h. \beta_0 + \alpha_0 \cdot \{r[\ell_1] \triangleright \ell_1 : \sigma \cdot \alpha_1\} \cdot h \rrbracket^\pi \{\ell_0/?\} \\
&= \left(\bigcup_{n>0} \llbracket f^n(\ell_0 : \{!\}, \ell_1 : \{!\}) \rrbracket^\pi \right) \{\ell_0/?\}
\end{aligned}$$

where $f(X) = \llbracket \beta_0 + \alpha_0 \cdot \{r[\ell_1] \triangleright \ell_1 : \sigma \cdot \alpha_1\} \cdot h \rrbracket^\pi_{\{X/h\}}$. The first approximation $f^1(\ell_0 : \{!\}, \ell_1 : \{!\})$ is:

$$\begin{aligned}
&\llbracket \beta_0 + \alpha_0 \cdot \{r[\ell_1] \triangleright \ell_1 : \sigma \cdot \alpha_1\} \cdot h \rrbracket^\pi_{\{(\ell_0:\{!\},\ell_1:\{!\})/h\}} \\
&= \llbracket \beta_0 \rrbracket^\pi \oplus \left(\llbracket \alpha_0 \rrbracket^\pi \odot \llbracket \{r[\ell_1] \triangleright \ell_1 : \sigma \cdot \alpha_1\} \rrbracket^\pi \odot \llbracket h \rrbracket^\pi_{\{(\ell_0:\{!\},\ell_1:\{!\})/h\}} \right) \\
&= (? : \{\beta_0\}) \oplus \left((? : \alpha_0) \odot (\ell_1 : \{\sigma\alpha_1\}) \odot (\ell_0 : \{!\}, \ell_1 : \{!\}) \right) \\
&= (? : \{\beta_0\}) \oplus (? : \{\alpha_0!\}, \ell_1 : \{\sigma\alpha_1!\}) \\
&= (? : \{\beta_0, \alpha_0!\}, \ell_1 : \{\varepsilon, \sigma\alpha_1!\})
\end{aligned}$$

The fixed point of f, after the substitution $\{\ell_0/?\}$, is:

$$\begin{aligned}
&(\ell_0 : \{\beta_0, \alpha_0!, \alpha_0\beta_0, \alpha_0\alpha_0!, \alpha_0\alpha_0\beta_0, \alpha_0\alpha_0\alpha_0! \dots\}, \\
&\quad \ell_1 : \{\varepsilon, \sigma\alpha_1, \sigma\alpha_1!, \sigma\alpha_1\sigma\alpha_1, \sigma\alpha_1\sigma\alpha_1!, \dots\})
\end{aligned}$$

The stateless semantics $\langle\!\langle H \rangle\!\rangle^\pi$ is the set:

$$(\ell_0 : \{\beta_0, \alpha_0!, \alpha_0\beta_0, \alpha_0\alpha_0!, \dots\}, \ell_1 : \{\varepsilon, \alpha_1, \alpha_1!\}) \qquad \square$$

Example 3. Consider the history expression:

$$H = \{r[\ell_0] \triangleright \ell_0 : \alpha\} \cdot \{r'[\ell_1] \triangleright \beta\}$$

The stateful semantics of H under $\pi = r[\ell_0] \mid r'[\ell_2]$ is:

$$\begin{aligned}
\llbracket H \rrbracket^\pi &= \llbracket \{r[\ell_0] \triangleright \ell_0 : \alpha\} \rrbracket^\pi \odot \llbracket \{r'[\ell_1] \triangleright \beta\} \rrbracket^\pi \\
&= (\ell_0 : \{\alpha\}) \odot (? : \bot) \\
&= (? : \bot)
\end{aligned}$$

In this case there are no σ, so the stateless and the stateful semantics coincide. $\square$

8.2   Validity

We now define when histories are valid, i.e. they arise from viable computations that do not violate any security constraint. Consider for instance $\eta_0 = \alpha_w \alpha_r \varphi[\alpha_w]$, where φ requires that no write α_w occurs after a read α_r. Then, η_0 is *not* valid according to our intended meaning, because the rightmost α_w occurs within a framing enforcing φ, and $\alpha_w \alpha_r \alpha_w$ does not obey φ. To be valid, a history η must obey all the policies within their scopes, determined by the framing events in η.

Definition 8. Safe sets and validity

The *safe sets* $S(\eta)$ of a history η are defined as:

$$S(\varepsilon) = \emptyset \qquad S(\eta\,\alpha) = S(\eta) \qquad S(\eta_0\,\varphi[\eta_1]) = S(\eta_0\,\eta_1) \cup \varphi[\eta_0^\flat\,(\eta_1^\flat)^\partial]$$

A history η is *valid* ($\models \eta$ in symbols) when:

$$\varphi[\mathcal{H}] \in S(\eta) \implies \forall \eta' \in \mathcal{H} : \eta' \models \varphi$$

A history expression H is π-*valid* when:

$$\langle\!\langle H \rangle\!\rangle^\pi \neq (? : \bot) \quad \text{and} \quad \forall \ell : \forall \eta \in \langle\!\langle H \rangle\!\rangle^\pi @\, \ell : \models \eta$$

where $(\ell_i : \mathcal{H}_i)_{i \in I} @\, \ell_j = \mathcal{H}_j$.

We formally define validity through the notion of *safe set*. For example, the safe set of η_0 is $\varphi[\{\alpha_w\alpha_r, \alpha_w\alpha_r\alpha_w\}]$. Intuitively, this means that the scope of the framing $\varphi[\cdots]$ spans over the histories $\alpha_w\alpha_r$ and $\alpha_w\alpha_r\alpha_w$. For each safe set $\varphi[\mathcal{H}]$, validity requires that *all* the histories in $\mathcal{H}$ obey φ.

Some notation is now needed. Let $\eta^\flat$ be the history obtained from η by erasing all the framing events, and let η^∂ be the set of all the prefixes of η, including the empty history ε. For example, if $\eta_0 = \alpha_w\alpha_r\varphi[\alpha_w]$, then $(\eta_0^\flat)^\partial = ((\alpha_w\alpha_r[_\varphi\alpha_w]_\varphi)^\flat)^\partial = (\alpha_w\alpha_r\alpha_w)^\partial = \{\varepsilon, \alpha_w, \alpha_w\alpha_r, \alpha_w\alpha_r\alpha_w\}$. Then, the safe set $S(\eta)$ and validity of histories and of history expressions are defined as in Def. 8.

Note that validity of a history expression is parametric with the given evaluation plan π, and it is defined location-wise on its semantics. If the plan contains unresolved choices for requests mentioned in H, then H is not π-valid, because the operators $\odot$ and $\oplus$ are strict on $\bot$.

Example 4. The safe sets of the history expression $H = \varphi[\alpha_0 \cdot \{r[\ell_1] \rhd \alpha_1, r[\ell_2] \rhd \varphi'[\alpha_2]\}] \cdot \alpha_3$, with respect to plans $r[\ell_1]$ and $r[\ell_2]$, are:

$$S(\langle\!\langle H \rangle\!\rangle^{r[\ell_1]}) = S([_\varphi\alpha_0\alpha_1]_\varphi\alpha_3) = \{\ \varphi[\{\varepsilon, \alpha_0, \alpha_0\alpha_1\}]\ \}$$
$$S(\langle\!\langle H \rangle\!\rangle^{r[\ell_2]}) = S([_\varphi\alpha_0[_{\varphi'}\alpha_2]_{\varphi'}]_\varphi\alpha_3)$$
$$= \{\ \varphi[\{\varepsilon, \alpha_0, \alpha_0\alpha_2\}], \varphi'[\{\alpha_0, \alpha_0\alpha_2\}]\ \}$$

Let φ require "never α_3", and let φ' require "never α_2". Then, H is $r[\ell_1]$-valid, because the histories ε, α_0, and $\alpha_0\alpha_1$ obey φ. Instead, H is not $r[\ell_2]$-valid, because the history $\alpha_0\alpha_2$ in the safe set $\varphi'[\{\alpha_0, \alpha_0\alpha_2\}]$ does not obey φ'. $\qquad\square$

8.3   Type and Effect System

We now introduce a type and effect system for our calculus, building upon [8]. Types and type environments, ranged over by τ and Γ, are mostly standard and are defined in the following table. The history expression H in the functional type $\tau \xrightarrow{H} \tau'$ describes the latent effect associated with an abstraction, i.e. one of the histories represented by H is generated when a value is applied to an abstraction with that type.

Definition 9. Types and Type Environments

$$\tau, \tau' ::= 1 \mid \tau \xrightarrow{H} \tau'$$
$$\Gamma ::= \emptyset \mid \Gamma; x : \tau \qquad \text{where } x \notin dom(\Gamma)$$

For notational convenience, we assume that the request type ρ in $\mathtt{req}_r\rho$ is a special type. E.g. we use $1 \xrightarrow{\varphi[\varepsilon]} (1 \xrightarrow{\varphi'[\varepsilon]} 1)$ for the request type of a service obeying φ and returning a function subject to the policy φ'. Additionally, we put some restrictions on request types. First, only functional types are allowed: this models services being considered as remote procedures (instead, initiators have type 1, so they cannot be invoked). Second, no constraints should be imposed over ρ_0 in a request type $\rho_0 \xrightarrow{\varphi} \rho_1$, i.e. in ρ_0 there are no annotations. This is because the constraints on the selected service should not affect its argument.

A typing judgment $\Gamma, H \vdash e : \tau$ means that the service e evaluates to a value of type τ, and produces a history denoted by the effect H. The auxiliary typing judgment $\Gamma, H \vdash_\ell e : \tau$ is defined as the least relation closed under the rules below, and we write $\Gamma, (\ell : H) \vdash e : \tau$ when the service e at ℓ is typed by $\Gamma, H \vdash_\ell e : \tau$. The effects in the rule for application are concatenated according to the evaluation order of the call-by-value semantics (function, argument, latent effect). The actual effect of an abstraction is the empty history expression, while the latent effect is equal to the actual effect of the function body. The rule for abstraction constraints the premise to equate the actual and latent effects, up to associativity, commutativity, idempotency and zero of $+$, associativity and zero of $\cdot$, α-conversion, and elimination of vacuous μ-binders. The next-to-last rule allows for weakening of effects. Note that our type system does not assign any type to $\mathtt{wait}$ expressions: indeed, waits are only needed in configurations, and not in service code.

We stipulated that the services provided by the network have certified types. Consequently, the typing relation is parametrized by the set W of services $\ell\langle e : \tau \rangle$ such that $\emptyset, \varepsilon \vdash_\ell e : \tau$. We assume W to be fixed, and we write $\vdash_\ell$ instead of $\vdash_{\ell,W}$. To enforce non-circular service composition, we require W to be partially ordered by $\prec$, where $\ell \prec \ell'$ if ℓ can invoke ℓ'; initiators are obviously the least elements of $\prec$, and they are not related to each other. Note that the up-wards cone of $\prec$ of an initiator represents the (partial) knowledge it has of the network.

Example 5. Consider the following λ^{req} expression:

$$e = \mathtt{if}\ b\ \mathtt{then}\ \lambda_z x.\, \alpha\ \mathtt{else}\ \lambda_z x.\, \alpha'$$

Definition 10. Typing services

$$\frac{\Gamma, H \vdash_\ell e : \tau}{\Gamma, \ell : H \vdash e : \tau} \quad \text{if } e \text{ is published at } \ell$$

$$\Gamma, \varepsilon \vdash_\ell * : 1 \qquad \Gamma, \alpha \vdash_\ell \alpha : 1 \qquad \Gamma, \varepsilon \vdash_\ell x : \Gamma(x)$$

$$\frac{\Gamma; x : \tau; z : \tau \xrightarrow{H} \tau', H \vdash_\ell e : \tau'}{\Gamma, \varepsilon \vdash_\ell \lambda_z x. \, e : \tau \xrightarrow{H} \tau'} \qquad \frac{\Gamma, H \vdash_\ell e : \tau \xrightarrow{H''} \tau' \quad \Gamma, H' \vdash_\ell e' : \tau}{\Gamma, H \cdot H' \cdot H'' \vdash_\ell e \, e' : \tau'}$$

$$\frac{\Gamma, H \vdash_\ell e : \tau}{\Gamma, \varphi[H] \vdash_\ell \varphi[e] : \tau} \qquad \frac{\Gamma, H \vdash_\ell e : \tau \quad \Gamma, H \vdash_\ell e' : \tau}{\Gamma, H \vdash_\ell \text{if } b \text{ then } e \text{ else } e' : \tau} \qquad \frac{\Gamma, H \vdash_\ell e : \tau}{\Gamma, H + H' \vdash_\ell e : \tau}$$

$$\frac{\tau = \uplus \{ \rho \boxplus_{r[\ell']} \tau' \mid \emptyset, \varepsilon \vdash_{\ell'} e : \tau' \quad \ell \prec \ell' \langle e : \tau' \rangle \quad \rho \approx \tau' \}}{\Gamma, \varepsilon \vdash_\ell \mathbf{req}_r \rho : \tau} \qquad \frac{\Gamma, H \vdash_\ell e : \tau}{\Gamma, H \vdash_\ell \{e\} : \tau}$$

Let $\tau = 1$, and $\Gamma = \{z : \tau \xrightarrow{\alpha + \alpha'} \tau; x : \tau\}$. Then, the following typing derivation is possible:

$$\frac{\dfrac{\dfrac{\Gamma, \alpha \vdash \alpha : \tau}{\Gamma, \alpha + \alpha' \vdash \alpha : \tau}}{\emptyset, \varepsilon \vdash \lambda_z x. \, \alpha : \tau \xrightarrow{\alpha + \alpha'} \tau} \qquad \dfrac{\dfrac{\Gamma, \alpha' \vdash \alpha' : \tau}{\Gamma, \alpha' + \alpha \vdash \alpha' : \tau}}{\emptyset, \varepsilon \vdash \lambda_z x. \, \alpha' : \tau \xrightarrow{\alpha' + \alpha} \tau}}{\emptyset, \varepsilon \vdash \text{if } b \text{ then } \lambda_z x. \, \alpha \text{ else } \lambda_z x. \, \alpha' : \tau \xrightarrow{\alpha + \alpha'} \tau}$$

Note that we can equate the history expressions $\alpha + \alpha'$ and $\alpha' + \alpha$, because $+$ is commutative. The typing derivation above shows the use of the weakening rule to unify the latent effects on arrow types. Let now:

$$e' = \lambda_w x. \, \text{if } b' \text{ then } * \text{ else } w(e \, x)$$

Let $\Gamma = \{w : \tau \xrightarrow{H} \tau, x : \tau\}$, where H is left undefined. Then, recalling that $\varepsilon \cdot H' = H' = H' \cdot \varepsilon$ for any history expression H', we have:

$$\frac{\Gamma, \varepsilon \vdash * : \tau \qquad \dfrac{\dfrac{\Gamma, \varepsilon \vdash w : \tau \xrightarrow{H} \tau \qquad \dfrac{\Gamma, \varepsilon \vdash e : \tau \xrightarrow{\alpha + \alpha'} \tau \quad \Gamma, \varepsilon \vdash x : \tau}{\Gamma, \alpha + \alpha' \vdash e \, x : \tau}}{\Gamma, (\alpha + \alpha') \cdot H \vdash w(e \, x) : \tau}}{\Gamma, \varphi[(\alpha + \alpha') \cdot H] \vdash \varphi[w(e \, x)] : \tau}}{\Gamma, \varepsilon + \varphi[(\alpha + \alpha') \cdot H] \vdash \text{if } b' \text{ then } * \text{ else } \varphi[w(e \, x)] : \tau}$$

To apply the typing rule for abstractions, the constraint $H = \varepsilon + \varphi[(\alpha + \alpha') \cdot H]$ must be solved. Let $H = \mu h. \, \varepsilon + \varphi[(\alpha + \alpha') \cdot h]$. It is easy to prove that:

$$\llbracket H \rrbracket = \llbracket \varepsilon + \varphi[(\alpha + \alpha') \cdot h] \rrbracket_{\{\llbracket H \rrbracket / h\}} = \{\varepsilon\} \cup \varphi[(\alpha + \alpha') \cdot \llbracket H \rrbracket]$$

We have then found a solution to the constraint above, so we can conclude that:

$$\emptyset, \varepsilon \vdash e' : \tau \xrightarrow{\mu h.\, \varepsilon + \varphi[(\alpha + \alpha') \cdot h]} \tau$$

Note in passing that a simple extension of the type inference algorithm of [43] suffices for solving constraints as the one above.   □

A service invocation $\mathtt{req}_r \rho$ has an empty actual effect, and a functional type τ, whose latent effect is a planned selection that picks from the network those services known by ℓ and matching the request type ρ.

To give a type to requests, we need some auxiliary technical notation. First we introduce $\approx$, $\boxplus$ and $\uplus$, with the help of a running example. We write $\rho \approx \tau$, and say ρ, τ *compatible*, whenever, omitting the annotations on the arrows, ρ and τ are equal. Formally:

$$1 \approx 1$$
$$(\rho_0 \xrightarrow{\varphi} \rho_1) \approx (\tau_0 \xrightarrow{H} \tau_1) \quad \text{iff } \rho_0 \approx \tau_0 \text{ and } \rho_1 \approx \tau_1$$

Example 6. Let $\rho = (\tau \rightarrow \tau) \xrightarrow{\varphi} (\tau \rightarrow \tau)$, with $\tau = 1$, be the request type in $\mathtt{req}_r \rho$, and consider two services $\ell_i \langle e_i : \tau_i \rangle$ with $\tau_i = (\tau \xrightarrow{h_i} \tau) \xrightarrow{\alpha_i \cdot h_i} (\tau \xrightarrow{\beta_i} \tau)$, for $i \in 1..2$. We have that $\tau_1 \approx \rho \approx \tau_2$, i.e. both the services are compatible with the request r.   □

The operator $\boxplus_{r[\ell]}$ combines a request type ρ and a type τ, when they are compatible. Given a request type $\rho = \rho_0 \xrightarrow{\varphi} \rho_1$ and a type $\tau = \tau_0 \xrightarrow{H} \tau_1$, the result of $\rho \boxplus_{r[\ell]} \tau$ is $\tau_0 \xrightarrow{\{r[\ell] \triangleright \ell : \varphi[\sigma \cdot H]\}} (\rho_1 \boxplus_{r[\ell]} \tau_1)$, where:

$$1 \boxplus_{r[\ell]} 1 = 1$$
$$(\rho_0 \xrightarrow{\varphi} \rho_1) \boxplus_{r[\ell]} (\tau_0 \xrightarrow{H} \tau_1) =$$
$$(\rho_0 \boxplus_{r[\ell]} \tau_0) \xrightarrow{\{r[\ell] \triangleright \varphi[H]\}} (\rho_1 \boxplus_{r[\ell]} \tau_1)$$

Example 6 (cont.). The request type ρ is composed with the service types τ_1 and τ_2 as follows:

$$\hat{\tau}_1 = (\tau \xrightarrow{h_1} \tau) \xrightarrow{\{r[\ell_1] \triangleright \ell_1 : \varphi[\sigma \cdot \alpha_1 \cdot h_1]\}} (\tau \xrightarrow{\{r[\ell_1] \triangleright \beta_1\}} \tau)$$
$$\hat{\tau}_2 = (\tau \xrightarrow{h_2} \tau) \xrightarrow{\{r[\ell_2] \triangleright \ell_2 : \varphi[\sigma \cdot \alpha_2 \cdot h_2]\}} (\tau \xrightarrow{\{r[\ell_2] \triangleright \beta_2\}} \tau)$$

where $\hat{\tau}_1 = \rho \boxplus_{r[\ell_1]} \tau_1$ and $\hat{\tau}_2 = \rho \boxplus_{r[\ell_2]} \tau_2$.   □

The top-level arrow carries a planned selection $\{r[\ell] \triangleright \ell : \varphi[\sigma \cdot H]\}$, meaning that, if the service at ℓ is chosen for r, then it generates (at location ℓ, and prefixed by σ) the behaviour H, subject to the policy φ. This top-level choice induces a dependency on the further choices for r recorded in $\rho_1 \boxplus_{r[\ell]} \tau_1$. In the example

$$\frac{\emptyset, \varepsilon \vdash_{\ell_0} \mathbf{req}_r \rho : \tau' \qquad \emptyset, \varepsilon \vdash_{\ell_0} (\lambda.\gamma) : \tau \xrightarrow{\gamma} \tau}{\emptyset, \{r[\ell_1] \rhd \ell_1 : \varphi[\sigma \cdot \alpha_1 \cdot \gamma], \ r[\ell_2] \rhd \ell_2 : \varphi[\sigma \cdot \alpha_2 \cdot \gamma]\} \vdash_{\ell_0} (\mathbf{req}_r \rho)(\lambda.\gamma) : \tau \xrightarrow{\{r[\ell_1] \rhd \beta_1, \ r[\ell_2] \rhd \beta_2\}} \tau}$$
$$\frac{}{\emptyset, \{r[\ell_1] \rhd \ell_1 : \varphi[\sigma \cdot \alpha_1 \cdot \gamma], \ r[\ell_2] \rhd \ell_2 : \varphi[\sigma \cdot \alpha_2 \cdot \gamma]\} \cdot \{r[\ell_1] \rhd \beta_1, \ r[\ell_2] \rhd \beta_2\} \vdash_{\ell_0} (\mathbf{req}_r \rho)(\lambda.\gamma)* : \tau}$$
$$\emptyset, \ell_0 : \{r[\ell_1] \rhd \ell_1 : \varphi[\sigma \cdot \alpha_1 \cdot \gamma], \ r[\ell_2] \rhd \ell_2 : \varphi[\sigma \cdot \alpha_2 \cdot \gamma]\} \cdot \{r[\ell_1] \rhd \beta_1, \ r[\ell_2] \rhd \beta_2\} \vdash (\mathbf{req}_r \rho)(\lambda.\gamma)* : \tau$$

Fig. 12. Typing derivation for Example 7

above, the service at ℓ_1 returns a function whose (latent) effect $\{r[\ell] \rhd \beta_1\}$ means that β_1 occurs in the location where the function will be actually applied.

Note that combining functional types never affects the type of the argument. This reflects the intuition that the type of the argument to be passed to the selected service cannot be constrained by the request.

Eventually, the operator $\mathbb{U}$ unifies the types obtained by combining the request type with the service types. Given two types $\tau = \tau_0 \xrightarrow{H} \tau_1$ and $\tau' = \tau_0' \xrightarrow{H'} \tau_1'$, the result of $\tau \mathbb{U} \tau'$ is $\tau_0'' \xrightarrow{H \cup H'} (\tau_1 \varsigma \mathbb{U} \tau_1' \varsigma)$, where ς unifies τ_0 and τ_0' (i.e. $\tau_0 \varsigma = \tau_0' \varsigma = \tau_0''$), and:

$$1 \mathbb{U} 1 = 1$$
$$(\tau_0 \xrightarrow{H} \tau_1) \mathbb{U} (\tau_0' \xrightarrow{H'} \tau_1') = (\tau_0 \mathbb{U} \tau_0') \xrightarrow{H \cup H'} (\tau_1 \mathbb{U} \tau_1')$$

Example 6 (cont.). We now unify the combination of the request type ρ with the service types, obtaining:

$$\tau' = (\tau \xrightarrow{h} \tau) \xrightarrow{\{r[\ell_1] \rhd \ell_1 : \varphi[\sigma \cdot \alpha_1 \cdot h], \ r[\ell_2] \rhd \ell_2 : \varphi[\sigma \cdot \alpha_2 \cdot h]\}}$$
$$(\tau \xrightarrow{\{r[\ell_1] \rhd \beta_1, \ r[\ell_2] \rhd \beta_2\}} \tau)$$

where $\varsigma = \{h/h_1, h/h_2\}$ is the selected unifier between $\tau \xrightarrow{h_1} \tau$ and $\tau \xrightarrow{h_2} \tau$. □

The following example further illustrates how requests and services are typed.

Example 7. Consider the request and the services of Example 6, and consider the initiator $(\mathbf{req}_r \rho)(\lambda.\gamma)*$ at site ℓ_0. Note that applying any service resulting from the request r to the function $\lambda.\gamma$ yields a new function, which we eventually apply to the value $*$. We have the typing derivation in Fig. 7. The stateful semantics $[\![H]\!]^\pi$ under $\pi = r[\ell_1]$ is:

$$[\![\{r[\ell_1] \rhd \ell_1 : \varphi[\sigma \cdot \alpha_1 \cdot \gamma], r[\ell_2] \rhd \ell_2 : \varphi[\sigma \cdot \alpha_2 \cdot \gamma]\}]\!]^\pi$$
$$\odot [\![\{r[\ell_1] \rhd \beta_1, \ r[\ell_2] \rhd \beta_2\}]\!]^\pi \{\ell_0/?\}$$
$$= (\ell_1 : \{\varphi[\sigma \alpha_1 \gamma]\}) \odot (? : \{\beta_1\})\{\ell_0/?\}$$
$$= (\ell_1 : \{\varphi[\sigma \alpha_1 \gamma]\}, \ell_0 : \{\beta_1\}) \qquad \qquad □$$

8.4 Type Safety

We now state two central results about our type and effect system. In this section we shall restrict our attention to the case where (i) services never become unavailable, and (ii) planning is only performed at start-up of execution, i.e. there is no dynamic replanning. Under these assumptions, rules PLN, FAIL and UNRES are never used. In Section 8.5 we shall come back on this issue.

A plan π is *well-typed* for a service at ℓ, $wt_{@\ell}(\pi)$, when, for each request $\mathrm{req}_r\rho$, the chosen service is compatible with ρ, while respecting the partial order $\prec$:

$$wt_{@\ell}(0)$$
$$wt_{@\ell}(\pi \mid \pi') \text{ if } wt_{@\ell}(\pi) \text{ and } wt_{@\ell}(\pi')$$
$$wt_{@\ell}(r[\ell']) \quad \text{if } \ell \prec \ell',\ \ell'\langle e : \tau \rangle \text{ and } \rho \approx \tau$$

The next theorem states that our type and effect system correctly over-approximates the actual run-time histories. Consider first a network with a single initiator e at location ℓ_1, and let its computed effect be H, with $\langle\!\langle H \rangle\!\rangle^\pi = (\ell_1 : \mathcal{H}_1, \ldots, \ell_k : \mathcal{H}_k)$ for a given plan π. For each site ℓ_i, the run-time histories occurring therein are prefixes of the histories in $\mathcal{H}_i$ (without framing events). Now, consider a network with $n < k$ initiators at the first n sites, each with its own plan π_j and effect H_j. Since initiators cannot invoke each other, we have $\langle\!\langle H_j \rangle\!\rangle^{\pi_j} = (\ell_1 : \emptyset, \ldots, \ell_j : \mathcal{H}_j, \ldots, \ell_n : \emptyset, \ell_{n+1} : \mathcal{H}_{n+1,j}, \ldots, \ell_k : \mathcal{H}_{k,j})$. For each service ℓ_i, the run-time histories at ℓ_i belong to (the prefixes of) one of the $\mathcal{H}_{i,j}$, with $1 \leq j \leq n$ (see Ex. 8). As usual, precision is lost when reducing the conditional construct to non-determinism, and when dealing with recursive functions.

Theorem 1. *Let $\{\ell_i\langle e_i : \tau_i\rangle\}_{i \in I}$ be a network, let N_0 be its initial configuration with all π_i well-typed, and let $\emptyset, H_i \vdash e_i : \tau_i$. If $N_0 \to^* \{\ell_i : \pi'_i \rhd \eta_i, e'_i\}_{i \in I}$, then:*

$$\eta_i \in \begin{cases} (\langle\!\langle H_i \rangle\!\rangle^{\pi_i} @ \ell_i)^{\flat\partial} & \text{if } \ell_i \text{ is an initiator} \\ (\sigma\langle\!\langle H_j \rangle\!\rangle^{\pi_j} @ \ell_i)^{\flat\partial} & \text{if } \ell_i \text{ is a service,} \\ & \text{for some initiator } \ell_j \end{cases}$$

Example 8. Consider an initiator $e_0 = \alpha_0; (\mathrm{req}_r\rho)*$ at site ℓ_0, with $\rho = 1 \to 1$, and a single service $e_1 = \lambda.\ \alpha_1; \varphi[\text{if } b \text{ then } \alpha_2 \text{ else } \alpha_3]$ at site ℓ_1, with φ requiring "never α_3". Assume that the guard b always evaluates to true, and that the execution monitor is off (we therefore omit it from configurations). Then, under the plan $\pi_0 = r[\ell_1]$, we have the following computation:

$$\ell_0 : \pi_0 \rhd \varepsilon, e_0 \parallel \ell_1 : 0 \rhd \varepsilon, *$$
$$\to \ell_0 : \pi_0 \rhd \alpha_0, \mathrm{req}_r\rho * \parallel \ell_1 : 0 \rhd \varepsilon, *$$
$$\to \ell_0 : \pi_0 \rhd \alpha_0, \mathrm{wait}\ \ell_1 \parallel \ell_1 : 0 \rhd \sigma, e_1 *$$
$$\to \ell_0 : \pi_0 \rhd \alpha_0, \mathrm{wait}\ \ell_1 \parallel \ell_1 : 0 \rhd \sigma\alpha_1, \varphi[\text{if} \cdots]$$
$$\to \ell_0 : \pi_0 \rhd \alpha_0, \mathrm{wait}\ \ell_1 \parallel \ell_1 : 0 \rhd \sigma\alpha_1, \varphi[\alpha_2]$$
$$\to \ell_0 : \pi_0 \rhd \alpha_0, \mathrm{wait}\ \ell_1 \parallel \ell_1 : 0 \rhd \sigma\alpha_1\alpha_2, \varphi[*]$$
$$\to \ell_0 : \pi_0 \rhd \alpha_0, \mathrm{wait}\ \ell_1 \parallel \ell_1 : 0 \rhd \sigma\alpha_1\alpha_2, *$$
$$\to \ell_0 : \pi_0 \rhd \alpha_0, * \parallel \ell_1 : 0 \rhd \varepsilon, *$$

The history expression H_0 extracted from e_0 is:

$$\ell_0 : \alpha_0 \cdot \{r[\ell_1] \rhd \ell_1 : \sigma \cdot \alpha_1 \cdot \varphi[\alpha_2 + \alpha_3]\}$$

Then, $\langle\!\langle H_0 \rangle\!\rangle^{\pi_0} = (\ell_0 : \{\alpha_0\}, \ell_1 : \{\alpha_1[_\varphi\alpha_2]_\varphi, \alpha_1[_\varphi\alpha_3]_\varphi\})$, and the run-time histories generated at site ℓ_1 are strictly contained in the set $(\sigma\langle\!\langle H_0 \rangle\!\rangle^{\pi_0}@\ell_1)^{\flat\partial} = \{\sigma\alpha_1[_\varphi\alpha_2]_\varphi, \sigma\alpha_1[_\varphi\alpha_3]_\varphi\}^{\flat\partial} = \{\sigma\alpha_1\alpha_2, \sigma\alpha_1\alpha_3\}^\partial = \{\varepsilon, \sigma, \sigma\alpha_1, \sigma\alpha_1\alpha_2, \sigma\alpha_1\alpha_3\}$. □

We can now state the type safety property. We say that a plan π is *viable* for e at ℓ when the evolution of e within a network, under plan π, does not go wrong at ℓ. A computation *goes wrong* at ℓ when it reaches a configuration whose state at ℓ is stuck. A state $\ell : \pi \rhd \eta, e$ is *not stuck* if either $e = v$, or $e = (\mathrm{req}_r\rho)v$, or $e = \mathtt{wait}\,\ell'$, or $\ell : \pi \rhd \eta, e \to \ell : \pi \rhd \eta', e'$. Note that we do not consider requests and waits to be stuck. To see why, consider e.g. the network configuration $\ell_1 : r[\ell_2] \rhd \eta_1, (\mathrm{req}_r\rho)v \parallel \ell_2 : \pi \rhd \eta_2, e \parallel \ell_3 : r[\ell_2] \rhd \eta_3, \mathtt{wait}\,\ell_2$. The initiator at ℓ_1 is not stuck, because a fair scheduler will allow it to access the service at ℓ_2, as soon as the initiator at ℓ_3 has obtained a reply.

Theorem 2 (Type Safety). *Let $\{\ell_i\langle e_i : \tau_i \rangle\}_{i\in I}$ be a network of services, and let $\emptyset, H_i \vdash e_i : \tau_i$ for all $i \in I$. If H_i is π_i-valid for π_i well-typed, then π_i is viable for e_i at ℓ_i.*

Example 9. Consider the network in Ex. 6, where we fix $e_i = \lambda x. (\alpha_i; (x*); (\lambda.\beta_i))$ for $i \in 1..2$. Assume the constraint φ on the request type ρ is true. Consider now the initiator $e_0 = \varphi_0[(\mathrm{req}_r\rho(\lambda.\gamma))*]$ at ℓ_0, where φ_0 requires "never β_2". Let $\pi = r[\ell_1]$. The history expression H_0 of e_0 (inferred as in Ex. 7) is π-valid. Indeed, $\langle\!\langle H_0 \rangle\!\rangle^\pi = (\ell_0 : \{\varphi_0[\beta_1]\}, \ell_1 : \{\varphi[\alpha_1\gamma]\})$, and both $\varphi_0[\beta_1]$ and $\varphi[\alpha_1\gamma]$ are valid. As predicted by Theorem 2, the plan π is viable for e_0 at ℓ_0:

$$\ell_0 : \pi \rhd \varepsilon, \varphi_0[(\mathrm{req}_r\rho(\lambda.\gamma))*] \parallel \ell_1 : 0 \rhd \varepsilon, *$$
$$\to \ell_0 : \pi \rhd \varepsilon, \varphi_0[(\mathtt{wait}\,\ell_1)*] \parallel \ell_1 : 0 \rhd \sigma, e_1(\lambda.\gamma)$$
$$\to \ell_0 : \pi \rhd \varepsilon, \varphi_0[(\mathtt{wait}\,\ell_1)*] \parallel \ell_1 : 0 \rhd \sigma\alpha_1, \gamma; (\lambda.\beta_1)$$
$$\to \ell_0 : \pi \rhd \varepsilon, \varphi_0[(\mathtt{wait}\,\ell_1)*] \parallel \ell_1 : 0 \rhd \sigma\alpha_1\gamma, (\lambda.\beta_1)$$
$$\to \ell_0 : \pi \rhd \varepsilon, \varphi_0[(\lambda.\beta_1)*] \parallel \ell_1 : 0 \rhd \varepsilon, *$$
$$\to \ell_0 : \pi \rhd \beta_1, \varphi_0[*] \parallel \ell_1 : 0 \rhd \varepsilon, *$$

Note that we have not displayed the state of the execution monitor (always off), nor the configurations at site ℓ_2, because irrelevant here. Consider now the plan $\pi' = r[\ell_2]$. Then H_0 is not π'-valid, because $\langle\!\langle H_0 \rangle\!\rangle^{\pi'} = (\ell_0 : \{\varphi_0[\beta_2]\}, \ell_2 : \{\varphi[\alpha_2\gamma]\})$, and the event β_2 violates φ_0. In this case the computation:

$$\ell_0 : \pi \rhd \varepsilon, \varphi_0[(\mathrm{req}_r\rho(\lambda.\gamma))*] \parallel \ell_2 : 0 \rhd \varepsilon, *$$
$$\to^* \ell_0 : \pi \rhd \varepsilon, \varphi_0[\beta_2] \parallel \ell_2 : 0 \rhd \varepsilon, *$$

is correctly aborted, because $\beta_2 \not\models \varphi_0$. □

8.5   A Planning Strategy

We now focus on the case where services may become unavailable, and planning may be performed at run-time. To do that, we shall complete the definition of the PLN and FAIL rules of the operational semantics of networks, by implementing the functions *plan* and *fail*. To do that, we adopt a planning strategy that mixes the replan and sandboxing strategies introduced in Section 5. To keep our presentation simple, we resort to the Greyfriars Bobby strategy to cope with disappearing services, and so we just wait that the disappeared services become available again. Definition 11 summarizes our planning and recovery strategies.

Consider you want to replan an expression e, when the current plan is π and the current state of the monitor flag is m. Our strategy constructs a new plan π' which is coherent with π on the choices already taken in the past (indeed, modifying past choices could invalidate the viability of the new plan, as shown in Ex. 10). To do that, we first update the global history expression (i.e. that used to compute the starting plan) with all the information about the newly discovered services, possibly discarding the services become unavailable. The result of this step is then analysed with the model-checker of Section 9 in search of viable plans. If a viable plan is found, then it is substituted for the old plan, and the execution proceeds with the execution monitor turned off. If no viable plan is found, the service repository is searched for services that fulfill the "syntactical" requirements of requests, i.e. for each $\mathsf{req}_r\rho$ to replan, the contract type ρ is compatible with the type of the chosen service. The execution then continues with the so-constructed plan, but the monitor is now turned on, because there is no guarantee that the selected services will obey the imposed constraints. If there are no services in the repository that obey this weaker condition, we still try to proceed with a plan with unresolved choices, keeping the execution monitor on and planning "on demand" each future request.

Example 10. Consider the following initiator service at location ℓ_0:

$$e_0 = \varphi[(\mathtt{let}\ f = \mathsf{req}_r 1 \to (1 \to 1)\ \mathtt{in}\ f\,*);$$
$$\{\mathtt{let}\ g = \mathsf{req}_{r'} 1 \to (1 \to 1)\ \mathtt{in}\ g\,*\}]$$

The service obtains a function f through the first request r, applies it, then it asks for a plan to get a second function g through r' and apply it. The policy φ requires that neither $\alpha\alpha$ nor $\beta\beta$ are performed at ℓ_0. Suppose the network repository consists just of the following two services, located at ℓ_1 and ℓ_2:

$$\ell_1\langle\lambda x.\lambda y.\,\alpha : 1 \to (1 \xrightarrow{\alpha} 1)\rangle \qquad \ell_2\langle\lambda x.\lambda y.\,\beta : 1 \to (1 \xrightarrow{\beta} 1)\rangle$$

The history expression of the initiator service is:

$$H = \ell_0 : \varphi[\{r[\ell_1] \rhd \alpha, r[\ell_2] \rhd \beta\} \cdot \{r'[\ell_1] \rhd \alpha, r'[\ell_2] \rhd \beta\}]$$

Definition 11. Planning and recovering strategies

Let $\bar{\pi}$ be the sub-plan of π containing all the already resolved choices.
Let H be the history expression of the initiator of the computation.
Let L be the set of newly-discovered available services.
Let H_L be the update of H with the information about the services in L.
Let $\pi' = \bar{\pi} \mid \pi''$ be a plan coherent with π on the already resolved choices.
Then:

$$plan(\pi, m, e) = \begin{cases} (\pi', \mathit{off}) & \text{if } H_L \text{ is } \pi'\text{-valid} \\ (\pi', \mathit{on}) & \text{if } \forall \mathtt{req}_r \rho \in e \ : \ r[\ell'] \in \pi' \wedge \ell' : \tau \implies \rho \approx \tau \\ (\bar{\pi} \mid \pi_?, \mathit{on}) & \text{otherwise, where } \pi_? \text{ maps each } r \notin \bar{\pi} \text{ to ?} \end{cases}$$

$$fail(\pi, m, e) = (\pi, m) \qquad \text{(Greyfriars Bobby)}$$

Assume that the execution starts with the viable plan $\pi = r[\ell_1] \mid r'[\ell_2]$, which would generate the history $\alpha\beta$ at ℓ_0, so obeying the policy φ.

$$\ell_0 : \pi \rhd \varepsilon, \mathit{off}, e_0 \parallel \ell_1 \rhd \varepsilon, \lambda x.\lambda y.\, \alpha \parallel \ell_2 \rhd \varepsilon, \lambda x.\lambda y.\, \beta$$
$$\to^* \ell_0 : \pi \rhd \alpha, \mathit{off}, \{\mathtt{let}\ g = \mathtt{req}_{r'} 1 \to (1 \to 1)\ \mathtt{in}\ g *\}$$
$$\parallel \ell_1 \rhd \varepsilon, \lambda x.\lambda y.\, \alpha \parallel \ell_2 \rhd \varepsilon, \lambda x.\lambda y.\, \beta$$

Just after the function f has been applied, the service at ℓ_2 becomes unavailable:

$$\to^* \ell_0 : \pi \rhd \alpha, \mathit{off}, \{\mathtt{let}\ g = \mathtt{req}_{r'} 1 \to (1 \to 1)\ \mathtt{in}\ g *\}$$
$$\parallel \ell_1 \rhd \varepsilon, \lambda x.\lambda y.\, \alpha \parallel \ell_2 \rhd \varepsilon, \mathsf{N/A}$$

Assume now that a new service is discovered at ℓ_3, with type $1 \to (1 \xrightarrow{\beta} 1)$:

$$\to^* \ell_0 : \pi \rhd \alpha, \mathit{off}, \{\mathtt{let}\ g = \mathtt{req}_{r'} 1 \to (1 \to 1)\ \mathtt{in}\ g *\}$$
$$\parallel \ell_1 \rhd \varepsilon, \lambda x.\lambda y.\, \alpha \parallel \ell_2 \rhd \varepsilon, \mathsf{N/A} \parallel \ell_3 \rhd \varepsilon, \lambda x.\lambda y.\, \beta$$

The planning strategy in Def. 11 determines that the plan $\pi' = r[\ell_1] \mid r'[\ell_3]$ is viable, and so the execution can safely proceed with π' and with the monitor turned off. Observe that the plan $\pi'' = r[\ell_3] \mid r'[\ell_1]$ is also viable, but it changes the choice already made for the request r. Using π'' instead of π' would lead to a violation of the policy φ, because of the history $\alpha\alpha$ generated at ℓ_0. $\qquad\square$

It is possible to extend the Type Safety result of Theorem 2 in the more general case that also the rules PLN, FAIL and UNRES can be applied. As before, as long as none of the selected services disappear and the initial plan is complete, we have the same static guarantees ensured by Theorem 2: starting from a viable plan will drive secure computations that never go wrong, so making the execution monitor unneeded. The same property also holds when the dynamic plan obtained through the rule PLN is a complete one, and the monitor is off.

Instead, when the new plan is not complete, we get a weaker property. The execution monitor guarantees that security will never be violated, but now there is no liveness guarantee: the execution may get stuck because of an attempted unsecure action, or because we are unable to find a suitable service for an unresolved request.

In the following section, we shall present a verification technique that extracts from a history expression the plans that make it valid.

9   Planning Secure Service Composition

Once extracted a history expression H from an expression e, we have to analyse H to find if there is any viable plan for the execution of e. This issue is not trivial, because the effect of selecting a given service for a request is not confined to the execution of that service. For instance, the history generated while running a service may later on violate a policy that will become active after the service has returned (see Example 11 below). Since each service selection affects the *whole* execution of a program, we cannot simply devise a viable plan by selecting services that satisfy the constraints imposed by the requests, only.

The first step of our planning technique (Section 9.1) consists then in lifting all the service choices $r[\ell]$ to the top-level of H. This semantic-preserving transformation, called *linearization*, results in effects of the form $\{\pi_1 \rhd H_1 \cdots \pi_n \rhd H_n\}$, where each H_i is free of further planned selection. Its intuitive meaning is that, under the plan π_i, the effect of the overall service composition e is H_i.

The other steps in our technical development allows for mechanically verifying the validity of history expressions that, like the H_i produced by linearization, have no planned selections. Our technique is based on model checking Basic Process Algebras (BPAs) with Finite State Automata (FSA). The standard decision procedure for verifying that a BPA process p satisfies a ω-regular property φ amounts to constructing the pushdown automaton for p and the Büchi automaton for the negation of φ. Then, the property holds if it is empty the (context-free) language accepted by the conjunction of the above, which is still a pushdown automaton. This problem is known to be decidable, and several algorithms and tools show this approach feasible [25].

Recall however that, as it is, our notion of validity is non-regular, because of the arbitrary nesting of framings. As an example, consider again the history expression $H = \mu h. \alpha + h \cdot h + \varphi[h]$. The language $[\![H]\!]^\pi$ is context-free and non-regular, because it contains unbounded pairs of balanced $[_\varphi$ and $]_\varphi$. Since context-free languages are not closed under intersection, the emptiness problem is undecidable.

To apply the procedure sketched above, we will first manipulate history expressions in order to make validity a regular property. This transformation, called *regularization*, is defined in Section 9.2, and it preserves validity of history expressions. In Section 9.3 we make history expression amenable to model-checking, by transforming them into BPAs. In Section 9.4 we construct the FSAs $A_{\varphi_{[]}}$ used for model-checking validity, by suitably transforming the automata A_φ defining security policies.

Summing up, we extract from an expression e a history expression H, we linearize it into $\{\pi_1 \triangleright H_1 \cdots \pi_k \triangleright H_k\}$, and if some H_i is valid, then we can deduce that H is π_i-valid. By Theorem 2, the plan π_i safely drives the execution of e, without resorting to any run-time monitor. To verify the validity of an history expressions that, like the H_i above, has no planned selections, we regularize H_i to remove redundant framings, we transform H_i into a BPA $BPA(H_i)$, and we model-check $BPA(H_i)$ with the FSAs $A_{\varphi_{[]}}$.

9.1 Linearization of History Expressions

Example 11. Let $e = (\lambda x. (\mathtt{req}_{r_2}\rho_2)x) ((\mathtt{req}_{r_1}\rho_1)*)$, be an initiator, $\rho_1 = \tau \to (\tau \to \tau)$ and $\rho_2 = (\tau \to \tau) \xrightarrow{\varphi} \tau$, where $\tau = 1$ and φ requires "never γ after β". Intuitively, the service selected upon the request r_1 returns a function, which is then passed as an argument to the service selected upon r_2. Assume the network comprises exactly the following four services:

$$\ell_1\langle e_{\ell_1} : \tau \xrightarrow{\alpha} (\tau \xrightarrow{\beta} \tau)\rangle \qquad \ell_2\langle e_{\ell_2} : (\tau \xrightarrow{h} \tau) \xrightarrow{h \cdot \gamma} \tau\rangle$$
$$\ell_1'\langle e_{\ell_1'} : \tau \xrightarrow{\alpha'} (\tau \xrightarrow{\beta'} \tau)\rangle \qquad \ell_2'\langle e_{\ell_2'} : (\tau \xrightarrow{h} \tau) \xrightarrow{\varphi'[h]} \tau\rangle$$

where φ' requires "never β'". Since the request type ρ_1 matches the types of e_{ℓ_1} and $e_{\ell_1'}$, both these services can be selected for the request r_1. Similarly, both e_{ℓ_2} and $e_{\ell_2'}$ can be chosen for r_2. Therefore, we have to consider four possible plans when evaluating the history expression H of e:

$$H = \{r_1[\ell_1] \triangleright \ell_1 : \sigma \cdot \alpha, r_1[\ell_1'] \triangleright \ell_1' : \sigma \cdot \alpha'\} \cdot$$
$$\{r_2[\ell_2] \triangleright \ell_2 : \varphi[\sigma \cdot \{\underline{r_1[\ell_1]} \triangleright \beta, \underline{r_1[\ell_1']} \triangleright \beta'\} \cdot \gamma],$$
$$r_2[\ell_2'] \triangleright \ell_2' : \varphi[\sigma \cdot \varphi'[\{\underline{r_1[\ell_1]} \triangleright \beta, \underline{r_1[\ell_1']} \triangleright \beta'\}]]\}$$

Consider first H under the plan $\pi_1 = r_1[\ell_1] \mid r_2[\ell_2]$, yielding $\langle\!\langle H \rangle\!\rangle^{\pi_1} = (\ell_0 : \emptyset, \ell_1 : \{\alpha\}, \ell_2 : \{\varphi[\beta\gamma]\})$. Then, H is not π_1-valid, because the policy φ is violated at ℓ_2. Consider now $\pi_2 = r_1[\ell_1'] \mid r_2[\ell_2']$, yielding $\langle\!\langle H \rangle\!\rangle^{\pi_2} = (\ell_0 : \emptyset, \ell_1' : \{\alpha'\}, \ell_2 : \{\varphi[\varphi'[\beta']]\})$. Then, H is not π_2-valid, because the policy φ' is violated. Instead, the remaining two plans, $r_1[\ell_1] \mid r_2[\ell_2']$ and $r_1[\ell_1'] \mid r_2[\ell_2]$ are viable for e. $\qquad\square$

As shown above, the tree-shaped structure of planned selections makes it difficult to determine the plans π under which a history expression is valid. Things become easier if we "linearize" such a tree structure into a set of history expressions, forming an equivalent planned selection $\{\pi_1 \triangleright H_1 \cdots \pi_k \triangleright H_k\}$, where no H_i has further selections. E.g., the linearization of H in Example 11 is:

$$\{r_1[\ell_1] \mid r_2[\ell_2] \triangleright \ell_1 : \sigma \cdot \alpha \cdot (\ell_2 : \varphi[\sigma \cdot \beta \cdot \gamma]),$$
$$r_1[\ell_1] \mid r_2[\ell_2'] \triangleright \ell_1 : \sigma \cdot \alpha \cdot (\ell_2' : \varphi[\sigma \cdot \varphi'[\beta]]),$$
$$r_1[\ell_1'] \mid r_2[\ell_2] \triangleright \ell_1' : \sigma \cdot \alpha' \cdot (\ell_2 : \varphi[\sigma \cdot \beta' \cdot \gamma]),$$
$$r_1[\ell_1'] \mid r_2[\ell_2'] \triangleright \ell_1' : \sigma \cdot \alpha' \cdot (\ell_2' : \varphi[\sigma \cdot \varphi'[\beta']]))\}$$

Formally, we say that H is *equivalent* to H' ($H \equiv H'$ in symbols) when $\langle\!\langle H \rangle\!\rangle^\pi = \langle\!\langle H' \rangle\!\rangle^\pi$, for each plan π. The following properties of $\equiv$ hold.

Theorem 3. *The relation $\equiv$ is a congruence, and it satisfies the following equations between planned selections:*

$$H \equiv \{0 \triangleright H\} \tag{1}$$

$$\{\pi_i \triangleright H_i\}_{i \in I} \cdot \{\pi'_j \triangleright H'_j\}_{j \in J} \equiv \{\pi_i \mid \pi'_j \triangleright H_i \cdot H'_j\}_{i \in I, j \in J} \tag{2}$$

$$\{\pi_i \triangleright H_i\}_{i \in I} + \{\pi'_j \triangleright H'_j\}_{j \in J} \equiv \{\pi_i \mid \pi'_j \triangleright H_i + H'_j\}_{i \in I, j \in J} \tag{3}$$

$$\varphi[\{\pi_i \triangleright H_i\}_{i \in I}] \equiv \{\pi_i \triangleright \varphi[H_i]\}_{i \in I} \tag{4}$$

$$\mu h. \{\pi_i \triangleright H_i\} \equiv \{\pi_i \triangleright \mu h. H_i\}_{i \in I} \tag{5}$$

$$\{\pi_i \triangleright \{\pi'_{i,j} \triangleright H_{i,j}\}_{j \in J}\}_{i \in I} \equiv \{\pi_i \mid \pi'_{i,j} \triangleright H_{i,j}\}_{i \in I, j \in J} \tag{6}$$

$$\ell : \{\pi_i \triangleright H_i\} \equiv \{\pi_i \triangleright \ell : H_i\}_{i \in I} \tag{7}$$

Example 12. Let $H = \mu h. \{r[\ell_1] \triangleright \alpha_1, \ r[\ell_2] \triangleright \alpha_2\} \cdot h$. Then, using equations (1), (2) and (6) of Theorem 3, and the identity of the plan 0, we obtain:

$$\begin{aligned}
H &\equiv \mu h. \{r[\ell_1] \triangleright \alpha_1, \ r[\ell_2] \triangleright \alpha_2\} \cdot \{0 \triangleright h\} \\
&\equiv \mu h. \{r[\ell_1] \mid 0 \triangleright \alpha_1 \cdot h, \ r[\ell_2] \mid 0 \triangleright \alpha_2 \cdot h\} \\
&= \mu h. \{r[\ell_1] \triangleright \alpha_1 \cdot h, \ r[\ell_2] \triangleright \alpha_2 \cdot h\} \\
&\equiv \{r[\ell_1] \triangleright \mu h. \alpha_1 \cdot h, \ r[\ell_2] \triangleright \mu h. \alpha_2 \cdot h\}
\end{aligned}$$

Note that the original H can choose a service among ℓ_1 and ℓ_2 at *each* iteration of the loop. Instead, in the linearization of H, the request r will be resolved into the *same* service at each iteration. ▢

Example 13. Let $H = \{r[\ell_1] \triangleright \alpha_1 \cdot \{r'[\ell'_1] \triangleright \beta_1, r'[\ell'_2] \triangleright \beta_2\}, \ r[\ell_2] \triangleright \alpha_2\}$. Applying equations (1), (2) and (7) of Theorem 3, we obtain:

$$\begin{aligned}
H &\equiv \{r[\ell_1] \triangleright \{0 \triangleright \alpha_1\} \cdot \{r'[\ell'_1] \triangleright \beta_1, r'[\ell'_2] \triangleright \beta_2\}, \ r[\ell_2] \triangleright \alpha_2\} \\
&\equiv \{r[\ell_1] \triangleright \{0 \mid r'[\ell'_1] \triangleright \alpha_1 \cdot \beta_1, 0 \mid r'[\ell'_2] \triangleright \alpha_1 \cdot \beta_2\}, \ r[\ell_2] \triangleright \alpha_2\} \\
&= \{r[\ell_1] \triangleright \{r'[\ell'_1] \triangleright \alpha_1 \cdot \beta_1, r'[\ell'_2] \triangleright \alpha_1 \cdot \beta_2\}, \ r[\ell_2] \triangleright \alpha_2\} \\
&\equiv \{r[\ell_1] \mid r'[\ell'_1] \triangleright \alpha_1 \cdot \beta_1, \ r[\ell_1] \mid r'[\ell'_2] \triangleright \alpha_1 \cdot \beta_2, \ r[\ell_2] \triangleright \alpha_2\} \quad ▢
\end{aligned}$$

We say that a history expression H is *linear* when $H = \{\pi_1 \triangleright H_1 \cdots \pi_k \triangleright H_k\}$, the plans are pairwise *independent* (i.e. $\pi_i \neq \pi_j \mid \pi$ for all $i \neq j$ and π) and no H_i has planned selections.

Given a history expression H, we obtain its linearization in three steps. First, we apply the first equation of Theorem 3 to each event, variable and ε in H. Then, we orient the equations of Theorem 3 from left to right, obtaining a rewriting system that is easily proved finitely terminating and confluent – up to the equational laws of the algebra of plans. The resulting planned selection $H' = \{\pi_1 \triangleright H_1 \cdots \pi_k \triangleright H_k\}$ has no further selections in H_i, but there may be non-independent plans (recall that we discard $\pi_i \triangleright H_i$ when π_i is ill-formed).

In the third linearization step, for each such pairs, we update H' by inserting $\pi_i \triangleright H_i + H_j$, and removing $\pi_j \triangleright H_j$.

The following result enables us to detect the viable plans for service composition: executions driven by any of them will never violate the security constraints on demand.

Theorem 4. *If $H = \{\pi_1 \triangleright H_1 \cdots \pi_k \triangleright H_k\}$ is linear, and H_i is valid for some $i \in 1..k$, then H is π_i-valid.*

9.2   Regularization of Redundant Framings

History expressions can generate histories with *redundant framings*, i.e. nesting of the same framing. For example, $\eta = \alpha\varphi[\alpha'\varphi'[\varphi[\alpha'']]]$ has an inner redundant framing φ around α''. Since α'' is already under the scope of the outermost φ-framing, it happens that η is valid if and only if $\alpha\varphi[\alpha'\varphi'[\alpha'']]$ is valid. Formally, the S-sets of η comprise $\varphi[\{\alpha, \alpha\alpha', \alpha\alpha'\alpha''\}]$ for the outer framing, and $\varphi[\{\alpha\alpha', \alpha\alpha'\alpha''\}]$ for the inner one. Validity requires that all the histories in $\{\alpha, \alpha\alpha', \alpha\alpha'\alpha''\}$ and $\{\alpha\alpha', \alpha\alpha'\alpha''\}$ obey φ. Since the second set is strictly included in the first one, then the *inner* framing is redundant.

Removing redundant framings from a history preserves its validity. But one needs the expressive power of a pushdown automaton, because framings openings and closings are to be matched in pairs. For example, consider the history:

$$\eta = \alpha \overbrace{[_\varphi \cdots [_\varphi}^{n} \overbrace{]_\varphi \cdots]_\varphi}^{m} [_\varphi$$

The last $[_\varphi$ is redundant if $n > m$; it is *not* redundant if $n = m$.

Below, we define a transformation that, given a history expression H, yields a H' that does not generate redundant framings, and H' is valid if and only if H is such. Recall that there is no need for regularizing planned selections, because, by Theorem 4, we will always verify the validity of history expressions with no selections.

Example 14. Let $H = \varphi[\alpha \cdot h_0 \cdot \varphi'[\alpha' + h_1]] \cdot h_2$, and let $\tilde{H} = \varphi[\alpha \cdot h_0 \cdot \varphi'[\alpha' + \bullet]] \cdot h_2$. Then, $H = \tilde{H}\{h_1/\bullet\}$, and so h_1 is guarded by $guard(\tilde{H}) = \{\varphi, \varphi'\}$. Similarly, h_0 is guarded by $\{\varphi\}$, and h_2 is unguarded (i.e. guarded by $\emptyset$). $\square$

Let H be a (possibly non-closed) history expression. Without loss of generality, assume that all the variables in H have distinct names. We define below $H\downarrow_{\Phi,\Omega}$, the history expression produced by the *regularization* of H against a set of policies Φ and a mapping Ω from variables to history expressions.

Intuitively, $H\downarrow_{\Phi,\Omega}$ results from H by eliminating all the redundant framings, and all the framings in Φ. The environment Ω is needed to deal with free variables in the case of nested μ-expressions. We feel free to omit the component Ω when unneeded, and, when H is closed, we abbreviate $H\downarrow_{\emptyset,\emptyset}$ with $H\downarrow$.

Definition 12. Guards

Let $\tilde{H}$ be a history expression with a hole $\bullet$, and let $H = \tilde{H}\{H'/\bullet\}$ be a history expression, for some H'. We say that H' is guarded by φ in H when $\varphi \in guard(\tilde{H})$, defined as the smallest set satisfying the following equations.

$$guard(H_0 \cdot H_1) = guard(H_i) \quad \text{if } \bullet \in H_i$$
$$guard(H_0 + H_1) = guard(H_i) \quad \text{if } \bullet \in H_i$$
$$guard(\varphi[H]) = \{\varphi\} \cup guard(H)$$
$$guard(\mu h.\, H) = guard(H)$$

The last three regularization rules would benefit from some explanation. Consider first a history expression of the form $\varphi[H]$ to be regularized against a set of policies Φ. To eliminate the redundant framings, we must ensure that H has neither φ-framings, nor redundant framings itself. This is accomplished by regularizing H against $\Phi \cup \{\varphi\}$.

Consider a history expression of the form $\mu h.H$. Its regularization against Φ and Ω proceeds as follows. Each free occurrence of h in H guarded by some $\Phi' \not\subseteq \Phi$ is unfolded and regularized against $\Phi \cup \Phi'$. The substitution Ω is used to bind the free variables to closed history expressions. Technically, the i-th free occurrence of h in H is picked up by the substitution $\{h/h_i\}$, for h_i fresh. Note also that $\sigma(h_i)$ is computed only if $\sigma'(h_i) = h_i$. As a matter of fact, regularization is a total function, and its definition above can be easily turned into a finitely terminating rewriting system.

Example 15. Consider the history expression $H_0 = \mu h.\, H$, where $H = \alpha + h \cdot h + \varphi[h]$. Then, H can be written as $H'\{h/h_i\}_{i \in 0..2}$, where $H' = \alpha + h_0 \cdot h_1 + \varphi[h_2]$. Since $guard(H'\{\bullet/h_2\}) = guard(\alpha + h_0 \cdot h_1 + \varphi[\bullet]) = \{\varphi\} \not\subseteq \emptyset$, then:

$$H_0 \downarrow_\emptyset = \mu h.\, H'\{h/h_0, h/h_1\} \downarrow_\emptyset \{H_0 \downarrow_\varphi /h_2\}$$
$$= \mu h.\, \alpha + h \cdot h + \varphi[H_0 \downarrow_\varphi]$$

To compute $H_0 \downarrow_\varphi$, note that no occurrence of h is guarded by $\Phi \not\subseteq \{\varphi\}$. Then:

$$H_0 \downarrow_\varphi = \mu h.\, (\alpha + h \cdot h + \varphi[h]) \downarrow_\varphi = \mu h.\, \alpha + h \cdot h + h$$

Since $[\![H_0 \downarrow_\varphi]\!] = \{\alpha\}^*$ has no φ-framings, we have that $[\![H_0 \downarrow]\!] = (\{\alpha\}^* \varphi[\{\alpha\}^*])^*$ has no redundant framings. □

Example 16. Let $H_0 = \mu h.\, H_1$, where $H_1 = \mu h'.\, H_2$, and $H_2 = \alpha + h \cdot \varphi[h']$. Since $guard(H_1\{\bullet/h\}) = \emptyset$, we have that:

$$H_0 \downarrow_{\emptyset,\emptyset} = \mu h.\, (H_1 \downarrow_{\emptyset,\{H_0/h\}})$$

Definition 13. Regularization of framings

$$\varepsilon\downarrow_{\Phi,\Omega} = \varepsilon \qquad (H \cdot H')\downarrow_{\Phi,\Omega} = H\downarrow_{\Phi,\Omega} \cdot H'\downarrow_{\Phi,\Omega}$$

$$h\downarrow_{\Phi,\Omega} = h \qquad \alpha\downarrow_{\Phi,\Omega} = \alpha \qquad (H + H')\downarrow_{\Phi,\Omega} = H\downarrow_{\Phi,\Omega} + H'\downarrow_{\Phi,\Omega}$$

$$\varphi[H]\downarrow_{\Phi,\Omega} = \begin{cases} H\downarrow_{\Phi,\Omega} & \text{if } \varphi \in \Phi \\ \varphi[H\downarrow_{\Phi\cup\{\varphi\},\Omega}] & \text{otherwise} \end{cases}$$

$$(\mu h. H)\downarrow_{\Phi,\Omega} = \mu h. (H'\sigma'\downarrow_{\Phi,\Omega\{(\mu h.H)\Omega/h\}} \sigma)$$

where $H = H'\{h/h_i\}_i$, h_i fresh, $h \notin fv(H')$, and

$$\sigma(h_i) = (\mu h.H)\Omega\downarrow_{\Phi\cup guard(H'\{\bullet/h_i\}),\Omega}$$

$$\sigma'(h_i) = \begin{cases} h & \text{if } guard(H'\{\bullet/h_i\}) \subseteq \Phi \\ h_i & \text{otherwise} \end{cases}$$

Note that H_2 can be written as $H_2'\{h/h_0\}$, where $H_2' = \alpha + h \cdot \varphi[h_0]$. Since $guard(H_2'\{\bullet/h_0\}) = \{\varphi\} \not\subseteq \emptyset$, it follows that:

$$\begin{aligned} H_1\downarrow_{\emptyset,\{H_0/h\}} &= \mu h'. H_2'\downarrow_{\emptyset,\{H_0/h, H_1\{H_0/h\}/h'\}} \{H_1\{H_0/h\}\downarrow_{\varphi,\{H_0/h\}}/h_0\} \\ &= \mu h'. \alpha + h \cdot \varphi[h_0] \{(\mu h'. \alpha + H_0 \cdot \varphi[h'])\downarrow_{\varphi,\{H_0/h\}}/h_0\} \\ &= \mu h'. \alpha + h \cdot \varphi[H_3\downarrow_{\varphi,\{H/h\}}] \\ &= \alpha + h \cdot \varphi[H_3\downarrow_{\varphi,\{H/h\}}] \end{aligned}$$

where $H_3 = \mu h'. \alpha + H_0 \cdot \varphi[h']$, and the last step is possible because the outermost μ binds no variable. Since $guard(\alpha + H_0 \cdot \varphi[\bullet]) = \{\varphi\} \subseteq \{\varphi\}$:

$$H_3\downarrow_\varphi = \mu h'. (\alpha + H_0 \cdot \varphi[h'])\downarrow_\varphi = \mu h'. \alpha + H_0\downarrow_\varphi \cdot h'$$

Since $\{\varphi\}$ contains both $guard(H_1\{\bullet/h\}) = \emptyset$, and $guard(H_2\{\bullet/h'\}) = \{\varphi\}$, then:

$$\begin{aligned} H_0\downarrow_\varphi &= \mu h. (\mu h'. \alpha + h \cdot \varphi[h'])\downarrow_\varphi = \mu h. \mu h'. (\alpha + h \cdot \varphi[h'])\downarrow_\varphi \\ &= \mu h. \mu h'. \alpha + h \cdot h' \end{aligned}$$

Summing up, we have that:

$$\begin{aligned} H_0\downarrow_\emptyset &= \mu h. \alpha + h \cdot \varphi[H_3\downarrow_\varphi] \\ H_3\downarrow_\varphi &= \mu h'. \alpha + (\mu h. \mu h'. \alpha + h \cdot h') \cdot h' \end{aligned} \qquad \square$$

We now establish the following basic properties of regularization, stating its correctness.

Theorem 5. *For all history expressions H:*

- *$H \downarrow$ has no redundant framings.*
- *$H \downarrow$ is valid if and only if H is valid.*

9.3 From History Expressions to Basic Process Algebras

Basic Process Algebras [11] (BPAs) provide a natural characterization of history expressions. BPA processes contain the terminated process 0, events α, that may stand for an access or framing event, the operators $\cdot$ and $+$ that denote sequential composition and (non-deterministic) choice, and variables X. To allow for recursion, a BPA is then defined as a process p and a set of definitions Δ for the variables X that occur therein.

Definition 14. Syntax of BPA processes

$$p, p' ::= 0 \mid \alpha \mid p \cdot p' \mid p + p' \mid X$$

Definition 15. LTS for Basic Process Algebras

The semantics $[\![P]\!]$ of a BPA $P = (p_0, \Delta)$ is the set of the histories labelling finite computations:

$$\{ \eta = a_1 \cdots a_i \mid p_0 \xrightarrow{a_1} \cdots \xrightarrow{a_i} p_i \}$$

where $a \in \mathsf{Ev} \cup \{\varepsilon\}$, and the relation $\xrightarrow{a}$ is inductively defined as:

$$0 \cdot p \xrightarrow{\varepsilon} p \qquad \alpha \xrightarrow{\alpha} 0 \qquad p + q \xrightarrow{\varepsilon} p \qquad p + q \xrightarrow{\varepsilon} q$$

$$\frac{p \xrightarrow{a} p'}{p \cdot q \xrightarrow{a} p' \cdot q} \qquad X \xrightarrow{\varepsilon} p \quad \text{if } X \triangleq p \in \Delta$$

We assume a finite set $\Delta = \{ X \triangleq p \}$ of definitions, such that, for each variable X, $X \triangleq p \in \Delta$ and $X \triangleq p' \in \Delta$ imply $p = p'$. The operational semantics of BPAs is in Def. 15.

We now introduce a mapping from history expressions to BPAs, in the line of [5,43]. Again, note that there is no need for transforming planned selections into BPAs, because we are only interested in the validity of history expressions with no selections.

Definition 16. Mapping history expressions to BPAs

$$BPA(\varepsilon, \Theta) = (0, \emptyset)$$

$$BPA(\alpha, \Theta) = (\alpha, \emptyset)$$

$$BPA(h, \Theta) = (\Theta(h), \emptyset)$$

$$BPA(H_0 \cdot H_1, \Theta) = (p_0 \cdot p_1, \Delta_0 \cup \Delta_1), \text{where } BPA(H_i, \Theta) = (p_i, \Delta_i)$$

$$BPA(H_0 + H_1, \Theta) = (p_0 + p_1, \Delta_0 \cup \Delta_1), \text{where } BPA(H_i, \Theta) = (p_i, \Delta_i)$$

$$BPA(\varphi[H], \Theta) = ([_\varphi \cdot p \cdot]_\varphi, \Delta), \text{where } BPA(H, \Theta) = (p, \Delta)$$

$$BPA(\mu h.H, \Theta) = (X, \Delta \cup \{X \triangleq p\}), \text{where } BPA(H, \Theta\{X/h\}) = (p, \Delta)$$

The mapping takes as input a history expression H and a mapping Θ from history variables h to BPA variables X, and it outputs a BPA process p and a finite set of definitions Δ. Without loss of generality, we assume that all the variables in H have distinct names.

The rules that transform history expressions into BPAs are rather natural. Events, variables, concatenation and choice are mapped into the corresponding BPA counterparts. A history expression $\varphi[H]$ is mapped to the BPA for H, surrounded by the opening and closing of the φ-framing. A history expression $\mu h.H$ is mapped to a fresh BPA variable X, bound to the translation of H in the set of definitions Δ.

We now state the correspondence between history expressions and BPAs. The semantics of $BPA(H)$ comprises all and only the prefixes of the histories generated by H (i.e. $[\![H]\!]^{0\,\partial}$).

Theorem 6. *For all history expressions H with no planned selection:*

$$\left([\![H]\!]^0\right)^\partial = [\![BPA(H)]\!]$$

9.4 Model-Checking Validity

Given a policy φ, we are interested in defining a FSA $A_{\varphi_{[]}}$ to be used in verifying the validity of a history η with respect to security policies within their framings. Since our histories are always finite and our properties are regular, FSA suffice.

The automaton $A_{\varphi_{[]}}$ is partitioned into two layers. The first layer is a copy of A_φ, where all the states are final. This models the fact that we are outside the scope of φ, i.e. the history leading to any state in this layer has balanced framings of φ (or none). The second layer is reachable from the first one when opening a framing for φ, while closing the framing gets back. The transitions in the second layer are a copy of those connecting accepting states in A_φ. Consequently, the states in the second layer are exactly the final states in A_φ. Since $A_{\varphi_{[]}}$ is only concerned with the verification of φ, the transitions for opening and closing framings $\varphi' \neq \varphi$ are rendered as self-loops.

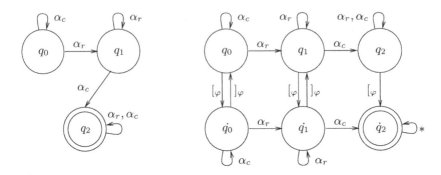

Fig. 13. Finite state automata A_φ (left) and $A_{\varphi_{[]}}$ (right)

Definition 17. Finite state automaton for $\varphi_{[]}$

$$A_{\varphi_{[]}} = (\Sigma', Q', q_0, \rho', F')$$
$$\Sigma' = \Sigma \cup \{\, [_{\varphi'},]_{\varphi'} \mid \varphi' \in \mathsf{Pol} \,\}$$
$$Q' = F' = Q \cup \{\, \dot{q} \mid q \in F \,\}$$
$$\rho' = \rho \cup \{\, (q, [_\varphi, \dot{q}) \mid q \in F \,\} \cup \{\, (\dot{q},]_\varphi, q) \mid q \in Q \,\}$$
$$\cup \{\, (\dot{q_i}, \alpha, \dot{q_j}) \mid (q_i, \alpha, q_j) \in \rho \wedge q_j \in F \,\}$$
$$\cup \{\, (q, [_{\varphi'}, q) \cup (q,]_{\varphi'}, q) \mid q \in Q' \wedge \varphi' \neq \varphi \,\}$$

For all histories η, we write $\eta \models \varphi_{[]}$ when η is accepted by $A_{\varphi_{[]}}$.

Example 17. Consider the policy φ saying that no event α_c can occur after an α_r. The FSA A_φ and $A_{\varphi_{[]}}$ are shown in Fig. 13, where the doubly-circled states are the offending ones (i.e. those modelling violation of the policy). It is immediate checking that the history $[_\varphi \alpha_r]_\varphi \alpha_c$ obeys the policy represented by $A_{\varphi_{[]}}$, while $\alpha_r [_\varphi \alpha_c]_\varphi$ does not.   □

We require that the history η to be verified against $A_{\varphi_{[]}}$ has no redundant framings, i.e. η has been regularized. Hereafter, let the formula φ be defined by the FSA $A_\varphi = (\Sigma, Q, q_0, \rho, F)$, which we assume to have a distinguished non-final sink state. The FSA $A_{\varphi_{[]}}$ is constructed as in Def. 17.

Although the policies enforced by the security framings can always inspect the whole past history, we can easily limit the scope from the side of the past. It suffices to mark in the history the point in time β_φ from which checking a policy φ has to start. The corresponding automaton ignores all the events before β_φ, and then behaves like the standard automaton enforcing φ.

Theorem 7. *Let η be a history with no redundant framings. Then, η is valid if and only if $\eta \models \varphi_{[]}$ for all φ occurring in η.*

Since finite state automata are closed under intersection, a valid history η is accepted by the intersection of the automata $A_{\varphi_{[]}}$ for all φ in η. Validity of a closed history expression H with no planned selections can be decided by showing that the BPA generated by the regularization of H satisfies the given regular formula. Together with Theorem 2, the execution of an expression in our calculus never violates security if its effect is verified valid. Thus we are dispensed from using an execution monitor to enforce the security properties.

Theorem 8. *Let H be a history expression H with no planned selections. Then, H is valid if and only if:*

$$[\![BPA(H\!\downarrow)]\!] \models \bigwedge_{\varphi \in H} \varphi_{[]}$$

10 Related Work

Process calculi techniques have been used to study the foundation of services. The main goal of some of these proposals, e.g. [26,18,32,35] is to formalise various aspects of standards for the description, execution and orchestration of services (WSDL, SOAP and WS-BPEL). The Global Calculus [21] addresses the problem of relating orchestration and choreography. As a matter of fact, our λ^{req} builds over the standard service infrastructure the above calculi formalise. Indeed, our call-by-contract supersedes standard invocation mechanisms and allows for verified planning.

The secure composition of components has been the main concern underlying the design of Sewell and Vitek's box-π [42], an extension of the π-calculus that allows for expressing safety policies in the form of *security wrappers*. These are programs that encapsulate a component to control the interactions with other (possibly untrusted) components. The calculus is equipped with a type system that statically captures the allowed causal information flows between components. Our safety framings are closely related to wrappers, but in [42] there is no analog of our liveness framings.

Gorla, Hennessy and Sassone [31] consider a calculus for mobile agents which may migrate between sites in a controlled manner. Each site has a *membrane*, representing both a security policy and a classification of external sites with respect to their levels of trust. A membrane guards the incoming agents before allowing them to execute. Three classes of membranes are studied, the most complex being the class of policies enforceable by finite state automata. When an agent comes from an untrusted site, *all* its code must be checked. Instead, an agent coming from a trusted site must only provide the destination site with a *digest* of its behaviour, so allowing for more efficient checks.

A different approach is Cook and Misra's Orc [38], a programming model for structured orchestration of services. The basic computational entities orchestrated by Orc expressions are sites. A site computation can start other orchestrations, locally store the effects of a computation, and make them visible to clients. Orc provides three basic composition operators, that can be used to model some common workflow patterns, identified by Van der Aalst et al. [23].

Another solution to planning service composition has been proposed in [36], where the problem of achieving a given composition goal is expressed as a constraint satisfaction problem.

From a technical point of view, the work of Skalka and Smith [43] is the closest to this paper. We share with them the use of a type and effect system and that of model checking validity of effects. In [43], a static approach to history-based access control is proposed. The λ-calculus is enriched with access events and local checks on the past event history. Local checks make validity a regular property, so regularization is unneeded. The programming model and the type system of [43] allow for access events parametrized by constants, and for let-polymorphism. We have omitted these features for simplicity, but they can be easily recovered by using similar techniques.

A related line of research addresses the issue of modelling and analysing resource usage. Igarashi and Kobayashi [34] introduce a type systems to check whether a program accesses resources according to a user-defined usage policy. Our model is less general than the framework of [34], but we provide a static verification technique, while [34] does not. Colcombet and Fradet [22] and Marriot, Stuckey and Sulzmann [37] mix static and dynamic techniques to transform programs in order to make them obey a given safety property. Besson, de Grenier de Latour and Jensen [12] tackle the problem of characterizing when a program can call a stack-inspecting method while respecting a global security policy. Compared to [22,37,12], our programming model allows for local policies, while the other only considers global ones.

Recently, increasing attention has been devoted to express service contracts as behavioural (or session) types. These synthetise the essential aspects of the interaction behaviour of services, while allowing for efficient static verification of properties of composed systems. Session types [33] have been exploited to formalize compatibility of components [46] and to describe adaptation of web services [19]. Security issues have been recently considered in terms of session types, e.g. in [17], which proves the decidability of type-checking in an extension of the π-calculus with session types and correspondence assertions [48]. Our λ^{req} has no explicit primitive for sessions. However, they can be suitably encoded, via higher-order functions.

Other papers have proposed type-based methodologies to check security properties of distributed systems. For instance, Gordon and Jeffrey [30] use a type and effect system to prove authenticity properties of security protocols. Web service authentication has been recently modelled and analysed in [13,14] through a process calculus enriched with cryptographic primitives. In particular, [15] builds security libraries using the WS-Security policies of [2]. These libraries are then mechanically analysed with ProVerif [16].

11   Conclusions

We have described a formal framework for designing and implementing secure service-oriented applications. The main features of our framework are its security-awareness, a call-by-contract service invocation, a formal semantics, and a system verification machinery, as well as a graphical modelling language. All the above items contribute to achieving static guarantees about planning, and graceful degradation when services disappear.

The formal foundation of our work is λ^{req}, a core calculus for services with primitives to express non-functional constraints on service composition. We focussed here on security properties, in particular on those expressible as safety properties of service execution histories. In other papers [8,6], we have also explored liveness properties.

We have then defined a type and effect system to safely approximate the run-time behaviour of services. These approximations are called *history expressions*. They are a sort of context-free grammars with special constructs to describe the (localized) histories produced by executing services, and the selection of services upon requests.

Analysing these approximations allowed us to single out the *viable plans* that drive secure service composition, i.e. those that achieve the task assigned while respecting all the security constraints on demand. To do that, we exploited model checking over Basic Process Algebras and Finite State Automata. This verification step required some pre-processing on history expressions: technically, we linearized and regularized them to expose the possible plans and to make model checking feasible.

As a further contribution, we proposed a graphical modelling language for services, supporting most of the features of λ^{req}. This calculus has a formal operational semantics in the form of a graph rewriting system. Services described in the graphical model can be naturally refined into more concrete λ^{req} programs. This can be done with the help of simple model transformation tools. One can then reuse all the λ^{req} tools, including its static machinery, and therefore rapidly build a working prototype of a service-based system.

As usual, a prototype can help in the design phase, because one can perform early tests on the system, e.g. by providing as input selected data, one can observe whether the outputs are indeed the intended ones. The call-by-contract mechanism makes this standard testing practice even more effective, e.g. one can perform a request with a given policy φ and observe the resulting plans. The system must then consider *all* the services that satisfy φ, and the observed effect is similar to running a *class* of tests. For instance, a designer of an online bookshop can specify a policy such as "order a book without paying" and then inspect the generated plans: the presence of viable plans could point out an unwanted behaviour, e.g. due to an unpredicted interaction between different special offers. As a matter of facts, standard testing techniques are yet not sophisticated enough to spot such kind of bugs. Thus, a designer may find the λ^{req} prototype useful to check the system, since unintended plans provide him with a clear description of the unwanted interactions between services.

Acknowledgments

This research has been partially supported by EU-FETPI Global Computing Project IST-2005-16004 SENSORIA (Software Engineering for Service-Oriented Overlay Computers).

References

1. Abadi, M., Fournet, C.: Access control based on execution history. In: Proc. 10th Annual Network and Distributed System Security Symposium (2003)
2. Atkinson, B., et al.: Web Services Security (WS-Security) (2002), http://www.oasis-open.org
3. Banerjee, A., Naumann, D.A.: History-based access control and secure information flow. In: Barthe, G., Burdy, L., Huisman, M., Lanet, J.-L., Muntean, T. (eds.) CASSIS 2004. LNCS, vol. 3362, Springer, Heidelberg (2005)
4. Barendregt, H.P., et al.: Term graph rewriting. In: Parallel Languages on PARLE: Parallel Architectures and Languages Europe (1987)
5. Bartoletti, M., Degano, P., Ferrari, G.L.: History based access control with local policies. In: Sassone, V. (ed.) FOSSACS 2005. LNCS, vol. 3441, Springer, Heidelberg (2005)
6. Bartoletti, M., Degano, P., Ferrari, G.L.: Planning and verifying service composition. Technical Report TR-07-02, Dip. Informatica, Univ. of Pisa. (to appear in Journal of Computer Security, 2007), http://compass2.di.unipi.it/TR/Files/TR-07-02.pdf.gz
7. Bartoletti, M., Degano, P., Ferrari, G.L., Zunino, R.: Types and effects for resource usage analysis. In: Proc. Foundations of Software Science and Computation Structures (Fossacs) (to appear, 2007)
8. Bartoletti, M., Degano, P., Ferrari, G.L.: Enforcing secure service composition. In: Proc. 18th Computer Security Foundations Workshop (CSFW) (2005)
9. Bartoletti, M., Degano, P., Ferrari, G.L.: Plans for service composition. In: Workshop on Issues in the Theory of Security (WITS) (2006)
10. Bartoletti, M., Degano, P., Ferrari, G.L.: Types and effects for secure service orchestration. In: Proc. 19th Computer Security Foundations Workshop (CSFW) (2006)
11. Bergstra, J.A., Klop, J.W.: Algebra of communicating processes with abstraction. Theoretical Computer Science, 37 (1985)
12. Besson, F., de Grenier de Latour, T., Jensen, T.: Interfaces for stack inspection. Journal of Functional Programming 15(2) (2005)
13. Bhargavan, K., Corin, R., Fournet, C., Gordon, A.D.: Secure sessions for web services. In: Proc. ACM Workshop on Secure Web Services (2004)
14. Bhargavan, K., Fournet, C., Gordon, A.D.: A semantics for web services authentication. In: Proc. ACM SIGPLAN-SIGACT Symposium on Principles of Programming Languages (POPL) (2004)
15. Bhargavan, K., Fournet, C., Gordon, A.D.: Verified reference implementations of WS-security protocols. In: Bravetti, M., Núñez, M., Zavattaro, G. (eds.) WS-FM 2006. LNCS, vol. 4184, Springer, Heidelberg (2006)
16. Blanchet, B.: An efficient cryptographic protocol verifier based on prolog rules. In: Computer Security Foundations Workshop (CSFW) (2001)

17. Bonelli, E., Compagnoni, A., Gunter, E.: Typechecking safe process synchronization. In: Proc. Foundations of Global Ubiquitous Computing. ENTCS, vol. 138(1) (2005)
18. Boreale, M., et al.: SCC: a service centered calculus. In: Bravetti, M., Núñez, M., Zavattaro, G. (eds.) WS-FM 2006. LNCS, vol. 4184, Springer, Heidelberg (2006)
19. Brogi, A., Canal, C., Pimentel, E.: Behavioural types and component adaptation. In: Rattray, C., Maharaj, S., Shankland, C. (eds.) AMAST 2004. LNCS, vol. 3116, Springer, Heidelberg (2004)
20. Bruni, R., Melgratti, H., Montanari, U.: Theoretical foundations for compensations in flow composition languages. In: Proc. of the 32nd ACM SIGPLAN-SIGACT Symposium on Principles of programming languages (POPL) (2005)
21. Carbone, M., Honda, K., Yoshida, N.: Structured global programming for communicating behaviour. In: European Symposium in Programming Languages (ESOP) (to appear, 2007)
22. Colcombet, T., Fradet, P.: Enforcing trace properties by program transformation. In: Proc. 27th ACM SIGPLAN-SIGACT Symposium on Principles of Programming Languages (POPL) (2000)
23. Van der Aalst, W., ter Hofstede, A., Kiepuszewski, B., Barros, A.: Workflow patterns. Distributed and Parallel Databases 14(1) (2003)
24. Edjlali, G., Acharya, A., Chaudhary, V.: History-based access control for mobile code. In: Vitek, J. (ed.) Secure Internet Programming. LNCS, vol. 1603, Springer, Heidelberg (1999)
25. Esparza, J.: On the decidability of model checking for several μ-calculi and Petri nets. In: Tison, S. (ed.) CAAP 1994. LNCS, vol. 787, Springer, Heidelberg (1994)
26. Ferrari, G.L., Guanciale, R., Strollo, D.: JSCL: A middleware for service coordination. In: Najm, E., Pradat-Peyre, J.F., Donzeau-Gouge, V.V. (eds.) FORTE 2006. LNCS, vol. 4229, Springer, Heidelberg (2006)
27. Fong, P.W.: Access control by tracking shallow execution history. In: IEEE Symposium on Security and Privacy (2004)
28. Garcia-Molina, H., Salem, K.: Sagas. In: Proc. ACM SIGMOD, ACM Press, New York (1987)
29. Gifford, D.K., Lucassen, J.M.: Integrating functional and imperative programming. In: ACM Conference on LISP and Functional Programming (1986)
30. Gordon, A., Jeffrey, A.: Types and effects for asymmetric cryptographic protocols. In: Proc. IEEE Computer Security Foundations Workshop (CSFW) (2002)
31. Gorla, D., Hennessy, M., Sassone, V.: Security policies as membranes in systems for global computing. Logical Methods in Computer Science 1(3) (2005)
32. Guidi, C., Lucchi, R., Gorrieri, R., Busi, N., Zavattaro, G.: SOCK: A calculus for service oriented computing. In: Dan, A., Lamersdorf, W. (eds.) ICSOC 2006. LNCS, vol. 4294, Springer, Heidelberg (2006)
33. Honda, K., Vansconcelos, V., Kubo, M.: Language primitives and type discipline for structures communication-based programming. In: Hankin, C. (ed.) ESOP 1998 and ETAPS 1998. LNCS, vol. 1381, Springer, Heidelberg (1998)
34. Igarashi, A., Kobayashi, N.: Resource usage analysis. In: Proc. 29th ACM SIGPLAN-SIGACT Symposium on Principles of Programming Languages (POPL) (2002)
35. Lapadula, A., Pugliese, R., Tiezzi, F.: A calculus for orchestration of web services. In: European Symposium in Programming Languages (ESOP) (to appear, 2007)
36. Lazovik, A., Aiello, M., Gennari, R.: Encoding requests to web service compositions as constraints. In: van Beek, P. (ed.) CP 2005. LNCS, vol. 3709, Springer, Heidelberg (2005)

37. Marriott, K., Stuckey, P.J., Sulzmann, M.: Resource usage verification. In: Ohori, A. (ed.) APLAS 2003. LNCS, vol. 2895, Springer, Heidelberg (2003)
38. Misra, J.: A programming model for the orchestration of web services. In: 2nd International Conference on Software Engineering and Formal Methods (SEFM 2004) (2004)
39. Nielson, F., Nielson, H.R.: Type and effect systems. In: Correct System Design (1999)
40. Nielson, F., Nielson, H.R., Hankin, C.: Principles of Program Analysis. Springer, Heidelberg (1999)
41. Schneider, F.B.: Enforceable security policies. ACM Transactions on Information and System Security (TISSEC) 3(1) (2000)
42. Sewell, P., Vitek, J.: Secure composition of untrusted code: box-π, wrappers and causality types. Journal of Computer Security 11(2) (2003)
43. Skalka, C., Smith, S.: History effects and verification. In: Chin, W.-N. (ed.) APLAS 2004. LNCS, vol. 3302, Springer, Heidelberg (2004)
44. Talpin, J.P., Jouvelot, P.: The type and effect discipline. Information and Computation 2(111) (1994)
45. Toma, I., Foxvog, D.: Non-functional properties in Web Services. WSMO Deliverable (2006)
46. Vallecillo, A., Vansconcelos, V., Ravara, A.: Typing the behaviours of objects and components using session types. In: Proc. of FOCLASA (2002)
47. Winskel, G.: The Formal Semantics of Programming Languages. The MIT Press, Cambridge (1993)
48. Woo, T.Y.C., Lam, S.S.: A semantic model for authentication protocols. In: IEEE Symposium on Security and Privacy (1993)

IT Security Analysis
Best Practices and Formal Approaches

Daniel Le Métayer

Inria Rhône-Alpes, Grenoble and
Trusted Logic, Versailles, France
Daniel.Le-Metayer@inrialpes.fr

Abstract. This tutorial provides an overview of the best industrial practices in IT security analysis followed by a sketch of recent research results in this area, especially results providing formal foundations and more powerful tools for security analysis. The conclusion suggests directions for further work to fill the gaps between formal methods and industrial practices.

1 Scope and Terminology

Information Technology (IT) security analysis is a vast domain whose frontiers and purpose are not defined in the same way by all actors and authors. Moreover alternative terms and expressions such as "risk analysis", "risk assessment", "risk mitigation", "threat modeling", "vulnerability analysis", etc. are often used to denote overlapping, similar, or connected concepts. To make the situation even more confusing, key words such as "threat" or "risk" are not used consistently in the IT security literature. Before diving into the core of the presentation, it is thus worth to start with precise definitions of the scope of this tutorial (Subsection 1.1) and the terminology used in the sequel (Subsection 1.2). Section 2 is devoted to the state of the art and best practices in industry while Section 3 provides a quick overview of recent research results in this area, especially results providing formal foundations and more powerful tools for security analysis. Section 4 concludes with suggestions for further work to fill the gap between the industrial and research views of security analysis.

1.1 Scope

Security analysis is the initial phase of a more general process called "security management" ("risk management" in [16]): the main goal of the risk analysis phase is to assess the situation with respect to the security of an IT product[1] in order to prepare the subsequent "decision making" step. The decision

---

[1] In this paper we use the words "product" or "IT product" as generic terms for IT products or systems.

A. Aldini and R. Gorrieri (Eds.): FOSAD 2006/2007, LNCS 4677, pp. 75–91, 2007.

may typically consist in the implementation of additional technical or organizational countermeasures to address the risks identified during the security analysis phase. The decision making task itself (which typically involves business related considerations) as well as the implementation and follow-up of the decisions are out of the scope of what we call "security analysis" here: they form the other main phases of the security management process.

Let us note that "to assess the situation with respect to the security of an IT product", as stated in the above paragraph, is a very broad characterization of the purpose of security analysis. In particular, it does not assume that a single piece of code of the product has already been developed. Indeed, it is desirable that a form of security analysis takes place during the design phase of the product to ensure that security issues are taken into account from the outset (rather than considered as an afterthought, to mitigate bad design choices, as it happens too often). Security analysis does not have to be confined to the design phase though. On the opposite, all best practices guides stress that security analysis and security management should be continuous processes, which should be applied, as part of a continuous improvement procedure, at every stage of the life cycle of a product.

Security analysis can also be performed as part of an evaluation process, either within an internal improvement procedure (as, e.g., in the OCTAVE[2] method [1]) or in the framework of an official certification procedure (as, e.g., in the Common Criteria[3] [4]). In the certification context the goal of the security analysis phase is not to prepare a decision concerning the evolution of the product but to answer a more precise question: considering a given security evaluation level targeted by the developer of the product and the security requirements associated with this level, does the product meet these requirements? The output of the security analysis is thus more or less a binary verdict in this context[4].

The nature of the context (namely decision making or certification) inevitably influences the focus and scope of the security analysis. Most concepts and techniques are quite similar though, and, for the sake of clarity and conciseness, we will not consider two different kinds of analysis in this tutorial. We will mainly focus on security analysis as part of a decision making process and occasionally refer to certification.

1.2 Terminology

Before embarking into the thick of the presentation, we provide in this subsection a short definition of the main technical terms used throughout this tutorial. These terms cover very basic notions but, as mentioned before, their meaning is subject to subtle variations. Hopefully, fixing this meaning from the outset will allow us to avoid any ambiguity in the rest of the paper.

---

[2] Octave is a registred trademark in the US Patent and Trademark Office.

[3] Common Criteria for Information Technology Security evaluation.

[4] In practice, the verdict comes with an evaluation report though [4], possibly with some reservations, precisions about the evaluation or limitations on the scope of the certificate.

- The primary notion in security analysis is the notion of *asset*. An asset can be anything (concrete or abstract, part of the IT product or under its control) which has a value and needs to be protected by a *security policy*.
- A *security breach* is a violation of the security policy with detrimental impact on the assets (asset destruction, asset disclosure, denial of service, etc.).
- A *vulnerability* is a flaw or weakness in the security procedures, design or implementation of the product that could be exercised and result in a security breach.
- A *threat* is a potential for an attacker to exercise a vulnerability.
- A *countermeasure* is a (technical or organizational) mechanism or measure to reduce vulnerabilities. Countermeasures are sometimes called *controls* [16].
- An *attack* is the manifestation of a threat or a succession of threats (by *attackers*) resulting in a security breach.
- The *risk* is a measure of the potential *impact* of attacks (or losses incurred as a consequence of attacks).

To illustrate these definitions, let us consider the information management system of a large hospital, managed by a private company:

- The most valuable *assets* are the patients health records. The *security policy* should, inter alia, protect them against disclosure to any unauthorized staff or third party.
- A *security breach* would be the disclosure of some health records to an unauthorized staff or third party.
- A *vulnerability* could be a lack of buffer overflow control in the implementation of the access control component of the information system.
- A *threat* could be the potential for exploitation of the vulnerability by a hacker to get root level privileges on the machine containing the health records.
- An *attack* could be the manifestation of the threat, followed by a copy of the health records of all patients and their publication on the Internet.
- A *countermeasure* could be a set of additional controls to avoid buffer overflows.
- The *risk* could be qualified as "high" because the *impact* on the image of the private company managing the system would be catastrophic; obviously the confidence of the patients in the hospital would also be undermined. Alternatively, the *risk* could be qualified as a precise amount of money (e.g. "ten millions of Euros"), which could be an assessment of direct damages - e.g. indemnities due to the hospital - and indirect damages such as loss of other customers.

2   Security Analysis: Best Practices

As set forth in the introduction we will focus on industrial methods and best practices in this section. A variety of security analysis methods are used in industry but they fall essentially into two categories [10]: commercial methods and standards. Examples of commercial methods include FRAAP [11], STRIDE [17,6], ASTRA [8] and Cigital method [10]. As far as standards are concerned, the most influential methods originate either from international organizations such as ISO (ISO/IEC 177799:2005, ISO/IEC 15408:20005) [4] or from national bodies such as SEI (Software Engineering Institute - Carnegie Mellon University) [1] or NIST (National Institute of Standards and Technology) [16]. Each of these methods has its own specificities, scope and emphasis. Some of them are general purpose (e.g. covering company wide security analysis as well as product analysis) when others are more focused (e.g. dedicated to product assessment); some of them provide general guidance when others are more constraining; some of them stress organizational issues when others are more technically oriented. However, beyond their differences of scope, focus and vocabulary, all methods are based on common notions and principles. Rather than sketching each of these methods in turn, we will thus present the main analysis steps which are shared by most methods (even if not always in the same application order and with the same emphasis) and refer to each of the methods in the course of the presentation to illustrate specific points. In the following subsections, we introduce successively the five main security analysis steps: identification of threats (Subsection 2.1), identification of vulnerabilities (Subsection 2.2), identification of countermeasures (Subsection 2.3), identification of attacks (Subsection 2.4) and risk analysis (Subsection 2.5). In Subsection 2.6, we provide hints on the final decision making step.

2.1   Identification of Threats

Threats can be defined by a number of attributes, such as:

- The attacker (also called the "threat agent", or "source of the threat" in the literature). Attackers can be insiders or outsiders, they can be individuals or organizations.
- The assets concerned by the threat. Usually a threat can concern, directly or indirectly, several assets because the security of an asset may depend on the security of other assets (e.g. passwords).
- The motivation of the threat agent. The motivations of the threat agent can be varied: first, he can be either negligent or malicious; in the second case, he can act for personal reasons (as a game, to become famous, etc.), for political reasons (terrorism, spying, etc.), for economic reasons (profit), criminal reasons (illicit trade, slander, etc.), etc.
- The resources of the attacker (expertise, material, funding, etc.). The level of resources can also vary a lot, depending on the nature of the attacker (individual or organization) and his motivation.
- The actions perpetrated by the attacker. Threats can lead to various kinds of security breaches (e.g. breach of confidentiality, of privacy, of integrity, denial of service, spoofing, etc.). They may involve technical actions (such as intrusion into the system, Trojan horse, exploitation of software bugs, viruses, etc.) as well as organizational or social actions (blackmail, bribery, deception, etc.).

Building a list of threat attributes for a category of product is useful not only for understanding threats and their criticality; it is also a valuable starting point for identifying the relevant threats in a security analysis phase. The "catalogue approach" put forward by several methods [6,16], consists in reviewing each type or combination of attributes to identify the applicable threats for the product under study. Obviously such a list can never be complete but, if based on previous experience and accumulated expertise, it may be very useful to avoid the most obvious oversights. In addition, as suggested in [6], the method can be used in combination with a review of all assets and/or vulnerabilities to envisage all possibly related threats. As an illustration of this approach, the classification put forward in [6] is based on the effects of the threats. It is called "STRIDE" for:

- Spoofing.
- Tampering.
- Repudiation.
- Information disclosure.
- Denial of service.
- Elevation of privilege.

Another, complementary, technique put forward in [17] consists in using data flow diagrams to represent the system and use them to identify its *entry points* (or interfaces) and the assets which can be reached through these entry points. Depending on the considered level of abstraction, an entry point can be a keypad, a port, an API, etc. The underlying principle is that a system can be attacked only if (1) the attacker has a way to interact with it and (2) he can get access to at least an asset through these interactions. The data flow diagrams used in [17] involve three types of nodes: processes (which perform actions on data), data stores (which serve as repositories for data) and external entities (which interact with the system). The arrows in the diagram represent the flows of data between the nodes. In addition, the diagrams are partitioned by boundaries reflecting privilege levels. Last but not least, data flow diagrams can be hierarchical, which makes them suitable for use in an iterative refinement process.

2.2   Identification of Vulnerabilities

Several techniques can be used to identify vulnerabilities but they can be classified into two main categories: "checklist based methods" and "testing methods". These two approaches are complementary but their applicability depends on the life cycle phase of the product: testing methods, which rely on the existence of the code, can obviously not be applied on a system which has not yet been developed.

Generally speaking, building checklists is a very effective way to capitalize on past experience and reduce the dependency of an organization with respect to a small group of experts. Checklists can also exploit public vulnerability databases, lists published by computer incident response teams or any other industry sources. Within a company, checklists are usually set up through information gathering techniques including interviews, questionnaires and document reviews [16]. Another type of checklist recommended in [16] is based on a set of security requirements identified beforehand: each requirement has to be considered to decide whether it is effectively met by the system or not. The security requirements can be technical (e.g. access control or authentication), operational (e.g. protection of computer rooms, data media access) or targeted towards the management of the company (e.g. periodic security reviews, security training, incident response capability, etc.).

When the system (or part of it) has been developed, checklist based methods should be complemented with testing methods which are targeted towards the assessment of the code itself. The code of the system can be evaluated in different ways:

- Static code analysis: the word "static" in this context refers to the fact that the code is not executed but scrutinized by another tool (a *static analyser*) or by human beings (*code review*). Static analysers may implement more or less sophisticated verification strategies ranging from semantical verifications [3] (which rely on a mathematical model of the program) to syntactic verifications and vulnerability scanning tools (which try to locate potentially dangerous programs or code patterns in the system). The most sophisticated techniques are usually the most precise (they detect more subtle vulnerabilities and issue less irrelevant warnings) but also the less general ones (e.g. they may be dedicated to a given programming language or type of application).
- Systematic testing: the system is tested in a systematic way based on a precise test plan. The testing can be more or less thorough, depending on the level of requirement and detail of the test plan. For example, for each level of evaluation, the Common Criteria [4] fix precise rules for the coverage and depth of the tests to be performed on the product (Class *Tests* of the *Security assurance requirements* catalogue).
- Penetration testing: in contrast with systematic testing, which considers the system from the designer point of view, penetration testing takes the position of the attacker. The goal of this phase is to deliberately try to circumvent the security of the product. The test suites can thus be seen as attack trials.

2.3   Identification of Countermeasures

Countermeasures were defined in Subsection 1.2 as technical or organizational mechanisms to reduce vulnerabilities. The role of countermeasures is thus to minimize the likelihood of an attacker exercising a vulnerability [16]. Most methods are based on catalogues of countermeasures which are supposed to be available to the security designer. These countermeasures are the results of decades of research in computer security and their presentation is much beyond the scope of this tutorial. In addition, as set forth in Section 1.1, their implementation and monitoring do not belong to the security analysis phase per se: they pertain to the subsequent phases of the security management process. Basically, the most valuable contribution of the methods discussed here with respect to countermeasures is their categorization and their integration within a broader security analysis process. This categorization makes it easier for security designers to find the most suitable countermeasure (or combination of countermeasures) to mitigate the vulnerabilities and alleviate the threats identified in the previous steps. For example, [16] distinguishes three main categories of countermeasures, respectively technical, operational and management oriented countermeasures. Each category itself is decomposed into three subcategories (1) preventive controls, (2) detective and recovery controls and (3) support controls. As an illustration, technical countermeasures include:

- Preventive controls: authentication, authorization, access control, non repudiation mechanisms (e.g. digital certificates), protection of communications (e.g. virtual private networks), etc.
- Detective and recovery controls: audit, intrusion detection, integrity checking, secure state restoring, virus detection, etc.
- Support controls[5]: identification, cryptographic key management, security administration, etc.

Operational and management countermeasures concern organizational issues such as the control of computing facilities, the establishment of security procedures, the assignment of responsibilities, staff training, security reviews, audits, etc.

Another categorization is proposed in the Common Criteria [4] (*Security functional requirements* catalogue) based on a list of *classes* (such as, e.g., indentification and authentication, privacy, trusted channels, security audit, user data protection, etc.), each class being itself decomposed into families (such as, e.g. security audit data generation, security audit analysis, etc.) defined as collections of individual components.

2.4   Identification of Attacks

Attacks were defined in Subsection 1.2 as manifestations of a threat *or a succession of threats* resulting in a security breach. Indeed, attacks against a system generally result from a combination of threats exploiting several vulnerabilities which are not mitigated by sufficient countermeasures. The attack analysis can thus be seen as the convergence point where the threats, vulnerabilities and countermeasures identified in the first three steps are combined to form the overall picture of the security of the system. One of the most natural way to represent attacks in a systematic way is to resort to *attack trees* [15] (also called *threat trees* in [17]). Attack trees can be seen as a security variant of the fault trees that have been used for decades in reliability analysis. Basically in an attack tree:

- The root represents the goal of the attack. An example of goal can be "Read a message sent by Alice to Bob".

---

[5] Support controls are pervasive techniques which are used by many other controls.

- The nodes represent subgoals. They are associated with boolean connectives ("AND" or "OR"). Continuing the previous example, possible subgoals are "Get the message from Bob's computer" OR "Get the message from the network" OR "Get the message from Alice's computer"; the second goal itself can be further decomposed into: "Intercept the message on the network" AND "Decrypt the message"; each subgoal can be further unfolded in an iterative process, leading to as many subtrees as necessary.
- The leaves represent unitary actions corresponding to the desired level of granularity. An example of leave can be "Cryptoanalysis of IDEA".
- Different kinds of attributes can be assigned to the leaves and propagated to the root. Typical examples of attributes include the minimal attack cost, the risk for the attacker, the required equipment or expertise, the probability of success, etc. The attributes of a node are derived from the attributes of the subnodes based on the boolean connectives. For example, the minimal cost of an "AND" attack node is the sum of the minimal costs of its subnodes while the minimal cost of an "OR" node is the minimum of the costs of its subnodes.

Attack trees are very popular in industry because they do not require a high initial investment: they can be used in a pragmatic, incremental process in which leaves requiring deeper investigation can be progressively decomposed into subtrees (or linked to pre-existing subtrees). Attack trees also favour knowledge sharing and reuse through attack tree patterns which can be defined to capture common attacks. Needless to say, various industrial tools have been proposed to manipulate attack trees. Last but not least, as discussed in Subsection 2.6, such tools can also be used directly by decision makers in order to assess the consequences of different assumptions. Attack trees also have limitations though, which are discussed in Section 3. In particular, they provide a convenient framework for presenting, categorizing and analyzing attacks but they offer little help (apart from encouraging a systematic decomposition approach) for the discovery of these attacks, which still relies on the expertise of the analyst. Another limitation of attack trees, as introduced here, is their lack of connection with any model of the system (whether informal or formal). This issue is addressed in Section 3 which also presents extensions of attack trees to deal with network security analysis.

2.5   Risk Analysis

Assuming that attacks have been identified as set forth in the previous subsection, the next step consists in assessing the risks associated with these attacks to be in a position to take appropriate decisions. Whereas the previous steps were essentially technical, risks have to do with the consequences of the attacks and their evaluation necessarily involves business related considerations such as, typically, the direct and indirect damages to the company's assets, to its customers' assets or to its whole business. The impact of an attack can result from the disclosure of confidential or personal data, from the destruction or inappropriate modification of data, from denial of service, etc. Two parameters are generally used to evaluate risks: the probability of successful attacks and their impact. The two parameters can be combined in different ways to establish a final estimation of the risk. For example, [16] recommends the use of risk-level matrices containing the two types of information:

- The magnitude of the impact, expressed in a range of three values: "High" if the attack may[6] "result in the highly costly loss of major tangible assets or resources"; "Medium" if the attack may "result in the costly loss of tangible assets or resources"; and "Low" if the attack may "result in the loss of some tangible assets or resources".
- The likelihood of the attack, expressed in a range of three values: "High" if the attacker is "highly motivated and sufficiently capable, and controls to prevent the vulnerability from being exercised are ineffective"; "Medium" if the attacker is "motivated and capable, but controls are in place that may impede successful exercise of the vulnerability"; "Low" if the attacker "lacks motivation or capability, or controls are in place to prevent, or at least significantly impede, the vulnerability from being exercised".

A rating can also be associated with each impact magnitude (e.g. 100, 50 and 10 for, respectively, High, Medium and Low) and attack likelihood (e.g. 1, 0.5 and 0.1 for, respectively, High, Medium and Low) and a numerical risk assessment derived as the product of the two values.

Risk assessment as described so far is called "qualitative" in the sense that it provides a relative evaluation of risks on a fixed and limited scale (e.g. three possible values for two parameters in the above example). The only possible use of the result of a qualitative analysis is to compare risks and define priorities. In contrast, "quantitative" risk assessments aim at measuring risks in terms of money. A typical way to get a quantitative measure of risk is to define it as the product of the estimated value of the threatened assets by the expected probability or frequency (e.g. annual rate) of successful attacks. The result is then an estimation of potential (direct) damages that can be balanced with the costs of potential countermeasures. The output of a quantitative risk assessment can thus be used directly by the decision maker to evaluate the return on investment for a given countermeasure. Not too surprisingly, quantitative risk assessments are commonly used by insurance companies and for security analysis in various industrial fields. They are not so popular for IT security analysis though. The main explanation lies in the difficulty to estimate the probability (or frequency) or successful attacks. First, statistical information on attacks is generally not available; in addition, many IT products are specific, or customized, and evolve over time; their environment is also changing (typically the attackers, their resources or motivations may vary; new attack techniques are discovered on a daily basis). This instability would make it very difficult to obtain precise forecasts of attack frequencies even if statistical materiel were available because their reliability would be very weak. An additional disadvantage of quantitative methods

---

[6] For the sake of conciseness, we just mention some of the conditions here; the reader may refer to [16] for a complete account.

is their cost and the increased effort required to interpret their results. For these reasons many authors and organizations recommend using simpler qualitative methods [11].

To conclude thus subsection, let us mention that several research proposals have been made to alleviate the drawbacks of quantitative methods. For example, [5] demonstrates the benefits of Monte-Carlo simulations for IT security analysis, the most important one being an estimation of the uncertainty of the result of the analysis (depending on the uncertainty of the estimates provided by the experts). A radically different approach is put forward in [14], based on economic principles: the key idea is to measure the security of a product as a function of the price of its vulnerabilities as fixed by a vulnerability market. The assumption is that, security breaches having a cost, vulnerabilities could be purchased and sold as any other good on a market. This approach has an additional payoff: it can be integrated within the development process to improve the security strength of the products before their delivery. Its limitations, however, stem from its bold assumptions not only on the development process (market based testing), but also on the organization of the economy (existence of a market for vulnerabilities).

2.6   Decision Making

The objective of all the previous security analysis steps was to prepare the final one, namely the decision making step[7]. The goal of the decision maker is to strike the best economic balance between the level of risk and the costs of potential technical, business and legal countermeasures. Basically, the main options available to the decision maker are the following:

- *Risk acceptance.* This can be seen as the ideal scenario for the organization: the level of risk is deemed acceptable (especially in comparison with the cost of potential countermeasures). In other words, the organization can live with the risk; no new countermeasure needs to be implemented.
- *Risk mitigation.* The level of risk is not acceptable in the current state of affairs but some countermeasures are not too expensive and are accepted: the risk will then be reduced at an acceptable level at a reasonable price.
- *Risk transference.* The level of risk is not acceptable and the proposed countermeasures are too expensive but the risk can be transferred to a third party at an acceptable price: this third party can typically be an insurance company or a business partner.
- *Risk avoidance.* The level of risk is not acceptable, the proposed countermeasures are too expensive and the risk cannot be transferred to a third party at an acceptable price. The decision is thus to avoid the risk: the

---

[7] The reader should keep in mind, however, the motto set forth in Section 1.1: security analysis is a continuous process, which should be applied, within a continuous improvement management procedure, at each stage of the life cycle of a system. By "final" step, what we mean here is thus the final step of a given security analysis session.

practical consequence can be the cancellation of a development plan or a change in marketing priorities (e.g. decision not to unroll a new product or functionality, or to postpone its deployment).

Strictly speaking, the decision step relies mostly on the decision maker's appraisal of the business and economic situation of the organization. However tools such as attack trees may provide a valuable help also at this stage. One useful possibility offered by attack trees is to play "what if" games. More precisely, attack trees make it easy to study the impact on the level of risk of different assumptions on the system (e.g. the presence or strength of a countermeasure) or on the environment (e.g. the motivation or expertise of the attacker). Decision makers can then assess the potential impact of their decisions to implement or not a given countermeasure or the consequences of a potential underestimation of adverse conditions in the environment.

3   Formal Approaches to Security Analysis

The first and implicit principle in terms of security is that perfection or total certainty are out of reach. The main objective of security analysis is thus to maximize the likelihood that a reasonable decision is taken at the end of the process. The two main origins of unfortunate decisions, which are also the two most challenging difficulties for security analysts are (1) the oversight of potential attacks and (2) the underestimation of their economic impact. Whereas the second difficulty is mostly business related, the first one is by essence more technical and calls for technical solutions. Indeed the main goal of all the approaches presented in Section 2 is to reduce, at each stage of the process, the likelihood of inadvertent omissions. The strategy to achieve this goal always boils down to the application procedures which are as methodical or systematic as possible. These procedures can roughly be classified into two categories:

- Check list based procedures: catalogues of threats in Subsections 2.1, of vulnerabilities in Subsection 2.2, or countermeasures in Subsection 2.3.
- Tool based procedures: data flow diagrams in Subsection 2.1, program analyzers in Subsection 2.2, attack trees in Subsection 2.4.

Tools are precious allies in this quest for comprehensiveness because they ensure that methods (which can potentially be complex) are applied systematically (or even automatically). However, as already mentioned in Section 2.4, tools are not a guarantee of completeness by themselves. Because they rely on mathematical models, formal approaches make it possible to go one step further and devise more powerful and more reliable tools. Such tools can be more powerful because they can exploit precise and complex information about the expected behaviour of the product; they can be more reliable because they can serve as a support for logical reasoning and allow for different kinds of consistency checks. These qualities help improving the effectiveness of the security analysis process and reducing the likelihood of bad decisions.

We first sketch in Subsection 3.1 recent research work aiming at enhancing attack trees with formal semantics. We proceed in Subsection 3.2 with attack graphs which alleviate some of the limitations of attack trees. Both attack trees and attack graphs are *vulnerability based* in the sense that they assume (and take as input) a pre-defined set of vulnerabilities. We sketch in Subsection 3.3 an alternative approach relying on a model of the system itself and discuss the pros and cons of each approach.

3.1 Formal Approaches Based on Attack Trees

As set forth in Subsection 2.4, the original definition of attack trees did not rely on any formal, mathematical semantics. Two main approaches have been followed to provide a formal framework for attack trees:

– The first approach consists in enhancing the attack tree notation with statements expressed in an attack specification language: the attack tree notation is then used as a structuring framework or glue syntax for the formal statements.
– The second approach is to endow the attack tree notation itself with a mathematical semantics, which makes it possible to study attack trees as mathematical objects of their own.

A representative of the first option is [18] which associates leaves and nodes of attack trees with preconditions and postconditions expressed in first order predicate logic. Leaf attributes are set by the analyst while node attributes can be derived automatically by composition. Preconditions define properties of the environment or configurations of the system which make an attack possible; postconditions characterize the modifications of the state of the system resulting from the attack (or attack step). The main benefit of the approach is to provide a setting for the systematic study of the composition of individual threats (or attack steps) to build larger attacks[8]. It thus contributes to reducing the likelihood of oversights in the consideration of potential attacks based on individual threats.

The second approach is followed by [9] which defines the denotational semantics of an attack tree as a set of attacks. Attacks themselves are multisets of actions (individual threats). Defining attack trees as sets of attacks implies that the ordering of individual actions is lost. In other words, the structure of the tree is not considered as an essential property of the attack tree, but rather as a "residual of the modeling strategy" [9]. The semantics of attack tree attributes is defined by three ingredients: (1) a domain, (2) a disjunctive operator and (3) a conjunctive operator. For example, the attribute "cost of the cheapest attack" can be defined with (1) the set of natural numbers, (2) the "min" operator for disjunction and (3) the "+" operator for conjunction. A significant payoff of the approach is that the semantics can be used to define criteria characterizing

---

[8] Basically two steps can be combined if the postcondition of the first one implies the precondition of the second one.

"reasonable" attributes [9]. For example, the "cost of the cheapest attack" as defined above is reasonable but the attribute "cost to defend against all attacks" defined with (1) the set of natural numbers, (2) the "+" operator for disjunction and (3) the "min" operator for conjunction, does not pass the criteria. The underlying reason is the lack of distributivity of the structure. In practical terms, unreasonable attributes are attributes which cannot be synthesized bottom-up, based on the structure of the attack tree.

3.2 From Attack Trees to Attack Graphs

Another limitation of attack trees is their inability to model cycles or attacks with common subgoals. Attack graphs are a natural generalization of attack trees which lift this limitation. They have been promoted in particular for the analysis of networks which is much more complex than the analysis of centralized systems due to the large number of states to be considered. Actually, the number of network states can be so large that attack trees or graphs cannot (or should reasonably not) be constructed and analyzed by hand. Most of the contributions in this area thus aim at proposing techniques for the automatic generation and analysis of attack graphs [2,7,12].

As a first illustration of this trend of work, [12] puts forward a graph generation algorithm based on:

- A configuration file which provides information about each device of the network, such as its hardware type, operating system, ports enabled, physical links, set of users, etc.
- An attacker profile defining the initial capabilities of the attacker (e.g. knowledge, physical access to devices, access rights, etc.).
- A database of attack templates. Each template represents a single step attack (or threat) defined by a precondition (condition on the state of the network and the capabilities of the attacker) and a postcondition (which characterizes the changes in the state of the system and the new capabilities of the attacker).

Graph generation can be carried out as a forward process starting from the initial state of the network or a backward exploration starting from a goal state (attack goal). At each generation step, the current (initial or goal) states are matched with preconditions or postconditions of attack templates in the database and the matching templates are applied to generate new nodes in the graph.

As far as the graph analysis is concerned, weights are associated with each edge and various graph algorithms can be applied to extract useful information from the graph such as, e.g., the least-cost attacks or the best defenses to decrease probabilities of successful attacks [12].

Another graph generation method is proposed in [7] based on a model checker which has been modified to generate all attack paths. Model checking is traditionally used to check whether a system satisfies a given property. If the property is not satisfied, the model checker produces a single counter-example, that is to say a sequence of operations leading to a violation of the property. In the present case, the property is a safety property and counterexamples represent attack paths. The algorithm proposed in [7] generates an attack graph from the set of attack paths returned by the model checker. In addition, it is shown that the generated attack graph is both complete (no missing state) and succinct (no unreachable state).

As far as graph analysis is concerned, [7] uses state marking and reachability algorithms to answer questions such as "What successful attacks are undetected by the intrusion detection system?" or "If all measures in the set M are implemented, does the system become safe?". Approximation algorithms can also be applied to answer N-P complete questions of the form "Given a set of measures M, what is the smallest subset of measures whose implementation makes the system safe?". In addition, attack graphs can also serve as a support for a probabilistic analysis: if probabilities are assigned to transitions, the graph can be interpreted as a Markov chain and used to answer questions such as "The implementation of which security measures will increase the likelihood of thwarting an attacker?". Attack graphs can thus be used in a quantitative risk analysis framework (Subsection 2.5).

To conclude this subsection, let us mention another, complementary, technique to tackle the scalability issue: [2] proposes a compact representation of attack graphs based on a monotonicity assumption. The assumption is that no action taken by an attacker can interfere with his ability to take any other action. In other words, the precondition of an attack step can never be invalidated, which means that attackers never need to backtrack. This assumption, which does not seem to be unrealistic in many cases, makes it possible to group attributes and factorize the set of states.

3.3   Formal Approaches Based on System Models

The main contribution of the methods presented in the two above subsections is to provide ways to deal with large state spaces, which is especially useful for network vulnerability analysis because network attack graphs are generally too large to be constructed and analyzed by hand. But these methods, whether based on attack trees or attack graphs, rely on the pre-existence of a database of known vulnerabilities or threats. Any oversight in the construction of this database can have dramatic effects on the result of the whole analysis. To put it another way, these techniques focus on the combination of well-identified atomic attacks but do not provide any help in discovering these atomic attacks in the first place. In addition, the lack of such database of vulnerabilities (which is not an unrealistic assumption for new, innovative IT products) make these techniques inapplicable or require the intervention of experts.

The only way to tackle this problem is to start from a model of the system itself (as opposed to a model of its vulnerabilities in the previous subsections). An illustrative example of this approach explicitly targeted at vulnerability analysis is presented in [13] which proposes a variant of CCS with algebraic data types to specify the behaviour of the system (or certain aspects of this behaviour which are deemed relevant for the security analysis). A variant of a model checking algorithm is then applied to check security properties. This algorithm implements a modified strategy to ensure that only finite portions of the infinite space are explored and all counter-examples (attack scenarios) are generated.

The main advantage of this approach is that it makes it possible discover as-yet-unknown vulnerabilities of the system. As a consequence, it does not require the availability of a pre-defined data base of vulnerabilities and it does not depend on assumptions about these vulnerabilities or on individual expertise. In addition, the results of the analysis are complete with respect to be behaviour of the system[9]: if the model used for the analysis is a faithful description of the behaviour of the system, all vulnerabilities will be discovered by the algorithm. The main limitation of this approach however is its cost, both in terms of design and computing resources: defining and analysing a formal model of a complete network would obviously be out of reach. Choices have thus to be made, both in terms of level of abstraction and features of the system to include within the model. Obviously, any error in these choices (e.g. overlooking a significant feature of the system or choosing a level of abstraction which hide serious vulnerabilities) can have a detrimental impact on the result of the analysis. In some sense, one can thus conclude that the sources of uncertainty are different in this approach, but they have not been eliminated.

4   Conclusion

The security analysis landscape pictured in this tutorial shows that a large variety of methods and techniques are available even if further progress has still to be made, especially to reduce the likelihood of oversights in the process. One of the lessons to be learned from this overview is that, just as in other areas of computer science, carefully designed formal methods can help a lot to tackle these issues because they can both enhance reliability in the results and serve as a basis for the design of powerful tools.

However, we believe that the range of methods referred to in Section 2 and Section 3 also brings to light several gaps:

- The first gap concerns the nature of the measures which are considered: some of the methods mentioned in Section 2 are very general and put emphasis on organizational issues whereas others focus on technical issues. At the extreme "technical" end, the formal frameworks presented in Section 3 do not concern organizational issues at all.
- The second gap has to do with the granularity of the analysis: the formal methods dilemma which appeared in Section 3 can roughly be expressed as a choice between a model of a *limited set of behaviours* of the *complete system* (behaviours leading to security breaches in vulnerability based approaches) or a model of *all possible behaviours* of a *small part of the system* (model based approaches).

---

[9] As specified by the model: obviously the specification itself may be flawed or may rely on wrong assumptions about the system or its environment.

Filling or reducing these gaps is crucial in order to be able to cope with the various aspects of IT security and to integrate all the relevant techniques in a consistent way. The main risk otherwise is that significant issues are overlooked or much energy and time are spent on minor issues when other, more significant, aspects, are underestimated. For example, since formal methods cannot be applied comprehensively to full-fledged systems, choices have to be made on the aspects of the system that are the best candidates for a deeper (and more expensive) analysis. It is important that these choices can be justified with respect to a global analysis of the system, which, as a matter of fact, cannot be completely formal. One of the main challenges in this area is thus to reconcile the global, encompassing view and the local view. A first attempt to achieve this reconciliation is described in [8] which proposes a semi-formal framework to detect and analyse the vulnerabilities of a product based on different security views. These views make it possible to track the assets in their different locations and identify the responsibilities of the actors involved. The method can deal with organizational as well as technical issues and allows for the detection of inconsistencies between the views of different stakeholders (e.g. customers, designers, developers). It is also helpful to elicit assumptions about the product and its environment and to provide a global security perspective. In its current state, the method relies on a static description of the product though, and it is targeted towards the study of invariant security properties such as confidentiality and integrity. Clearly, more work remains to be done in this area, and any new results in this direction can also provide new impetus for formal methods and encourage their use in practical situations.

References

1. Alberts, C., Dorofee, A., Stevens, J., Woody, C.: Introduction to the OCTAVE approach. Carnegie Mellon, SEI (2003)
2. Ammann, P., Wijesekera, D., Kaushik, S.: Scalable, graph-based network vulnerability analysis. In: Proceedings of the 9th ACM conference on Computer and Communications Security CCS'02 (2002)
3. Besson, F., Jensen, T., Le Métayer, D., Thorn, T.: Model checking security properties of control flow graphs. Journal of Computer Security 9 (2001)
4. Common Criteria for Information Technology Security evaluation, http://www.commoncriteriaportal.org/
5. Conrad, J.R.: Analyzing the risks of information security investments with Monte-Carlo simulations. In: IEEE Workshop on the Economics of Information Society (2005)
6. Howard, M., LeBlanc, D.: Writing secure code. Microsoft Press, Redmond (2003)
7. Jha, S., Sheyner, O., Wing, J.: Two formal analyses of attack graphs. In: Proceedings of the 15th Computer Security Foundations Workshop, IEEE Computer Society, Los Alamitos (2002)
8. Le Métayer, D., Loiseaux, C.: ASTRA: a security analysis method based on systematic asset tracking (to appear)
9. Maw, S., Oostdijk, M.: Foundations of attack trees. In: Won, D.H., Kim, S. (eds.) ICISC 2005. LNCS, vol. 3935, Springer, Heidelberg (2006)

10. McGraw, G.: Software security: building security in. Addison Wesley Professional, Reading (2006)
11. Peltier, T.R.: Information Security Risk Analysis. Auerbach Publications (2005)
12. Phillips, C., Swiler, L.P.: A graph-based system for network-vulnerability analysis. In: Proceedings of the 1998 Workshop on New Security Paradigms, ACM Press, New York (1998)
13. Ramakrishan, C.R., Sekar, R.: Model-based vulnerability analysis of computer systems. In: Second International Workshop on Verification, Model Checking and Abstract Interpretation (VMCAI'98) (1998)
14. Schechter, S.E.: Computer security strengths and risks: a quantitative approach. PhD Thesis, Harvard University (2004)
15. Schneier, B.: Attack trees, modeling security threats. Dr Dobbs Journal (1999)
16. Stoneburner, G., Goguen, A., Feringa, A.: Risk management guide for information technology systems. NIST Special Publication, pp. 800–830 (2002)
17. Swiderski, F., Snyder, W.: Threat modeling. Microsoft Press, Redmond (2004)
18. Tidwell, T., Larson, R., Fitch, K., Hale, J.: Modeling internet attacks. In: Proceedings of the 2001 IEEE Workshop on Information Assurance and Security, IEEE Computer Society Press, Los Alamitos (2001)

Low-Level Software Security: Attacks and Defenses

Úlfar Erlingsson

Microsoft Research, Silicon Valley
and
Reykjavík University, Iceland

Abstract. This tutorial paper considers the issues of low-level software security from a language-based perspective, with the help of concrete examples. Four examples of low-level software attacks are covered in full detail; these examples are representative of the major types of attacks on C and C++ software that is compiled into machine code. Six examples of practical defenses against those attacks are also covered in detail; these defenses are selected because of their effectiveness, wide applicability, and low enforcement overhead.

1 Introduction

Computers are often subject to external attacks that aim to control software behavior. Typically, such attacks arrive as data over a regular communication channel and, once resident in program memory, trigger pre-existing, low-level software vulnerabilities. By exploiting such flaws, these low-level attacks can subvert the execution of the software and gain control over its behavior.

The combined effects of these attacks make them one of the most pressing challenges in computer security. As a result, in recent years, many mechanisms have been proposed for defending against these attacks. However, these defenses, as well as the attacks, are strongly dependent on low-level minutiae, such as the exact semantics of high-level language constructs, the precise syntax of machine-code opcodes, and the layout of code and data into memory. Therefore, in the literature, it is rare to find the full details of concrete attacks, or precisely how particular defenses prevent those attacks. This tutorial paper aims to partially remedy this situation.

The remainder of this introductory section gives more background about low-level software security, as well as notes on the presentation of low-level details. Next, Section 2 gives four examples that represent some of the important classes of low-level software attacks. These attacks apply to software written in C and C++, or similar languages, and compiled into executable machine-code for commodity, x86 hardware. These attacks are described in enough detail to be understood even by readers without a background in software security, and without a natural inclination for crafting malicious attacks. Then, Section 3 explains in detail the motivation, detailed mechanisms, and limitations of six important, practical defenses. A final Section 4 offers a brief summary and discussion.

A. Aldini and R. Gorrieri (Eds.): FOSAD 2006/2007, LNCS 4677, pp. 92–134, 2007.

Throughout, the attacks and defenses are placed in perspective by showing how they are both facilitated by the gap between the semantics of the high-level language of the software under attack, and the low-level semantics of machine code and the hardware on which the software executes.

1.1 Low-Level Software Security in Languages Other Than C and C++

It is not only in languages such as C and C++ that the issues of low-level software security must be considered. Low-level attacks may be possible whenever software is translated from a higher-level language into a lower-level language, without a guarantee that this translation preserves the higher-level abstractions.

Software programmers express their intent using the abstractions of the higher-level language. If these abstractions are not preserved in low-level execution, then this discrepancy can cause the software to behave in unexpected ways. Often, an attacker will be able to exploit this discrepancy, and divert the low-level execution of the software to perform arbitrary functionality of the attackers choosing.

Unfortunately, in practice, compilers from high-level to low-level languages do not guarantee full abstraction. This is true even for type-safe languages, such as Java and Microsoft's C#. As a result, low-level software attacks are also possible in such languages.

For instance, in Java, variables can be declared to be "private" to classes, in such a way that only the code in the declaring class is able to access the variables. In the Java language, this is a strong guarantee that a programmer might rely on—e.g., to implement a bank account whose sum can be updated only through well-defined deposit and withdraw operations in the declaring class.

However, Java is executed indirectly through compilation into a lower-level language, "JVML bytecode", whose semantics are different, As a result, when a class declares nested classes its private variables are actually not private, but are accessible to all the code in a set of classes. Often, this set may be dynamically extended by the Java virtual machine that executes JVML bytecode; these new classes may originate from third parties, as long as the type safety of the JVML bytecode can be verified.

As a result, attackers may be able to directly craft low-level JVML bytecode that pretends to be in the set of nested classes, and thereby circumvents the high-level Java language semantics of the software [1]. In this case, private variables may be subject to arbitrary modification by code written by attackers—e.g., artificially inflating a bank-account sum that is stored in a private variable.

Similarly, C# code is compiled into "CLR bytecode" with different semantics that create possibilities for low-level attacks. For instance, it is impossible in C# to invoke object constructors more than once, so a variable initialized during construction, and not modified from then on, may be assumed to be immutable in C# software—and it is easy to see how programmers might depend on this property. However, at the lower level of CLR bytecode, an object constructor is just another function that may be invoked multiple times [28]. Thus, in fact, a

```
int unsafe( char* a, char* b )        int safe( char* a, char* b )
{                                     {
    char t[MAX_LEN];                      char t[MAX_LEN] = { '\0' };
    strcpy( t, a );                       strcpy_s( t, _countof(t), a );
    strcat( t, b );                       strcat_s( t, _countof(t), b );
    return strcmp( t, "abc" );            return strcmp( t, "abc" );
}                                     }
```

(a) An unchecked C function   (b) A safer version of the function

Fig. 1. Two C functions that both compare whether the concatenation of two input strings is the string "abc". The first, unchecked function contains a security vulnerability if the inputs are untrusted. The second function is not vulnerable in this manner, since it uses new C library functions that perform validity checks against the lengths of buffers. Modern compilers will warn about the use of older, less safe library functions, and strongly suggest the use of their newer variants.

"C# immutable" variable may be modified arbitrarily often by an attack that operates at the lower level of CLR bytecode. Here, as in the case of Java, the semantic gap between languages allows attackers to introduce valid, type-safe low-level code that can invalidate properties of the high-level software.

Low-level software security can also be relevant in the context of very different high-level languages, such as the scripting languages embedded within Web pages. For instance, consider a Web application that prompts the user for her name and sends a greeting back to the Web browser. To perform this task, a statement like `response.println("<p>Hello, " + userName + ".</p>");` might be executed by the Web server. This statement may well be written in a high-level programming language that requires explicit declaration of all scripts to be executed in the Web browser. However, scripts are just text strings, and if the string `userName` can be chosen by an attacker, then that attacker may be able to cause arbitrary behavior. The low-level execution in the Web browser will ignore the intent of the higher-level language and execute script code found anywhere, even embedded within `userName` [34].

Therefore, the concepts discussed in this tutorial are applicable more broadly than might appear. Of course, since low-level software security is closely bound to system particulars, the details will be different in contexts other than C and C++ software compiled into machine code. However, in those other contexts there may still be a direct relationship to the attacks and defenses in this tutorial. For instance, defenses based on randomization and secrets much like those in Section 3 have recently been successfully used to prevent low-level attacks on scripting languages in Web applications [26].

1.2   The Difficulty of Eliminating Low-Level Vulnerabilities

Figure 1 is representative of the attacks and defenses presented in this tutorial. The attacks in Section 2 all exploit vulnerabilities similar to that in Figure 1(a), where a buffer overflow may be possible. For the most part, the defenses in Section 3 use techniques like those in Figure 1(b) and prevent exploits by maintaining additional information, validating that information with runtime checks, and halting execution if such a check fails.

Unfortunately, unlike in Figure 1, it is often not so straightforward to modify existing source code to use new, safer methods of implementing its functionality. For most code there may not be a direct correspondence between well-known, unsafe library functions and their newer, safer versions. Indeed, existing code can easily be unsafe despite not using any library routines, and vulnerabilities are often obscured by pointer arithmetic or complicated data-structure traversal. (To clarify this point, it is worth comparing the code in Figure 1 with the code in Figure 3, on page 98, where explicit loops implement the same functionality.)

Furthermore, manual attempts to remove software vulnerabilities may give a false sense of security, since they do not always succeed and can sometimes introduce new bugs. For example, a programmer that intends to eliminate buffer overflows in the code of Figure 1(a) might change the strcpy and strcat function calls as in Figure 1(b), but fail to initialize t to be the empty string at the start of the function. In this case, the strcmp comparison will be against the unmodified array t, if both strings a and b are longer than MAX_LEN.

Thus, a slight omission from Figure 1(b) would leave open the possibility of an exploitable vulnerability as a result of the function reporting that the concatenation of the inputs strings is "abc", even in cases when this is false. In particular, this may occur when, on entry to the function, the array t contains "abc" as a residual data value from a previous invocation of the function.

Low-level software security vulnerabilities continue to persist due to technical reasons, as well as practical engineering concerns such as the difficulties involved in modifying legacy software. The state of the art in eliminating these vulnerabilities makes use of code review, security testing, and other manual software engineering processes, as well as automatic analyses that can discover vulnerabilities [23]. Furthermore, best practice also acknowledges that some vulnerabilities are likely to remain, and make those vulnerabilities more difficult to exploit by applying defenses like those in this tutorial.

1.3   The Assumptions Underlying Software, Attacks, and Defenses

Programmers make many assumptions when creating software, both implicitly and explicitly. Some of these assumptions are valid, based on the semantics of the high-level language, as discussed in Section 1.1. For instance, C or C++ programmers may assume that execution does not start at an arbitrary place within a function, but at the start of that function.

Programmers may also make questionable assumptions, such as about the execution environment of their software. For instance, software may be written without concurrency in mind, or in a manner that is dependent on the address encoding in pointers, or on the order of heap allocations. Any such assumptions hinder portability, and may result in incorrect execution when the execution environment changes even slightly.

Finally, programmers may make invalid, mistaken assumptions. For example, in C or C++, programmers may assume that the int type behaves a true, mathematical integer, or that a memory buffer is large enough for the size of the content it may ever need to hold. All of the above types of assumptions are relevant to low-level software security, and each may make the software vulnerable to attack.

At the same time, attackers also make assumptions, and low-level software attacks rely on a great number of specific properties about the hardware and software architecture of their target. Many of these assumptions involve details about names and the meaning of those names, such as the exact memory addresses of variables or functions and how they are used in the software. These assumptions also relate to the software's execution environment, such as the hardware instruction set architecture and its machine-code semantics.

For example, the Internet Worm of 1988 was successful in large part because of an attack that depended on the particulars of the commonly-deployed VAX hardware architecture, the 4 BSD operating system, and the fingerd service. On other systems that were popular at the time, that same attack failed in a manner that only crashed the fingerd service, due to the differences in instruction sets and memory layouts [43]. In this manner, attack code is often fragile to the point where even the smallest change prevents the attacker from gaining control, but crashes the target software—effecting a denial-of-service attack.

Defense mechanisms also have assumptions, including assumptions about the capabilities of the attacker, about the likelihood of different types of attacks, about the properties of the software being defended, and about its execution environment. In the attacks and defenses that follow, a note will be made of the assumptions that apply in each case. For instance, of the defenses in Section 3, Defense 1 assumes that attacks make use of a contiguous stack-based buffer overflow, and Defense 4 provides strong guarantees by assuming that Defense 3 is also in place. Also, many defenses (including most of the ones in this tutorial) assume that denial-of-service is not the attacker's goal, and halt the execution of the target software upon the failure of runtime validity checks.

1.4   The Presentation of Technical Details in This Tutorial

The presentation in this tutorial paper assumes a basic knowledge of programming languages like C and C++, and their compilation, as might be acquired in an introductory course on compilers. For the most part, relevant technical concepts are introduced when needed. In fact, a large fraction of the technical content is shown in numbered figures whose captions are written to be understandable independent of the main text and without much prior knowledge of low-level software security issues.

As well as giving a number of examples of vulnerable C and C++ software, this tutorial shows many details relating to software execution, such as machine code and execution stack content. Throughout, the details shown will reflect software execution on one particular hardware architecture—a 32-bit x86, such as the IA-32 [11]—but demonstrate properties that also apply to most other hardware platforms.

The examples show many concrete, hexadecimal values and—in order to avoid confusion—the reader should remember that on the little-endian x86, when four bytes are displayed as a 32-bit integer value, their printed order will be reversed from the order of the bytes in memory. Thus, if the hexadecimal bytes 0xaa, 0xbb, 0xcc, and 0xdd occur in memory, in that order, then those bytes encode the 32-bit integer 0xddccbbaa.

2   A Selection of Low-Level Attacks on C and C++ Software

This section presents four low-level software attacks in full detail and explains how each attack invalidates a property of target software written in the C or C++ languages. The attacks are carefully chosen to be representative of four major classes of attacks: stack-based buffer overflows, heap-based buffer overflows, jump-to-libc attacks, and data-only attacks.

No examples are given below of a "format-string attack" or of an "integer-overflow vulnerability". Format-string vulnerabilities are particularly simple to eliminate [12]; therefore, although they have received a great deal of attention in the past, they are no longer a significant, practical concern in well-engineered software. Integer-overflow vulnerabilities [8] do still exist, and are increasingly being exploited, but only as a first step towards attacks like those described below. In this section, Attack 4 is one example where an integer overflow might be the first step in the exploit crafted by the attacker.

As further reading, the survey of Pincus and Baker gives a good general overview of low-level software attacks like those described in this section [38].

2.1   Attack 1: Corruption of a Function Return Address on the Stack

It is natural for C and C++ programmers to assume that, if a function is invoked at a particular call site and runs to completion without throwing an exception, then that function will return to the instruction immediately following that same, particular call site.

Unfortunately, this may not be the case in the presence of software bugs. For example, if the invoked function contains a local array, or buffer, and writes into that buffer are not correctly guarded, then the return address on the stack may be overwritten and corrupted. In particular, this may happen if the software copies to the buffer data whose length is larger than the buffer size, in a *buffer overflow*.

Furthermore, if an attacker controls the data used by the function, then the attacker may be able to trigger such corruption, and change the function return address to an arbitrary value. In this case, when the function returns, the attacker can direct execution to code of their choice and gain full control over subsequent behavior of the software. Figure 2 and Figure 3 show examples of C functions that are vulnerable to this attack.

```
int is_file_foobar( char* one, char* two )
{
    // must have strlen(one) + strlen(two) < MAX_LEN
    char tmp[MAX_LEN];
    strcpy( tmp, one );
    strcat( tmp, two );
    return strcmp( tmp, "file://foobar" );
}
```

Fig. 2. A C function that compares the concatenation of two input strings against "file://foobar". This function contains a typical stack-based buffer overflow vulnerability: if the input strings can be chosen by an attacker, then the attacker can direct machine-code execution when the function returns.

```
int is_file_foobar_using_loops( char* one, char* two )
{
    // must have strlen(one) + strlen(two) < MAX_LEN
    char tmp[MAX_LEN];
    char* b = tmp;
    for( ; *one != '\0'; ++one, ++b ) *b = *one;
    for( ; *two != '\0'; ++two, ++b ) *b = *two;
    *b = '\0';
    return strcmp( tmp, "file://foobar" );
}
```

Fig. 3. A version of the C function in Figure 2 that copies and concatenates strings using pointer manipulation and explicit loops. This function is also vulnerable to the same stack-based buffer overflow attacks, even though it does not invoke strcpy or strcat or other C library functions that are known to be difficult to use safely.

This attack, sometimes referred to as *return-address clobbering*, is probably the best known exploit of a low-level software security vulnerability; it dates back to before 1988, when it was used in the fingerd exploit of the Internet Worm. Indeed, until about a decade ago, this attack was seen by many as the only significant low-level attack on software compiled from C and C++, and "stack-based buffer overflow" were widely considered a synonym for such attacks. More recently, this attack has not been as prominent, in part because other methods of attack have been widely publicized, but also in part because the underlying vulnerabilities that enable return-address clobbering are slowly being eliminated (e.g., through the adoption of newer, safer C library functions).

To give a concrete example of this attack, Figure 4 shows a normal execution stack for the functions in Figures 2 and 3, and Figure 5 shows an execution stack for the same code just after a overflow of the local array—potentially caused by an attacker that can choose the contents of the two string provided as input.

Of course, an attacker would choose their input such that the buffer overflow would not caused by "asdfasdfasdfasdf", but another string of bytes. In particular, the attacker might choose 0x48, 0xff, and 0x12, in order, as the final three

```
address      content
0x0012ff5c  0x00353037  ; argument two pointer
0x0012ff58  0x0035302f  ; argument one pointer
0x0012ff54  0x00401263  ; return address
0x0012ff50  0x0012ff7c  ; saved base pointer
0x0012ff4c  0x00000072  ; tmp continues 'r' '\0' '\0' '\0'
0x0012ff48  0x61626f6f  ; tmp continues 'o' 'o' 'b' 'a'
0x0012ff44  0x662f2f3a  ; tmp continues ':' '/' '/' 'f'
0x0012ff40  0x656c6966  ; tmp array:      'f' 'i' 'l' 'e'
```

Fig. 4. A snapshot of an execution stack for the functions in Figures 2 and 3, where the size of the tmp array is 16 bytes. This snapshot shows the stack just before executing the return statement. Argument one is "file://", and argument two is "foobar", and the concatenation of those strings fits in the tmp array. (Stacks are traditionally displayed with the lowest address at the bottom, as is done here and throughout this tutorial.)

```
address      content
0x0012ff5c  0x00353037  ; argument two pointer
0x0012ff58  0x0035302f  ; argument one pointer
0x0012ff54  0x00666473  ; return address      's' 'd' 'f' '\0'
0x0012ff50  0x61666473  ; saved base pointer 's' 'd' 'f' 'a'
0x0012ff4c  0x61666473  ; tmp continues      's' 'd' 'f' 'a'
0x0012ff48  0x61666473  ; tmp continues      's' 'd' 'f' 'a'
0x0012ff44  0x612f2f3a  ; tmp continues      ':' '/' '/' 'a'
0x0012ff40  0x656c6966  ; tmp array:         'f' 'i' 'l' 'e'
```

Fig. 5. An execution-stack snapshot like that in Figure 4, but where argument one is "file://" and argument two is "asdfasdfasdfasdf". The concatenation of the argument strings has overflowed the tmp array and the function return address is now determined by the last few characters of the two string.

character bytes of the two argument string—and thereby arrange for the function return address to have the value 0x0012ff48. In this case, as soon as the function returns, the hardware instruction pointer would be placed at the second character of the two argument string, and the hardware would start executing the data found there (and chosen by the attacker) as machine code.

In the example under discussion, an attacker would choose their input data so that the machine code for an *attack payload* would be present at address 0x0012ff48. When the vulnerable function returns, and execution of the attack payload begins, the attacker has gained control of the behavior of the target software. (The attack payload is often called *shellcode*, since a common goal of an attacker is to launch a "shell" command interpreter under their control.)

In Figure 5, the bytes at 0x0012ff48 are those of the second to fifth characters in the string "asdfasdfasdfasdf", namely 's', 'd', 'f', and 'a'. When executed as machine code, those bytes do not implement an attack. Instead, as described in Figure 6, an attacker might choose 0xcd, 0x2e, 0xeb, and 0xfe as a very simple attack payload. Thus, an attacker might call the operating system to

```
machine code
opcode bytes        assembly-language version of the machine code
   0xcd 0x2e             int 0x2e  ; system call to the operating system
   0xeb 0xfe          L: jmp L    ; a very short, direct infinite loop
```

Fig. 6. The simple attack payload used in this tutorial; in most examples, the attacker's goal will be to execute this machine code. Of these four bytes, the first two are a x86 `int` instruction which performs a system call on some platforms, and the second two are an x86 `jmp` instruction that directly calls itself in an infinite loop. (Note that, in the examples, these bytes will sometimes be printed as the integer `0xfeeb2ecd`, with the apparent reversal a result of x86 little-endianness.)

enable a dangerous feature, or disable security checks, and avoid detection by keeping the target software running (albeit in a loop).

Return-address clobbering as described above has been a highly successful attack technique—for example, in 2003 it was used to implement the Blaster worm, which affected a majority of Internet users [5]. In the case of Blaster, the vulnerable code was written using explicit loops, much as in Figure 3. (This was one reason why the vulnerability had not been detected and corrected through automatic software analysis tools, or by manual code reviews.)

Attack 1: Constraints and Variants

Low-level attacks are typically subject to a number of such constraints, and must be carefully written to be compatible with the vulnerability being exploited.

For example, the attack demonstrated above relies on the hardware being willing to execute the data found on the stack as machine code. However, on some systems the stack is not executable, e.g., because those systems implement the defenses described later in this tutorial. On such systems, an attacker would have to pursue a more indirect attack strategy, such as those described later, in Attacks 3 and 4.

Another important constraint applies to the above buffer-overflow attacks: the attacker-chosen data cannot contain null bytes, or zeros—since such bytes terminate the buffer overflow and prevent further copying onto the stack. This is a common constraint when crafting exploits of buffer overflows, and applies to most of the attacks in this tutorial. It is so common that special tools exist for creating machine code for attack payloads that do not contain any embedded null bytes, newline characters, or other byte sequences that might terminate the buffer overflow (one such tool is Metasploit [18]).

There are a number of attack methods similar to return-address clobbering, in that they exploit stack-based buffer overflow vulnerabilities to target the function-invocation control data on the stack. Most of these variants add a level of indirection to the techniques described above.

One notable attack variant corrupts the base pointer saved on the stack (see Figures 4 and 5) and not the return address sitting above it. In this variant, the vulnerable function may return as expected to its caller function, but, when

```
typedef struct _vulnerable_struct
{
    char buff[MAX_LEN];
    int (*cmp)(char*,char*);
} vulnerable;

int is_file_foobar_using_heap( vulnerable* s, char* one, char* two )
{
    // must have strlen(one) + strlen(two) < MAX_LEN
    strcpy( s->buff, one );
    strcat( s->buff, two );
    return s->cmp( s->buff, "file://foobar" );
}
```

Fig. 7. A C function that sets a heap data structure as the concatenation of two input strings, and compares the result against "file://foobar" using the comparison function for that data structure. This function is vulnerable to a heap-based buffer overflow attack, if an attacker can choose either or both of the input strings.

that caller itself returns, it uses a return address that has been chosen by the attacker [30]. Another notable variant of this attack targets C and C++ exception-handler pointers that reside on the stack, and ensures that the buffer overflow causes an exception—at which point a function pointer of the attacker's choice may be executed [32].

2.2   Attack 2: Corruption of Function Pointers Stored in the Heap

Software written in C and C++ often combines data buffers and pointers into the same data structures, or objects, with programmers making a natural assumption that the data values do not affect the pointer values. Unfortunately, this may not be the case in the presence of software bugs. In particular, the pointers may be corrupted as a result of an overflow of the data buffer—regardless whether the data structures or objects reside on stack, or in heap memory. Figure 7 shows C code with a function that is vulnerable to such an attack.

To give a concrete example of this attack, Figure 8 shows the contents of the `vulnerable` data structure after the function in Figure 7 has copied data into the `buff` array using the `strcpy` and `strcmp` library functions. Figure 8 shows three instances of the data structure contents: as might occur during normal processing, as might occur in an unintended buffer overflow, and, finally, as might occur during an attack. These instances can occur both when the data structure is allocated on the stack, and also when it is allocated on the heap.

In the last instance of Figure 8, the attacker has chosen the two input strings such that the `cmp` function pointer has become the address of the start of the data structure. At that address, the attacker has arranged for an attack payload to be present. Thus, when the function in Figure 7 executes the `return` statement, and invokes `s->cmp`, it transfers control to the start of the data structure, which contains data of the attacker's choice. In this case, the attack payload is the

	buff (char array at start of the struct)			cmp
address:	0x00353068 0x0035306c	0x00353070	0x00353074	0x00353078
content:	0x656c6966 0x662f2f3a	0x61626f6f	0x00000072	0x004013ce

(a) A structure holding "file://foobar" and a pointer to the strcmp function

	buff (char array at start of the struct)			cmp
address:	0x00353068 0x0035306c	0x00353070	0x00353074	0x00353078
content:	0x656c6966 0x612f2f3a	0x61666473	0x61666473	0x00666473

(b) After a buffer overflow caused by the inputs "file://" and "asdfasdfasdf"

	buff (char array at start of the struct)			cmp
address:	0x00353068 0x0035306c	0x00353070	0x00353074	0x00353078
content:	0xfeeb2ecd 0x11111111	0x11111111	0x11111111	0x00353068

(c) After a malicious buffer overflow caused by attacker-chosen inputs

Fig. 8. Three instances of the vulnerable data structure pointed to by s in Figure 7, where the size of the buff array is 16 bytes. Both the address of the structure and its 20 bytes of content are shown. In the first instance, the buffer holds "file://foobar" and cmp points to the strcmp function. In the second instance, the pointer has been corrupted by a buffer overflow. In the third instance, an attacker has selected the input strings so that the buffer overflow has changed the structure data so that the simple attack payload of Figure 6, page 100, will be executed.

four bytes of machine code 0xcd, 0x2e, 0xeb, and 0xfe described in Figure 6, page 100, and used throughout this tutorial.

It is especially commonplace for C++ code to store object instances on the heap and to combine—within a single object instance—both data buffers that may be overflowed and potentially exploitable pointers. In particular, C++ object instances are likely to contain *vtable pointers*: a form of indirect function pointers that allow dynamic dispatch of virtual member functions. As a result, C++ software may be particularly vulnerable to heap-based attacks.

As a concrete example of vulnerable C++ code, Figure 9 shows the body and supporting classes for a function that performs string concatenation and comparison that should, by now, be familiar.

The C++ code in Figure 9 is vulnerable in much the same manner as the code in Figure 7. In particular, the memory layout of Vulnerable objects mirrors that of the vulnerable data structure: an array bytes followed by a pointer to allow for different types of string comparison. However, in this case, the pointer is a not a direct function pointer, but a pointer to the vtables of one of the two Comparer classes.

The extra level of indirection to a function pointer requires the attacker to slightly change their attack. As shown in Figure 10, the attacker can place the attack payload four bytes into the overflowed buffer, place the payload address at the start of the buffer, and place in the vtable pointer the address of the start of the buffer. Thereby, the attack payload will be executed when the function in

Figure 9 invokes `s->cmp`, and makes use of the `m_cmp` member of the `Vulnerable` class. (However, note that, in Figure 10, if the object instance were located at a memory address that contained embedded null bytes, then the attacker would have difficulty writing that address in the buffer overflow.)

```
class Comparer
{
public:
    virtual int compare(char* a, char* b) { return stricmp(a,b); }
};

class CaseSensitiveComparer : public Comparer
{
public:
    virtual int compare(char* a, char* b) { return strcmp(a,b); }
};

class Vulnerable
{
    char m_buff[MAX_LEN];
    Comparer m_cmp;
public:
    Vulnerable(Comparer c) : m_cmp(c) {}
    void init(char* str) { strcpy(m_buff, str); }
    void append(char* str) { strcat(m_buff, str); }
    int cmp(char* str) {
        return m_cmp.compare( m_buff, str );
    }
};

int is_file_foobar_using_cpp( Vulnerable* s, char* one, char* two )
{
    // must have strlen(one) + strlen(two) < MAX_LEN
    s->init( one );
    s->append( two );
    return s->cmp( "file://foobar" );
}
```

Fig. 9. A C++ version of the code in Figure 7, which uses virtual methods to allow for different types of string comparison. This code is also vulnerable to a heap-based attack, using one level of indirection more than the attack on the code in Figure 7.

	m_buff (char array at start of the object)			m_cmp (vtable)
address:	0x05101010	0x05101014	0x05101018	0x0510101c	0x05101020
content:	0x05101014	0xfeeb2ecd	0x11111111	0x11111111	0x05101010

Fig. 10. The address and contents of a `Vulnerable` object, with a 16 byte buffer, in the case of a buffer overflow attack designed to execute the attack payload from Figure 6. This attack payload is found at address `0x05101014`, four bytes into the buffer.

Attack 2: Constraints and Variants

Heap-based attacks are often constrained by their ability to determine the address of the heap memory that is being corrupted, as can be seen in the examples above. This constraint applies in particular, to all indirect attacks, where a heap-based pointer-to-a-pointer is modified—such as in the C++ attack example above. Furthermore, the exact bytes of those addresses may constrain the attacker, e.g., if the exploited vulnerability is that of a string-based buffer overflow, in which case the address data cannot contain null bytes.

The examples above demonstrate attacks where heap-based buffer overflow vulnerabilities are exploited to corrupt pointers that reside within the same data structure or object as the data buffer that is overflowed. There are two important attack variants, not described above, where heap-based buffer overflows are used to corrupt pointers that reside in other structures or objects, or in the heap metadata.

In the first variant, two data structures or objects reside consecutively in heap memory, the initial one containing a buffer that can be overflowed, and the subsequent one containing a direct, or indirect, function pointer. Heap objects are often adjacent in memory like this when they are functionally related and are allocated in order, one immediately after the other. Whenever these conditions hold, attacks similar to the above examples may be possible, by overflowing the buffer in the first object and overwriting the pointer in the second object.

In the second variant, the attack is based on corrupting the metadata of the heap itself through a heap-based buffer overflow, and exploiting that corruption to write an arbitrary value to an arbitrary location in memory. This is possible because heap implementations contain code such as `p->prev->next = p->next;` to manage doubly-linked lists in their metadata. An attacker that can corrupt the metadata can choose the values of `p->prev` and `p->next`, and thereby choose what is written where. The attacker can then use this capability to write a pointer to the attack payload in the place of any soon-to-be-used function pointer sitting at a known address. For example, in a published attack on the GDI+ JPEG flaw in Windows the attacker overwrote the C++ vtable pointer of a global object whose virtual destructor was invoked as part of error recovery [16].

2.3   Attack 3: Execution of Existing Code Via Corrupt Pointers

If software does not contain any code for certain functionality—such as performing floating-point calculations, or making system calls to interact with the network—then the programmers may naturally assume that execution of the software will not result in this behavior, or functionality.

Unfortunately, for C or C++ software, this assumption may not hold in the face of bugs and malicious attacks, as demonstrated by attacks like those in this tutorial. As in the previous two examples of attacks, the attacker may be able to cause arbitrary behavior by *direct code injection*: by directly modifying the hardware instruction pointer to execute machine code embedded in attacker-provided input data, instead of the original software. However, there are other

```
int median( int* data, int len, void* cmp )
{
    // must have 0 < len <= MAX_INTS
    int tmp[MAX_INTS];
    memcpy( tmp, data, len*sizeof(int) );   // copy the input integers
    qsort( tmp, len, sizeof(int), cmp );    // sort the local copy
    return tmp[len/2];                      // median is in the middle
}
```

Fig. 11. A C function that computes the median of an array of input integers by sorting a local copy of those integers. This function is vulnerable to a stack-based buffer overflow attack, if an attacker can choose the set of input integers.

means for an attacker to cause software to exhibit arbitrary behavior, and these alternatives can be the preferred mode of attack.

In particular, an attacker may find it preferable to craft attacks that execute the existing machine code of the target software in a manner not intended by its programmers. For example, the attacker may corrupt a function pointer to cause the execution of a library function that is unreachable in the original C or C++ source code written by the programmers—and should therefore, in the compiled software, be never-executed, dead code. Alternatively, the attacker may arrange for reachable, valid machine code to be executed, but in an unexpected order, or with unexpected data arguments.

This class of attacks is typically referred to as *jump-to-libc* or *return-to-libc* (depending on whether a function pointer or return address is corrupted by the attacker), because the attack often involves directing execution towards machine code in the libc standard C library.

Jump-to-libc attacks are especially attractive when the target software system is based on an architecture where input data cannot be directly executed as machine code. Such architectures are becoming commonplace with the adoption of the defenses such as those described later in this tutorial. As a result, an increasingly important class of attacks is *indirect code injection*: the selective execution of the target software's existing machine code in a manner that enables attacker-chosen input data to be subsequently executed as machine code. Figure 11 shows a C function that is vulnerable to such an attack.

The function in Figure 11 actually contains a stack-based buffer overflow vulnerability that can be exploited for various attacks, if an attacker is able to choose the number of input integers, and their contents. In particular, attackers can perform return-address clobbering, as described in Attack 1. However, for this particular function, an attacker can also corrupt the comparison-function pointer cmp before it is passed to qsort. In this case, the attacker can gain control of machine-code execution at the point where qsort calls its copy of the corrupted cmp argument. Figure 12 shows the machine code in the qsort library function where this, potentially-corrupted function pointer is called.

To give a concrete example of a jump-to-libc attack, consider the case when the function in Figure 11 is executed on some versions of the Microsoft Windows

```
...
push    edi              ; push second argument to be compared onto the stack
push    ebx              ; push the first argument onto the stack
call    [esp+comp_fp]    ; call comparison function, indirectly through a pointer
add     esp, 8           ; remove the two arguments from the stack
test    eax, eax         ; check the comparison result
jle     label_lessthan   ; branch on that result
...
```

Fig. 12. Machine code fragment from the qsort library function, showing how the comparison operation is called through a function pointer. When qsort is invoked in the median function of Figure 11, a stack-based buffer overflow attack can make this function pointer hold an arbitrary address.

address	machine code opcode bytes	assembly-language version of the machine code
0x7c971649	0x8b 0xe3	mov esp, ebx ; change the stack location to ebx
0x7c97164b	0x5b	pop ebx ; pop ebx from the new stack
0x7c97164c	0xc3	ret ; return based on the new stack

Fig. 13. Four bytes found within executable memory, in a system library. These bytes encode three machine-code instructions that are useful in the crafting of jump-to-libc attacks. In particular, in an attack on the median function in Figure 11, these three instructions may be called by the qsort code in Figure 12, which will change the stack pointer to the start of the local tmp buffer that has been overflowed by the attacker.

operating system. On these systems, the qsort function is implemented as shown in Figure 12 and the memory address 0x7c971649 holds the four bytes of executable machine code, as shown in Figure 13.

On such a system, the buffer overflow may leave the stack looking like that shown in the "malicious overflow contents" column of Figure 14. Then, when the qsort function is called, it is passed a copy of the corrupted cmp function-pointer argument, which points to a *trampoline* found within existing, executable machine code. This trampoline is the code found at address 0x7c971649, which is shown in Figure 13. The effect of calling the trampoline is to, first, set the stack pointer esp to the start address of the tmp array, (which is held in register ebx), second, read a new value for ebx from the first integer in the tmp array, and, third, perform a return that changes the hardware instruction pointer to the address held in the second integer in the tmp array.

The attack subsequently proceeds as follows. The stack is "unwound" one stack frame at a time, as functions return to return addresses. The stack holds data, including return addresses, that has been chosen by the attacker to encode function calls and arguments. As each stack frame is unwound, the return instruction transfers control to the start of a particular, existing library function, and provides that function with arguments.

Figure 15 shows, as C source code, the sequence of function calls that occur when the stack is unwound. The figure shows both the name and address of the Windows library functions that are invoked, as well as their arguments.

stack address	normal stack contents	benign overflow contents	malicious overflow contents	
0x0012ff38	0x004013e0	0x1111110d	0x7c971649	; cmp argument
0x0012ff34	0x00000001	0x1111110c	0x1111110c	; len argument
0x0012ff30	0x00353050	0x1111110b	0x1111110b	; data argument
0x0012ff2c	0x00401528	0x1111110a	0xfeeb2ecd	; return address
0x0012ff28	0x0012ff4c	0x11111109	0x70000000	; saved base pointer
0x0012ff24	0x00000000	0x11111108	0x70000000	; tmp final 4 bytes
0x0012ff20	0x00000000	0x11111107	0x00000040	; tmp continues
0x0012ff1c	0x00000000	0x11111106	0x00003000	; tmp continues
0x0012ff18	0x00000000	0x11111105	0x00001000	; tmp continues
0x0012ff14	0x00000000	0x11111104	0x70000000	; tmp continues
0x0012ff10	0x00000000	0x11111103	0x7c80978e	; tmp continues
0x0012ff0c	0x00000000	0x11111102	0x7c809a51	; tmp continues
0x0012ff08	0x00000000	0x11111101	0x11111101	; tmp buffer starts
0x0012ff04	0x00000004	0x00000040	0x00000040	; memcpy length argument
0x0012ff00	0x00353050	0x00353050	0x00353050	; memcpy source argument
0x0012fefc	0x0012ff08	0x0012ff08	0x0012ff08	; memcpy destination arg.

Fig. 14. The address and contents of the stack of the median function of Figure 11, where tmp is eight integers in size. Three versions of the stack contents are shown, as it would appear just after the call to memcpy: a first for input data of the single integer zero, a second for a benign buffer overflow of consecutive integers starting at 0x11111101, and a third for a malicious jump-to-libc attack that corrupts the comparison function pointer to make qsort call address 0x7c971649 and the machine code in Figure 13.

```
// call a function to allocate writable, executable memory at 0x70000000
VirtualAlloc(0x70000000, 0x1000, 0x3000, 0x40); // function at 0x7c809a51

// call a function to write the four-byte attack payload to 0x70000000
InterlockedExchange(0x70000000, 0xfeeb2ecd);     // function at 0x7c80978e

// invoke the four bytes of attack payload machine code
((void (*)())0x70000000)();                      // payload at 0x70000000
```

Fig. 15. The jump-to-libc attack activity caused by the maliciously-corrupted stack in Figure 14, expressed as C source code. As the corrupted stack is unwound, instead of returning to call sites, the effect is a sequence of function calls, first to functions in the standard Windows library kernel32.dll, and then to the attack payload.

The effect of these invocations is to create a new, writable page of executable memory, to write machine code of the attacker's choice to that page, and to transfer control to that attack payload.

After the trampoline code executes, the hardware instruction pointer address is 0x7c809a51, which is the start of the Windows library function VirtualAlloc, and the address in the stack pointer is 0x0012ff10, the third integer in the tmp array in Figure 14. As a result, when VirtualAlloc returns, execution will continue at address 0x7c80978e, which is the start of the Windows library function InterlockedExchange. Finally, the InterlockedExchange function returns to the address 0x70000000, which at that time holds the attack payload machine code in executable memory.

(This attack is facilitated by two Windows particulars: all Windows processes load the library kernel32.dll into their address space, and the Windows calling convention makes library functions responsible for popping their own arguments off the stack. On other systems, the attacker would need to slightly modify the details of the attack.)

Attack 3: Constraints and Variants

A major constraint on jump-to-libc attacks is that the attackers must craft each such attack with a knowledge of the addresses of the target-software machine code that is useful to the attack. An attacker may have difficulty in reliably determining these addresses, for instance because of variability in the versions of the target software and its libraries, or because of variability in the target software's execution environment. Artificially increasing this variability is a useful defense against many types of such attacks, as discussed later in this tutorial.

Traditionally, jump-to-libc attacks have targeted the system function in the standard system libraries, which allows the execution of an arbitrary command with arguments, as if typed into a shell command interpreter. This strategy can also be taken in the above attack example, with a few simple changes. However, an attacker may prefer indirect code injection, because it requires launching no new processes or accessing any executable files, both of which may be detected or prevented by system defenses.

For software that may become the target of jump-to-libc attacks, one might consider eliminating any fragment of machine code that may be useful to the attacker, such as the trampoline code shown in Figure 13. This can be difficult for many practical reasons. For instance, it is difficult to selectively eliminate fragments of library code while, at the same time, sharing the code memory of dynamic libraries between their instances in different processes; however, eliminating such sharing would multiply the resource requirements of dynamic libraries. Also, it is not easy to remove data constants embedded within executable code, which may form instructions useful to an attacker. (Examples of such data constants include the jump tables of C and C++ switch statements.)

Those difficulties are compounded on hardware architectures that use variable-length sequences of opcode bytes for encoding machine-code instructions. For example, on some versions of Windows, the machine code for a system call is encoded using a two-byte opcode sequence, 0xcd, 0x2e, while the five-byte sequence 0x25, 0xcd, 0x2e, 0x00, and 0x00 corresponds to an arithmetic operation (the operation and eax, 0x2ecd, in x86 assembly code). Therefore, if an instruction for this particular and operation is present in the target software, then jumping to its second byte can be one way of performing a system call. Similarly, any x86 instruction, including those that read or write memory, may be executed through a jump into the middle of the opcode-byte sequence for some other x86 machine-code instruction.

Indeed, for x86 Linux software, it has been recently demonstrated that it is practical for elaborate jump-to-libc attacks to perform arbitrary functionality while executing *only* machine-code found embedded within other instructions [40]. Much as in the above example, these elaborate attacks proceed through the unwinding of the stack, but they may also "rewind" the stack in order to encode loops of activity. However, unlike in the above example, these elaborate attacks may allow the attacker to achieve their goals without adding any new, executable memory or machine code to target software under attack.

Attacks like these are of great practical concern. For example, the flaw in the `median` function of Figure 11 is in many ways similar to the recently discovered "animated cursor vulnerability" in Windows [22]. Despite existing, deployed defenses, that vulnerability is subject to a jump-to-libc attack similar to that in the above example.

2.4 Attack 4: Corruption of Data Values That Determine Behavior

Software programmers make many natural assumptions about the integrity of data. As one example, an initialized global variable may be assumed to hold the same, initial value throughout the software's execution, if it is never written by the software. Unfortunately, for C or C++ software, such assumptions may not hold in the presence of software bugs, and this may open the door to malicious attacks that corrupt the data that determine the software's behavior.

Unlike the previous attacks in this tutorial, data corruption may allow the attacker to achieve their goals without diverting the target software from its expected path of machine-code execution—either directly or indirectly. Such attacks are referred to as *data-only*, or *non-control-data*, attacks [10]. In some cases, a single instance of data corruption can be sufficient for an attacker to achieve their goals. Figure 16 shows an example of a C function that is vulnerable to such an attack.

As a concrete example of a data-only attack, consider how the function in Figure 16 makes use of the environment string table by calling `getenv` routine in the standard C library. This routine returns the string that is passed to another standard routine, `system`, and this string argument determines what external command is launched. An attacker that is able to control the function's two integer inputs is able to write an arbitrary data value to a nearly-arbitrary location in memory. In particular, this attacker is able to corrupt the table of the environment strings to launch an external command of their choice.

Figure 17 gives the details of such an attack on the function in Figure 16, by selectively showing the address and contents of data and code memory. In this case, before the attack, the environment string table is an array of pointers starting at address `0x00353610`. The first pointer in that table is shown in Figure 17, as are its contents: a string that gives a path to the "all users profile". In a correct execution of the function, some other pointer in the environment string

```
void run_command_with_argument( pairs* data, int offset, int value )
{
    // must have offset be a valid index into data
    char cmd[MAX_LEN];
    data[offset].argument = value;
    {
        char valuestring[MAX_LEN];
        itoa( value, valuestring, 10 );
        strcpy( cmd, getenv("SAFECOMMAND") );
        strcat( cmd, " " );
        strcat( cmd, valuestring );
    }
    data[offset].result = system( cmd );
}
```

Fig. 16. A C function that launches an external command with an argument value, and stores in a data structure that value and the result of the command. If the offset and value can be chosen by an attacker, then this function is vulnerable to a data-only attack that allows the attacker to launch an arbitrary external command.

address	attack command string data as integers	as characters
0x00354b20	0x45464153 0x4d4d4f43 0x3d444e41 0x2e646d63	SAFECOMMAND=cmd.
0x00354b30	0x20657865 0x2220632f 0x6d726f66 0x632e7461	exe /c "format.c
0x00354b40	0x63206d6f 0x3e20223a 0x00000020	om c:" >

address	first environment string pointer
0x00353610	0x00353730

address	first environment string data as integers	as characters
0x00353730	0x554c4c41 0x53524553 0x464f5250 0x3d454c49	ALLUSERSPROFILE=
0x00353740	0x445c3a43 0x6d75636f 0x73746e65 0x646e6120	C:\Documents and
0x00353750	0x74655320 0x676e6974 0x6c415c73 0x7355206c	Settings\All Us
0x00353760	0x00737265	ers

address	opcode bytes	machine code as assembly language
0x004011a1	0x89 0x14 0xc8	mov [eax+ecx*8], edx ; write edx to eax+ecx*8

Fig. 17. Some of the memory contents for an execution of the function in Figure 16, including the machine code for the data[offset].argument = value; assignment. If the data pointer is 0x004033e0, the attacker can choose the inputs offset = 0x1ffea046 and value = 0x00354b20, and thereby make the assignment instruction change the first environment string pointer to the "format" command string at the top.

table would be to a string, such as SAFECOMMAND=safecmd.exe, that determines a safe, external command to be launched by the system library routine.

However, before reading the command string to launch, the machine-code assignment instruction shown in Figure 17 is executed. By choosing the offset and value inputs to the function, the attacker can make ecx and edx hold arbitrary values. Therefore, the attacker can make the assignment write any value to nearly any address in memory, given knowledge of the `data` pointer. If the `data` pointer is `0x004033e0`, then that address plus `8*0x1ffea046` is `0x00353610`, the address of the first environment string pointer. Thus, the attacker is able to write the address of their chosen attack command string, `0x00354b20`, at that location. Then, when `getenv` is called, it will look no further than the first pointer in the environment string table, and return a command string that, when launched, may delete data on the "C:" drive of the target system.

Several things are noteworthy about this data-only attack and the function in Figure 16. First, note that there are multiple vulnerabilities that may allow the attacker to choose the `offset` integer input, ranging from stack-based and heap-based buffer overflows, through integer overflow errors, to a simple programmer mistake that omitted any bounds check. Second, note that although `0x1ffea046` is a positive integer, it effectively becomes negative when multiplied by eight, and the assignment instruction writes to an address before the start of the `data` array. Finally, note that this attack succeeds even when the table of environment strings is initialized before the execution starts, and the table is never modified by the target software—and when the table should therefore logically be read-only given the semantics of the target software.

Attack 4: Constraints and Variants

There are two major constraints on data-only attacks. First, the vulnerabilities in the target software are likely to allow only certain data, or a certain amount of data to be corrupted, and potentially only in certain ways. For instance, as in the above example, a vulnerability might allow the attacker to change a single, arbitrary four-byte integer in memory to a value of their choice. Such vulnerabilities exist in some heap implementations, as described on page 104; there, an arbitrary write is possible through the corruption of heap metadata, most likely caused by the overflow of a buffer stored in the heap. Many real-world attacks have exploited this vulnerability, including the GDI+ JPEG attack in Windows [16,10].

Second, even when an attacker can replace any amount of data with arbitrary values, and that data may be located anywhere, a data-only attack will be constrained by the behavior of the target software when given arbitrary input. For example, if the target software is an arithmetic calculator, a data-only attack might only be able to cause an incorrect result to be computed. However, if the target software embeds any form of an interpreter that performs potentially dangerous operations, then a data-only attack could control the input to that interpreter—allowing the attacker to perform the dangerous operations. The `system` standard library routine is an example of such an interpreter; many applications, such as Web browsers and document viewers, embed other interpreters for scripting languages.

To date, data-only attacks have not been prominent. Rather, data corruption has been most frequently utilized as one step in other types of attacks, such as direct code injection, or an jump-to-libc attack. This may change with the increased deployment of defenses, including the defenses described below.

3 Defenses That Preserve C and C++ Language Properties

This section presents, in detail, six effective, practical defenses against low-level software attacks on x86 machine-code software, and explains how each defense is based on preserving a property of target software written in the C or C++ languages. These defenses are stack canaries, reordering of stack variables, non-executable data, control-flow integrity, encrypted pointers, and address-space layout randomization. They have been selected based on their efficiency, and ease-of-adoption, as well as their effectiveness.

In particular, this section describes neither defenses based on instruction-set randomization [27], nor defenses based on dynamic information flow tracking, or tainting, or other forms of data-flow integrity enforcement [9,36]. Such techniques can offer strong defenses against all the attacks in Section 2, although, like the defenses below, they also have limitations and counterattacks. However, these defenses have drawbacks that make their deployment difficult in practice.

For example, unless they are supported by specialized hardware, they incur significant overheads. On unmodified, commodity x86 hardware, defenses based on data-flow integrity may double the memory requirements, and may make execution up to 37 times slower [36]. Because these defenses also double the number of memory accesses, even the most heavily optimized mechanism is still likely to run software twice as slow [9]. Such overheads are likely to be unacceptable in many scenarios, e.g., for server workloads where a proportional increase in cost may be expected. Therefore, in practice, these defenses may never see widespread adoption—especially since equally good protection may be achievable using a combination of the below defenses.

This section does not attempt a comprehensive survey of the literature on these defenses. However, related material can be found with a search based on the papers referenced in this section, and their discussion of other work.

3.1 Defense 1: Checking Stack Canaries on Function Return Addresses

The C and C++ languages do not specify how function return addresses are represented in stack memory. Rather, these, and many other programming languages, hold abstract most elements of a function's invocation stack frame in order to allow for portability between hardware architectures and to give compilers flexibility in choosing an efficient low-level representation. This flexibility enables an effective defense against some attacks, such as the return-address clobbering of Attack 1.

In particular, on function calls, instead of storing return addresses directly onto the stack, C and C++ compilers are free to generate code that stores

```
address     content
0x0012ff5c  0x00353037  ; argument two pointer
0x0012ff58  0x0035302f  ; argument one pointer
0x0012ff54  0x00401263  ; return address
0x0012ff50  0x0012ff7c  ; saved base pointer
0x0012ff4c  0x00000000  ; all-zero canary
0x0012ff48  0x00000072  ; tmp continues 'r' '\0' '\0' '\0'
0x0012ff44  0x61626f6f  ; tmp continues 'o' 'o' 'b' 'a'
0x0012ff40  0x662f2f3a  ; tmp continues ':' '/' '/' 'f'
0x0012ff3c  0x656c6966  ; tmp array:      'f' 'i' 'l' 'e'
```

Fig. 18. A stack snapshot like that shown in Figures 4 where a "canary value" has been placed between the tmp array and the saved base pointer and return address. Before returning from functions with vulnerabilities like those in Attack 1, it is an effective defense to check that the canary is still zero: an overflow of a zero-terminated string across the canary's stack location will not leave the canary as zero.

return addresses in an encrypted and signed form, using a local, secret key. Then, before each function return, the compiler could emit code to decrypt and validate the integrity of the return address about to be used. In this case, assuming that strong cryptography is used, an attacker that did not know the key would be unable to cause the target software to return to an address of their choice as a result of a stack corruption—even when the target software contains an exploitable buffer overflow vulnerability that allows such corruption.

In practice, it is desirable to implement an approximation of the above defense, and get most of the benefits without incurring the overwhelming cost of executing cryptography code on each function call and return.

One such approximation requires no secret, but places a public *canary* value right above function-local stack buffers. This value is designed to warn of dangerous stack corruption, much as a coal-mine canary would warn about dangerous air conditions. Figure 18 shows an example of a stack with an all-zero canary value. Validating the integrity of this canary is an effective means of ensuring that the saved base pointer and function return address have not been corrupted— given the assumption that attacks are only possible through stack corruption based on the overflow of a string buffer. For improved defenses, this public canary may contain other bytes, such as newline characters, that frequently terminate the copying responsible for string-based buffer overflows. For example, some implementations have used the value 0x000aff0d as the canary [14].

Stack-canary defenses may be improved by including in the canary value some bits that should be unknown to the attacker. For instance, this may help defend against return-address clobbering with an integer overflow, such as is enabled by the memcpy vulnerability in Figure 11. Therefore, some implementations of stack canary defenses, such as Microsoft's /GS compiler option [7], are based on a random value, or *cookie*.

Figure 19 shows the machine code for a function compiled with Microsoft's /GS option. The function preamble and postamble each have three new instructions that set and check the canary, respectively. With /GS, the canary placed

```
function_with_gs_check:
      ; function preamble machine code
      push ebp                          ; save old base pointer on the stack
      mov  ebp, esp                     ; establish the new base pointer
      sub  esp, 0x14                    ; grow the stack for buffer and cookie
      mov  eax, [__security_cookie]     ; read cookie value into eax
      xor  eax, ebp                     ; xor base pointer into cookie
      mov  [ebp-4], eax                 ; write cookie above the buffer
      ...
      ; function body machine code
      ...
      ; function postamble machine code
      mov  ecx, [ebp-4]                 ; read cookie from stack, into ecx
      xor  ecx, ebp                     ; xor base pointer out of cookie
      call __security_check_cookie      ; check ecx is cookie value
      mov  esp, ebp                     ; shrink the stack back
      pop  ebp                          ; restore old, saved base pointer
      ret                               ; return

__security_check_cookie:
      cmp  ecx, [__security_cookie]     ; compare ecx and cookie value
      jnz  ERR                          ; if not equal, goto an error handler
      ret                               ; else return
ERR:  jmp __report_gsfailure            ; report failure and halt execution
```

Fig. 19. The machine code for a function with a local array in a fixed-size, 16-byte stack buffer, when compiled using the Windows /GS implementation of stack cookies in the most recent version of the Microsoft C compiler [7,24]. The canary is a random cookie value, combined with the base pointer. In case the local stack buffer is overflowed, this canary is placed on the stack above the stack buffer, just below the return address and saved base pointer, and checked before either of those values are used.

on the stack is a combination of the function's base pointer and the function's *module cookie*. Module cookies are generated dynamically for each process, using good sources of randomness (although some of those sources are observable to an attacker running code on the same system). Separate, fresh module cookies are used for the executable and each dynamic library within a process address space (each has its own copy of the __security_cookie variable in Figure 19). As a result, in a stack with multiple canary values, each will be unique, with more dissimilarity where the stack crosses module boundaries.

Defense 1: Performance, Limitations, Variants, and Counterattacks

The is little enforcement overhead from stack canary defenses, since they are only required in functions with local stack buffers that may be overflowed. (An overflow in a function does not affect the invocation stack frames of functions it calls, which are lower on the stack; that function's canary will be checked before any use of stack frames that are higher on the stack, and which may have been corrupted by the overflow.) For most C and C++ software this overhead amounts to a few percent [14,15]. Even so, most implementations aim to reduce this overhead even further, by only initializing and checking stack canaries in functions that contain a local string `char` array, or meet other heuristic requirements. As a result, this defense is not always applied where it might be useful—as evidenced by the recent ANI vulnerability in Windows [22].

Stack canaries can be an efficient and effective defense against Attack 1, where the attacker corrupts function-invocation control data on the stack. However, stack canaries only check for corruption at function exit. Thus, they offer no defense against Attacks 2, 3, and 4, which are based on corruption of the heap, function-pointer arguments, or global data pointers.

Stack canaries are a widely deployed defense mechanism. In addition to Microsoft's /GS, StackGuard [14] and ProPolice [15] are two other notable implementations. Given its simple nature, it is somewhat surprising that there is significant variation between the implementations of this defense, and these implementations have varied over time [7,21]. In part, this reflects the ongoing arms race between attackers and defenders; however, it is also because stack-canaries have been combined with other defenses, such as Defense 2 below.

Stack canary defenses are subject to a a number of counterattacks. Most notably, even when the only exploitable vulnerability is a stack-based buffer overflow, the attackers may be able to craft an attack that is not based on return-address clobbering. For example, the attack may corrupt a local variable, an argument, or some other value that is used before the function exits.

Also, the attacker may attempt to guess, or learn the stack-canary values, which can lead to a successful attack given enough luck or determination. The success of this counterattack will depend on the exploited vulnerability, the attacker's access to the target system, and the particulars of the target software. (For example, if stack canaries are based on random cookies, then the attacker may be able to exploit certain format-string vulnerabilities to learn which canary values to embed in the data of the buffer overflow.)

3.2   Defense 2: Moving Function-Local Variables Below Stack Buffers

Most details about the function-invocation stack frame are left unspecified in the C and C++ languages, to give flexibility in the compilation of those language aspects down to a low-level representation. In particular, the compiler is free to lay out function-local variables in any order on the stack, and to generate code that operates not on function arguments, but on copies of those arguments. This flexibility enables an efficient defense against attacks based on stack corruption, such as Attacks 1 and 3.

In this defense, the compiler places arrays and other function-local buffers above all other function-local variables on the stack. Also, the compiler makes copies of all function arguments into new, function-local variables that also sit below any buffers in the function. As a result, these variables and arguments are not subject to corruption through an overflow of those buffers. Figure 20 shows an example of how this defense might prevent the stack-based exploit in

stack address	stack contents	overflow contents	
0x0012ff38	0x004013e0	0x1111110d	; cmp argument
0x0012ff34	0x00000001	0x1111110c	; len argument
0x0012ff30	0x00353050	0x1111110b	; data argument
0x0012ff2c	0x00401528	0x1111110a	; return address
0x0012ff28	0x0012ff4c	0x11111109	; saved base pointer
0x0012ff24	0x00000000	0x11111108	; tmp final 4 bytes
0x0012ff20	0x00000000	0x11111107	; tmp continues
0x0012ff1c	0x00000000	0x11111106	; tmp continues
0x0012ff18	0x00000000	0x11111105	; tmp continues
0x0012ff14	0x00000000	0x11111104	; tmp continues
0x0012ff10	0x00000000	0x11111103	; tmp continues
0x0012ff0c	0x00000000	0x11111102	; tmp continues
0x0012ff08	0x00000000	0x11111101	; tmp buffer starts
0x0012ff04	0x004013e0	0x004013e0	; *local copy of cmp argument*
0x0012ff00	0x00000004	0x00000040	; memcpy length argument
0x0012fefc	0x00353050	0x00353050	; memcpy source argument
0x0012fef8	0x0012ff08	0x0012ff08	; memcpy destination argument

Fig. 20. A version of the stack shown in Figure 14 for the median function of Figure 11, showing the contents for both valid inputs and in the case of a benign buffer overflow. A local copy of the cmp argument has been placed at address 0x0012ff04, below tmp; therefore, this copy cannot be corrupted by an overflow of the tmp buffer. If the code in the body of the function makes use of this copy, not the original argument, then this prevents attacks based on the vulnerability exploited by Attack 3.

Attack 3. In this example, a local copy has been made of the cmp function-pointer argument corrupted by the attack; since this local copy resides below the buffer on the stack, it cannot be corrupted in an overflow of that buffer.

Defense 2: Performance, Limitations, Variants, and Counterattacks

Placing local variables and copies of function arguments below any buffers in a function's stack frame has negligible enforcement overheads: reordering local variables has effectively zero overhead, and the overhead of local argument copies is also close to zero. Furthermore, this overhead applies only to functions with local stack buffers that may be overflowed. As a result, in practice, the overhead of this defense is often too small to be reliably measured [15].

This defense is both efficient and effective, but it is also limited. In particular, this defense offers no protection against Attacks 2 and 4 or other attacks that do not exploit stack-based buffer overflow vulnerabilities.

However, this defense does not completely prevent an attacker from exploiting the effects of a stack-based buffer overflow. For instance, although local variables or arguments may not be corrupted, these variables may contain pointers into a region of the stack that may possibly be corrupted by the attacker. Thus, in the case of a string pointer function argument, the attacker may not be able to change the address in the pointer, but they will be able to change the contents of the string itself—as long as the buffer overflow reaches up to the location on the stack where the string resides.

This defense is combined with stack canaries in most implementations, such as ProPolice and Microsoft's /GS. This is a good fit, since both techniques defend against the effects of stack-based buffer overflow, but only stack canaries offer a means of detecting when stack corruption may have occurred. There is some variation between these implementations. In particular, in order to further reduce enforcement overhead, not all function arguments may be copied, but only code and data pointers and other arguments that meet some heuristic requirements. (Of course, this may permit some attacks that might otherwise not be possible.)

There are few counterattacks to this defense. An attacker may attempt to craft a more indirect stack-based buffer overflow exploit that corrupts the contents of pointers into the stack. However, the attacker is also likely to turn their attention from attacks based on stack-based buffer overflow to other means of attack, such as those described in Attacks 2 and 4.

3.3   Defense 3: Making Data Not Be Executable as Machine Code

Many high-level languages allow code and data to reside in two, distinct types of memory. The C and C++ languages follow this tradition, and do not specify what happens when code pointers are read and written as data, or what happens when a data pointer is invoked as if it were a function pointer. This under-specification brings important benefits to the portability of C and C++ software, since it must sometimes run on systems where code and data memory are truly different. It also enables a particularly simple and efficient defense against direct-code-injection exploits, such as those in Attacks 1 and 2.

If data memory is not executable, then Attacks 1 and 2 fail as soon as the hardware instruction pointer reaches the first byte of the attack payload (e.g., the bytes 0xfeeb2ecd described in Figure 6, and used throughout this tutorial). Even when the attacker manages to control the flow of execution, they cannot simply make control proceed directly to their attack payload. This is a simple, useful barrier to attack, which can be directly applied to most software, since, in practice, most software never treats data as code.

(Some legacy software will execute data as a matter of course; other software uses self-modifying code and writes to code memory as a part of regular, valid execution. For example, this behavior can be seen in some efficient, just-in-time interpreters. However, such software can be treated as a special case, since it is uncommon and increasingly rare.)

Defense 3: Performance, Limitations, Variants, and Counterattacks

In its implementation on modern x86 systems, non-executable data has some performance impact because it relies on double-size, extended page tables. The NX page-table-entry bit, which flags memory as non-executable, is only found in PAE page tables, which are double the size of normal tables, and are otherwise not commonly used. The precise details of page-table entries can significantly impact the overall system performance, since page tables are a frequently-consulted part of the memory hierarchy—with thousands of lookups a second and, in some cases, a lookup every few instructions. However, for most workloads, the overhead should be in the small percents, and will often be close to zero.

Non-executable data defends against direct code injection attacks, but offers no barrier to exploits such as those in Attacks 3 and 4. For any given direct code-injection attack, it is likely that an attacker can craft an indirect jump-to-libc variant, or a data-only exploit [10]. Thus—although this defense can be highly useful when used in combination with other defenses—by itself, it is not much of a stumbling block for attackers.

On Microsoft Windows, and most other platforms, software will typically execute in a mode where writing to code memory generates a hardware exception. In the past, some systems have also generated such an exception when the hardware instruction pointer is directed to data memory, i.e., upon an attempt to execute data as code. However, until recently, commodity x86 hardware has only supported such exceptions through the use of segmented memory—which runs counter to the flat memory model that is fundamental to most modern operating systems. (Despite being awkward, x86 segments have been used to implement non-executable memory, e.g., stacks, but these implementations are limited, for instance in their support for multi-threading and dynamic libraries.)

Since 2003, and Windows XP SP2, commodity operating systems have come to support the x86 extended page tables where any given memory page may be marked as non-executable, and x86 vendors have shipped processors with the required hardware support. Thus, it is now the norm for data memory to be non-executable, in particular when running the Windows operating system.

On most legacy x86 processors that use unmodified page tables, it is actually possible to make data pages be non-executable using a clever technique first implemented in the PaX project [37]. This technique builds on the fact that, at the very top of the memory hierarchy on those x86 processors, code and data is separated into two distinct memories: the code *i-cache* and data *d-cache*. By maintaining an invariant, this technique can ensure that data memory is never present in the i-cache, and therefore that data memory is never executed. Although ingenious, this technique does not work on all x86 processors; it can also have significant performance overhead and has a race condition on multi-processor systems. Therefore, it never saw significant adoption before being superseded by the current x86 hardware support for non-executable data pages.

(The technique works as follows: all data pages in the page table are marked as invalid, thereby preventing data memory from entering either of the two top-level memories. Rather, an access to a data memory address will cause a page-fault handler to be invoked; this handler can load the data memory into the d-cache only, by briefly marking as valid the page-table entry for the data memory and reading the data memory, e.g., using the mov instruction. As a result, until it is evicted from the d-cache, the memory will be accessible as data. However, because its page-table entry remains marked as invalid, the memory will never enter the i-cache, and therefore never be executable.)

Indirect code injection, jump-to-libc attacks, and data-only attacks are all effective counterattacks to this defense Even so, non-executable data can play a key role in an overall defense strategy; for instance, when combined with Defense 6 below, this defense can prevent an attacker from knowing the location of any executable memory bytes that could be useful to an attack.

3.4   Defense 4: Enforcing Control-Flow Integrity on Code Execution

As in all high-level languages, it is not possible for software written in the C and C++ languages to perform arbitrary control-flow transfers between any two points in its code. Compared to the exclusion of data from being executed as code, the policies on control-flow between code are much more fine-grained.

For example, the behavior of function calls is only defined when the callee code is the start of a function—even when the caller invokes that code through a function pointer. Also, it is not valid to place a label into an expression, and goto to that label, or otherwise transfer control into the middle of an expression being evaluated. Transferring control into the middle of a machine code instruction is certainly not a valid, defined operation, in any high-level language—even though the hardware may allow this, and this may be useful to an attacker (see Attack 3, page 109).

Furthermore, within the control flow that a language permits in general, only a small fraction will, in fact, be possible in the semantics of a particular piece of software written in that language. For most software, control flow is either completely static (e.g., as in a C goto statement), or allows only a small number of possibilities during execution.

For example, consider the case when the entire high-level language software consists of the C++ code of Figure 9 on page 103. There, in the cmp function, it is only possible for the invocation of m_cmp.compare to pass control to the start of a compare member function in one of the two Comparer classes. Also, it is clear that when either of those compare functions returns, it can only be to the call site in the cmp function. Similarly, for all C or C++ software, any indirect control transfers, such as through function pointers or at return statements, will have only a small number of valid targets.

Dynamic checks can ensure that the execution of low-level software does not stray from a restricted set of possibilities allowed by the high-level software. The runtime enforcement of such a Control-Flow Integrity, or CFI, security policy is a highly effective defense against low-level software attacks [2,3].

As a concrete example of the benefits of CFI enforcement, consider the published attack on the GDI+ JPEG flaw in Windows [16]. This attack starts by causing a heap memory corruption that results in a global variable being overwritten; this variable holds a C++ object pointer. When this pointer is later used for calling a virtual destructor, the attacker has the possibility of executing code of their choice, much as in the C++ example in Attack 2. A CFI check at

```
class Vulnerable
{
    char m_buff[MAX_LEN];
    Comparer m_cmp;
public:
    Vulnerable(Comparer c) : m_cmp(c) {}
    // ... elided code ...
    int cmp(char* str) {
        if( (m_cmp.compare == &Comparer::compare) ||
            (m_cmp.compare == &CaseSensitiveComparer::compare) )
        {
            return m_cmp.compare( m_buff, str );
        }
        else throw report_memory_corruption_error();
    }
};
```

Fig. 21. An excerpt of the C++ code in Figure 9 with explicit CFI checks that only allow valid comparison methods to be invoked at runtime—thereby preventing the exploit in Attack 2. (This code may not be accepted by modern C++ compilers, because of how it reads the address of a virtual member function in an object instance.)

```
int is_file_foobar_using_heap( vulnerable* s, char* one, char* two )
{
    // ... elided code ...
    if( (s->cmp == strcmp) || (s->cmp == stricmp) ) {
        return s->cmp( s->buff, "file://foobar" );
    } else {
        return report_memory_corruption_error();
    }
}
```

Fig. 22. An excerpt of the C code in Figure 7 with explicit CFI checks that only allow the proper comparison methods to be invoked at runtime—assuming only strcmp and stricmp are possible. These CFI checks prevent the exploit on this function in Attack 2.

this callsite can prevent this exploit, for instance by restricting valid destinations to the C++ virtual destructor methods of the GDI+ library.

There are several strategies possible in the implementation of CFI enforcement. For instance, CFI may be enforced by dynamic checks that compare the target address of each computed control-flow transfer to a set of allowed destination addresses. Such a comparison may be performed by the machine-code equivalent of a switch statement over a set of constant addresses. Programmers can even make CFI checks explicitly in their software, as shown in Figures 21 and 22. However, unlike in Figures 21 and 22, it is not possible to write software that explicitly performs CFI checks on return addresses, or other inaccessible pointers; for these, CFI checks must be added by the compiler, or some other

```
bool lt(int x, int y) {
    return x < y;
}
bool gt(int x, int y) {
    return x > y;
}
sort2(int a[], int b[], int len)
{
    sort( a, len, lt );
    sort( b, len, gt );
}
```

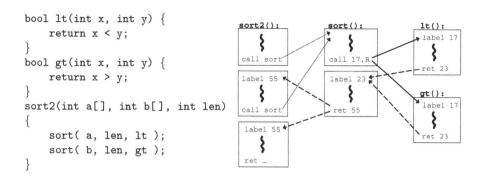

Fig. 23. Three C functions and an outline of their possible control flow, as well as how an CFI enforcement mechanism based on CFI labels might apply to the functions. In the outline, the CFI labels 55, 17, and 23 are found at the valid destinations of computed control-flow instructions; each such instruction is also annotated with a CFI label that corresponds to its valid destinations.

mechanism. Also, since the set of allowed destination addresses may be large, any such sequence of explicit comparisons is likely to lead to unacceptable overhead.

One efficient CFI enforcement mechanism, described in [2], modifies according to a given control-flow graph, both the *source* and *destination* instructions of computed control-flow transfers. Two destinations are *equivalent*, when the CFG contains edges to each from the same set of sources. At each destination, a *CFI label* is inserted, that identifies equivalent destinations, i.e., destinations with the same set of possible sources. The CFI labels embed a value, or bit pattern, that distinguishes each; these values need not be secret. Before each source instruction, a dynamic CFI check is inserted that ensures that the runtime destination has the proper CFI label.

Figure 23 shows a C program fragment demonstrating this CFI enforcement mechanism. In this figure, a function sort2 calls a qsort-like function sort twice, first with lt and then with gt as the pointer to the comparison function. The right side of Figure 23 shows an outline of the machine-code blocks for these four functions and all control-flow-graph edges between them. In the figure, edges for direct calls are drawn as light, dotted arrows; edges from source instructions are drawn as solid arrows, and return edges as dashed arrows. In this example, sort can return to two different places in sort2. Therefore, there are two CFI labels in the body of sort2, and an CFI check when returning from sort, using 55 as the CFI label. (Note that CFI enforcement does not guarantee to which of the two callsites sort must return; for this, other defenses, such as Defense 1, must be employed.)

Also, in Figure 23, because sort can call either lt or gt, both comparison functions start with the CFI label 17, and the call instruction, which uses a function pointer in register R, performs a CFI check for 17. Finally, the CFI label 23 identifies the block that follows the comparison callsite in sort, so both comparison functions return with a CFI check for 23.

machine-code opcode bytes	machine code in assembly
...	...
0x57	push edi
0x53	push ebx
0x8b 0x44 0x24 0x24	mov eax, [esp+comp_fp]
0x81 0x78 0xfc 0x78 0x56 0x34 0x12	cmp [eax-0x4], 0x12345678
0x75 0x13	jne cfi_error_label
0xff 0xd0	call eax
0x0f 0x18 0x80 0xdd 0xcc 0xbb 0xaa	prefetchnta [0xaabbccdd]
0x83 0xc4 0x08	add esp, 0x8
0x85 0xc0	test eax, eax
0x7e 0x02	jle label_lessthan
...	...

Fig. 24. A version of Figure 12, showing how CFI checks as in [2] can be added to the qsort library function where it calls the comparison function pointer. Before calling the pointer, it is placed in a register eax, and a comparison establishes that the four bytes 0x12345678 are found immediately before the destination code, otherwise execution goes to a security error. After the call instruction, an executable, side-effect-free instruction embeds the constant 0xaabbccdd; by comparing against this constant, the comparison function can establish that it is returning to a valid call site.

Figure 24 shows a concrete example of how CFI enforcement based on CFI labels can look, in the case of x86 machine-code software. Here, the CFI label 0x12345678 identifies all comparison routines that may be invoked by qsort, and the CFI label 0xaabbccdd identifies all of their valid call sites. This style of CFI enforcement has good performance, and also gives strong guarantees. By choosing the bytes of CFI labels carefully, so they don't overlap with code, even an attacker that controls all of data memory cannot divert execution from the permitted control-flow graph—assuming that data is also non-executable.

The CFI security policy dictates that software execution must follow a path of a control-flow graph, determined ahead of time, that represents all possible valid executions of the software. This graph can be defined by analysis—source-code analysis, binary analysis, or execution profiling. This graph does not need to be perfectly accurate, but needs only be a conservative approximation of the control-flow graph possible in the software, as written in its high-level programming language. To be conservative, the graph must err on the side of allowing all valid executions of the software, even this may entail allowing some invalid executions as well. For instance, the graph might conservatively permit the start of a few-too-many functions as the valid destinations of a source instruction where a function pointer is invoked.

Defense 4: Performance, Limitations, Variants, and Counterattacks

CFI enforcement incurs only modest overhead. With the CFI enforcement mechanism in [2], which instruments x86 machine code much as is shown in Figure 24, the reported code-size increase is around 8%, and execution slowdown ranges from 0% to 45% on a set of processor benchmarks, with a mean of 16% Even so, this overhead is significant enough that CFI enforcement has, to date, seen only limited adoption. However, a form of CFI is enforced by the Windows SafeSEH mechanism, which limits dispatching of exceptions to a set of statically-declared exception handlers; this mechanism does not incur measurable overheads.

CFI enforcement offers no protection against Attack 4 or other data-only attacks. However, CFI can be an highly effective defense against all attacks based on controlling machine-code execution, including Attacks 1, 2, and 3.

In particular, CFI enforcement is likely to prevent all variants of Attack 3, i.e., jump-to-libc attacks that employ trampolines or opportunistic executable byte sequences such as those found embedded within machine-code instructions. This is the case even if CFI enforces only a coarse-grained approximation of the software control-flow graph, such as allowing function-pointer calls to the start of any function with the same argument types, and allowing functions to return to any of their possible call sites [2].

CFI enforcement mechanisms vary both in their mechanisms and in their policy. Some mechanisms establish the validity of each computed control transfer by querying a separate, static data structure, which can be a hash table, a bit vector, or a structure similar to multi-level page tables [42]. Other mechanisms execute the software in a fast machine-code interpreter that enforces CFI on control flow [29]. Finally, a coarse-grained form of CFI can be enforced by making all computed-control-flow destinations be aligned on multi-word boundaries. (However, in this last case, any "basic block" is effectively a valid destination, so trampolines and elaborate jump-to-libc attacks are still feasible.) The complexity and overheads of these CFI mechanisms varies, but is typically greater than that described above, based on CFI labels.

In a system with CFI enforcement, any exploit that does not involve controlling machine-code execution is a likely counterattack; this includes not only data-only attacks, such as Attack 4, but also other, higher-level attacks, such as social engineering and flaws in programming interfaces [4]. In addition, depending on the granularity of CFI enforcement policy, and how it is used in combination with other defenses, there may still exist possibilities for certain jump-to-libc attacks, for instance where a function is made to return to a dynamically-incorrect, but statically-possible, call site.

3.5   Defense 5: Encrypting Addresses in Code and Data Pointers

The C and C++ languages do not exactly specify how pointers encode memory addresses, since this representation is highly platform specific. Just as C and C++ hold return addresses abstract, which allows Defense 1, other pointers are only subject to a few, well-defined operations that hold abstract their address value. Therefore, one promising line of defense is to encrypt the addresses stored in data and code pointers using a secret key, unknown to the attacker.

All of the attacks in Section 2 depend on pointer corruption in some way. As long as all pointers contain encrypted addresses—including direct and indirect function pointers, return addresses, base pointers, and pointers to data—then

	buff (char array at start of the struct)				cmp
address:	0x00353068	0x0035306c	0x00353070	0x00353074	0x00353078
content:	0x656c6966	0x662f2f3a	0x61626f6f	0x00000072	0xbd6ba903

Fig. 25. A version of the data structure in Figure 8(a). The structure holds the string "file://foobar" and a pointer to the strcmp function, whose address is 0x004013ce. In this example, the address has been explicitly encrypted using the Windows EncodePointer library function, and is stored as 0xbd6ba903 in the data structure.

this defense can thwart all of these attacks. For instance, encrypted pointers can prevent Attack 4, where a pointer in the environment string table is corrupted. When crafting this attack, if the attacker does not know the pointer encoding, then they cannot know what integer value to write as an address in the environment string table.

Unfortunately, in practice, software is most commonly written for expediency and efficiency, not portability. Thus, existing C and C++ software often contains elaborate pointer arithmetic, and operates on pointers cast into integral types in ways that make it difficult to adopt defenses based on encrypted pointers. This is in stark difference from the other defenses in this section: it is far more common for software to rely on the address encoding in pointers than, say, for software to make use of self-modifying code, or execute data as code. As a result, defense mechanisms such as PointGuard [13], which attempt to pervasively and automatically apply encrypted pointers, have seen very limited adoption.

However, if encrypted pointers are used explicitly by programmers, then the programmers can ensure that no pointer arithmetic is invalidated by the encryption. Such explicit, selective application of encrypted pointers is a useful defense for security-critical code that is a likely target of attacks. Figure 25 shows the contents of a data structure where a function pointer has been explicitly encrypted using a library function available on Windows.

This defense has seen significant adoption in security-conscious software systems. For instance, in recent versions of the Windows heap implementation, many heap metadata pointers are explicitly encrypted to prevent certain forms of heap-based attacks discussed on page 104, in Attack 2.

Figure 26 shows how, on Windows, programmers can use pointer encoding to make the C++ function in Figure 9 less vulnerable to attack. In this code fragment, Windows library routines are explicitly invoked to encrypt and decrypt the address in the comparison pointer, using a per-process random value. Thus this address will always appear encrypted in the object instance contents, requiring the attacker to guess or learn the key in order to perform attacks such as that shown in Figure 10.

Defense 5: Performance, Limitations, Variants, and Counterattacks

The performance effects of this defense will vary based on how pervasively pointers are encrypted, and what encryption method is used. To keep overheads low,

```
class LessVulnerable
{
    char m_buff[MAX_LEN];
    void* m_cmpptr;
public:
    LessVulnerable(Comparer* c) {
        m_cmpptr = EncodePointer( c );
    }
    // ... elided code ...
    int cmp(char* str) {
        Comparer* mcmp;
        mcmp = (Comparer*) DecodePointer( m_cmpptr );
        return mcmp->compare( m_buff, str );
    }
};
```

Fig. 26. An excerpt of a variant of the C++ code in Figure 9 where the comparison pointer is encoded using a random value specific to the process executing the software. This code invokes library routines for the encoding and decoding; these particular routines are present on Windows XP SP2 and more recent versions of Microsoft Windows.

only a weak form of encryption is typically used, e.g., xor-ing pointers with a secret value. When encryption is simply an inline xor operation, its performance effects will be limited to a few percent, even when applied widely [13]. In Windows, encryption is based on an xor operation and a bit-wise rotation, using either per-process or system-wide random values established using good sources of randomness [20]; one system call is performed when using a per-process secret. As applied in Windows utilities and systems software, this defense has enforcement overheads that are small enough to be hard to measure for most workloads.

The main limitation of this defense is that encrypted pointers must be selectively applied to existing software, due to their potential incompatibility with pointer arithmetic. Also, in the common case where encryption does not include any signature or integrity check, this defense may not detect attempted attacks.

Many variants of this defense are possible, depending on which pointers are encrypted. In particular, the encoding of addresses held in pointers does not need to be the same for all pointers in a given piece of software. Instead, pointers could be assigned into equivalence classes, or "colors", and each color could be given a different encoding, as long as no instruction that accessed a pointer made use of more than one color. This variant can make defenses more fine grained and, if applied pervasively to all or most pointers, can approximate the benefits of other, general constraints on the software's data flow [9].

The counterattacks to this defense depend on which pointers are encrypted, and, of course, attacks that do not involve pointers are still possible. In particular, this defense may not prevent attacks based on corrupting the contents of data, such as a buffer overflow of a boolean value that signifies successful authentication [10]. Such attacks do not corrupt pointers, but still require the attacker to know, in some form, the location of the data contents to be corrupted.

3.6   Defense 6: Randomizing the Layout of Code and Data in Memory

The C and C++ languages specify neither where code is located in memory, nor the location of variables, arrays, structures, or objects. For software compiled from these languages, the layout of code and data in memory is decided by the compiler and execution environment. This layout directly determines all concrete addresses used during execution—and attacks, including all of the attacks in Section 2, typically depend on these concrete addresses.

Therefore, a simple, pervasive form of address encryption can be achieved by shuffling, or randomizing, the layout of software in the memory address space, in a manner that is unknown to the attacker. Defenses based on such Address-Space Layout Randomization, or ASLR, can be a highly practical, effective barrier against low-level attacks. Such defenses were first implemented in the PaX project [37] and have recently been deployed in Windows Vista [19,24].

ASLR defenses can be used to change the addresses of all code, global variables, stack variables, arrays, and structures, objects, and heap allocations; with ASLR those addresses are derived from a random value, chosen for the software being executed and the system on which it executes. These addresses, and the memory-layout shuffling, may be public information on the system where the software executes. However, low-level software attacks—including most worms, viruses, adware, spyware, and malware—are often performed by remote attackers that have no existing means of running code on their target system, or otherwise inspect the addresses utilized on that system. To overcome ASLR defenses, such attackers will have to craft attacks that do not depend on addresses, or somehow guess or learn those addresses.

ASLR is not intended to defend against attackers that are able to control the software execution, even to a very small degree. Like many other defenses that rely on secrets, ASLR is easily circumvented by an attacker that can read the software's memory. Once an attacker is able to execute even the smallest amount of code of their choice (e.g., in a jump-to-libc attack), it should be safely assumed that the attacker can read memory and, in particular, that ASLR is no longer an obstacle. Fortunately, ASLR and the other defenses in this tutorial can be highly effective in preventing attackers from successfully executing even a single machine-code instruction of their choice.

As a concrete example of ASLR, Figure 27 shows two execution stacks for the median function of Figure 11, taken from two executions of that function on Windows Vista, which implements ASLR defenses. These stacks contain code addresses, including a function pointer and return address; they also include addresses in data pointers that point into the stack, and in the data argument which points into the heap. All of these addresses are different in the two executions; only the integer inputs remain the same.

On many software platforms, ASLR can be applied automatically, in manner that is compatible even with legacy software. In particular, unlike Defense 5, ASLR changes only the concrete values of addresses, not how those addresses are encoded in pointers; this makes ASLR compatible with common, legacy programming practices that depend on the encoding of addresses.

stack one		stack two		
address	contents	address	contents	
0x0022feac	0x008a13e0	0x0013f750	0x00b113e0	; cmp argument
0x0022fea8	0x00000001	0x0013f74c	0x00000001	; len argument
0x0022fea4	0x00a91147	0x0013f748	0x00191147	; data argument
0x0022fea0	0x008a1528	0x0013f744	0x00b11528	; return address
0x0022fe9c	0x0022fec8	0x0013f740	0x0013f76c	; saved base pointer
0x0022fe98	0x00000000	0x0013f73c	0x00000000	; tmp final 4 bytes
0x0022fe94	0x00000000	0x0013f738	0x00000000	; tmp continues
0x0022fe90	0x00000000	0x0013f734	0x00000000	; tmp continues
0x0022fe8c	0x00000000	0x0013f730	0x00000000	; tmp continues
0x0022fe88	0x00000000	0x0013f72c	0x00000000	; tmp continues
0x0022fe84	0x00000000	0x0013f728	0x00000000	; tmp continues
0x0022fe80	0x00000000	0x0013f724	0x00000000	; tmp continues
0x0022fe7c	0x00000000	0x0013f720	0x00000000	; tmp buffer starts
0x0022fe78	0x00000004	0x0013f71c	0x00000004	; memcpy length argument
0x0022fe74	0x00a91147	0x0013f718	0x00191147	; memcpy source argument
0x0022fe70	0x0022fe8c	0x0013f714	0x0013f730	; memcpy destination arg.

Fig. 27. The addresses and contents of the stacks of two different executions of the
same software, given the same input. The software is the median function of Figure 11,
the input is an array of the single integer zero, and the stacks are snapshots taken at
the same point as in Figure 14. The snapshots are taken from two executions of that
function on Windows Vista, with a system restart between the executions. As a result
of ASLR defenses, only the input data remains the same in the two executions. All
addresses are different; even so, some address bits remain the same since, for efficiency
and compatibility with existing software, ASLR is applied only at a coarse granularity.

However, ASLR is both easier to implement, and is more compatible with
legacy software, when data and code is shuffled at a rather coarse granularity.
For instance, software may simultaneously use more than a million heap allocations; however, on a 32-bit system, if an ASLR mechanism randomly spread
those allocations uniformly throughout the address space, then only small contiguous memory regions would remain free. Then, if that software tried to allo-
cate an array whose size is a few tens of kilobytes, that allocation would most
likely fail—even though, without this ASLR mechanism, it might certainly have
succeeded. On the other hand, without causing incompatibility with legacy software, an ASLR mechanism could change the base address of all heap allocations,
and otherwise leave the heap implementation unchanged. (This also avoids trig-
gering latent bugs, such as the software's continued use of heap memory after
deallocation, which are another potential source of incompatibility.)

In the implementation of ASLR on Windows Vista, the compilers and the
execution environment have been modified to avoid obstacles faced by other
implementations, such as those in the PaX project [37]. In particular, the software executables and libraries of all operating system components and utilities
have been compiled with information that allows their relocation in memory at
load time. When the operating system starts, the system libraries are located

sequentially in memory, in the order they are needed, at a starting point chosen randomly from 256 possibilities; thus a jump-to-libc attack that targets the concrete address of a library function will have less than a 0.5% chance of succeeding. This randomization of system libraries applies to all software that executes on the Vista operating system; the next time the system restarts, the libraries are located from a new random starting point.

When a Windows Vista process is launched, several other addresses are chosen randomly for that process instance, if the main executable opts in to ASLR defenses. For instance, the base of the initial heap is chosen from 32 possibilities. The stacks of process threads are randomized further: the stack base is chosen from 32 possibilities, and a pad of unused memory, whose size is random, is placed on top of the stack, for a total of about 16 thousand possibilities for the address of the initial stack frame. In addition, the location of some other memory regions is also chosen randomly from 32 possibilities, including thread control data and the process environment data (which includes the table corrupted in Attack 4). For processes, the ASLR implementation chooses new random starting points each time that a process instance is launched.

An ASLR implementation could be designed to shuffle the memory layout at a finer granularity than is done in Windows Vista. For instance, a pad of unused memory could be inserted within the stack frame of all (or some) functions; also, the inner memory allocation strategy of the heap could be randomized. However, in Windows Vista, such an ASLR implementation would incur greater overhead, would cause more software compatibility issues, and might be likely to thwart mostly attacks that are already covered by other deployed defenses. In particular, there can be little to gain from shuffling the system libraries independently for each process instance [41]—and such an ASLR implementation would be certain to cause large performance and resource overheads.

Defense 6: Performance, Limitations, Variants, and Counterattacks

The enforcement overhead of ASLR defenses will vary greatly depending on the implementation. In particular, implementations where shared libraries may be placed at different addresses in different processes will incur greater overhead and consume more memory resources.

However, in its Windows Vista implementation, ASLR may actually slightly improve performance. This improvement is a result of ASLR causing library code to be placed contiguously into the address space, in the order that the code is actually used. This encourages a tight packing of frequently-used page table entries, which has performance benefits (cf. the page-table changes for non-executable data, discussed on page 117).

ASLR can provide effective defenses against all of the attacks in Section 2 of this tutorial, because it applies to the addresses of both code and data. Even so, as discussed on page 125 for Defense 5, some data-only attacks remain possible, where the attacks do not depend on concrete addresses, but rely on corrupting the contents of the data being processed by the target software.

The more serious limitation of ASLR is the small number of memory layout shuffles that are possible on commodity 32-bit hardware—especially given the coarse shuffling granularity that is required for efficiency and compatibility with existing software. As a result, ASLR creates only at most a few thousand possibilities that an attacker must consider, and any given attack will be successful against a significant (albeit small) number of target systems. The number of possible shuffles in an ASLR implementation can be greatly increased on 64-bit platforms, which are starting to be adopted. However, current 64-bit hardware is limited to 48 usable bits and can therefore offer at most a 64-thousand-fold increase in the number of shuffles possible [44].

Furthermore, at least on 32-bit systems, the number of possible ASLR shuffles is insufficient to provide a defense against scenarios where the attacker is able to retry their attack repeatedly, with new addresses [41]. Such attacks are realistic. For example, because a failed attack did not crash the software in the case of the recent ANI vulnerability in Windows [22], an attack, such as a script in a malicious Web page, could try multiple addresses until a successful exploit was found. However, in the normal case, when failed attacks crash the target software, attacks based on retrying can be mitigated by limiting the number of times the software is restarted. In the ASLR implementation in Windows Vista, such limits are in place for many system components.

ASLR defenses provide one form of software diversity, which has been long known to provide security benefits. One way to achieve software diversity is to deploy multiple, different implementations of the same functionality. However, this approach is costly and may offer limited benefits: its total cost is proportional to the number of implementations and programmers are known to make the same mistakes when implementing the same functionality [33].

A more attractive defense—which can offer more diversity, at little cost—is to artificially perturb some of the low-level properties of existing, deployed implementations [17]. ASLR is one, relatively coarse-grained variant of this defense. Other, finer-grained variants exist, including techniques based on automatically creating multiple software versions through randomized obfuscation of the high-level software specification [39]. While preserving the software's high-level semantics, such obfuscation can change the semantics as well as the addresses of low-level code and data. However, unlike ASLR, defenses based on finer-grained diversity have many costs, including performance overheads and increases to the cost of software-engineering processes such as testing and debugging.

ASLR has a few counterattacks other than the data-only, content-based attacks, and the persistent guessing of an attacker, which are both discussed above. In particular, an otherwise harmless information-disclosure vulnerability may allow an attacker to learn how addresses are shuffled, and circumvent ASLR defenses. Although unlikely, such a vulnerability may be present because of a format-string bug, or because the contents of uninitialized memory are sent on the network when that memory contains residual addresses.

Another type of counterattack to ASLR defenses is based on overwriting only the low-order bits of addresses, which are predictable because ASLR is applied at

a coarse granularity. Such overwrites are sometimes possible through buffer overflows on little-endian architectures, such as the x86. For example, in Figure 27,
if there were useful trampoline machine-code to be found seven bytes into the
cmp function, then changing the least-significant byte of the cmp address on the
stack from 0xe0 to 0xe7 would cause that code to be invoked. An attacker that
succeeded in such corruption might well be able to perform a jump-to-libc attack much like that in Attack 3. (However, for this particular stack, the attacker
would not succeed, since the cmp address will always be overwritten completely
when the vulnerability in the median function in Figure 11 is exploited.)

Despite the above counterattacks, ASLR is an effective barrier to attack,
especially when combined with the defenses described previously in this section.
Indeed, with such a combination of defenses, an attacker may be most likely to
counter with a higher-level attack, such as one based on higher-level interfaces
such as Web scripting languages, or simply based on social engineering.

4   Summary and Discussion

The distinguishing characteristic of low-level software attacks is that they are
dependent on the low-level details of the software's executable representation
and its execution environment. As a result, defenses against such attacks can be
based on changing those details in ways that are compatible with the software's
specification in a higher-level programming language.

As in Defense 1, integrity bits can be added to the low-level representation of
state, to make attacks more likely to be detected, and stopped. As in Defense 2,
the low-level representation can be reordered and replicated to move it away from
corruption possibilities. As in Defenses 3 and 4, the low-level representation can
be augmented with a conservative model of behavior and with runtime checks
that ensure execution conforms to that model. Finally, as in Defenses 1, 5, and 6,
the low-level representation can be encoded with a secret that the attacker must
guess, or otherwise learn, in order to craft functional attacks.

However, defenses like those in this tutorial fall far short of a guarantee that
the software exhibits only the low-level behavior that is possible in the software's higher-level specification. Such guarantees are hard to come by. For languages like C and C++, there are efforts to build certifying compilers that can
provide such guarantees, for correct software [6,31]. Unfortunately, even these
compilers offer few, or no guarantees in the presence of bugs, such as buffer-
overflow vulnerabilities. Many of these bugs can be eliminated by using other,
advanced compiler techniques, like those used in the Cyclone [25], CCured [35],
and Deputy [45] systems. But these techniques are not widely applicable: they
require pervasive source-code changes, runtime memory-management support,
restrictions on concurrency, and result in significant enforcement overhead.

In comparison, the defenses in this tutorial have very low overheads, require
no source code changes but at most re-compilation, and are widely applicable
to legacy software written in C, C++, and similar languages. For instance, they
have been applied pervasively to recent Microsoft software, including all the

Table 1. A table of the relationship between the attacks and defenses in this tutorial. None of the defenses completely prevent the attacks, in all of their variants. The first two defenses apply only to the stack, and are not an obstacle to the heap-based Attack 2. Defenses 3 and 4 apply only to the control flow of machine-code execution, and do not prevent the data-only Attack 4. Defense 5 applies only to pointers that programmers can explicitly encode and decode; thus, it cannot prevent the return-address clobbering in Attack 1. When combined with each other, the defenses are stronger than when they are applied in isolation.

	Attack 1	Attack 2	Attack 3	Attack 4
Defense 1	Partial defense		Partial defense	Partial defense
Defense 2	Partial defense		Partial defense	Partial defense
Defense 3	Partial defense	Partial defense	Partial defense	
Defense 4	Partial defense	Partial defense	Partial defense	
Defense 5		Partial defense	Partial defense	Partial defense
Defense 6	Partial defense	Partial defense	Partial defense	Partial defense

components of the Windows Vista operating system. As in that case, these defenses are best used as one part of a comprehensive software-engineering methodology designed to to reduce security vulnerabilities. Such a methodology should include, at least, threat analysis, design and code reviews for security, security testing, automatic analysis for vulnerabilities, and the rewriting of software to use safer languages, interfaces, and programming practices [23].

The combination of the defenses in this tutorial forms a substantial, effective barrier to all low-level attacks—although, as summarized in Table 1, each offers only partial protection against certain attacks. In particular, they greatly reduce the likelihood that an attacker can exploit a low-level security vulnerability for purposes other than a denial-of-service attack. Because these defenses are both effective, and easy to adopt in practice, in the next few years, they are likely to be deployed for most software. Their adoption, along with efforts to eliminate buffer overflows and other underlying security vulnerabilities, offers some hope that, for C and C++ software, low-level software security may become less of a concern in the future.

Acknowledgments. Thanks to Martín Abadi for suggesting the structure of this tutorial, and to Yinglian Xie for proofreading and for suggesting useful improvements to the exposition.

References

1. Abadi, M.: Protection in programming-language translations. In: Larsen, K.G., Skyum, S., Winskel, G. (eds.) ICALP 1998. LNCS, vol. 1443, pp. 868–883. Springer, Heidelberg (1998) (Also Digital Equipment Corporation Systems Research Center report No. 154, April 1998)
2. Abadi, M., Budiu, M., Erlingsson, Ú., Ligatti, J.: Control-Flow Integrity: Principles, implementations, and applications. In: Proceedings of the ACM Conference on Computer and Communications Security (2005) (Also as Microsoft Research Technical Report MSR-TR-05-18 February 2005)
3. Abadi, M., Budiu, M., Erlingsson, Ú., Ligatti, J.: A theory of secure control flow. In: Proceedings of the 7th International Conference on Formal Engineering Methods (2005) (Also as Microsoft Research Technical Report MSR-TR-05-17 May 2005)
4. Anderson, R.J.: Security Engineering: A Guide to Building Dependable Distributed Systems. John Wiley & Sons, Inc., New York (2001)
5. Bailey, M., Cooke, E., Jahanian, F., Watson, D., Nazario, J.: The Blaster worm: Then and now. IEEE Security and Privacy 03(4), 26–31 (2005)
6. Blazy, S., Dargaye, Z., Leroy, X.: Formal verification of a C compiler front-end. In: Misra, J., Nipkow, T., Sekerinski, E. (eds.) FM 2006. LNCS, vol. 4085, pp. 460–475. Springer, Heidelberg (2006)
7. Bray, B.: Compiler security checks in depth (2002), http://msdn2.microsoft.com/en-us/library/aa290051(vs.71).aspx
8. Brumley, D., Chiueh, T.C., Johnson, R., Lin, H., Song, D.: Efficient and accurate detection of integer-based attacks. In: Proceedings of the 14th Annual Network and Distributed System Security Symposium (NDSS'07) (February 2007)
9. Castro, M., Costa, M., Harris, T.: Securing software by enforcing data-flow integrity. In: USENIX'06: Proceedings of the 7th conference on USENIX Symposium on Operating Systems Design and Implementation, Berkeley, CA, USA, USENIX Association, pp. 11–11 (2006)
10. Chen, S., Xu, J., Sezer, E.C., Gauriar, P., Iyer, R.: Non-control-data attacks are realistic threats. In: Proceedings of the Usenix Security Symposium, pp. 177–192 (2005)
11. Intel Corporation: Intel IA-32 architecture, software developer's manual, Volumes 1–3 (2007), http://developer.intel.com/design/Pentium4/documentation.htm
12. Cowan, C., Barringer, M., Beattie, S., Kroah-Hartman, G., Frantzen, M., Lokier, J.: FormatGuard: Automatic protection from printf format string vulnerabilities. In: Proceedings of the Usenix Security Symposium (2001)
13. Cowan, C., Beattie, S., Johansen, J., Wagle, P.: PointGuard: Protecting pointers from buffer overflow vulnerabilities. In: Proceedings of the Usenix Security Symposium, pp. 91–104 (2003)
14. Cowan, C., Pu, C., Maier, D., Walpole, J., Bakke, P., Beattie, S., Grier, A., Wagle, P., Zhang, Q., Hinton, H.: StackGuard: Automatic adaptive detection and prevention of buffer-overflow attacks. In: Proceedings of the Usenix Security Symposium, pp. 63–78 (1998)
15. Etoh, H., Yoda, K.: ProPolice—improved stack smashing attack detection. IPSJ SIGNotes Computer Security (CSEC), 14 (October 2001)
16. Florio, E.: GDIPLUS VULN - MS04-028 - CRASH TEST JPEG (September 15, 2004), Forum message sent, full-disclosureatlists.netsys.com
17. Forrest, S., Somayaji, A., Ackley, D.: Building diverse computer systems. In: HOTOS '97: Proceedings of the 6th Workshop on Hot Topics in Operating Systems (HotOS-VI), p. 67. IEEE Computer Society, Washington, DC (1997)

18. Foster, J.C.: Metasploit Toolkit for Penetration Testing, Exploit Development, and Vulnerability Research. Syngress Publishing (2007)
19. Howard, M.: Alleged bugs in Windows Vistas ASLR implementation (2006), http://blogs.msdn.com/michael_howard/archive/2006/10/04/ Alleged-Bugs-in -Windows-Vista_1920_s-ASLR-Implementation.aspx
20. Howard, M.: Protecting against pointer subterfuge (redux) (2006), http://blogs.msdn.com/michael_howard/archive/2006/08/16/702707.aspx
21. Howard, M.: Hardening stack-based buffer overrun detection in VC++ 2005 SP1 (2007), http://blogs.msdn.com/michael_howard/archive/2007/04/03/ hardening-stack-based-buffer-overrun-detection-in-vc-2005-sp1.aspx
22. Howard, M.: Lessons learned from the animated cursor security bug (2007), http://blogs.msdn.com/sdl/archive/2007/04/26/ lessons-learned-from-the-animated-cursor-security-bug.aspx
23. Howard, M., Lipner, S.: The Security Development Lifecycle. Microsoft Press, Redmond, WA (2006)
24. Howard, M., Thomlinson, M.: Windows Vista ISV security (April 2007), http://msdn2.microsoft.com/en-us/library/bb430720.aspx
25. Jim, T., Morrisett, G., Grossman, D., Hicks, M., Cheney, J., Wang, Y.: Cyclone: A safe dialect of C. In: Proceedings of the Usenix Technical Conference, pp. 275–288 (2002)
26. Johns, M., Beyerlein, C.: SMask: Preventing injection attacks in Web applications by approximating automatic data/code separation. In: SAC '07: Proceedings of the 2007 ACM symposium on Applied computing, pp. 284–291. ACM Press, New York (2007)
27. Kc, G.S., Keromytis, A.D., Prevelakis, V.: Countering code-injection attacks with instruction-set randomization. In: CCS '03: Proceedings of the 10th ACM conference on Computer and communications security, pp. 272–280. ACM Press, New York (2003)
28. Kennedy, A.: Securing the .NET programming model. special issue of Theoretical Computer Science. In: Earlier version presented at APPSEM II Workshop, in Munich, Germany, September 12-15, 2005 (to appear, 2007)
29. Kiriansky, V., Bruening, D., Amarasinghe, S.: Secure execution via program shepherding. In: Proceedings of the Usenix Security Symposium, pp. 191–206 (2002)
30. Klog.: The frame pointer overwrite. Phrack 9(55) (1999)
31. Leroy, X.: Formal certification of a compiler back-end, or: programming a compiler with a proof assistant. In: 33rd symposium Principles of Programming Languages, pp. 42–54. ACM Press, New York (2006)
32. Litchfield, D.: Defeating the stack buffer overflow prevention mechanism of Microsoft Windows 2003 Server (2003), http://www.nextgenss.com/papers/defeating-w2k3-stack-protection.pdf
33. Littlewood, B., Popov, P., Strigini, L.: Modeling software design diversity: a review. ACM Comput. Surv. 33(2), 177–208 (2001)
34. Livshits, B., Erlingsson, Ú.: Using Web application construction frameworks to protect against code injection attacks. In: PLAS '07: Proceedings of the 2007 workshop on Programming languages and analysis for security, pp. 95–104. ACM Press, New York (2007)
35. Necula, G.C., McPeak, S., Weimer, W.: CCured: Type-safe retrofitting of legacy code. In: Proceedings of the 29th ACM Symposium on Principles of Programming Languages, pp. 128–139 (2002)

36. Newsome, J., Song, D.: Dynamic taint analysis for automatic detection, analysis, and signature generation of exploits on commodity software. In: Proceedings of the 12th Annual Network and Distributed System Security Symposium (NDSS'07) (February 2005)
37. PaX Project: The PaX project (2004), http://pax.grsecurity.net/
38. Pincus, J., Baker, B.: Beyond stack smashing: Recent advances in exploiting buffer overruns. IEEE Security and Privacy 2(4), 20–27 (2004)
39. Pucella, R., Schneider, F.B.: Independence from obfuscation: A semantic framework for diversity. In: CSFW '06: Proceedings of the 19th IEEE workshop on Computer Security Foundations, pp. 230–241. IEEE Computer Society, Washington, DC (2006) (Expanded version available as Cornell University Computer Science Department Technical Report TR 2006-2016)
40. Shacham, H.: The geometry of innocent flesh on the bone: Return-into-libc without function calls (on the x86). In: submission (2006), http://hovav.net/dist/geometry.pdf
41. Shacham, H., Page, M., Pfaff, B., Goh, E.-J., Modadugu, N., Boneh, D.: On the effectiveness of address-space randomization. In: CCS '04: Proceedings of the 11th ACM conference on Computer and communications security, pp. 298–307. ACM Press, New York (2004)
42. Small, C.: A tool for constructing safe extensible C++ systems. In: Proceedings of the 3rd Conference on Object-Oriented Technologies and Systems (1997)
43. Spafford, E.H.: The Internet worm program: An analysis. SIGCOMM Comput. Commun. Rev. 19(1), 17–57 (1989)
44. Wikipedia: x86-64 (2007), http://en.wikipedia.org/wiki/X86-64
45. Zhou, F., Condit, J., Anderson, Z., Bagrak, I., Ennals, R., Harren, M., Necula, G., Brewer, E.: SafeDrive: Safe and recoverable extensions using language-based techniques. In: USENIX'06: Proceedings of the 7th conference on USENIX Symposium on Operating Systems Design and Implementation, Berkeley, CA, USA, USENIX Association, pp. 4–4 (2006)

Enhancing Java Security with History Based Access Control*

Fabio Martinelli and Paolo Mori

Istituto di Informatica e Telematica
Consiglio Nazionale delle Ricerche
via Moruzzi, 1 - 56124 Pisa, Italy
{fabio.martinelli, paolo.mori}@iit.cnr.it

Abstract. Java language has become very popular in the last few years. Due to its portability, Java applications are adopted in distributed environment, where heterogeneous resources cooperate. In this context, security is a fundamental issue, because each resource could execute applications that have been developed by possibly unknown third parties.

This paper recalls several solutions for improving the Java native security support. In particular, it discusses an approach for history based access control of Java applications. This paper also describes the application of this solution to two common use cases: grid computing and mobile devices (such as mobile phones or PDAs).

1 Introduction

Java language has become very popular in the last few years, for many reasons, such as the ease of programming, the robustness, the memory management, and also the cross platform capability. "Write once, run anywhere" is a slogan that was created by Sun Microsystems to illustrate the cross-platform benefits of the Java language. As a matter of fact, the portability of the Java language allows to compile a Java application once, on a given architecture with a given operating system, and to execute the resulting bytecode on any architecture with any operating system that supports a Java Virtual Machine.

For this reason, Java applications are adopted in distributed environment, i.e. environment where there must be cooperation among distinct devices that run different operating systems. Moreover, Java is also adopted for developing applets, i.e. programs that are downloaded from remote sites and that run within an internet browser on behalf of the user that downloaded them. In this case too, the applet can be downloaded and executed by a browser running on any architecture with any operating system.

Security is a fundamental issue in this context. As a matter of fact, a Java application that has been developed by third parties, e.g. an application that

---

* Work partially supported by EU-funded projects *Trust and Security for Next Generation Grids*, GridTrust, IST-033817, *Security of Software and Services for Mobile Systems*, S3MS, IST-27004, and ARTIST2 Network of Excellence, IST-004527.

A. Aldini and R. Gorrieri (Eds.): FOSAD 2006/2007, LNCS 4677, pp. 135–159, 2007.

has been downloaded from internet, could contain errors, or even malicious code that could damage the system or could obtain unauthorised accesses to system resources. Since this application runs on the system on behalf of the user that downloaded it, i.e. with the same rights of this user, the security support must guarantee that this application will not damage the system. Here and in the following, we consider security from the point of view of the computational resource that executes Java applications, i.e. the security support must guarantee that the Java application does not perform dangerous operations that could harm the system executing it, or that could damage other system entities, like processes or users.

Java 2 Standard Edition (J2SE) provides a set of security mechanisms that address the most common security requirements. However, sometimes the security model provided by Java is too restrictive, because authorisation is based on rules that evaluate static factors, and that do not take into account the current state of the computation. For example, we could be interested in enforcing a security policy that, at the beginning of the execution, allows the application to read file A or file B, but when the application reads one of the two files, then it cannot read the other one anymore.

This paper describes an enhancement to Java security by integrating an history based access control system in the Java runtime environment. This system is based on the application behaviour, i.e. the Java application is authorized to perform a given action depending on the actions it has previous performed. In this way, the rights granted to an application are not static, but they depend on the application behaviour. Hence, a right that was granted to the application at the beginning of the execution, could be revoked after that the application has performed a given action, or a right that was not granted at the beginning of the execution could be granted after that another action has been performed by the application.

This paper is structured as follows. Section 2 presents a short overview of the security support provided by the standard Java security architecture, and Section 3 presents other attempts to enhance the security architecture of Java. Section 4 describes the history based acess control system for Java we propose, and Section 5 describes two use cases where the proposed security enhanced Java Virtual Machine has been exploited.

2   Java Security Architecture

Java 2 Standard Edition is the standard package released by Sun Microsystems for the development and the execution of Java applications. The security model implemented by J2SE, [2] [22], is defined as *sandbox*, and provides built-in language features, such as strong data typing, and run time security features, such as automatic memory management, bytecode verification and secure class loading. Moreover, another security mechanism provided by J2SE is the Java Security Manager, that implements an authorisation system. Through these mechanisms, untrusted Java applications, such as the applets downloaded from internet, are executed in a restricted environment, where a limited access to system resources is provided.

The bytecode verification ensures that only legitimate Java bytecodes are loaded and executed by the Java Virtual Machine. The class loader is the mechanism that reads files containing the bytecode into the Java Virtual machine. Hence, securing the class loader is critical to restrict the environment where the Java application is executed. Moreover, the access to the resources of the underlying operating system is always mediated by the Java Virtual Machine, that exploits the Security Manager to determine whether the Java application has the right to access a given resource. These rights are defined through a security policy.

Figure 1 shows the architecture of the Java runtime environment, including security components.

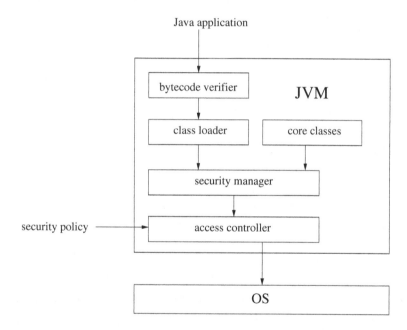

Fig. 1. Java runtime environment

In the following, we focus our attention on the runtime enforcing of security policies.

2.1 Security Manager

The Security Manager is an access control system provided by the security support of the J2SE. The aim of the Security Manager is to control whether a given action of the running application should be permitted or not. The Security Manager is automatically activated when executing an Applet, while it must be explicitly activated when executing a local application. It is a Java object that performs runtime checks on the invocation of methods that access the resources. Actually, the implementation of the methods of the core Java classes that access resources includes the invocation to a proper method of the Security Manager that checks whether the access to the resource can be granted to the application. For example, the implementation of constructor java.net.socket(host,port) that accesses the network to establish a TCP connection with a remote host, includes the invocation to the Security Manager method CheckConnect(host,port). If the access right is not granted, a security exception is returned to the application. It is also possible to invoke a method of the Security Manager within a Java application, to check whether a given permission will be granted to this application. To determine whether an access should be granted or not, the Security Manager exploits a security policy. The security policy is a set of entry, called permissions. A permission refers to an action that the application is allowed to perform. Each permission consists of a type, that indicates the resource type this permission refers to, a name that specify the resource this permission refers to, and the action that can be performed on this resource. As an example, a permission could be: (java.net.SocketPermission, miohost.iit.cnr.it, connect). This permission allows the Java application to set up a socket connection with the remote host miohost.iit.cnr.it. The Java Access Controller is the mechanism that the Security Manager actually exploits to enforce the security policy.

3 Related Work

This section describes the most relevant works aimed at enhancing the security architecture of Java by performing runtime enforcement of security policies. These works are grouped according to the approach they use to introduce the security controls in the Java Security Architecture.

3.1 Security Manager Extension

The standard mechanism provided by the Java security architecture to define a customised authorisation system is the extension of the Security Manager. As a matter of fact, it is possible to extend the Security Manager class to define a customised Security Manager. In this way, one can redefine some (or even all) of the methods of the Security Manager to define customised controls when accessing certain resources. Hence, when a core Java class invokes the Security Manager before accessing a resource, the user defined access control procedure is executed instead of the standard one. As an example, one could be interested to redefine only the methods related to network access, because it wants lo limit the number of simultaneous TCP connections. In this case, the methods checkConnect and checkAccept could be extended to take into account the current number of opened connections. However, since the Security Manager methods are invoked directly by the Java Virtual Machine, the user cannot define a customised set of events to be controlled, but he must use the ones defined by the Security Manager methods.

3.2   System Library

A first approach to protect the resources of the underlying system from the actions performed by a Java application is the one that acts on the system libraries that implement the accesses to those resources.

A simple solution is the one that modifies these system libraries to insert the pieces of code that implement the controls of the security policy. This solution is quite common, it has no load time overhead, and a little runtime overhead, i.e. only the one to evaluate the policy. However, this solution is not very flexible. For example, if the policy is encoded in the system libraries, the update of such a policy requires the update of the whole system libraries. This approach has been adopted in [9] and [24].

A similar solution is the one that wraps system libraries instead of modifying them. The wrapper function is executed instead of the actual system library function, and it includes the code that performs the security checks needed before the invocation of the system library function, the actual invocation to the system library function, and sometimes the code that performs the security checks after the execution of the action, for instance to check some conditions on the result of the action.

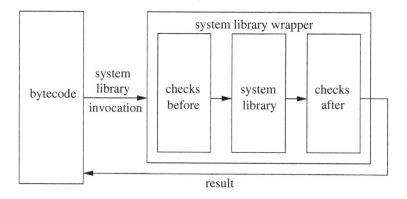

Fig. 2. System libraries wrapping

The *name space management* security mechanism, described in [51] and [52], exploits the system library wrapping approach to enforce security policies. This mechanism controls how the class names are resolved into runtime classes, by adopting a modified version of the Java class loader. Hence, given the same class name, depending on the security policy that has to be enforced, the modified class loader loads the class implementation that embeds the corresponding security policy code. In this case the system libraries that are wrapped are the Java core classes that implements the accesses to resources.

Naccio, [16], is another security tool that adopts the same approach. In Naccio, to enforce the security policy, the bytecode must be modified to call the wrapper functions instead of the actual system library ones. Security policies are expressed in terms of abstract resource manipulation, and then are transformed in the actual control code to be executed at run time by customising them for the specific platform, defined by a platform interface description. The *policy generator* is the Naccio component that takes as input the resource description, the security policy to be enforced, the platform interface and the platform library and produces a policy description file, that contains the transformation rule to enforce the security policy on the given platform. The *application transformer*, instead, is the component that read the policy description file and the target application and produces a version of the application that has been instrumented to invoke the controls that implement the security policy. The same policy description file can be applied to distinct applications to enforce the same security policy.

3.3   Java Stack Inspection

The stack inspection is a technique that, for each critical operation that is invoked by an application, controls the sequence of invocations that leaded to such operation. This technique exploits the Java runtime stack. As a matter of fact, during the execution of a Java application, a sequence of methods are invoked by the bytecode, and each time a method is invoked, a new frame referring to this method is pushed on the Java runtime stack, while each time a method returns, the related frame is popped from the stack. Hence, at a given time of the execution, the stack contains a sequence of frames that refer to the sequence of methods that have been invoked by the application. Distinct threads exploit distinct stacks.

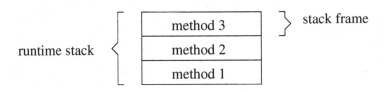

Fig. 3. Java runtime stack

The Java runtime stack inspection, consists in the inspection of the stack frames during the execution of an application to determine whether the methods of untrusted applications are performing hostile activities. To enable the stack inspection, each stack frame, besides the name of the invoked method, includes also two other fields: *privilege flag*, that determines whether full privilege are paired with this method, and the *principal field* that indicates whether the method is part of a system class or of a user one.

When a method that performs a critical operation is invoked, a stack inspection is executed. This means that all the frames that are currently on the stack are examined, from the newest to the oldest. If at least one of this frame is untrusted, the operation cannot be executed. As a matter of fact, this means that

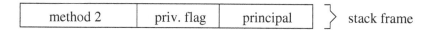

Fig. 4. Java runtime stack frame

the critical operation has been invoked, directly or indirectly, by an untrusted application. To decide whether a frame is trusted or not we take into account the privilege flag and the principal field. For instance, all the frames whose principal is System are trusted. The research of untrusted frames into the stack is implemented exploiting four basic primitives, that we represent with:

- enablePrivilege
- disablePrivilege
- revertPrivilege
- checkPrivilege

When an application method wants to access a resource R, it must invoke enablePrivilege(R). Then, the local policy is checked to determine whether the permission on R can be granted to the application. If the right is granted, the stack frame of the current method records this privilege with a flag. When the application actually performs the operation to access R, the checkPrivilege(R) is invoked. This primitive examines the stack frames looking for the privilege flag, to check whether the access permission to R has been already granted to the application. The other two primitives are used to revoke the permissions that have been granted. These controls are performed by the runtime support, because the Java runtime stack is not directly accessible by the Java applications. This technique performs the permission decision process taking into account only the application methods that have been invoked and that have not been terminated yet. As a matter of fact, when a method terminates, the related frame is removed from the Java runtime stack. This technique has been described and exploited in [51] and [53]. An alternative approach is described in [14], that merges an Inlined Reference Monitor (IRM) into the Java application bytecode, to enforce a security policy exploiting the stack inspection technique.

3.4   Java Log Auditing

The Java log auditing is a technique that examines the interactions of an application with the system resources by inspecting the execution logs, to detect attacks that attempt to circumvent the existing security mechanisms. This technique has been presented in [46]. Since J2SE does not provide a native support for logging the operation performed by a Java application during its execution, this support must be added in the JVM itself, by modifying and recompiling its source code. The security relevant events that have been considered in this approach, and that are caught by the event logging system, are:

- class events: class loading and creation of user-defined class loaders;
- system calls;

– JNI events: calls to non Java routines;
– thread events: methods invoked by a thread that might cause interferences with the execution of other threads.

Moreover, since this approach works on the execution logs, it detects a violation only after that this violation has been already executed by the application.

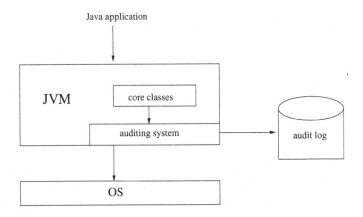

Fig. 5. Java runtime environment

The approach presented in [46] exploits an intrusion detection framework called STAT [50]. The STAT framework provides a generic signature based host intrusion detection engine that can be extended to be used in a specific context. Hence, it requires the definition of a set of models of known faulty application behaviours (attack signatures) that will be recognised by the tool. This set must be updated each time a new faulty application behaviour has been discovered.

3.5 Code Inlining

The code inlining is a technique that inserts the code that monitors the application directly in the bytecode, thus obtaining a secure version of the bytecode. The code inlining is performed before or when the application is loaded, and the Java Virtual Machine executes the secure version of the bytecode. The new code is inserted in the bytecode before the invocation of the security relevant actions and sometimes even after, and can directly include the security checks or the invocation to a library that implements these checks. In this way, the JVM, while executing the bytecode of the Java application, also performs the security checks. This approach is based on the assumption that the bytecode is not allowed to modify itself.

The code inlining approach has been adopted in [14], where an Inlined Reference Monitor (IRM) is inserted into Java Virtual Machine Language bytecode files to enforce security policies like stack inspection. The Policy Enforcement Toolkit (PoET) synthesizes the reference monitor for a given policy and inserts

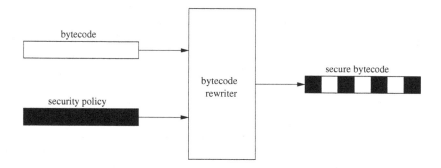

Fig. 6. Code inlining

it in the application code. Security policies for PoET are specified through the Policy Specification Language (PSLang) [13], while the reference monitor are generated exploiting the security automata approach described in [15].

The code inlining approach has been adopted also in [44]. In this case too, a tool generates the control code and integrates it in the application bytecode before it is loaded in the Java Virtual Machine. In particular, when the Java class loader loads a class, an *access constraint compiler* determines the resources exploited by this class, retrieves the related resource access constraints and generates the control code and a set of editing instructions that regulate the access to these resources. The *bytecode editor* exploits these instructions to embed the control code in the bytecode, and the resulting program is loaded into the Java Virtual Machine and executed. The security policy is expressed through a declarative policy language that allows to specify a set of constraints on accesses to resources. These constraints can take into account also the state of the application or of the resources. Hence, this approach also provides a limited mechanism for history based access control.

Another tool that exploits the code inlining approach is Polymer [5]. In this case too, a *policy compiler* compiles program monitors defined by the security policy into plain Java and then into bytecode, and a *bytecode rewriter* processes the application bytecode inserting calls to the monitor in all the necessary places. The Polymer security policy contains three main elements: 1) a decision procedure that determines how to react to each security relevant action performed by the application, 2) a security state that keeps track of the application activities, and 3) methods to update the security state. Polymer exploits edit automata [36].

Finally, *Naccio*, described in Section 3.2, adopts code inlining to substitute the invocation to system library functions to wrapper functions in the application bytecode.

3.6   Proof Carrying Code

Proof Carrying Code technique, [42], does not enforce the security policy at runtime, but it requires an off line static analysis of the application code. As a matter of fact, the code developer produces a safety proof, that states that the code adheres to a given policy. This proof is generated when the application is compiled, and it is embedded in the application code. On the executing resource side, before the execution of the application, a proof validator checks whether the proof is valid. If the proof is valid, the code respects the given policy and can be executed on the resource. On one hand, this technique reduces the runtime overhead, because the time consuming phase, that is the policy verification, is performed only once, when the code is compiled on the code developer side, while the proof validation can be performed with efficient algorithms. On the other hand, two major drawbacks of this technique are that the size of the proof could be very large, especially for complex policies, and the proof is hard to generate.

The solutions described in [10] and [43] exploit simplified versions of this approach.

4 History Based Access Control System

This paper describes the integration of an history based access control system within the Java runtime environment. The access control system is history based because it does not simply allow the execution of an action by exploiting authorisation rules that take into account only static factors, but it monitors the behaviour of the Java application, i.e. the sequence of actions performed by the application. Hence, to decide whether an action can be executed, the whole trace of execution of the application is evaluated. In this way, some dependencies among the actions performed by the application can be imposed by the policy. For example, a policy could state that an action γ can be executed only if actions α and β have been already executed in any order.

The approach adopted to embed the security controls in the Java runtime environment exploits the wrapping of system libraries, that has been described in Section 3.2. Hence, some system libraries functions have been wrapped, and the wrapper functions include all the checks that are required to enforce the security policy. However, in this case we do not wrap the Java core classes, but the invocations to operating system libraries. The security relevant actions that are monitored by the access control system are the system calls that are paired with the functions that have been wrapped.

In the following of this section we describe the security policy enforced by the system, the system architecture and some implementation details.

4.1 Process-Algebra Based Security Policy

The security policy describes the allowed behaviour of the Java applications, i.e. the sequences of security relevant actions that the applications are allowed to perform during their execution. Our approach implements the *default deny* model, i.e. any action that does not comply with the behaviour described in the policy is denied by default. Distinct policies can be applied to execute applications on behalf of distinct users, because the policy to be enforced can be chosen according to some user attribute, such as the trust level.

Some languages for the security policy specification have been developed. Some of these languages describe policies in terms of subject, objects and rights granted to subjects on objects [11] [32]. Other languages, instead, describe policies through attack sequences. As an example, the STATL language [12] describes attacks using the State Transition Analysis Technique. Since our approach requires the description of the admitted behaviour of the applications in terms of sequences of system calls, with their parameters and results, we use our policy language. The language is based on constructs from process algebras as CSP [28] [45] and CryptoCCS [38], that have been shown very useful to describe process behavior in security sensitive scenarios.

Indeed, the policy describes the order in which the system calls can be performed (traces), the value of the input parameters and of the results of these calls, and other various conditions, represented through predicates. The policy results from the composition of system calls, predicates and variable assignments through some composition operators, as described by the following grammar:

$$P ::= \perp \, \| \, \top \, \| \, \alpha(\boldsymbol{x}).P \, \| \, p(\boldsymbol{x}).P \, \| \, \boldsymbol{x} := \boldsymbol{e}.P \, \| \, P \, or \, P \, \| \, P par_{\alpha_1,..,\alpha_n} P \, \| \, \{P\} \, \| \, Z$$

where P is a policy, $\alpha(\boldsymbol{x})$ is a system call, $p(\boldsymbol{x})$ is a predicate, $\boldsymbol{x}$ are variables and Z is a constant process definition $Z \doteq P$. The informal semantics is the following:

- $\perp$ is the *deny-All* operator;
- $\top$ is the *allow-All* operator;
- $\alpha(\boldsymbol{x}).P$ is the *sequential operator*, and represents the possibility of performing a system call $\alpha(\boldsymbol{x})$ and then behave as P;
- $p(\boldsymbol{x}).P$ behaves as P in the case the predicate $p(\boldsymbol{x})$ is true;
- $\boldsymbol{x} := \boldsymbol{e}.P$ assigns to variables $\boldsymbol{x}$ the values of the expressions $\boldsymbol{e}$ and then behaves as P;
- $P_1 or P_2$ is the *alternative operator*, and represents the non deterministic choice between P_1 and P_2;
- $P_1 par_{\alpha_1,...,\alpha_n} P_2$ is the *synchronous parallel operator*. It expresses that both P_1 and P_2 policies must be simultaneously satisfied. This is used when the two policies deal with common system calls (in $\alpha_1, \ldots, \alpha_n$);
- $\{P\}$ is the *atomic evaluation*, and represents the fact that P is evaluated in an atomic manner, by allowing at the same time testing and writing of variables. Here P may contain only predicates, assignments and at most one system call;
- Z is the constant process. We assume that there is a specification for the process $Z \doteq P$ and Z behaves as P.

Other derived operators may be considered. For instance, $P_1 par P_2$ is the *parallel operator*, and represents the interleaved execution of P_1 and P_2. It is used when the policies P_1 and P_2 deal with disjoint system calls. The policy sequence operator $P_1; P_2$ may be implemented using the policy languages operators (and control variables) (e.g., see [28]). It allows to put two process behaviors in sequence. By using the constant definition, the iteration and replication operators, i(P) and r(P) resp., can be easily derived. Informally, i(P) behaves as the continuous iteration of P. It can be modeled in our framework by defining a constant $Z \doteq P; Z$. Thus i(P) is Z. Similarly, the replication is the parallel composition of the same process an unbounded number of times. It can be modeled in our framework by defining a constant $Z \doteq P par Z$. Thus r(P) is Z.

As an example, given that α and β represent system calls and p and q are predicates, the following rule:

$$\mathrm{p}(\boldsymbol{x}).\alpha(\boldsymbol{x}).\mathrm{q}(\boldsymbol{y}).\beta(\boldsymbol{y})$$

describes a behaviour that includes the system call α, whose parameters $\boldsymbol{x}$ enjoy the conditions represented by the predicate p, followed by the system call β, whose parameters $\boldsymbol{y}$ enjoy the conditions represented by the predicate q. Hence, this rule defines an ordering among the system calls represented by α and β, because β can be executed only after α. The predicate p specifies the controls to be performed on the parameters and on the results of α, through conditions on $\boldsymbol{x}$, as shown in the next example. However, the predicate q could also include conditions on $\boldsymbol{x}$ to test the result of α. For the sake of simplicity, we omit the deny-All operator at the end of each policy. The following example shows in more details a simple policy:

[(x_1 = ''/tmp/*''), (of < 9)].open(x_1, x_2, x_3, x_4)

This policy allows the execution of the **open** system call if the first parameter x_1, i.e. the file name, is equal to /tmp/*. As usual, the symbol * represents any string. The other condition in the predicate, (of < 9), concerns the execution state and says that the **open** system call can be performed only if the number of files currently opened by this application, represented by the variable of, is smaller than 9. Hence, this policy initially grants to the application the right to open any file in the /tmp directory. However, this right is revoked when 8 files are currently opened by the application.

Many different execution patterns may be described with this language. For instance, if we wish that the system call d is performed only after that a, b and c have been performed (in any order) we may define the following policy:

(a par b par c); d

The difference between the synchronous parallel composition and the asynchronous one may be exemplified as follows. The admissible traces of the policy

(a par b)

are a,b,ab and ba. So the admissible traces of

(a par a)

are a and aa. Instead, the admissible traces of

(a par$_a$ a)

is simply a, since the two parallel as must synchronize.

Orchestrating several policies. Our language, through its usage of predicates, allows actually also the possibility to invoke at a given time, different kind of policies. Predicates could also include properties that concern the evaluation of factors that do not involve only system calls and their parameters. The exploitation of external factors provides a flexible way to evaluate distinct kinds of conditions, i.e. to integrate other policies with the behavioral one. For example, the policy could include properties that involve the evaluation of the set of credentials (e.g., X.509 digital certificates) submitted by the user, as described in [35]. The definition of an integrated framework for the specification and analysis for security and trust in complex and dynamic scenarios was introduced in [39], where a similar language of our policy one has been shown to be useful to model also trust and reputation parameters, through a clever usage of logical rules (added to the main policy language). Such a capability of integrating different policies and different aspects of resource usage is a key feature of our approach and is particularly exploited in grid systems, where heterogeneous resources should be collected and managed in a uniform way.

An example. A simple example of security policy is shown in Figure 7. In this example, AF_INET, STREAM, TCP, AH, CF and READ are constants. CF is a file name, while AH is an host name. The variable `cr` indicates whether the critical file CF has been opened, and it is initialized with false. The policy from line 2 to line 7 describes the behaviour of an application that communicates with remote hosts through TCP client sockets. The first system call is the `socket` one (line 2), preceded by a predicate that allows to open TCP sockets only. In the `socket` case, the first three parameters, x_1, x_2, x_3, are the input one, while the forth, sd, represents the output. When the call is executed, the value of the socket descriptor that is returned is stored in sd. The second system call is the `connect` one (line 3), that connects the socket descriptor stored in sd with the host represented by the constant AH. Obviously, AH could also represent a set of host names. Then, the rule allows to send or to receive messages on the previously connected TCP socket. As a matter of fact, two system calls, `send`

---

cr := false.	line 1
(([(x_1=AF_INET),(x_2=STREAM),(x_3=TCP)].socket(x_1,x_2,x_3,sd).	line 2
[(x_5=sd),(x_6=AH)].connect(x_5, x_6, x_7, x_8).	line 3
i({[(x_9=sd),(cr=false)].send(x_9, x_{10}, x_{11}, x_{12}, x_{13})}	line 4
or	line 5
[(x_{14}=sd)].recv(x_{14}, x_{15}, x_{16}, x_{17}, x_{18}));	line 6
[(x_{20}=sd)].close(x_{20},x_{21}))	line 7
par	line 8
({[(x_{22}=CF),(x_{23}=READ)].open(x_{22},x_{23},x_{24},fd).cr:=true}.	line 9
i([(x_{26}=fd)].read(x_{26}, x_{27}, x_{28}, x_{29}));	line 10
[(x_{30}=fd)].close(x_{30}, x_{31})))	line 11

Fig. 7. Security policy

and `recv`, composed through the `or` operator, are included within the iterative operator. However, the `send` system call in line 4 is preceded by a predicate that includes the condition (`cr = false`), to check whether the value of the variable `cr` is equal to false. The value of `cr` is initialised to false in line 1, and is set to true in line 9 when the critical file has been opened. Hence, this simple policy states that, when the application starts, the right to send information to the remote host AH using TCP sockets is granted by default, but this right is revoked during its execution as soon as the application opens the critical file CF in read mode. The opening of CF in write mode, instead, is denied by this policy, because it is not explicitly allowed.

4.2   Architecture

The architecture of our system mainly consists of two components, the *Application Monitor* (AM), and the *Policy Decision Point* (PDP), that have been integrated in the Java runtime architecture, as described in Figure 8.

AM is the component that monitors the behaviour of the application, by intercepting the security relevant actions that the application tries to perform on the system resources. Since the JVM is a virtual machine, it mediates all the interactions between the application and the resource. The application interacts with the JVM only, the JVM translates the bytecode into invocations to operating system libraries functions and performs them on the system resources. Hence, in our approach, the security relevant actions are represented by the system calls that are executed by the JVM on the operating system to access the system resources. For example, the implementation of the `java.io.FileInputStream` Java core class, that accesses a file on the file system, exploits the operating system library function `open`. To intercept the system call invocations, the system libraries wrapping approach has been exploited (see Section 3.2), and the operating system libraries that implement the system calls that provide access to the system resource have been wrapped by the AM. With reference to the previous example, the invocation to the `open` operating system library function is wrapped by the AM. Hence, AM consists of a set of wrapper functions that are executed when the JVM invokes the corresponding functions of the system libraries. To substitute the invocations to the original system libraries functions with the wrapper ones, the JVM has been recompiled, as detailed in the implementation details section.

An exception is represented by the Java Native Interface (JNI). As a matter of fact, JNI allows the application to execute arbitrary code (not developed in Java) without the JVM mediation. The main aim of JNI is the execution of legacy code that exploit some specific features of the underlying system. Since the legacy code is not portable, we always deny the use of JNI.

AM mainly executes three steps. First, it invokes the PDP to perform the policy check on the current action with the current parameters. Second, if the result returned by the PDP is positive, i.e. the execution of the system call is allowed by the security policy, then the system call is executed. Third, the PDP is invoked again. The PDP invocation after the system call execution is aimed

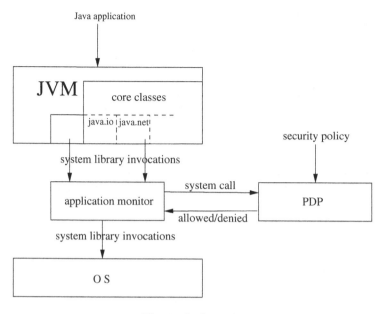

Fig. 8. Architecture

at controlling the value of the result returned by the system call, or the values of fields that could have been modified by the system call execution (e.g. the system call parameters), because the security policy could define controls on these values too. For example, in case of an `accept` system call, the control after the execution can check the address of the remote host that has been connected with the local server socket. As a matter of fact, this value is available only after that the system call has been executed. If the result of the second PDP check is positive too, the execution of the application is resumed. Otherwise, an error can be returned to the application, or the application can be stopped.

The PDP is the component that, given an action, decides whether the policy allows it or not in the current state. In this case, actions are represented by system calls, but the same PDP can be applied to other kind of actions. As a matter of fact, the main difference when enforcing policies that adopts a different kind of actions, is in the AM, that performs the task of detecting the actions. To determine whether, at a given time of the execution of the application, a system call matches the permitted behaviour, both the security policy and the system calls that have been previously executed by the application, i.e. the history of the application, have to be considered. Hence, the PDP stores also information about the state of the execution.

4.3   Implementation Details

Our prototype has been implemented on a machine running the Linux operating system, and exploiting the IBM jikes Research Java Virtual Machine, RVM,

[1], that is a research oriented and open source Java Virtual Machine, and that follows both the *Java Language Specification* [33] and the *Java Virtual Machine Specification* [37].

The implementation of the application monitor involves the wrapping of the invocations to the operating system libraries functions that execute the system calls in the Jikes RVM source code. This has been implemented by exploiting a feature of the gcc compiler [21] that tells the linker to substitute the references to a given function with another function. The new function is invoked every time that the original one is invoked in the source code. However, the original function can be invoked in the new function exploiting a special name for it. Hence, no modifications to the original JVM source code are required to wrap the system libraries invocation. The only modifications that have been done are on the configuration files (Makefiles) that describe the compilation parameters of the JVM sources to change the gcc invocation parameters. Moreover, a new source file including the implementation of the wrapper functions has been added to the JVM source code. The system library functions that have been wrapped represent a subset of those offered by the system libraries, and are the ones that access the system resources we are interested to monitor, such as files or sockets. Moreover, not all the functions that access a given resource have been wrapped, but only the ones that are exploited in the JVM source code.

The PDP runs in a POSIX thread that is created by the JVM during its initialisation, before starting the execution of the bytecode. This required a modification to the JVM source code to insert the command that creates the PDP thread. After its initialisation, where the PDP reads the policy from a file and builds the data structures to represent it, the PDP suspends itself on a semaphore. The PDP is reactivated by the application monitor thought the semaphore each time the JVM executes a system call for the Java application. The communication between the application monitor, that runs in the JVM thread, and the PDP, that runs in its own thread, has been implemented through shared variables.

5 Use Cases

This section presents two scenarios in which the history based access control system for Java described in the previous section has been adopted: the Computational Services shared in the Grid environment and the execution of Java applications on mobile devices, such as mobile phones or Personal Digital Assistants (PDAs).

5.1 Grid Computing

Grid computing technology is aimed at the definition of a very large cooperation environment, where a dynamic set of participants both provide services to other participants, and exploit service provided by other participants. The grid environment can be successfully exploited for the execution of computational or data intensive applications, such as very large scale simulations (e.g. earthquake simulation [47]) or image analysis (e.g. astronomy or climate study). The design of this environment introduces some problems, such as coordination, integration, interoperability and also security [19] [20]. Alternative toolkits have been implemented for the deployment of grid environments, such as Gridbus [4], Legion [8], Globus [17] [18], and others. In the following, we refer to Globus, that is a widely used one.

Security is a challenging issue in the grid environment. As a matter of fact, this environment supports the collaboration among a very large and dynamic set of entities, where no trust relationships may exist a priori and where one could be interested in monitoring the appropriate usage of these relationships. [29] and [41] describe the security requirements of the grid environment, such as authentication, delegation, authorisation, privacy, message confidentiality and integrity, trust, policy and access control enforcement. Access control enforcement concerns the enforcement on the local resource of a security policy that controls the interactions between the applications executed on behalf of the grid users and the local resource itself. This is necessary to detect attacks that try to circumvent the other security mechanisms, such as the authentication one.

Computational Services. Various services can be shared on the grid, such as: storage services, data base services, computational services and others. Computational services provide computational resources where the grid participants can execute their applications. Hence, computational service providers allow the execution on their local resources of unknown applications on behalf of unknown grid users. From the resource provider point of view, the execution of an untrusted application represents a threat for the integrity of his local resource. The platform independence of Java language addresses the interoperability problem of the grid environment, due to the high heterogeneity of the resources shared in this environment. Hence, Java language is suitable to develop applications to be executed on the grid.

The approach we proposed in [3] and [40] improves the security of the Globus computational service by integrating into the Globus security architecture the history based access control system described in Section 4. This component enforces a fine grain security policy that consists in an highly detailed description of the correct behaviour of the applications executed on computational service.

The current implementation of Globus does not perform this kind of controls. It provides a coarse grained access control to the resource. As a matter of fact, once Globus has authenticated a grid user, this user is mapped onto a local account according to the settings in the gridmap file, and the security policy that is enforced is only the one defined by the privileges paired with this account by the operating system. Alternative proposals, described in [34], [49], [6] and [7] address this issue by integrating well known authorization systems, such as Akenti or PERMIS, within the Globus toolkit.

Integration with Globus. The Globus architecture implements the sharing of computational resources through the Globus Resource Allocation Manager, GRAM, service [23], [54]. GRAM consists of two components: the Master Hosting

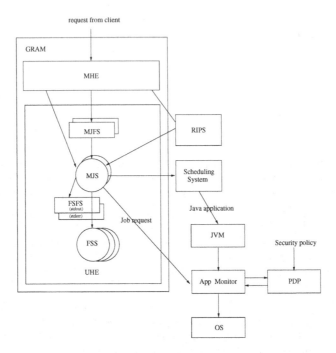

Fig. 9. Integration within Globus GRAM Architecture

Environment, MHE and the User Hosting Environment, UHE. The MHE is executed with the privilege of the "globus" user, and receives the request for the creation of a new instance of the computational service coming from a remote grid user. Then, Master Managed Job Factory Service, MMJFS, of the MHE checks the grid user certificate, authorises the request, maps the remote grid user in a local user through the gridmap file, and activates the UHE for the local user. The UHE runs with the privileges of the local user and, once activated, it does not terminate, but it waits for other requests from the same local account. Notice that the gridmap file can be configured in a way such that distinct grid users are mapped on the same local account. Once the UHE is activated, the MHE requests to the Master Job Factory Service, MJFS, that runs in the UHE the creation of a new instance of Managed Job Service, MJS, to manage the job request. The MJS reads the job request, translates and submits it to the local scheduling system, and monitors the job status.

Due to the high modularity of the Globus toolkit design, the integration of our security enhanced JVM was easy. As previously stated, our prototype implements a computational service devoted to the execution of Java jobs. To properly describe this kind of jobs in the job request, the RSL schema could was updated to include the "java" jobs as a new job type. The MJS, that manages the job requests, to execute java applications, invokes the JVM. This was easily implemented by updating the GRAM perl scripts that submits the application to the local scheduling system. Obviously, the invoked JVM is our security enhanced one. The PDP is activated by the JVM, and reads both the policy file and the job request to create the restricted environment for the execution of the application. As a matter of fact, the PDP extracts from the job request the limits to be applied to the resource usage. Since Java application is executed in the local user environment, the MJS, that is execute in this environment, has been modified to export the job request to the PDP. This modification is straightforward because the MJS Java implementation includes a proper class to manage the gram attributes of the job request. Obviously, the bytecode of the application has to be previously downloaded by the grid user on the computational resource by exploiting the grid ftp service.

This solution is described by Figure 9, that extends the GRAM architecture that is presented in [23].

5.2 Java on Mobile Devices

Nowadays mobile devices, such as mobile phones or Personal Digital Assistants (PDAs), are very widespread and most of the people are used to them. These modern mobile devices often have a considerable computational power, and they are able to execute Java applications, called MIDlets. To this aim, these devices are equipped with a customised version of the Java runtime environment: Java 2 Micro Edition (J2ME). The J2ME architecture mainly consists of three distinct layers, the Mobile Information Device Profile (MIDP, JSR 118) [30], the Connection Limited Device Configuration (CLDC, JSR 139) [31] and the Kilo Virtual Machine (KVM), as described in Figure 10.

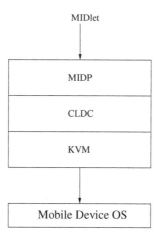

Fig. 10. Java 2 Micro Edition runtime environment

This architecture can be integrated by a set of optional packages aimed at implementing specific functionality. For example, the Wireless Messaging API (WMA, JSR 120, JSR 205) [26] [27] is an optional package to manage wireless communication resources, like Short Message Service (SMS) or Cell Broadcast Service (CBS).

In this context, security is very important, because MIDlets are downloaded from remote sites and executed on mobile devices. The MIDlets could include even malicious code, that could harm the device, or that could use device resources to execute actions that the user does not want, such as creating network connections and transferring the address book to a remote party, sending sms messages to the contacts in the address book, and so on.

The standard security mechanisms provided by J2ME are not very flexible, because allow to define a static set of permissions that depends only on the MIDlet source. Moreover, since complex conditions cannot be defined with the standard security support, when writing the security policy one typically decide to prompt the mobile device user every time that the condition that determines the right to perform the current action cannot be expressed.

J2ME Security. Each layer of J2ME implements its own security mechanisms. The security support provided by CLDC concerns the low level and the application level security. In particular, to execute the MIDlet, the CLDC adopts a sandbox model, that requires that: the MIDlet must be preverified to ensure that is a valid java class; the MIDlet cannot bypass or alter standard class loading mechanisms of the KVM; only a predefined set of APIs are available to the MIDlet; the MIDlet can only load classes from the archive it comes from (Jar file); the classes of the system packages cannot be overridden or modified.

The MIDP, [25], instead, defines a set of protection domains, and pairs with each of these domains a set of permissions. A protection domain is assigned to a MIDlet depending on the provider of the MIDlet itself. In particular, each MIDlet can be signed by a principal, and the Certification Authority that issued the certificate of this principal determines the protection domain of the MIDlet. The standard protection domains that are defined in MIDP 2.0 are: *1) Manufacturer; 2) Operator; 3) Identified Third Parthy; 4) Unidentified Third Parthy*. If the MIDlet is not signed, than is assigned to the Unidentified Third Party protection domain. The permissions refer to the operations that the MIDlet can perform during its execution. For example, if the MIDlet uses http protocol to interact with a remote server, this MIDlet must have the permission to open http connection, i.e. `javax.microedition.io.Connector.http`.

Further permissions are added to the standard ones when optional packages are installed. For example, the Wireless Messaging API introduces the following permissions that refers to Short Message Service and Cell Broadcast Service, such as `javax.microedition.io.Connector.sms` or `javax.wireless.messaging.sms.send`.

Integration with J2ME. In this use case, the history based access control system has been integrated in the J2ME runtime architecture. As a matter of fact, as described in the previous section, the standard security support of J2ME defines static permission, i.e. it does not take into account the state of the computation. Hence, the security support will grant to the MIDlet the same permission every time that the MIDlet perform the same action during its execution. Instead, to enhance the security of the device that executes the MIDlets, a user could be interested in defining security policies where the right of a MIDlet to execute a given action depends on the actions that the MIDlet has previously executed. For example, a policy could state that a MIDlet can send only two sms messages to the same telephone number. In this case, the right of the MIDlet to send a sms to a given telephone number depends on the state of the computation, in particular depends on whether the MIDlet has already sent other two sms messages to the same telephone number.

The solution adopted to embed the application monitor in the J2ME architecture follows the approach described in 3.2. In particular, the system library that has been exploited is the one that implements the MIDP permission support. This solution requires the modification of the Security Token[1], that is a light version of the security manager that manages MIDP permissions, to insert the code that implements the application monitor. The advantage of this solution is that the Security Token is invoked every time that an action paired with a MIDP permission is executed, hence the application monitor is always invoked when a security relevant action is executed. The limitation imposed by this solution, instead, is that this approach defines as security relevant actions the ones that are also paired with a MIDP permission, and is not possible to monitor other actions. The standard controls executed by the Security Token can be left in place or can be disabled.

The Sun Simulation Environment. To ease the development and the test of J2ME applications, several simulation environments are currently available. These simulators reproduce on a desktop computer, a platform that supports CLCD and MIDP, where is possible to develop and run applications using J2ME. In particular, the development of an J2ME application consists of the following steps. First, the java application is written using the API of CLDC and MIDP. Then, the application is compiled exploiting the java compiler (javac) of a Java Standard Edition (J2SE) installation. Then, the resulting bytecode is verified through the preverifier tool provided by the MIDP package. Finally, the resulting code can be run in the simulation environment.

The Sun's web site [48] allows the downloading of a full simulation environment for Desktop computers; in particular, currently it provides both the MIDP v2.0 and the CLDC 1.1 Reference Implementations. Moreover, the implementation of other optional packages is available too, such as the Wireless Messaging API (WMA) and others.

The implementation of the application monitor involves the modification of the MIDP code that implements the Security Token to insert the code that invokes the PDP as described in Figure 11.

As described in 4.3, in this case too, the PDP runs in a POSIX thread that is created by the KVM during its initialization, before starting the execution of the MIDlet bytecode. The PDP thread creation code has been inserted in the KVM

---

[1] We refer to Sun MIDP and CLDC Reference Implementation.

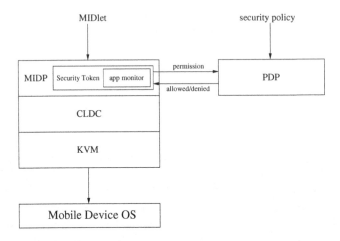

Fig. 11. Integration within the Java 2 Micro Edition runtime environment

source file. The Security Token, instead, is a Java class in the MIDP package. The application monitor is simply an invocation to a Java class that has been inserted in the Security Token source code before the execution of the permission evaluation. This class, in turn, through the Kilo Native Interface (KNI), invokes the PDP to evaluate the security policy. If the result returned by the PDP is "denied", then the application monitor throws a Security Exception, that will be managed by the application.

6 Conclusions

This paper presented a history based access control system that has been integrated within the Java runtime architecture to enhance the security when executing Java applications. This access control system enhances the security of the resource executing Java application, and can be adopted in distributed environments, where third party unknown applications are executed on the computational resource. To validate our approach, the paper describes the adoption of the proposed access control system in two common scenarios where Java is adopted: grid computing and mobile devices.

References

1. Alpern, B., Attanasio, C.R., Barton, J.J., et al.: The jalapeño virtual machine. IBM System Journal 39(1) (2000)
2. Anderson, A.: Java access control mechanisms. Technical report, Sun Microsystems (2002)
3. Baiardi, F., Martinelli, F., Mori, P., Vaccarelli, A.: Improving grid service security with fine grain policies. In: Meersman, R., Tari, Z., Corsaro, A. (eds.) On the Move to Meaningful Internet Systems 2004: OTM 2004 Workshops. LNCS, vol. 3292, pp. 123–134. Springer, Heidelberg (2004)

4. Baker, M., Buyya, R., Laforenza, D.: Grids and grid technologies for wide-area distributed computing. International Journal of Software: Practice and Experience 32(15), 1437–1466 (2002)

5. Bauer, L., Ligatti, J., Walker, D.: Composing security policies with polymer. In: PLDI '05: Proceedings of the 2005 ACM SIGPLAN conference on Programming language design and implementation, pp. 305–314. ACM Press, New York (2005)

6. Chadwick, D.W., Otenko, O.: The permis x.509 role based privilege management infrastructure. In: Proceedings of the 7th ACM symposium on Access control models and technologies (SACMAT 02), pp. 135–140. ACM Press, New York (2002)

7. Chadwick, D.W., Otenko, S., Welch, V.: Using SAML to Link the GLOBUS Toolkit to the PERMIS Authorisation Infrastructure. In: Proceedings of Eighth Annual IFIP TC-6 TC-11 Conference on Communications and Multimedia Security (September 2004)

8. Chapin, S.J., Katramatos, D., Karpovich, J., Grimshaw, A.: Resource management in Legion. Future Generation Computer Systems 15(5-6), 583–594 (1999)

9. Ciaschini, V., Gorrieri, R.: Contrasting malicious java applets by modifying the java virtual machine. In: 19th Int.l Information Security Conference (SEC'04), pp. 47–64. Kluwer, Dordrecht (2004)

10. Colby, C., Lee, P., Necula, G.C., Blau, F., Plesko, M., Cline, K.: A certifying compiler for Java. ACM SIGPLAN Notices 35(5), 95–107 (2000)

11. Damianou, N., Dulay, N., Lupu, E., Sloan, M.: The ponder policy specification language. In: Sloman, M., Lobo, J., Lupu, E.C. (eds.) POLICY 2001. LNCS, vol. 1995, pp. 18–39. Springer, Heidelberg (2001)

12. Eckmann, S., Vigna, G., Kemmerer, R.: Statl: An attack language for state-based intrusion detection. Journal of Computer Security 10(1/2), 71–104 (2002)

13. Erlingsson, U.: The inlined reference monitor approach to security policy enforcement. PhD thesis, Cornell University, Adviser-Fred B. Schneider (2004)

14. Erlingsson, U., Schneider, F.B.: IRM enforcement of Java stack inspection. In: IEEE Symposium on Security and Privacy, pp. 246–255 (2000)

15. Erlingsson, U., Schneider, F.B.: SASI enforcement of security policies: A retrospective. In: WNSP: New Security Paradigms Workshop, ACM Press, New York (2000)

16. Evans, D., Twyman, A.: Flexible policy-directed code safety. In: IEEE Symposium on Security and Privacy, pp. 32–45 (1999)

17. Foster, I.: Globus toolkit version 4: Software for service-oriented systems. In: Jin, H., Reed, D., Jiang, W. (eds.) NPC 2005. LNCS, vol. 3779, pp. 2–13. Springer, Heidelberg (2005)

18. Foster, I., Kesselman, C.: The globus project: A status report. In: Proceedings of IPPS/SPDP '98 Heterogeneous Computing Workshop, pp. 4–18 (1998)

19. Foster, I., Kesselman, C., Nick, J.M., Tuecke, S.: The physiology of the grid: An open grid service architecture for distributed system integration. Globus Project (2002), http://www.globus.org/research/papers/ogsa.pdf

20. Foster, I., Kesselman, C., Tuecke, S.: The anatomy of the grid: Enabling scalable virtual organizations. International Journal of Supercomputer Applications 15(3), 200–222 (2001)

21. GCC: the GNU compiler collection, http://gcc.gnu.org/

22. Gong, L.: Inside Java2 Platform Security, 2nd edn. Addison-Wesley, Reading (1999)

23. Globus GRAM architecture,
http://www-unix.globus.org/developer/gram-architecture.html

24. Grimm, R., Bershad, B.N.: Separating access control policy, enforcement, and functionality in extensible systems. ACM Transactions on Computer Systems 19(1), 36–70 (2001)
25. JSR 118 Expert Group: Security for GSM/UMTS compliant devices recommended practice. addendum to the mobile information device profile. Technical report, Java Community Process (November 2002),
    http://www.jcp.org/aboutJava/communityprocess/maintenance/jsr118/
26. JSR 120 Expert Group: Wireless messaging api (wma) for Java 2 micro edition. Technical Report JSR 120, Java Community Process (2003),
    http://jcp.org/aboutJava/communityprocess/final/jsr120/
27. JSR 205 Expert Group: Wireless messaging api 2.0 (wma) for Java 2 micro edition. Technical Report JSR 205, Java Community Process (2004),
    http://jcp.org/aboutJava/communityprocess/final/jsr205/
28. Hoare, C.A.R.: Communicating sequential processes. Commun. ACM 21(8), 666–677 (1978)
29. Humphrey, M., Thompson, M.R., Jackson, K.R.: Security for grids. Proceedings of the IEEE 93(3), 644–652 (2005)
30. Sun Microsystems Inc. Mobile Information Device Profile for Java 2 micro edition. Technical Report JSR 118, Java Community Process (November 2002),
    http://jcp.org/aboutJava/communityprocess/final/jsr118/index.html
31. Sun Microsystems Inc. The Connected Limited Device Configuration specification. Technical Report JSR 139, Java Community Process (March 2003),
    http://jcp.org/aboutJava/communityprocess/final/jsr139/
32. Jajodia, S., Samarati, P., Subrahmanian, V.S.: A logical language for expressing authorizations. In: Proceedings of the 1997 IEEE Symposium on Security and Privacy, pp. 31–42. IEEE Press, Los Alamitos (1997)
33. Gosling, J., Joy, B., Steele, G., Bracha, G.: The Java Language Specification. Sun Microsystems (2000)
34. Keahey, K., Welch, V.: Fine-grain authorization for resource management in the grid environment. In: Parashar, M. (ed.) GRID 2002. LNCS, vol. 2536, pp. 199–206. Springer, Heidelberg (2002)
35. Koshutanski, H., Martinelli, F., Mori, P., Vaccarelli, A.: Fine-grained and history-based access control with trust management for autonomic grid services. In: Proceedings of the 2nd International Conference on Autonomic and Autonomous Systems (ICAS'06), IEEE Computer Society, Los Alamitos (2006)
36. Ligatti, J., Bauer, L., Walker, D.: Edit automata: Enforcement mechanisms for run-time security policies. International Journal of Information Security 4(1-2), 2–16 (2005)
37. Lindholm, T., Yellin, F.: The Java Virtual Machine Specification. Sun Microsystems (1999)
38. Martinelli, F.: Analysis of security protocols as open systems. Journal of Computer Security 290(1), 1057–1106 (2003)
39. Martinelli, F.: Towards an integrated formal analysis for security and trust. In: Steffen, M., Zavattaro, G. (eds.) FMOODS 2005. LNCS, vol. 3535, pp. 115–130. Springer, Heidelberg (2005)
40. Martinelli, F., Mori, P., Vaccarelli, A.: Towards continuous usage control on grid computational services. In: Proceedings of Joint International Conference on Autonomic and Autonomous Systems and International Conference on Networking and Services (ICAS-ICNS 2005), p. 82. IEEE Computer Society, Los Alamitos (2005)

41. Nagaratnam, N., Janson, P., Dayka, J., Nadalin, A., Siebenlist, F., Welch, V., Foster, I., Tuecke, S.: Security architecture for open grid services. In: GGF OGSA Security Working Group (2003)
42. Necula, G.C.: Proof-carrying code. In: Conference Record of POPL '97: The 24th ACM SIGPLAN-SIGACT Symposium on Principles of Programming Languages, pp. 106–119 (1997)
43. Necula, G.C., Lee, P.: The design and implementation of a certifying compiler. In: Proceedings of the 1998 ACM SIGPLAN Conference on Prgramming Language Design and Implementation (PLDI), pp. 333–344 (1998)
44. Pandey, R., Hashii, B.: Providing fine-grained access control for Java programs via binary editing. Concurrency: Practice and Experience 12(14), 1405–1430 (2000)
45. Ryan, P., Schneider, S., Goldsmith, M., Lowe, G.: The modelling and analysis of security protocols: the CSP approach. Addison-Wesley, Reading (2000)
46. Soman, S., Krintz, C., Vigna, G.: Detecting malicious java code using virtual machine auditing. In: 12th USENIX Security Symposium (2003)
47. Spencer, B., Finholt, T.A., Foster, I., Kesselman, C., Beldica, C., Futrelle, J., Gullapalli, S., Hubbard, P., Liming, L., Marcusiu, D., Pearlman, L., Severance, C., Yang, G.: Neesgrid: A distributed collaboratory for advanced earthquake engineering experiment and simulation. In: 13th World Conference on Earthquake Engineering (2004)
48. http://java.sun.com/javame/downloads/index.jsp
49. Thompson, M.R., Essiari, A., Keahey, K., Welch, V., Lang, S., Liu, B.: Fine-grained authorization for job and resource management using akenti and the globus toolkit. In: Proceedings of Computing in High Energy and Nuclear Physics (2003)
50. Vigna, G., Eckmann, S., Kemmerer, R.: The stat tool suite. In: DISCEX 2000, Hilton Head, South Carolina, IEEE Computer Society Press, Los Alamitos (2000)
51. Wallach, D.S.: A New Approach to Mobile Code Security. PhD thesis, Princeton University, New Jersey (1999)
52. Wallach, D.S., Balfanz, D., Dean, D., Felten, E.W.: Extensible security architectures for Java. In: 16th Symposium on Operating Systems Principles, pp. 116–128 (1997)
53. Wallach, D.S., Felten, E.W.: Undestanding java stack inspection. In: IEEE Symposium on Security and Privacy, IEEE Computer Society, Los Alamitos (1998)
54. Welch, V., Siebenlist, F., Foster, I., Bresnahan, J., Czajkowski, K., Gawor, J., Kesselman, C., Meder, S., Pearlman, L., Tuecke, S.: Security for grid services. In: 12th IEEE International Symp. on High Performance Distributed Computing (2003)

On the Protection and Technologies of Critical Information Infrastructures

Javier Lopez, Cristina Alcaraz, and Rodrigo Roman

Computer Science Department
University of Malaga, Spain
{jlm, alcaraz, roman}@lcc.uma.es

Abstract. Critical Infrastructures are complex and highly interconnected systems that are crucial for the well-being of the society. Any type of failure can cause significant damage, affecting one or more sectors due to their inherent interdependency. Not only the infrastructures are critical, but also the information infrastructures that manage, control and supervise them. Due to the seriousness of the consequences, the protection of these critical (information) infrastructures must have the highest priority. It is the purpose of this book chapter to review and discuss about these infrastructures, to explain their elements, and to highlight their research and development issues. This chapter will also discuss the role of Wireless Sensor Network (WSN) technology in the protection of these infrastructures.

1 Introduction

The well-being of the national and international economy, security and quality of life, is becoming increasingly dependent on the safety and the robustness of *Critical Infrastructures* (CI), such as energy, banking, transport, and others. These infrastructures are extremely complex, since they are composed of both physical facilities and highly interconnected national (and international) software-based control systems. These information systems can also be considered critical by themselves, and are commonly called *Critical Information Infrastructures* (CII). Not only the internal elements of critical (information) infrastructures are highly interconnected with each other, but also the infrastructures themselves need other infrastructures in order to function properly.

The notion of criticality in the context of infrastructures is intertwined with the nature of the threats that affect those infrastructures and the possible effects of a single failure. In fact, due to their complexity and their existing interdependences, infrastructures are affected by a diverse number of security risks and vulnerabilities. Such vulnerabilities can be exploited both locally and remotely by a wide range of attackers, like terrorists and malicious/negligent insiders. Lastly, because of those interdependences, any kind of accidental or provoked failure can cascade through and between infrastructures, with unpredictable and extremely damaging consequences.

A. Aldini and R. Gorrieri (Eds.): FOSAD 2006/2007, LNCS 4677, pp. 160–182, 2007.
© Springer-Verlag Berlin Heidelberg 2007

Protecting CII is an extremely complex task. It is necessary to have clear what the exact meaning of 'infrastructure' is, and what (and why) are the exact sectors that should be considered critical. It is also essential to consider which the differences between CI and CII are in order to effectively discover their specific threats and vulnerabilities. Then it becomes possible to identify who are the different actor groups that need to participate in the protection processes, and what are the challenges that these groups need to overcome in order to adequately protect the infrastructures.

The purpose of this book chapter is to discuss on the previous topics, thus allowing the reader to have a clear understanding of the importance of the protection of critical infrastructures and the existing challenges. The chapter will be mainly focused on CII and will include a discussion on the most important electronic control systems, as well as an introduction to one of its underlying technologies, *wireless sensor networks* (WSN). Moreover, the chapter will provide an overview of the research projects that use such a technology as a foundation.

2 Critical Infrastructures

In order to fully understand what the term Critical Infrastructures refers to, it is necessary to have clear what an infrastructure exactly is. The dictionary definition of the word '*infrastructure*' is "the underlying foundation or basic framework" and "the resources (as personnel, buildings, or equipment) required for an activity" [1]. Such definition is obviously general, and can refer to a broad range of structural elements. Still, it suits to the infrastructures on which we want to focus: civil infrastructures, i.e. the infrastructures that are integral to the social, political, and economic life of a nation. Examples of those infrastructures can be mass transit infrastructures and water treatment systems.

These infrastructure systems have grown in complexity during the course of history: from very simple structures to pervasive, complex, and varied systems. An example can be found in water supply and treatment systems. In ancient towns, citizens had to walk directly to the sources of water, such as rivers or wells. Cities started to grow, and it was necessary to create structures like aqueducts which would carry the water straight from the source. These simple constructions finally evolved into intricate systems that not only transport the water, but also are in charge of treating both the natural water and the wastewater.

The underlying elements of present-day infrastructures are deeply interconnected, and they depend heavily from each other. There are three major elements in an infrastructure: Administration, Physical, and Information System. Administration includes the human aspects (both decision-makers and workforce), and economic, regulatory, and organizational aspects. Physical corresponds to the material aspect of the resource supply system. Finally, the Information System corresponds to the underlying Information and Communications Technologies (such as SCADA, Distributed Control Systems, and others) that manage the infrastructure.

The infrastructures themselves are not the only thing that has evolved over time. During the last 20 years, the actual definition of the word infrastructure in policy terms has evolved as well. Many sectors have been included or excluded from being public infrastructure depending on the definition used at that time. A possible reason is their inherent heterogeneity: each sector is different historically and technically, as well as in their professional practices, financing problems, and public attitudes towards them [2].

Nowadays, the concept of infrastructure in policy terms is more or less stable. In the EU, an Infrastructure is considered as a "framework of (inter)dependent networks and systems comprising identifiable industries, institutions (including people and procedures), and/or distribution capabilities that provide a reliable flow of products, supplies and/or services, for the smooth functioning of governments at all levels, the economy, the society as a whole, and of other infrastructures" [3]. Note that a comprehension of infrastructure may span also their operating procedures, management practices, and development policies [2].

Once the concept of infrastructure is clear, it is possible to apply the concept of critical in this specific context. The word 'critical' can be seen as the combination of two words: *important* ("marked by or indicative of significant worth or consequence") and *indispensable* ("not subject to being set aside or neglected") [4]. As a consequence, formally speaking, an infrastructure can be considered critical if it has a strong influence over its environment, so strong that if it is not available for a period of time the possible effects are not negligible.

Moving on to the definition of Critical Infrastructures, we realize that such definition is no unique. According to the European Commission, Critical Infrastructures consist of "those physical and information technology facilities, networks, services and assets which, if disrupted or destroyed, would have a serious impact on the health, safety, security or economic well-being of citizens or the effective functioning of governments in the Member States" [5]. On the other hand, the United States consider Critical Infrastructures as "those systems and assets, whether physical or virtual, so vital to the United States that the incapacity or destruction of such systems and assets would have a debilitating impact on security, national economic security, national public health or safety, or any combination of those matters" [6].

Regardless of their definition, most CI share four key properties: interdependencies, private ownership, ICT dependence, and global boundaries [7].

- Exhibit strong and mutual dependences. A failure in one single infrastructure will cascade and affect others. Due to the inherent complexity of the infrastructures and their relationships, it is extremely difficult to anticipate the scope of such interdependences.
- Mostly (but not only) owned and operated by the private sector due to privatization processes. Note that the private sector is not the only actor group that has influence over these infrastructures (cf. Section 4.1).
- Becoming increasingly dependent on Information Systems, since they basically depend on highly interconnected national (and even international) electronic control systems for their smooth, reliable, and continuous operation.
- Becoming increasingly more international. This is a logical consequence of the increasing globalisation of commerce. As a result, it is not enough to simply develop a purely national methodology for protecting the critical infrastructures.

Differences among between countries can be observed not only in the definition of the term CI, but also in the definition of which are the critical sectors. The conceptualization of whether an infrastructure is critical or not depends on their strategic position within the whole system and the socio-political context, and it is also influenced by specific geographical and historical preconditions. There are also two differing, but interrelated perceptions of criticality: Systemic and Symbolic [8]. In the systemic approach, an infrastructure is critical due to its structural position and its interdependences with other systems. On the other hand, in the symbolic approach the importance of an infrastructure mainly depends on its role or function in society.

The most frequently mentioned critical sectors in all countries are the following: Banking and Finance, Central Government / Government Services, Information and Communication Technologies, Emergency / Rescue Services, Energy / Electricity, Health Services, Transportation / Logistics, and Water management systems. Other important sectors are Food / Agriculture, Information Services / Media, Military Defence, Oil and Gas Supply, and Public Administration. Note, however, that it is broadly acknowledged that the focus on sectors is far too artificial to represent the realities of complex infrastructure systems, thus it is deemed necessary to evolve beyond the conventional "sector"-based focus and to look at the services, the physical and electronic (information) flows, their role and function for society, and especially the core values that are delivered by the infrastructures [9].

All these infrastructures are menaced by certain threats that may hinder their functionality or render them temporarily or permanently useless. Precisely, it is the existence and the possible consequences of these threats what drives the need of considering the criticality of an infrastructure. From a global perspective, threats can be organized into three distinct categories: natural threats (in the form of disasters such as floods, fires, and landslides), environmental threats (e.g. long-term power failure, pollution, infrastructure decay, and others), and human threats. Note that human threats, which are originated from human sources, can be accidental or intentional, and may come from inside or outside the infrastructure [10][11].

One of the key human threats against the security of infrastructures is terrorism. A large number of factors, like regional conflicts and the proliferation of Weapons of Mass Destruction, can fuel the existence of terrorist groups. Such groups can act worldwide, with dramatic consequences both in human and financial terms. Note that there are still other relevant human threats, like corporate espionage and malicious/negligent insiders [10]. Although the probability of the occurrence of these threats is different for a certain socio-economical context, any of the previously presented type of threats can be able to hinder the provisioning of the infrastructures' services, thus there is a need of quantifying the potential risk of any threat.

Not only the potential risk of existing threats is of importance, it is also significant to measure whether a certain infrastructure is more critical than others. For the EU, the selection criteria of what infrastructures are critical and their different degrees of criticality depends on the following three factors [5]:

- *Scope:* The loss of a critical infrastructure element is rated by the extent of the geographic area, which could be affected by its loss or unavailability.
- *Magnitude:* The degree of the impact or loss can be assessed according to the following criteria: public impact (population affected), economic (significance of economic loss, present and future), environmental (impact on the location), interdependency (between other critical infrastructures), and political (regarding the confidence on the government).
- *Time:* This criterion ascertains at what point the loss of an element could have a serious impact, and at what point it would be possible to recover the functionality of that element.

2.1 Dependencies and Interconnectivity

Generally speaking, a CI is based on a set of collaborative and adaptive components [12], with capability to learn of past experiences. These components communicate with each other in a certain context, and receive as inputs the outputs corresponding from other components. Moreover, a specific input could produce a certain effect on the state of a component. This way of establishing connexions between components can also be applied to the relationships between complex entities such as infrastructures. In other words, most infrastructures depend on other infrastructures. As explained before, this is one of the key properties of critical infrastructures.

Connectivity of infrastructures can be done through dependent or interdependent connections. When the relation between two infrastructures is individual and unidirectional, it is considered a simple dependency connection. This can be seen as a linkage between two points i, j, where i depends on j, but j does not depend on i, and any problem in j affects on i, but not on the contrary. However, in the real life the connections of infrastructures are much more complex. Every infrastructure is connected to other by means of bidirectional links (j depends on i, and i depends on j), known as interdependency connection. This relation implicates that any state of each infrastructure influences on the behaviour of other and vice versa, involving an inter-block between them.

There are four main types of interdependencies that are not mutually exclusive: physical, cyber, geographic, and logical. When an infrastructure depends on the material output (commodities or resources) of other, then the interdependency is *physical*. In this case, any change in the state of an infrastructure could affect upon the other. Other kind of interdependency is the *cyber*, which appeared with the pervasive computing and the need of automating the infrastructures. It is related to the information transmitted through the information infrastructure by means of electronic or communications lines. In this type of interdependency, the states of the next infrastructures will depend on the output of the current information infrastructure. For large systems, the operation is based on computerized or specialized systems, as for example *supervisory control and data acquisition systems* (SCADA). A *geographic* interdependency occurs when the infrastructures are spatially distributed and close to each other. This proximity could implicate devastating consequences if an unexpected event (fired or explosion) takes place in a determined point of the environmental. Finally, a *logical* interdependency consists of control mechanisms or regulations used to interlink components of different infrastructures without requiring of physical, cyber or geographic connections. Also the human decisions and actions may play an important role in the logic interdependency because any incorrect decision or action could involve serious problems in a system.

3   Critical Information Infrastructures

As previously noted, a CI is highly dependent on ICT because information systems are one of the three major components. The principal task of ICT is to manage, control and supervise the infrastructures, thus allowing their smooth, reliable and continuous operation. However, ICT can be considered as critical infrastructures themselves, because in most cases they are indispensable for the operation of the infrastructures [13]. Thus, the concept of CII arises.

For example, the power industry relies heavily on information technology to regulate power generation, optimize power production, and control demands and power distribution, amongst other things. Such monitoring is carried out by electronic control systems such as SCADA, which are also used to integrate electric companies into regional or national power grids for optimization and redundancy purposes. Another specific example is the Internet because it is used to manage essential services such as financial transactions, emergency community alerts, and military communications [14].

There is no exact definition of the term CII, probably because the information systems can be considered just as an essential part of CI. This is backed up by the definition given in the CI2RCO FP6 project, where CII are "Information processes supported by Information and Communication Technology (ICT) which form critical infrastructures for themselves or that are critical for the operation of other critical infrastructures" [3]. Nevertheless, even if CI and CII cannot and should not be discussed as completely separate concepts due to their interrelationship, it is necessary to distinguish them, at least in conceptual terms.

The need to separate both ideas primarily comes from the specific threats inherent to the information infrastructures, which are specialized in targeting its immaterial contents: the information that flows through the infrastructure, the knowledge that is created from such information, and the services that are provided. Those attacks can be launched simultaneously from anywhere by unknown actors, resulting on great damage not only to the logical infrastructure but to the physical infrastructure as well [15]. By separating CII from CI, it is possible to have a clear view of the challenges that the CII have to overcome and to be more precise in the development of programs and activities that pursue their overall protection.

Although nature and environmental threats are important to CII, most specialized attacks against these information infrastructures come from humans. A successful attack can disclose sensitive data from an infrastructure, falsify or corrupt its

information flow, hinder the functionality of its services, or provide an unlimited –
and unauthorized – access to the monitoring and control mechanisms that could be
exploited later. Most of these attacks are carried out using ICT (e.g. system
penetration and tampering), although attackers can use other non-technological
methods, such as social engineering and blackmail, to obtain information that could
be used in future attacks.

4   Critical Information Infrastructure Protection

It is necessary to admit the criticality of the information infrastructures and locate the
most important threats against their normal operation. However, these are not
sufficient conditions for assuring their proper behaviour. Using that knowledge as a
foundation, it is indispensable to create and establish certain procedures that
efficiently protect the CII against the attacks that may come, anytime, anywhere, from
those threats. *Critical Information Infrastructure Protection* (CIIP) can be formally
defined as follows: "The programs and activities of infrastructure owners,
manufacturers, users, operators, R&D institutions, governments, and regulatory
authorities which aim at keeping the performance of critical (information)
infrastructures in case of failures, attacks, or accidents above a defined minimum
level of service and aim at minimising the recovery time and damage" [3].

The importance of any protection mechanism is dependent on the nature of
the existing threats and their possible harmful effects. And in case of these
infrastructures, there is no room for discussions. The threats are numerous, and due
to cascading effects, the effects of a simple failure can be devastating in both
economic and human terms. For example, in 2002, a remote intrusion into a SCADA
system of a sewage plant resulted in the dispersion of around 1,2 million litres of
sewage into the environment. Also, in 2004, a fault in the air-conditioning system of
an important Telco node near Rome affected most of the check-in desks of the
Fiumicino airport at Rome. These and other episodes [16] are just a small subset of
the possible situations that justify the significance of the protection mechanisms
for CII.

Similarly to the previous case, there is a narrow line between CIP and CIIP.
Nevertheless, the key focus of CIIP is relatively clear: the protection of the
information systems and its services on which the infrastructures depend. Also, due to
the existent and future challenges within the CIIP context, to consider CIIP as a
separate issue from CIP is becoming increasingly important. Those challenges are the
following [17]:

- The protection of the CII has generally become more important due to the
  increasing role of the ICT in the management of infrastructures and their
  interlinking position between various infrastructure sectors.
- The number of computer and network vulnerabilities is expected to remain high,
  mainly due to the ongoing technological evolution and the unbelievable low
  priority of security as a design factor. Therefore, future infrastructures will have
  many critical points of failure due to an ill-understood behaviour of the underlying
  systems and hidden vulnerabilities.

- The threats targeting CII are evolving rapidly both in terms of their nature (e.g. becoming highly distributed) and of their capability to cause harm (e.g. affecting a physical element with a simple operation).

As this book chapter is mainly focused on CII, the remainder of this section will focus on the protection of such infrastructures. Nevertheless, since CII can be considered as an essential part of CI, the following contents can be also of relevance for the protection of these ones. As an example, the actor groups that have a large influence on CIIP also retain that influence regarding CIP.

4.1 Protection Requirements and Actor Groups

The creation of protection mechanisms for critical information infrastructures is a daunting task. Not only are those protection mechanisms extremely important, but also especially complex. There must be different layers of protection that are in charge of ensuring the safety of the infrastructures before, during and after attacks occur. The existence of these layers is consistent with the special operational requirements of these infrastructures: the main purpose of a certain protection mechanism is to assure that the protected system is operating as it should, and a CII must provide its services at all times. Moreover, there are many different actor groups, such as the public/private sector, the academic community, and the individual consumers that affect or are affected by the protection policies and measures; hence, they must be involved in the creation and maintenance of these mechanisms.

It is possible to divide the protection requirements of CII into four groups [18]: dependability, survivability, law enforcement, and national security. Regarding *dependability*, the existence of basic information security services that provide confidentiality, integrity and authentication to the elements of the infrastructure and their information flow are not enough to consider that the dependability properties are preserved. There should be other methods that assure the availability and reliability of the system, alongside with procedures that analyze the existing interdependences between infrastructures and their inherent risks. Concerning *survivability*, the protection mechanisms that must keep the system safe against abnormal situations should recognize the attacks and the extent of their damage, react automatically to mitigate the effects of those attacks, and maintain a certain level of service in the most critical *processes*. After those abnormal situations take place, the system must recover their essential services as soon as possible and provide an output about the situation that could help on improving the robustness of the system against future attacks.

The existence of the other two groups, *law enforcement* and *national security*, is justified by the interdisciplinary nature of the CII: there must be a legal framework and a policy framework working beyond the scope of a single infrastructure or set of infrastructures. In particular, for law enforcement, policies are needed that facilitate the cooperation between the different actors, allowing the existence of mutual agreements. Also, through that cooperation, the private sector must be capable of identifying and localizing the infrastructures with the highest priority in their socio/economical context. Beyond law enforcement, all relevant actors must have the necessary procedures to prevent and react against any problematic situation of relevance at a (inter)national level. Those procedures include building awareness about a certain problem, providing information in case of emergency, and reacting/mitigating against the emergency scenarios.

As previously noted, there are many actor groups dealing with CIIP. The public sector consists of governments and their different agencies. They are responsible of the economy of their countries and the well-being of their citizens, and have a strategic role due to their global point of view and capacity to provide assessment, coordination, and leadership. The private sector owns and administers most infrastructures due to the privatization processes (since the 1980's in Europe and much before in US) [19], thus has the task of actually implementing the protection policies. The third actor group is the academic community, that is capable of undertake medium and long-term research on many fields related to infrastructure protection, ranging from the technical issues to the socio-economical dimensions of the topic. Finally, the individual users or consumers can be considered as the final actor group. The existence of efficient protection mechanisms is difficult to achieve without the participation and cooperation of all the actor groups involved.

All these actors do not have a single perspective on CIIP since all consider the topic from different perspectives and with different motivations. As a result, there can be different, yet equally valid, viewpoints that discuss about what needs to be protected, by whom, with which measures, and so on. The answers may vary depending on the scenario, and are linked to the question of which protection efforts, goals, strategies, and instruments are appropriated for problem solution in a certain context [20]. Such viewpoints are observed below:

- The system-level, technical viewpoint: CIIP is approached as an IT-security or information assurance issue, with a strong focus on internet security. Threats to the information infrastructure are to be confronted just by technical means such as firewalls, anti-virus software, or intrusion and detection software. The establishment of early warning approaches such as Computer Emergency Response Teams (CERTs) is an example of this perspective.
- The business viewpoint: here, CIIP is seen as an issue of "business continuity", especially in the context of e-business. This requires not only permanent access to IT infrastructures, but also permanently available business processes to ensure satisfactory business performance. Protection mechanisms used in this perspective include the ideas used on the technical viewpoint, but also includes organizational and human activities. This perspective is also reflected in some countries' protection approaches that mainly aim to support the information society.
- The law-enforcement viewpoint: CIIP is seen as an issue for protecting the networked society against technology-enabled crimes of major and minor scale. This type of protection involves more or less traditional law-enforcement strategies and is assisted by adopting appropriate legislation and fostering international co-operation.

- The national-security viewpoint: this is a very comprehensive view of CIIP where the whole society is perceived as being endangered, so action must be taken at a variety of levels (e.g., at the technical, legislative, organizational, or international levels). Actors involved in protection efforts include government officials from different agencies, as well as representatives of the private sector and of the general public.

4.2 Research and Development Issues

Once the protection requirements and the different actor groups are known, it is possible to enumerate which are the most important Research and Development topics that pursue the fulfilment of such requirements. Those topics can be divided into eight categories, and are presented below. Each category have been gathered from the different research communities and government agencies and then verified by relevant actor groups [3].

1. *Holistic system security.* This research topic considers the security of the CII as a whole, rather than the security of its individual parts. Therefore, research efforts in this area deal with the discovery and analysis of interdependences between infrastructures. In addition, it is also necessary to create realistic simulation models that could both serve as a testbed and provide an insight on the effects of future attacks. This research topic mainly comprises (inter)dependency and complexity theory and cascading theory, alongside with simulation and modelling of complex systems.

2. *Risk management and vulnerability analysis.* In order to know how to effectively protect a particular infrastructure, there should be certain procedures that evaluate their inherent risks, analysing the impact on CII of attack scenarios and the present or future reaction of the elements of the infrastructures under such circumstances. It mainly comprises risk and vulnerability awareness, assessment, and management, as well as information security and scenario management.

3. *Prevention and Detection.* Security on CII must be proactive rather than reactive, i.e. it has to act in advance to deal with an expected difficulty. Therefore, both the human and computer elements of the system should be warned against any possible or ongoing abnormal situation that is taking place. This research topic mainly comprises *Early Warning Systems* and *Intrusion/Malware detection*, plus setting up information sharing networks.

4. *Incident Response and Recovery.* Just as CII must function properly and provide their services anytime, unforeseen events and attacks can also happen anytime. As a result, these complex networks must be designed to rapidly respond to any adverse situation and recover their functionality as soon as possible. It comprises the existence of support tools for Computer *Emergency Response Teams (CERTs)* and incident analysis, response, and recovery.

5. *Survivability of Systems.* Detecting and Reacting against external or internal malicious events is not enough for a CII. The protection mechanisms must concentrate all their efforts on allowing the business continuity by means of adequate optimisation strategies and survivable systems and architectures. Mainly,

it comprises security and resilience of hardware components, operating systems, and the process of software engineering, along with procedures for redundancy and service continuity.

6. *Policies and legal environment.* As many actor groups participate and are affected by the CII, it is necessary to provide a set of legal frameworks where the protection of the infrastructures can be effectively negotiated and enforced. Due to the (inter)national nature of CIIP and the different actor groups motivations, the creation of these frameworks and cooperation networks is really challenging. This topic mainly comprises (cyber) crime legal frameworks and development of CIIP policy and information sharing frameworks.

7. *Fundamental research and development.* There are some fundamental problems that the underlying elements of CII must deal with in order to provide a strong foundation for secure infrastructures. These problems are mostly of technical nature, and their overall objective is to build secure, scalable, and reliable systems. It comprises secure protocols and architectures, standardisation, fault tolerant systems, and management of trust and resilience.

8. *Non-technology issues compromising CIIP.* There are a number of non-technological factors, such as human and organisational aspects, that can affect positively or negatively the performance of the system. This research topic mainly comprises training programmes for increasing public awareness, treating humans as another element of the CIIP, planning common concept developments, and tools for cost/benefit analysis of investments on CIIP.

5 Electronic Control Systems

5.1 SCADA and PLC

Supervisory control and data acquisition systems, or SCADA [21], can be seen as a complex system comprised by a set of hardware (for instance, controllers) and software (for instance, database or programmes) components that are interconnected. The main goal of this type of systems is to control and supervise the state and/or condition of every element (products, machines, materials, and even the staff) of an infrastructure, as well as to carry out in real time a set of operations. SCADA systems can monitor large infrastructures, thus it requires long and secure communication networks to send and receive the control packets and measurements obtained from its components. In fact, depending on the overall dimensions of the infrastructure, it may be necessary to establish connectivity with outside networks.

A SCADA system is basically composed of five fundamental elements, which are represented in the figure 1. The infrastructure is supervised and monitored by an operator using a central system known as *Human Machine Interface* (*HMI*). The HMI works like a mediator between the system and operator, and shows all the data obtained from every part of the system by means of graphical interfaces (schemes, windows, graphics, and so on). All the information is recollected by a *Master Terminal Unit* (*MTU*), which also retransmits the operator's control signals to remote parts of the system. Both the recollected data and the control signals are sent out using a *communication infrastructure*, such as Internet, wired networks, wireless network, or public telephone network. Finally, the control signals are received by *Remote Terminal Units (RTU)*, which retransmit them to the individual devices of the system. The measurements coming from those devices, such as flow or voltage, are also gathered by the RTU and sent to the MTU. Note that a RTU may be a Programmable Logic Controller (PLC).

A PLC is a small computer used for automation of real-world processes, such as control of machinery on factory assembly lines. More specifically, the PLC is a microprocessor based device with the specific purpose of reading data from sensors connected to its input ports and controlling actuators through its output ports. These sensors can read limit switches, dual-level devices, temperature indicators, and others. Also, the actuators can drive any kind of electric motor, pneumatic or hydraulic cylinders or diaphragms, magnetic relays or solenoids, and so on.

Fig. 1. General representation of SCADA system architecture

Traditional systems consisted of hard-wired relay logic, which had virtually no control system and applications. As a result, the design engineers had to manually monitor the processes in order to prepare specifications and reports for the contractor. On the contrary, SCADA systems allow the engineers to design the appropriated functionality that the system should have, facilitating the operation of the whole system. A concrete example of the applicability of SCADA systems are water treatment or wastewater treatment infrastructures [22], which are composed of a set of applications, programmable controllers, distributed control systems, and computer-based operator interface stations to control all the facilities. The applications must be unique for each facility because they have to manage specific processes at every individual plant, such as pump control algorithms, equipment control, and so on.

5.2 Vulnerabilities in Electronic Control Systems

The *Electronic Control Systems (ECS)* are very vulnerable to threats mostly because of two reasons. Firstly, the communication infrastructure is based on wired or wireless networks, and sometimes, depending on the distance between its elements, it requires to keep connectivity with outside networks such as the Internet. Secondly, these ECS are essential parts of critical infrastructures, and any failure (logical or physical) in a component could bring severe and devastating consequences. If an attacker penetrates in an ECS, for example a SCADA system of a refinery, he could access, manipulate, control and change all its behaviour – from passwords to measurements and devices (HMI, MTU and RTU).

The specific threats that may affect ECS are physical and logical in nature. For example, a ECS could be targeted by a cyberattack (e.g. autonomous worms, denial of service attacks, viruses), a failure or attack in the communication infrastructure (e.g. lack of connectivity, vulnerability in subnetworks, lack of authentication, confidentiality and privacy methods in the underlying protocols), a natural disaster (e.g. hurricanes, tornadoes, flooding, earthquakes), a deliberate action (e.g. terrorism, organized crime), a human or technical error (e.g. radio interferences, unsuitable applications software) or an accident.

Therefore, ECS must be able to detect and warn of the type of threat and its localization to the human operator as soon as possible, and also automatically respond in real-time to reach a stable and reliable system. However, including methods of detection, alerting and protection in such complex systems is not an easy task, since it requires of secure and specialized mechanisms (for instance, specially designed *Intrusion Detection Systems*), as well as extremely robust and reliable secure communication protocols. Still, it is mandatory to apply security primitives to protect the information, and to provide confidentiality, authentication and privacy to all the elements and services of the ECS.

6 Wireless Sensor Networks in CIP/CIIP

The protection of Critical Information Infrastructures faces numerous challenges, for example managing the secure interaction between peers, assuring the resilience and robustness of the overall system, or deploying warning and alert systems. For carrying out such proposals, suitable and intelligent technologies (for instance, Wireless Sensor Networks) are required for providing support to such protection. Indeed, Wireless Sensor Networks technology possesses appropriate properties and capabilities to control and work in diverse scenarios. Therefore, the main focus of this section is to justify why Wireless Sensor Networks technology is suitable for providing security in determined critical scenarios, describing its structure, behavior, advantages, disadvantages, and its role in the overall scheme of protecting the Critical Information Infrastructures.

6.1 Wireless Sensor Networks

A *Wireless Sensor Network* (WSN) [23] is composed of small and autonomous devices, deployed over a certain region, that cooperate with each other in order to achieve the same objective. These devices, called sensor nodes, make use of different types of sensors to monitor the physical state of a specific object or to examine the environmental conditions of its surroundings. Thanks to these attractive features, this technology is increasingly being applied in diverse scenarios and applications (from simple, complex to critical) of very different sectors (such as agricultural, business, environment, health care, homeland security, industry, and so on).

Sensor nodes can measure a wide range on environmental conditions, like temperature, humidity, lighting, radiation, noise, and others. Such information must be transmitted to the end user (a human being or computer) with the purpose of obtaining, evaluating, and studying relevant samples. However, there is no direct link between the real world, where dozens, hundreds and thousands of sensor nodes are deployed, and the end user. Between both points, there should exist devices whose resources and capabilities have to be more powerful than sensor nodes. Those devices are known as B*ase Stations*. Any device with enough capabilities to manage the services offered by the sensor network, such as a laptop or a PDA handed by a user, can become a base station.

Regarding the services offered by a WSN, sensor nodes not only can monitor the environment, but also can issue warnings and receive queries about the state of the network or a certain property. Indeed, all measurements perceived (e.g. radiation) and processed by the nodes must be sent to the closest base station, being later retransmitted to the end user. Besides, nodes must be able to detect any kind of anomalous activity of the environment (e.g. high levels of radiation) and alert the end users. Finally, the base stations can request to the nodes information about a specific feature of the network or environment, which is provided "on-demand". Note that base stations can also send control packets in order to reconfigure the network without using an additional infrastructure, since the nodes have the capability of self-configuring themselves. Therefore, the channel of communication between the sensor nodes and base station is totally bidirectional.

It must be noted that there are two types of architectures in WSN, which are represented in the figure 2: hierarchical (HWSN) and distributed (DWSN). In a hierarchical network, the sensor nodes are organized into groups, known as clusters. In every cluster there exists a special node, called "cluster head", entrusted to manage certain tasks in the cluster, as for example data aggregation. In contrast, in a distributed network the sensor nodes are completely independent, making their own decisions and determining which their next actions are by themselves. Note that it is possible to have both architectures in a sensor network at the same time (i.e. hybrid), thus improving the resilience and robustness of the network in case the "spinal cord" (i.e. the "cluster heads") fails.

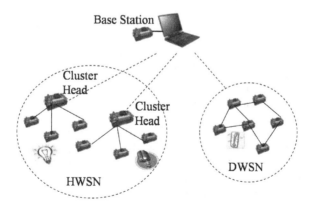

Fig. 2. General representation of a Wireless Sensor Network architecture

6.2   Sensor Node Hardware

A sensor node has four principal components: processor unit, sensing unit, power unit, and transceiver. Concretely speaking, the *processing unit*, also known as microcontroller, is a highly-constrained computer integrated on a chip. This unit also has memory and input/output interfaces. The *sensing unit* is composed of a set of sensors such as temperature, humidity, vibration, light, air, radiation, and so on. The power unit, which in most cases consists of batteries, is the responsible for supplying energy to every element of the system. With a finite energy source a node can subsist long periods of time, even a year with an optimal configuration. Finally, the *transceiver* is the responsible of sending and receiving messages through a wireless antenna, allowing the nodes to support multiple communication paths and providing routing capabilities.

In the design of a wireless sensor network is important to take into account the possible computational and communicational capabilities of sensor nodes, with the purpose of analyzing whether they are suitable for carrying out a determined application. Actually, it is possible to classify sensor nodes into three categories according to the features of their microcontrollers: "weak", "normal", and "heavy duty". Additionally, there are two major types of transceivers: wideband radios and narrowband radios. Note that any type of node category is able to support both narrowband and wideband radios.

The class "weak" represents those sensor nodes whose capabilities are extremely constrained (i.e. less than 2kB of instruction memory and 64B of RAM), but still enough to execute very simple applications (such as monitoring the temperature in a region). Conversely, the class "normal" represents those nodes that are able to fulfill any kind of sensing and collaborative applications. A node belonging to this class usually has a microcontroller of 4-8Mhz, with 48kB-128kB of instruction memory and 4kB-10kB of RAM. Finally, nodes belonging to the "heavy-duty" class are expensive PDA-like devices that are able to execute any kind of application, from simple, complex to critical. Their microprocessors are quite powerful, with around 180Mhz, 4MB-32MB of instruction memory and 256kB-512kB of RAM.

On the other hand, regarding the type of transceivers, wideband radios are faster and more robust, working at frequencies such as 2.4Ghz, but are also power-demanding and slower to wake up. Narrowband radios have less throughput (i.e. work at lower frequencies, such as 868Mhz) and are more susceptible to noise, but they have less power consumption and faster wakeup times. Note that most nodes use wideband-based transceivers that follow the IEEE 802.15.4 standard.

A question that may surface at this point is what nodes are suitable for being used on a critical infrastructure. The answer is simple: it depends on the tasks assigned to those nodes: "weak" nodes can behave as mere data collectors, forwarding the data to a node of higher capabilities; "normal" nodes can both obtain data from their surroundings and preprocess them, or even more, make organizational decisions in pure distributed or hybrid networks; "heavy-duty" nodes can behave as "cluster heads" in hierarchical networks, or act as surrogated base stations in control of one section of the network.

6.3 Role of Sensor Networks in CIP/CIIP

The scientific community and national governments consider WSN technology as a fundamental part in CIP and CIIP, since the sensors can be embedded into systems and provide attractive operations such as monitoring, tracking, detecting, reporting and collecting. For these reasons, in 2004 the U.S Department for Homeland Security

[24] declared as one of their strategic goals "to provide a *National Common Operating Picture* (COP)" for Critical Infrastructures, where the core of the systems would be an intelligent, self-monitoring, and self-healing sensor network. Also, the Australian government suggested sensor network technology as part of their new R&D proposals to develop several topics based on research and commercialization of CIP in Australia, known as "*Cooperative Research Center for Security* (CRC-SAFE)".

From an academic point of view, the scientific community is interested in applying the WSN technology in many critical applications. In fact, at present there are several applications running, or even finished. An example is the CoBIs project [25] developed by BP in a petrochemical plant in Hull (UK) [26]), where sensor nodes are attached on chemical containers and storage facilities to control both the nearness of incompatible dangerous products and their safety during their storage or transportation. Intel [27] also led an experiment in a plant of Oregon to control the vibrations of its semiconductor fabrication equipments. Another project associated to industry infrastructures is SMEPP project [28], which aims to supervise the radiation levels of nuclear power plants. Moreover, the U.K. (EPSRC) is involved in other specific projects (Underground M3 and Smart Infrastructure - WINES II project [29]) related to ageing of civil infrastructures (bridges, tunnels, water supplies and sewer systems).

Finally, other sector that is also critical is the quality and treatment of water. On this matter, the DISCOVERY project [30], also known as Distributed Intelligence, Sensing and Coordination in Variable Environment, consists of the deployment of an underwater sensor network to control oil spills, and in extreme cases, to respond and seal off a perimeter containing contaminated water. In the same way, the University of California is leading two projects [31] to measure the amount of arsenic in Bangladesh groundwater, and the nitrate propagation in soils and ground water in California.

As already mentioned, WSN are also appropriated to secure the protection and safety of the information in critical infrastructures. For that purpose, it would be advisable to have available and configured an *Early Warning System* (EWS) and a *Dynamic Reconfiguration Systems* (DRS) in order to detect anomalous events, specify the exact location of a problem, alert and attend the problem as soon as possible, and in certain situations, to re-configure the different components of the CII taking as input the output of EWS.

6.4 Research Challenges and Security

As already seen in previous sections, there are many scenarios where sensor networks play a major role. However, this type of technology has some research issues that need to be solved, and the security is one of the most relevant. Sensor nodes are highly vulnerable to attacks, due to their constrained nature in terms of computational and memory capabilities, and also due to the wireless nature of the communication channel [32]. Hence, it is necessary to discover and design secure, robust and effective architectures, protocols (such as routing, aggregation and time synchronization) and applications.

In the WSN context there are two major types of attacks: physical and logical. A malicious adversary can carry out any of them in order to compromise and manipulate the network (locally or globally) for its own convenience. Generally, physical attacks are caused by the implicit and explicit nature of the nodes, that is, most of them are not tamper-resistant and can be easily accessible by intruders, respectively. As a consequence of physical attacks, the sensitive information of the node can be retrieved, but also the node itself can be reprogrammed. However, it is also important to know that there are some mechanisms to protect a node against data stealing, such as *data and code obfuscation* schemes, which generate new software version of the sensor nodes [33]. Even more, a node could check the state of another one simply calling to the procedure *code attestation* [34].

On the other hand, logical attacks are caused by the weaknesses inherent to the communication channel. Any device, equipped with a wireless antenna and located in the vicinity of the network, can easily access the information exchange. Therefore, a minimal protection is required to assure the confidentiality and authenticity between peers, and the integrity in the communication channel and the messages. Such protection mechanisms are necessary, but not sufficient conditions for guaranteeing the viability of the services offered. These services are based on certain "core" protocols, such as *data aggregation* (to filter all the information collected in a single message), *routing* (to route a message from a source to a target node) and *time synchronization* (to synchronize the clocks of each sensor node). At present, there are many specific implementations of these protocols, but any of them guarantees neither the correct functionality of the network nor its robustness against any kind of threat or failure.

The nodes must have integrated and implemented the basic security primitives to assure a minimal protection of the information flow in the communication channel. Those primitives are *Symmetric Key Cryptography* schemes (SKC), *Message Authentication Codes* (MAC), and even *Public Key Cryptography* (PKC). There are many existing implementations of software-based SKC primitives for sensor networks (cf. [35]). Regarding MAC, it is possible to implement that primitive using SKC operations (e.g. by using CB-MAC). Finally, until 2004 the PKC implementations for sensor networks were considered technically "impossible", since they required very high computational capabilities. However, that idea was changed by, among others, Gura et. al. [36]. They introduced the possibility of using *Elliptic Curve Cryptography* (ECC) as a efficient PKC primitive, with keys of 163 bit and point multiplications.

Primitives are the foundation for the protection of the information flow, but they need of security credentials such as secret keys in order to work properly. At the moment, there are many *Key Management System* (KMS) proposed for sensor networks, and every one is oriented for a specific context with certain properties. As these properties are associated to the requirements of every scenario, it is necessary to use a tool that identifies [37] the Key Management System more suitable for a specific application domain. Aside from all these advances in security, it is important to research other areas such as *Intrusion Detection Systems* (IDS) for network monitoring and self-configuration, trust management, delegation of privileges, secure management of mobile nodes, and so on.

As a final note, it can be pointed out that there are some similarities between a SCADA system and a wireless sensor network, since both offer special services that can be useful for the management of the infrastructure, such as monitoring, and both also present vulnerabilities of internal and external attacks against the system. However, the SCADA system is more complex, and its elements have higher processing capacity, memory and energy, than a sensor node.

7 Research Projects

As of 2007, the protection of CII is one of the priority areas for research in the context of the European Community. For instance, in the *VII Framework Programme* (FP7), this topic is part of the first ICT challenge, "Pervasive and Trusted Network and Service Infrastructures". CIIP has been also considered as an important area in the previous European research programmes. There have been more than 20 projects in the last years mainly oriented to solve the interdisciplinary challenges of European infrastructures [38]. In this section we present some of those projects, alongside with other non-European projects that have used sensor network technology.

7.1 VITUS

VITUS (*Video Image analysis for TUnnel Safety*) project [39] is included in the Program I2 "Intelligence Infrastructure" (2002-2006), and supported by the Austrian Federal Ministry of Transport, Innovation and Technology. The objective of VITUS is to provide automatic safety in tunnel roads of Europe using automated visual video surveillance systems. Analogue CCTV-systems have been used in the past to monitor traffic incidents, but they are not very robust and reliable. The need to develop such intelligent system arises from the concrete measures issued by the EU in 2001 [40] aimed to prevent serious disasters such as the Mont Blanc tunnel incident.

This project was divided in two subprojects, known as VITUS-1 [41] and VITUS-2 [39]. Specifically, VITUS-1 has been the responsible of analyzing the viability part of the project, with the partial tasks of identifying the appropriated mechanisms and sensors to detect abnormal and dangerous events, as well as of mechanisms to alert to the tunnel operators in serious situations. On the other hand, VITUS-2 was the responsible of developing and evaluating the prototype defined in VITUS-1. VITUS-2 has been organized in several partial tasks, such as the installation of electronic components and calibrated digital cameras, recording of scenes for the video database, development of algorithms for detecting and tracking static or dynamic objects in the tunnel, classification of objects, detection of unexpected events or irregular behaviors, the development of framework and interfaces prototypes, evaluations, documentation and dissemination, and management of documents.

7.2 CoBIS

CoBIS (*Collaborative Business Items*) is a 6th European Framework Programme (FP6) project [25]. This project was finalized on 2007, and its objective was to develop a platform to embed business logic in physical entities, such as materials, machine parts, modules, clothing, and so on. These items had to be able to provide services and to adequately solve problematic situations, by cooperating and communicating with each other. In this platform, every item must have associated an unique RFID tag to be identified, and a sensor node to monitor both its current state and the environmental conditions. This way of handle services provides more reliability and scalability than traditional systems, since the intelligent objects can help in reducing manual data collection.

Partial tasks of this project were identification and classification of services, development of collaborative and technology frameworks, design and implementation of management services, and evaluation in an oil and gas industry. Indeed, and as mentioned in previous sections, a BP petrochemical plant in Hull in the United Kingdom [26] carried out the first evaluations, attaching sensor nodes on chemical containers and storage facilities. As a result, it was possible to control the proximity of incompatible dangerous products and both their state and environmental conditions during their storage or transportation. On the other hand, CoBIS also intended to guarantee workplace safety using smart clothing. Note that although evaluations had been made in oil and gas industries, this project could be extended and applied in other sectors whose products (for example, food, pharmaceuticals or healthcare) could suffer severe damage by environmental conditions.

7.3 CenSCIR Projects

The *Center for Sensed Critical Infrastructure Research* (CenSCIR) [42] is housed in Carnegie Mellon University's College of Engineering (CIT) Institute for Complex Engineered Systems (ICES). This center runs several projects whose objectives are to monitor and supervise infrastructures of critical importance, such as decaying road systems, oil and gas pipelines, unstable electric power grids, leaking water distribution systems, water treatment plants, telecommunications networks systems, and commercial and industrial facilities. Specific objectives are the development of data interpretation techniques, data models, decision support frameworks, sensor data driven decision support, and so on.

Examples of projects carried out inside CenSCIR are the projects led by Akinci et. al. [43] and Singhvi et. al. [44]. The first one supervises the construction deviations of buildings, with the goal of reducing unexpected impacts or undesired damages, and even minimizes the maintenance costs. Indeed, most constructions suffer deviations by quality or ageing of materials, lack of inspection of construction work or unskilled workers. All of these cause an increase of 12% in construction costs. The second one aims to optimize the user comfort by minimizing the energy costs in intelligent homes. For that purpose, they used wireless sensor network to create a intelligent lighting control system.

7.4 WINES II

WINES II (*Wireless Intelligent Networked Systems - Smart Infrastructure*) project [29], is funded by the EPSRC (Engineering and Physical Sciences Research Council), with a duration of three years (2006-2009). In this project, specialists of very different areas are involved with the aim of investigating the best way of controlling the ageing of civil infrastructures of United Kingdom (such as bridges, tunnels, and water supply and sewer systems), primarily by using wireless sensor networks. In fact, most of the research challenges suggested for this project, such as maximizing scalability and resolve the problems related to security and power supply, are associated with WSN.

The foundations of this project were based on the problematic of maintaining the civil infrastructures in UK, which are around a hundred years old. This is the case of tunnels in the London underground (LUL) and pipelines of Thames Water. On the other hand, there are around 150,000 bridges in the UK which are related to critical links corresponding both roads and rail infrastructures. The use of WSN technology allows the autonomous control of every previously mentioned infrastructure, and it is important to note that all the information retrieved from those networks is sent to a same common system by means of wireless systems or the Internet.

8 Future Directions

It has been clear during the course of this chapter that CIIP is a very young and interdisciplinary research topic that needs to be addressed by many actors with different points of view. There is, however, a sense of emergency attached to this topic. The nature of its threats and the possible effects of a single failure demand for a fast and coordinated action from all stakeholders involved. If no solutions are devised soon, the chances of problematic incidents that can globally affect the safety of a nation will grow steadily. While it is not possible to completely eliminate the possibility of such events taking place, it is necessary to keep them under control.

The statements presented in the previous paragraph could be perceived as catastrophic, in the sense that the actual risk of a certain critical infrastructure failing and the influence of such failure on its socio-economical surroundings are mostly unknown. Nevertheless, there are some global and infrastructure-related trends that clearly will affect the well-being CII [45]. From a global point of view privatization and outsourcing are growing, thus it will be more difficult to coordinate all interested parties, amongst other things. Also, globalization is growing, so the already complex interdependences between infrastructures will become even more transnational.

Infrastructure-specific trends range from social ones to technological ones. Our society is becoming more and more dependent on the unfailing operation of critical infrastructures: it is difficult to picture life as we live it now without the services provided by such infrastructures. The increasing complexity of their underlying systems and computer networks multiply the chances of a single failure, failure that can be provoked anywhere, anyhow, anytime. These problems in a single component of an infrastructure could easily cascade to other infrastructures, due to their inherent interdependences.

There are many challenges that all actor groups have to overcome so as to provide an appropriate protection to the actual and future CII. As of 2007, the major challenges on the area of CIIP are the following [3]:

- Design and development of integrated protection architectures and technologies for the pervasive and ubiquitous secure computing environment that become part of the CII (resilient and secure hardware/software architectures).
- Tools and platforms for dependencies and inter-dependencies analysis and anti-cascading protection measures.

- Tools for intrusion detection.
- Tools and platforms for trusted sharing of sensitive information.
- Tools for dealing with uncertain dynamic threats to CII and the preparation for proper and efficient and effective incident management including optimization strategies in risk reduction.
- Organizational, technical and operational policies and good practices for intra-sector, cross-sector, cross-border and public-private partnership establishment and conditioning.
- Forensics tools for critical infrastructures (Network Forensics)

References

1. Definition of the word Infrastructure. Merriam Webster's Collegiate Dictionary (11th edn.), Springfield, MA (2003)
2. National Research Council, Dahms, L.: Infrastructure for the 21st century - framework for a research agenda. National Academy Press, Washington, D.C. (1987)
3. Critical Information Infrastructure Research Co-ordination (CI2RCO). Deliverable D12, ICT R&D for CIIP: Towards a European Research Agenda (April 13th, 2007)
4. Definition of the word Critical: Merriam Webster's Collegiate Dictionary (11th edn.), Springfield, MA (2003)
5. Commission of the European Communities: Communication from the Commission to the Council and the European Parliament: Critical Infrastructure Protection in the Fight Against Terrorism, COM (2004) 702 final, Brussels (2004)
6. Congress of the United States of America: USA PATRIOT ACT. Public Law, 107–156, Washington, D.C. (2001)
7. Analysis and Assessment for Critical Infrastructure Protection (ACIP). Deliverable D1.1 (August 31, 2002)
8. Metzger, J.: The Concept of Critical Infrastructure Protection (CIP). In: Business and Security: Public-Private Sector Relationships in a New Security Environment, pp. 197–209. Oxford University Press, Oxford (2004)
9. Dunn, M., Abele-Wigert, I.: The International CIIP Handbook 2006: An Inventory of Protection Policies in 20 Countries and 6 International Organizations (Vol. I) (Zurich, Center for Security Studies, 2006)
10. Stoneburner, G., Goguen, A., Feringa, A.: Risk Management Guide for Information Technology Systems. In: Recommendations of the National Institute of Standards and Technology. NIST Special Publication 800-30, Washington, D.C. (2002)
11. Radvanovksy, R.: Critical Infrastructure: Homeland Security and Emergency Preparedness. CRC Press, Boca Raton (2006)
12. Rinaldi, S., Peerenboom, J., Kelly, T.: Identifying, understanding, and analyzing Critical infrastructure interdependencies. IEEE Control Systems Magazine 21, 11–25 (2001)
13. President's Commission on Critical Infrastructure Protection (PCCIP): Critical Foundations: Protecting America's Infrastructures. Washington, D.C. (1997)
14. Landau, S., Stytz, M.R., Landwehr, C.E., Schneider, F.B.: Overview of Cyber Security: A Crisis of Prioritization. IEEE Security and Privacy 03(3), 9–11 (2005)
15. Dunn, M.: Threat Frames in the US Cyber-Terror Discourse. In: Paper presentation at the 2004 British International Studies Association (BISA) Conference, Warwick (2004)

16. Bologna, S., Setola, R.: The need to improve local self-awareness in CIP/CIIP. In: Proceedings of First IEEE International Workshop on Critical Infrastructure Protection (IWCIP 2005), Darmstadt, Germany, pp. 84–89 (2005)
17. Dunn, M.: Understanding Critical Information Infrastructures: An Elusive Quest. In: Dunn, M., Mauer, V. (eds.) The International CIIP Handbook 2006: Analyzing Issues, Challenges, and Prospects (Zürich, Forschungsstelle für Sicherheitspolitik, 2006), vol. II, pp. 27–53 (2006)
18. Critical Information Infrastructure Research Co-ordination (CI2RCO): Deliverable D1, Common Understanding of CI2RCO-Basics (March 1, 2005)
19. Henriksen, S.: The Shift of Responsibilities within Government and Society. In: CRN Workshop Report. Societal Security and Crisis Management in the 21st Century, Stockholm, pp. 60–63 (2004)
20. Dunn, M.: The Socio-Political Dimensions of Critical Information Infrastructure Protection (CIIP). International Journal for Critical Infrastructure Protection 1(2/3), 258–268 (2005)
21. Krutz, R.L.: Securing SCADA Systems. Wiley Publishing, Chichester (2005)
22. Malcolm Pirnie: Why Malcolm Pirnie Can your Configuration Needs. White Paper (2000), http://www.pirniecentral.com/Docs/MPI_Configure.html
23. Akyildiz, I.F., Su, W., Sankarasubramaniam, Y., Cayirci, E.: Wireless sensor networks: a survey. Computer Networks: The International Journal of Computer and Telecommunications Networking 38(4), 393–422 (2002)
24. The Department of Homeland Security, Science and Technology Directorate: The National Plan for Research and Development in Support of Critical Infrastructure Protection. Washington, D.C. (2005)
25. Collaborative Business Items project (CoBIS) (2004-2007), http://www.cobis-online.de
26. Collin, J.: BP Tests RFID Sensor Network at U.K. Plant (2006), http://www.rfidjournal.com/article/articleview/2443/
27. Sensor Nets / RFID. Intel Corporation, http://www.intel.com/research/exploratory/wireless sensors.htm
28. SMEPP Secure Middleware for Embedded Peer-to-Peer Systems (FP6-2005-IST-5) (2007), http://www.smepp.org
29. WINES II – Smart Infrastructure University of Cambridge and Imperial College, London (2006), http://www.winesinfrastructure.org
30. Distributed Intelligence, Sensing and Coordination in Variable Environments. CSIRO (2006), http://www.ict.csiro.au/page.php?cid=97
31. Ramanathan, N., Balzano, L., Estrin, D., Hansen, M., Harmon, T., Jay, J., Kaiser, W.J., Sukhatme, G.: Designing Wireless Sensor Networks as a Shared Resource for Sustainable Development. In: Proceedings of the International Conference on Information and Communication Technologies and Development (ICTD 2006), Berkeley, USA (2006)
32. Walters, J.P., Liang, Z., Shi, W., Chaudhary, V.: Wireless Sensor Network Security: A Survey. In: Xiao, Y. (ed.) Security in Distributed, Grid, and Pervasive Computing, Auerbach Publications, CRC Press, Boca Raton (2006)
33. Alarifi, A., Du, W.: Diversifying Sensor Nodes to Improve Resilience Against Node Compromise. In: Proceedings of the 4th ACM Workshop on Security of Ad Hoc and Sensor Networks (SASN 2006), Alexandria, USA (2006).
34. Park, T., Shin, K.G.: Soft Tamper-Proofing via Program Integrity Verification in Wireless Sensor Networks. IEEE Transactions on Mobile Computing 4(3), 297–309 (2005)
35. Law, Y.W., Doumen, J., Hartel, P.: Survey and Benchmark of Block Ciphers for Wireless Sensor Networks. ACM Transactions on Sensor Networks 2(1), 65–93 (2006)

36. Gura, N., Patel, A., Wander, A.: Comparing elliptic curve cryptography and RSA on 8-bit CPUs. In: Joye, M., Quisquater, J.-J. (eds.) CHES 2004. LNCS, vol. 3156, Springer, Heidelberg (2004)

37. Alcaraz, C., Roman, R.: Applying Key Infrastructures for Sensor Networks in CIP/CIIP Scenarios. In: Lopez, J. (ed.) CRITIS 2006. LNCS, vol. 4347, Springer, Heidelberg (2006)

38. Critical Information Infrastructure Research Co-ordination (CI2RCO). Deliverable D10, Gap analysis of existing CIIP R&D programmes at regional, national and EU level. (September 29, 2006)

39. Schwabach, H., Harrer, M., Waltl, A., Horst, B., Tacke, A., Zoffmann, G., Beleznai, C., Strobl, B., Helmut, G., Fernández, G.: VITUS: Video based Image analysis for Tunnel Safety. In: International Conference on Tunnel Safety and Ventilation (2006)

40. Commission of the European Communities: European transport policy for 2010: Time to decide. White Paper 370 (2001)

41. Schwabach, H., Harrer, M., Holzmann, W., Bischof, Fernández Domínguez, H.G., Nölle, M., Pflugfelder, R., Strobl, B., Tacke, A., Waltl, A.: Video Based Image Analysis for Tunnel Safety – VITUS-1: A Tunnel Video Surveillance and Traffic Control System. In: 12th World Congress on Intelligent Transport Systems (2005)

42. Center for Sensed Critical Infrastructure Research (CenSCIR) (2006), http://www.ices.cmu.edu/censcir/

43. Akinci, B., Boukamp, F., Gordon, C., Huber, D., Lyons, C., Park, K.: A formalism for utilization of sensor systems and integrated project models for active construction quality control. Carnegie Mellon University, Pittsburgh, United States, ScienceDirect (2005)

44. Singhvi, V., Krause, A., Guestrin, C., Matthews, H.S., Garrett, J.H., Matthews, H.: Intelligent Lighting Control using Sensor Networks. In: Proceedings of SenSys'05, San Diego, California, USA (2005)

45. Critical Information Infrastructure Research Co-ordination (CI2RCO): Deliverable D6, Report on the analysis and evaluation of CIIP R&D programmes (June 2, 2006)

An Interpretation of
Identity-Based Cryptography

Liqun Chen

Hewlett-Packard Laboratories, Bristol, UK
liqun.chen@hp.com

Abstract. Identity-based cryptography (IBC) is an asymmetric key cryptographic technology with a special feature, in which a user's public key can be an identifier of the user and the corresponding private key is created by binding the identifier with a system master secret. This paper is based on the author's lecture notes in this area[1]. In this paper, we introduce the concept of IBC by explaining some basic cryptographic primitives, such as identity-based encryption, signatures, combined encryption/signing and key-agreement. We also introduce two types of implementation techniques, which are based on integer factorization and discrete logarithm from pairings respectively. In order to make the technology easier to understand, we describe a small number of mechanisms in each primitive. Some of the mechanisms have been adopted by international standard bodies. At the end of the paper, we briefly cover the key escrow issue and a few well-known security models for these primitives.

1 Introduction

The concept of Identity-Based Cryptography (IBC) was proposed by Shamir in 1984 [69]. In an IBC system, a user's public and private key pair is set up in a special way, i.e. the public key presents an identifier of the user, and the private key is created by binding the identifier with a system master secret. The master secret is owned by a trusted authority, called Key Generation Center (KGC), and the key generation mechanism is called an identity-based key extraction algorithm.

In the same paper, Shamir provided the first key extraction algorithm based on the integer factorization problem, and presented an identity-based signature scheme. He believed that identity-based cryptosystems exist and encouraged researchers to look for such systems.

By following Shamir's IBC concept and identity-based key extraction algorithm, many Identity-Based Signature (IBS) schemes and Identity-Based Key Agreement (IBKA) protocols were proposed after 1984. The following are several examples.

---

[1] The lecture was given by the author in the 6th International School on Foundations of Security Analysis and Design (FOSAD), which took place in Bertinoro University Residential Centre Italy in September 2006.

A. Aldini and R. Gorrieri (Eds.): FOSAD 2006/2007, LNCS 4677, pp. 183–208, 2007.
© Springer-Verlag Berlin Heidelberg 2007

Signatures. Fiat and Shamir proposed an IBS scheme in 1986 [38]. Guillou and Quisquater in 1988 [43] proposed another IBS scheme. Girault and Stern in 1994 [42] developed a modification of the Guillou and Quisquater scheme. In 1998, ISO/IEC 14888-2 was published [47], and included two IBS schemes based on the works from [42,43]. The standard ISO/IEC 14888 is current in the revision process.

Key agreement. Okamoto in 1986 [57] presented an IBKA scheme, and Tanaka and Okamoto slightly modified it in [74]. In 1990, Girault and Paillès [41] developed an identity-based system, which can be used for non-interactive key agreement schemes. In 1999, ISO/IEC 11770-3 was published [46], and included an identity-based key agreement scheme based on the works from [57, 74, 41]. This ISO/IEC standard is now also in the revision process.

However, constructing a practical Identity-Based Encryption (IBE) scheme remained an open problem for many years. The following lists a few significant tries:

- 1986. Desmedt and Quisquater [36] made a proposal for implementing identity-based cryptosystems by using tamper-proof hardware devices.
- 1987. Tanaka [73] proposed an identity-based public key distribution scheme, which becomes insecure if a number of users combine their private keys together, since it will allow them to jointly recover the master secret.
- 1987. Okamoto [58] described a key distribution system based on identification information. In this system, the user's identity is only part of the key generation process and a public directory is still required for off-line communication between users.
- 1991. Maurer and Yacobi [56] proposed an identity-based public key distribution scheme, which requires a big computational effort on the KGC.
- 1997. Vanstone and Zuccherato [75] proposed an identity-based key distribution scheme. This system failed to provide adequate security, since the composite modulus used in the system can be factored easily and the computational effort required on the KGC was not much less than that required to break the system by an unauthorized user.

Seventeen years after Shamir's conjecture, three IBE solutions were proposed in 2001 by Boneh and Franklin [16], Cocks [35] and Sakai *et al.* [65] respectively. The Cocks scheme uses quadratic residuos, and the security of the scheme is based on the hardness of the integer factorization problem. Both the Boneh and Franklin scheme and the Sakai *et al.* scheme use bilinear pairings on elliptic curves [71], and the security of their schemes is based on the hardness of the Bilinear Diffie-Hellman (BDH) problem [16]. Their schemes are efficient in practice. Boneh and Franklin defined a well-formulated security model for IBE in [16]. The Boneh-Franklin scheme has received much attention owing to the fact that it was the first IBE scheme to have a proof of security in an appropriate model.

After that, many researchers have worked on using pairings to develop various identity-based cryptographic primitives, including authenticated IBE, IBE with threshold decryption, identity-based KEM, identity-based blind signatures, identity-based group signatures, identity-based ring signatures, identity-based concurrent signatures, identity-based proxy encryption and signatures, hierarchical IBE, fuzzy IBE, identity-based signcryption and so on. A number of researchers have provided surveys on the identity-based cryptographic primitives and pairing based cryptographic primitives, e.g. [34,37]. Another resource for obtaining the relative papers in these primitives is Barreto's pairing-based crypto lounge [5], which has a good collection of IBC mechanisms from pairings.

The purpose of this paper is not to provide a full overview of IBC, but to give a simple introduction of this research area for tutorial purposes. In order to make the concept of IBC and its applications understandable for as many readers as possible, we introduce a small number of mechanisms in each major primitive category. The most materials listed in this paper were used in the lecture given in the 6th International School on Foundations of Security Analysis and Design in 2006. Some selected mechanisms have been adopted by ISO (the International Organization for Standardization) and IEC (the International Electrotechnical Commission). Some of them have been submitted to IEEE P1363.3 [49].

The remaining part of the paper is organized as follows. we revisit the basic concept of IBC in the next section. In section 3, we introduce three IBC mechanisms based on integer factorization. After that, we recall some preliminaries of pairings in Section 4. In Sections 5 - 8, we explain a few IBE, IBS, IBKA and IB-Signcryption mechanisms from pairings. We then introduce some solutions for reducing the key escrow problem in IBC. Finally, we briefly mention some well-known security models for analysis of the major cryptographic primitives, and then conclude the paper.

2   What Is Identity-Based Cryptography?

Identity-Based Cryptography (IBC) is a specific type of asymmetric cryptographic technology. Compared with a traditional asymmetric cryptographic system based on a Public Key Infrastructure (PKI), such as the one defined in ISO/IEC 9594-8 [45], this technology has an interesting property. A public key can be derived from an arbitrary data string, and the corresponding private key is created by binding this string with a system master secret owned by a trusted authority. As a result, two processes of verifying a user's public key and using the public key are handled in a single algorithm. Whilst in PKI, verifying a public key and using the public key are normally achieved by using two separate algorithms.

Let us consider a common situation in many asymmetric cryptographic applications, e.g. encryption, authentication, digital signatures, key agreement etc. For the purpose of verifying the validation of a user's public key, a Trusted Third Party (TTP) is involved to make an authenticated link between the public key and the user's identity. This party plays a different role in an IBC system to the one played in a PKI system.

In a PKI system, the TTP is a Certificate Authority (CA). Having given a user's identity and public key, the CA first authenticates the user by checking whether the user owns the identity and whether he knows the value of the corresponding private key. If the authentication succeeds, the CA then issues a certificate, which includes a signature on the public key and identity signed under the CA's private signing key. Anybody, who would like to have an authenticated copy of the public key of the user, must verify the certificate by using the CA's public key.

In an IBC system, the TTP is a Key Generation Center (KGC). Once a user's identity has been given, the KGC only needs to verify whether the user owns the identity. If the verification succeeds, the KGC creates a private key for the user by combining the identity with the KGC's own private key. Anybody requiring an authenticated copy of the user's public key can simply involve the KGC's public key in every usage. The validation of the user public key is guaranteed by such a combination.

Thus, a more interesting result can be achieved, namely the creation of a non-pre-interactive communication between two players, such as an encrypter and a decrypter. For example, if Alice wants to send a secure email to Bob at bob@hp.com, she simply encrypts her message using the public key presenting bob@hp.com. There is no need for Alice to obtain a certificate of Bob's public key in advance. In order to make sure that only Bob is able to decrypt the message, Alice includes a public key of a chosen KGC in the encryption. After receiving the encrypted email, Bob authenticates himself to the KGC by proving the ownership of the email address and then obtains his private key from the KGC. Note that unlike the existing PKI based secure email infrastructure, Alice can send the encrypted email to Bob even if Bob has not yet got his private key. Alice can even choose any meaningful information, such as a photo, a phone number, a post address, a time, a role, a title, a policy and any terms and conditions, as Bob's public key and she can choose any trustworthy party as the KGC.

The disadvantage of the IBC technology is that we cannot escape the property of key escrow. It is obvious that the KGC knows the user's private key. A potential problem is that the KGC may impersonate a user and a user might be able to deny what he has done (for example signed a message). In an ordinary PKI system we have a similar problem. A CA can generate a key pair, and (falsely) certify that the public key belongs to a specific user. The CA can then impersonate the user to any other users. In both IBC and PKI we therefore always assume that the TTP (KGC or CA) will not impersonate users.

However, in PKI, the problem can be solved if we add an extra process (which is actually recommended by many applications), that the possession of the user's private key is verified every time the user uses the key. So, if a user has demonstrated that he knows the value of the private key, he cannot then deny his responsibility for the usage of the key. Unfortunately, we cannot offer the same solution for IBC because key escrow is inherent in IBC. As a result, an identity-based signature is not able to provide the property of non-repudiation (even if the ownership of a private signing key has been proved by a user), since there is always more than one entity knowing the private signing key. Many researchers have worked on this area to reduce the problem.

In the next a few sections, we will introduce several IBC mechanisms in major cryptographic primitives: encryption, signatures, key agreement and signcryption, and will also cover some solutions of removing key escrow problem. In the mechanism description, particularly in Figures, we omit the modulo operation, as long as the explained meaning is clear to the readers. Throughout the paper, $x\|y$ is used to denote concatenation of two data strings x and y, and $\alpha \in_R \beta$ is used to denote that an element α is picked from a set β uniformly and randomly.

3 Integer Factorization Based Mechanisms

In this section, we introduce three IBC mechanisms. Security of these mechanisms are based on the computational hardness of the integer factorization problem, i.e., given a large positive integer, finding its prime factorization is computationally infeasible.

3.1 The Shamir IBS Scheme

Like all Identity-Based Signature (IBS) solutions, Shamir's IBS scheme involves three players: A (Alice) is a signature signer, B (Bob) is a signature verifier and T (Trent) is a Key Generation Center (KGC).

T owns a pair of system master public and private key. The master public key is an RSA type public key including the values e and n, where $n = pq$, p and q are two large primes, and e is a prime and does not divide $(p-1)(q-1)$. The master private key is the corresponding RSA private key including the value d, satisfying $d = 1/e \bmod (p-1)(q-1)$.

Players: A - signer, B - verifier and T - KGC.

System setup: Public parameters are (n, e, H), and T's private key is d.

Key extract: Given ID_A, presenting A's identity, T generates A's private key as

$$g = ID_A^d.$$

Signature generation: To sign a message $m \in \{0,1\}^*$, A chooses $r \in_R \mathbb{Z}_n^*$, and computes the signature pair (s,t) as

$$t = r^e, \quad s = g \cdot r^{H(t\|m)}.$$

Verification: Given (ID_A, m, t, s), B verifies the signature as follows:

If $s^e \equiv ID_A \cdot t^{H(t\|m)}$, accept the signature; otherwise reject it.

Fig. 1. The Shamir IBS scheme

A has a pair of private signing key and public verification key. Her public key presents her identity ID_A, which could be a digest of a meaningful identifier, e.g., her email address, alice@hp.com. In that case, $ID_A = H_0(\text{alice@hp.com})$, where H_0 is a secure hash-function, $H_0 : \{0,1\}^* \rightarrow \mathbb{Z}_n^*$. Shamir's identity-based key extraction algorithm is an RSA signing algorithm. A's private key d_A is generated by T as $d_A = ID_A^d \bmod n$.

The system parameters include another secure hash-function, $H : \{0,1\}^n \times \{0,1\}^* \rightarrow \mathbb{Z}_n^*$. The Shamir IBS scheme is shown in Figure 1.

3.2   The IBKA Scheme in ISO/IEC 11770-3

We now introduce an Identity-Based Key Agreement (IBKA) protocol from ISO/IEC 11770-3 [46]. This standard was published in 1999, and it is currently in the revising process.

The protocol involves three players: A (Alice) and B (Bob) are two users, and T (Trent) is a KGC. The system master public key includes a modulus n and exponent e, which are the same as in the Shamir IBS scheme of Section 3.1, plus two elements h and g satisfying $g = h^e \bmod n$. The master private key is the value d, which is again the same as in the Shamir IBS scheme.

Each user X (either A or B) has a private key denoted as d_X, satisfying $(d_X)^e \cdot ID_X = 1 \bmod n$. The value d_X is computed by T as $d_X = (1/ID_X)^d \bmod n$, where ID_X presents X's identity.

The key agreement protocol is shown in Figure 2. As a result of the protocol, A and B end up with the same value g^{ab}. They then use this value as their shared secret to retrieve a set of shared keys and to add a key confirmation process if requested. This part is standard and well-known, and is not special for identity-based systems. The readers with interests of knowing the details are recommended to check [46].

Players: A and B - two users and T - KGC.

System setup: Public parameters are (n, e, h, g), where $g = h^e$, and T's private key is d.

Key extract: Let ID_X present X's identity, where $X = \{A, B\}$. X's private key is generated by T as $d_X = (1/ID_X)^d$.

Protocol:

$$
\begin{array}{cc}
A & B \\
a \in_R \mathbb{Z}_n^* & b \in_R \mathbb{Z}_n^* \\
\end{array}
$$

$$\xrightarrow{\quad t_A = d_A \cdot h^a \quad}$$

$$\xleftarrow{\quad t_B = d_B \cdot h^b \quad}$$

$$
\begin{array}{cc}
K_{AB} = ((t_B)^e \cdot ID_B)^a = g^{ab} & K_{BA} = ((t_A)^e \cdot ID_A)^b = g^{ab}
\end{array}
$$

Fig. 2. The IBKA scheme in ISO/IEC 11770-3

3.3   The Cocks IBE Scheme

In 2001, Cocks proposed an Identity-Based Encryption (IBE) Scheme [35], which uses quadratic residues modulo a large composite integer. Based on the author's best knowledge, except a very recent work [17]this is the only practical IBE scheme that does not use pairings.

Security of this scheme is based on the hardness of the quadratic residues problem, i.e. given two values y and n, find the value x satisfying $x = y^2 \bmod n$, where $n = pq$ and p and q are two large primes. The scheme encrypts a data string bit by bit, and it requires $(\log n)$ bits of ciphertext per bit of plaintext, but the scheme is quite fast. The scheme is shown in Figure 3.

Players: A - encrypter, B - decrypter and T - KGC.

System setup: Public parameters are (n, H), and T's private key is (p, q).

Key extract: Let ID_B present B's identity and $a = H(ID_B)$. Bob's private key r is a square root of either a or $-a$ modulo n, which is generated by T as

$$r = a^{\frac{n+5-(p+q)}{8}} \bmod n.$$

Encryption: To encrypt a data string $D \in \{1, 0\}^*$, A first presents D as a bit string. Let x be a single bit of D, coded as $+1$ or -1, A chooses $t \in_R \mathbb{Z}_n$, such that the Jacobi symbol $(\frac{t}{n})$ equals x. A then outputs $s_+ = t + a/t \bmod n$ or $s_- = t - a/t \bmod n$ or both as the ciphertext of x.

Decryption: B recovers the bit x by computing the Jacobi symbol $(\frac{s+2r}{n})$, where s is either s_+ or s_-.

Fig. 3. The Cocks IBE scheme

Three players are involved: Alice (A) is an encrypter, Bob (B) is a decrypter and Trent (T) is a KGC. The master key pair are generated as follows. Generate two large primes p and q, where p and q are both congruent to 3 mod 4, and compute $n = pq$. The value n then is published as the master public key, and the master private key is (p, q).

Let ID_B present B's identity. Let H denote a secure hash-function and a denote an output of H with the input ID_B, i.e., $a = H(ID_B)$, such that the Jacobi symbol $(\frac{a}{n}) = +1$. Bob's private key r is a square root of either a or $-a$ modulo n.

To encrypt a message $m \in \{0, 1\}^*$, Alice first generates a transport key, denoted as D in Figure 3, and uses it to encrypt m using any symmetric encryption algorithm. She sends to Bob each bit of D in turn as follows: Let x be a single bit of D, coded as $+1$ or -1. Then Alice chooses a value t at random modulo n, such that the Jacobi symbol $(\frac{t}{n})$ equals x. Then she sends Bob $s = t + a/t \bmod n$, if she knows a is the square for which Bob holds the root, or $s = t - a/t \bmod n$, if she knows $-a$ is the square. If Alice does not know which of a or $-a$ is the square, she will have to replicate the above, using different randomly chosen t

values to send the same x bits, and transmitting both $s_1 = t + a/t \bmod n$ and $s_- = t - a/t \bmod n$ to Bob at each step.

Bob recovers the bit x by computing the Jacobi symbol $(\frac{s+2r}{n})$. As $s + 2r = t(1 + r/t)^2 \bmod n$, it follows that the Jacobi symbol $(\frac{s+2r}{n}) = (\frac{t}{n}) = x$. Since Bob knows the value of r, he can calculate the Jacobi symbol easily.

4 Preliminaries of Pairings

In this section, we recall the well-known preliminaries of pairings, including the definition of bilinear pairings, some related problems and assumptions and two pairing-based key extraction algorithms.

4.1 Bilinear Groups and Some Assumptions

Here we briefly recall some basic facts of pairings.

Definition 1. *A pairing is a bilinear map* $\hat{e} : \mathbb{G}_1 \times \mathbb{G}_2 \to \mathbb{G}_T$ *between three groups* $\mathbb{G}_1$, $\mathbb{G}_2$ *and* $\mathbb{G}_T$ *of exponent* q, *which has the following properties:*

1. *Bilinear:* $\forall (P_1, P_2) \in \mathbb{G}_1 \times \mathbb{G}_2$ *and* $\forall (a, b) \in \mathbb{Z}_q \times \mathbb{Z}_q$, *we have* $\hat{e}(aP_1, bP_2) = \hat{e}(P_1, P_2)^{ab}$.
2. *Non-degenerate: There exist non-trivial points* $P_1 \in \mathbb{G}_1$ *and* $P_2 \in \mathbb{G}_2$ *both of order* q *such that* $\hat{e}(P_1, P_2) \neq 1$.
3. *Computable:* $\forall (P_1, P_2) \in \mathbb{G}_1 \times \mathbb{G}_2$, $\hat{e}(P_1, P_2)$ *is efficiently computable.*

Some recent researches have made use of different types of pairing system, e.g. Chen, Cheng and Smart in [24] discussed how to use four types of pairings in IBKA protocols, where three types were taken from [39] whilst the fourth was from [67]. However, for the purpose of this paper, we do not specify which types of pairing system can be used in each mechanism. The readers with interests of finding the details are recommended to read these papers.

There are a batch of assumptions related to the bilinear groups. We list a few assumptions below, which are relative to these IBC mechanisms that we are going to introduce in the remaining part of the paper. Cheng and Chen in [31] listed a large number of assumptions and showed how they are related to each other.

Assumption 1 (Diffie-Hellman (DH)). *For* $x, y \in_R \mathbb{Z}_q^*$, $P \in \mathbb{G}_1^*$, *given* (P, xP, yP), *computing* xyP *is hard.*

Assumption 2 (Bilinear DH (BDH)) [16]. *For* x, y, $z \in_R \mathbb{Z}_q^*$, $P_2 \in \mathbb{G}_2^*$, $P_1 = \psi(P_2)$, $\hat{e} : \mathbb{G}_1 \times \mathbb{G}_2 \to \mathbb{G}_T$, *given* $(P_1, P_2, xP_2, yP_2, zP_2)$, *computing* $\hat{e}(P_1, P_2)^{xyz}$ *is hard.*

Assumption 3 (Decisional Bilinear DH (DBDH)). *For* x, y, z, $r \in_R \mathbb{Z}_q^*$, $P_2 \in \mathbb{G}_2^*$, $P_1 = \psi(P_2)$, $\hat{e} : \mathbb{G}_1 \times \mathbb{G}_2 \to \mathbb{G}_T$, *distinguishing between the distributions* $(P_1, P_2, xP_2, yP_2, zP_2, \hat{e}(P_1, P_2)^{xyz})$ *and* $(P_1, P_2, xP_2, yP_2, zP_2, \hat{e}(P_1, P_2)^r)$ *is hard.*

Assumption 4 (DH Inversion (k-DHI) [54]). *For an integer k, and $x \in_R$ $\mathbb{Z}_q^*$, $P \in \mathbb{G}_1^*$, given $(P, xP, x^2P, \ldots, x^kP)$, computing $\frac{1}{x}P$ is hard.*

Assumption 5 (Bilinear DH Inversion (k-BDHI) [14]). *For an integer k, and $x \in_R \mathbb{Z}_q^*$, $P_2 \in \mathbb{G}_2^*$, $P_1 = \psi(P_2)$, $\hat{e} : \mathbb{G}_1 \times \mathbb{G}_2 \to \mathbb{G}_T$, given $(P_1, P_2, xP_2, x^2P_2, \ldots, x^kP_2)$, computing $\hat{e}(P_1, P_2)^{1/x}$ is hard.*

4.2   Identity-Based Key Extraction

There are a number of different key extraction algorithms to achieve identity-based cryptographic mechanisms from pairings. In this section, we introduce two algorithms, which have been widely used in many mechanisms of different cryptographic primitives, including all of the mechanisms we have selected in this paper.

In the first key extraction algorithm (called **Extract 1**), an identity string is mapped to a point on an elliptic curve and the corresponding private key is computed by multiplying the mapped point with the master secret of the KGC. This key extraction algorithm was first shown in Sakai *et al.*'s work [64] in 2000 as the preparation step of an identity-based key establishment protocol. Apart from the Boneh-Franklin IBE scheme [16] and the Sakai *et al.* IBE scheme [65], many other IBC mechanisms have made use of this key extraction algorithm, such as the signature schemes [21,44], the authenticated key agreement schemes [29,72], and the signcryption schemes [19,30].

The second key extraction algorithm (called **Extract 2**) requires much simpler hashing than Extract 1 and therefore improves performance. More specifically, it maps an identity string to an element $h \in \mathbb{Z}_q^*$ instead of a point on an elliptic curve. The corresponding private key is generated as follow: first, compute the inverse of the sum of the master key (a random integer from $\mathbb{Z}_q^*$) and the mapped h; secondly, multiply a point of the elliptic curve (which is the generator of an order q subgroup of the group of points on the curve) with the inverse (obtained in the first step). The algorithm was presented by Sakai and Kasahara in 2003 [63]. The idea of this algorithm can be tracked back to the work in 2002 [54]. After the paper [63] was appeared, a number of other identity-based schemes based on this key extraction algorithm have been published, for example [52,53].

Chen, Cheng and Smart in [24] described two variants for each of the two key extraction algorithms. We recall their description as follows:

Setup of KGC. Both Extract 1 and Extract 2 use the same setup algorithm to create the KGC master key pair. Given the security parameter k, the algorithm first selects a set of pairing parameters of the correct form, including generation of three cyclic groups $\mathbb{G}_1$, $\mathbb{G}_2$ and $\mathbb{G}_T$ of prime order q, an isomorphism ψ from $\mathbb{G}_2$ to $\mathbb{G}_1$, and a bilinear pairing map $\hat{e} : \mathbb{G}_1 \times \mathbb{G}_2 \to \mathbb{G}_T$. Let P_1 be the generator of $\mathbb{G}_1$ and P_2 be the generator of $\mathbb{G}_2$. The master private key is $s \in_R \mathbb{Z}_q^*$, and the master public key is either $R = sP_1 \in \mathbb{G}_1$ or $R' = sP_2 \in \mathbb{G}_2$ or both (R, R').

Extract 1. We refer to two variants of this algorithm as Extract 1 and Extract 1'. In Extract 1 given the pairing parameters, an identity string ID_A for a user A, a hash-function $H_1 : \{0,1\}^* \rightarrow \mathbb{G}_1$, the master private key $s \in \mathbb{Z}_q^*$, and the master public key, either $R = sP_1 \in \mathbb{G}_1$ or $R' = sP_2 \in \mathbb{G}_2$ or both, the algorithm computes $Q_A = H_1(ID_A) \in \mathbb{G}_1$ and $d_A = sQ_A \in \mathbb{G}_1$. Extract 1' is the same, except that H_1 is now a hash function with codomain $\mathbb{G}_2$, and hence Q_A and d_A lie in $\mathbb{G}_2$. In both cases, the values Q_A and d_A will be used as the public and private key pair corresponding to A's identity ID_A.

Extract 2. We refer to two variants of this algorithm as Extract 2 and Extract 2'. In Extract 2, given the pairing parameters, an identity string ID_A for a user A, a hash-function $H_1 : \{0,1\}^* \rightarrow \mathbb{Z}_q^*$, the master private key $s \in \mathbb{Z}_q^*$, and the master public key $R = sP_1 \in \mathbb{G}_1$, the algorithm computes $\alpha = H_1(ID_A) \in \mathbb{Z}_q^*$ and $d_A = \frac{1}{s+\alpha}P_2 \in \mathbb{G}_2$. The values $T_A = \alpha P_1 + R = (s+\alpha)P_1 \in \mathbb{G}_1$. In Extract 2', $R' = sP_2 \in \mathbb{G}_2$ and $T_A = \alpha P_2 + R' = (s+\alpha)P_2 \in \mathbb{G}_2$ and $d_A = \frac{1}{s+\alpha}P_1 \in \mathbb{G}_1$. In both cases, T_A and d_A will be used as the public and private key pair corresponding to A's identity ID_A.

In the remaining part of the paper, the following notation is used in the specification of IBC mechanisms from pairings:

- $\mathbb{G}_1$, $\mathbb{G}_2$, $\mathbb{G}_T$ are three groups of prime order q,
- $\hat{e} : \mathbb{G}_1 \times \mathbb{G}_2 \rightarrow \mathbb{G}_T$ is a bilinear map,
- $P_1 \in \mathbb{G}_1$, $P_2 \in \mathbb{G}_2$ and $\psi(P_2) = P_1$,
- $g = \hat{e}(P_1, P_2)$,
- $s \in_R \mathbb{Z}_q^*$ is the master private key,
- $R = sP_1 \in \mathbb{G}_1$ and $R' = sP_2 \in \mathbb{G}_2$,
- n is a chosen integer, which is dependent on the security parameter. Note that in some mechanisms, the value n equals to the message space.

5   Encryption Mechanisms from Pairings

In this section, we introduce two Identity-Based Encryption (IBE) schemes and one Identity-Based Key Encapsulation Mechanism (IB-KEM).

5.1   The Boneh-Franklin IBE Scheme

Boneh and Franklin [16] proposed an IBE scheme and defined a security model for IBE. Their scheme was the first IBE scheme to have a proof of security in an appropriate model. The security of the scheme was proved under the BDH assumption in the random oracle model [9]. The scheme makes use of the symmetric pairing setting, i.e. $\mathbb{G}_1 = \mathbb{G}_2$ and $P_1 = P_2 = P$, and the key extraction algorithm Extract 1, as specified in Section 4.2. The scheme is shown in Figure 4, in which four hash-functions are used: $H_1 : \{0,1\}^* \to \mathbb{G}_1$, $H_2 : \mathbb{G}_T \to \{0,1\}^n$, $H_3 : \{0,1\}^n \times \{0,1\}^n \to \mathbb{Z}_q^*$ and $H_4 : \{0,1\}^n \to \{0,1\}^n$.

Players: A - encrypter, B - decrypter and T - KGC.

System setup: The system parameters are $(q, \mathbb{G}_1, \mathbb{G}_T, \hat{e}, n, P, R, H_1, H_2, H_3, H_4)$, and the master private key is s.

Key extract: Let $ID_B \in \{0,1\}^*$ present B's identity, B's private key d_B is generated by T as $d_B = sQ_B$ where $Q_B = H_1(ID_B)$.

Encryption: A performs the following steps to encrypt $m \in \{0,1\}^n$ for B:

1. Choose $\sigma \in_R \{0,1\}^n$, and compute $r = H_3(\sigma\|m)$ and $g_B = \hat{e}(Q_B, R)$.
2. Output the ciphertext C as
$$C = (U, V, W) = (rP, \sigma \oplus H_2(g_B^r), m \oplus H_4(\sigma)).$$

Decryption: To recover m from (U, V, W), the following steps are performed by B:

1. Compute $\sigma = V \oplus H_2(\hat{e}(d_B, U))$, $m = W \oplus H_4(\sigma)$ and $r = H_3(\sigma\|m)$.
2. If $U \equiv rP$, return m; else return "invalid".

Fig. 4. The Boneh-Franklin IBE scheme

5.2   The SK-IBE Scheme

The original scheme was proposed by Sakai and Kasahara in 2003 [63]. Here we describe a modified version, which was introduced by Chen and Cheng in [22].

Players: A - encrypter, B - decrypter and T - KGC.

System setup: The system parameters are $(q, \mathbb{G}_1, \mathbb{G}_2, \mathbb{G}_T, \psi, \hat{e}, n, P_1, P_2, R, g, H_1, H_2, H_3, H_4)$, and the master private key is s.

Key extract: Let $ID_B \in \{0,1\}^*$ present B's identity, B's private key d_B is generated by T as $d_B = \frac{1}{s+H_1(ID_B)}P_2$.

Encryption: To encrypt $m \in \{0,1\}^n$ for B, A performs the following steps:

1. Choose $\sigma \in_R \{0,1\}^n$, and compute $r = H_3(\sigma\|m)$ and $Q_B = H_1(ID_B)P_1 + R$.
2. Output the ciphertext C as
$$C = (U, V, W) = (rQ_B, \sigma \oplus H_2(g^r), m \oplus H_4(\sigma)).$$

Decryption: To recover m from (U, V, W), the following steps are performed by B:

1. Compute $\sigma = V \oplus H_2(\hat{e}(U, d_B))$, $m = W \oplus H_4(\sigma)$ and $r = H_3(\sigma\|m)$.
2. If $U \equiv r(H_1(ID_B)P_1 + R)$, return m; else return "invalid".

Fig. 5. The SK-IBE scheme

The security of the scheme was proved under the k-BDHI assumption in the random oracle model. The scheme uses the key extraction algorithm Extract 2, as described in Section 4.2. The scheme is shown in Figure 5, in which four hash-functions are used: $H_1 : \{0,1\}^* \rightarrow \mathbb{Z}_q^*$, $H_2 : \mathbb{G}_T \rightarrow \{0,1\}^n$, $H_3 : \{0,1\}^n \times \{0,1\}^n \rightarrow \mathbb{Z}_q^*$ and $H_4 : \{0,1\}^n \rightarrow \{0,1\}^n$.

5.3   The CCMS IB-KEM Scheme

A natural way to protect arbitrarily long messages is to use hybrid encryption. A hybrid encryption scheme consists of two basic operations. One operation uses a public-key encryption technique (a so called key encapsulation mechanism or KEM) to derive a shared key; the other operation uses the shared key in a symmetric-key algorithm (a so called data encapsulation mechanism or DEM) to encrypt the actual message. Cramer and Shou [32] formalised the notion of hybrid encryption and presented sufficient conditions for a KEM and a DEM to construct IND-CCA2 secure public key encryption. Bentahar et al. [12] extended the KEM concept to the identity-based setting and gave three constructions of such an IB-KEM.

Based on the Bentahar et al. solution, Chen, Cheng, Malone-Lee and Smart [23] developed an more efficient identity-based key encapsulation mechanism in 2005. As shown in Figure 6, the mechanism uses the key extraction algorithm, Extract 2, as described in Section 4.2. An extended work has been submitted to IEEE P1363.3 by Barbosa et al., which is available at [4]. The security of this scheme was proved under the k-BDHI assumption in the random oracle model. Note that the scheme uses the same four hash-functions as in the SK-IBE scheme of Section 5.2.

Players: A - encrypter, B - decrypter and T - KGC.

System setup: The same as it in the SK-IBE scheme.

Key extract: The same as it in the SK-IBE scheme.

Key encapsulation: To encapsulate an encryption key k, the following steps are performed by A:

1. Choose $m \in_R \{0,1\}^n$.
2. Compute $r = H_3(m)$, $Q_B = H_1(ID_B)P_1 + R$ and $k = H_4(m)$.
3. Output the key encapsulation text C as

$$C = (U, V) = (rQ_B, m \oplus H_2(g^r)).$$

Key retrieval: To retrieve k from (U, V), the following steps are performed by B:

1. Compute $m = V \oplus H_2(\hat{e}(U, d_B))$ and $r = H_3(m)$.
2. If $U \equiv r(H_1(ID_B)P_1 + R)$, compute $k = H_4(m)$ and return k; else return "invalid".

Fig. 6. The CCMS IB-KEM scheme

6   Signature Mechanisms from Pairings

A number of Identity-Based Signature (IBS) schemes from pairings have been published since 2000, for example, the Sahai *et al.* scheme [64], the Paterson scheme [59], the Hess scheme [44], the Cha and Cheon scheme [21] and the Yi scheme [81].

In this section, we introduce three signature schemes. The first two have been adopted by ISO and IEC in ISO/IEC 14888-3 [48].

6.1   The First IBS Scheme in ISO/IEC 14888-3

The ISO/IEC 14888-3 IBS-1 scheme is based on the Hess IBS Scheme [44]. The security of this scheme was proved under the Diffie-Hellman assumption in the random oracle model by using the technique from [60,61].

The scheme uses the key extraction algorithm Extract 1, as described in Section 4.2, with the symmetric pairing setting, i.e. $\mathbb{G}_1 = \mathbb{G}_2$ and $P_1 = P_2 = P$.

The scheme is shown in Figure 7, where H_1 and H_2 denote two hash-functions, $H_1 : \{0,1\}^* \to \mathbb{G}_1$ and $H_2 : \{0,1\}^n \times \mathbb{G}_1 \to \mathbb{Z}_q^*$.

Players: A - singer, B - verifier and T - KGC.

System setup: The system parameters are $(q, \mathbb{G}_1, \mathbb{G}_T, \hat{e}, n, P, R, H_1, H_2)$, and the master private key is s.

Key extract: Given ID_A presenting A's identity, T generates A's private key as $d_A = sQ_A$, where $Q_A = H_1(ID_A)$.

Signing: To sign $m \in \{0,1\}^n$, A performs the following steps:

– Pick $k \in_R \mathbb{Z}_q^*$.
– Compute $U = \hat{e}(sQ_A, P)^k$, $h = H_2(m\|U)$ and $S = (k - h)d_A$.
– Outputs (h, S) as a signature.

Verification: To verify the signature (h, S), B performs the following steps:

– Computes $U = \hat{e}(S, P)\hat{e}(Q_A, R)^h$.
– If $h \equiv H_2(m\|U)$, return "accept". Else, return "reject".

Fig. 7. ISO/IEC 14888-3 IBS-1 scheme

6.2   The Second IBS Scheme in ISO/IEC 14888-3

The ISO/IEC 14888-3 IBS-2 scheme is based on the Cha-Cheon IBS Scheme [21]. The security of this scheme was proved under the Diffie-Hellman assumption in the random oracle model.

The scheme, as the same as IBS-1, uses the key extraction algorithm Extract 1, as described in Section 4.2, with the symmetric pairing setting, i.e. $\mathbb{G}_1 = \mathbb{G}_2$ and $P_1 = P_2 = P$. The scheme is shown in Figure 8, where H_1 and H_2 denote two hash-functions, $H_1 : \{0,1\}^* \to \mathbb{Z}_q^*$ and $H_2 : \{0,1\}^n \times \mathbb{G}_1 \to \mathbb{Z}_q^*$.

Players: A - singer, B - verifier and T - KGC.

System setup: The system parameters are $(q, \mathbb{G}_1, \mathbb{G}_T, \hat{e}, n, P, R, H_1, H_2)$, and the master private key is s.

Key extract: Given ID_A presenting A's identity, T generates A's private key as $d_A = sQ_A$, where $Q_A = H_1(ID_A)$.

Signing: To sign $m \in \{0, 1\}^n$, A performs the following steps:

- Pick $r \in_R \mathbb{Z}_q^*$.
- Compute $U = rQ_A$, $h = H_2(m\|U)$ and $S = (r + h)d_A$.
- Outputs (U, S) as a signature.

Verification: To verify the signature (U, S), B performs the following steps:

- Computes $h = H_2(m\|U)$.
- If $\hat{e}(P, S) \equiv \hat{e}(R, U + hQ_A)$, return "accept". Else, return "reject".

Fig. 8. ISO/IEC 14888-3 IBS-2 scheme

6.3   The BLMQ IBS Scheme

This IBS scheme was proposed by Barreto *et al.* in [6]. It has been submitted to IEEE P1363.3 and is available at [7]. The security of this scheme was proved under the k-DHI assumption in the random oracle model.

The scheme uses the key extraction algorithm Extract 2, as described in Section 4.2. The scheme is shown in Figure 9, where two hash-functions are used: $H_1 : \{0, 1\}^* \to \mathbb{Z}_q^*$ and $H_2 : \{0, 1\}^n \times \mathbb{G}_T \to \mathbb{Z}_q^*$.

Players: A - signer, B - verifier, and T - KGC.

System setup: The system parameters are $(q, \mathbb{G}_1, \mathbb{G}_2, \mathbb{G}_T, \psi, \hat{e}, n, P_1, P_2, R', g, H_1, H_2)$, and the master private key is s.

Key extract: Let ID_A present A's identity. A's private key is generated by T as $d_A = \frac{1}{s+H_1(ID_A)}P_1$.

Signing: To sign $m \in \{0, 1\}^n$, A performs the following steps:

- Pick $x \in_R \mathbb{Z}_q^*$.
- Compute $r = g^x$, $h = H_2(m\|r)$ and $S = (x + h)d_A$.
- Output (h, S) as a signature.

Verification: To verify the signature (U, S), B performs the following steps:

- Computes $r = \hat{e}(S, H_1(ID_A)P_2 + R')g^{-h}$
- If $h \equiv H_2(m\|r)$, return "accept". Else, return "reject".

Fig. 9. The BLMQ IBS scheme

7   Key Agreement Mechanisms from Pairings

A large number of Identity-Based Key Agreement (IBKA) protocols from pairings have been published in the past several years, e.g. [18, 29, 33, 50, 53, 62, 66, 70, 72, 76, 79, 80]. Chen, Cheng and Smart [24] gave an overview of these IBKA schemes. In this section, we introduce one of the protocols as follows.

In 2002, Smart [72] proposed an IBKA protocol. After that, Chen and Kudla [29] modified the Smart scheme in order to make it more efficient and, more interestingly, to let it hold the new property of KGC forward security, which they defined to mean that the compromise of the KGC's private key will not compromise previously established session keys. We refer the modified Smart scheme as the Smart-Chen-Kudla IBKA scheme. The security of this scheme has been proved by Chen, Cheng and Smart [24] using the Bellare-Rogaway key agreement security model [10, 13] under the BDH assumption and the random oracle model [9]. The scheme has been submitted to IEEE P1363.3 [49]. We describe the scheme using Extract 1 with the symmetric pairing setting in Figure 10. Note that actually the scheme works with different types of pairings, and the details can be found in [24].

Players: A and B - two users, and T - KGC.

System setup: Public parameters are $(q, \mathbb{G}_1, \mathbb{G}_T, \hat{e}, n, P, R)$ and $H : \{0,1\}^* \to \mathbb{G}_1$, and T's private key is s.

Key extract: Let ID_X present user X's identity, where $X = \{A, B\}$. X's private key is generated by T as $d_X = sQ_X$, where $Q_X = H(ID_X)$.

Protocol:

$$
\begin{array}{cc}
A & B \\
a \in_R \mathbb{Z}_q^* & b \in_R \mathbb{Z}_q^*
\end{array}
$$

$$\xrightarrow{\quad t_A = aP \quad}$$
$$\xleftarrow{\quad t_B = bP \quad}$$

$$
\begin{array}{cc}
s_{AB} = & s_{BA} = \\
abP\|\hat{e}(d_A, t_B)\hat{e}(Q_B, asP) & abP\|\hat{e}(d_B, t_A)\hat{e}(Q_A, bsP)
\end{array}
$$

Fig. 10. The Smart-Chen-Kudla IBKA protocol

It is clear that in the end of the protocol, A and B will establish a shared secret $s_{AB} = s_{BA}$, since $\hat{e}(d_A, t_B)\hat{e}(Q_B, asP) = \hat{e}(d_B, t_A)\hat{e}(Q_A, bsP) = \hat{e}(bQ_A + aQ_B, sP)$.

It is required that in applications of the scheme, a cryptographic hash-function (namely key derivation function in the literature) should be used to retrieve a session key (or a set of session keys) from a data string including the two-party identities, the protocol transcripts, the shared secret etc. If key confirmation between A and B is required, a well-known method is to make use of a secure message authentication code (MAC) algorithm, which as defined in [11] takes a key and a message as input and outputs a tag on the message. A and B each generate such a tag by using the shared session key derived from the key derivation function and a selected message that could include A and B's identifiers, the protocol transcripts and a message index showing who has created this tag. A and B then exchange their tags to confirm that they have got the shared session key.

8   Signcryption Mechanisms from Pairings

The primitive of signcryption was proposed by Zheng in 1997 [83]. The idea of a signcryption scheme is to combine the functionality of an encryption scheme with that of a signature scheme. It must provide privacy and unforgeability. This should be done in a more efficient manner than a composition of an encryption scheme with a signature scheme.

The idea of Identity-Based Signcryption (IB-Signcryption) was first proposed by Malone-Lee [55]. He proposed a security model dealing with notions of privacy and unforgeability and also proposed a scheme but no proofs of security. A weakness in the Malone-Lee scheme was subsequently pointed out by Libert and Quisquater [51], where a new scheme was proposed. The new scheme came with proofs of security in the model of [55]. The model of security for IB-Signcryption was further developed by Boyen in [19], where two new security notions were added: ciphertext authentication and ciphertext anonymity. A scheme was also proposed in [19] and analyzed in the enhanced model. Chen and Malone-Lee [30] proposed a modification of the Boyen scheme that is considerably more efficient. They also proved that the new scheme secure in the model of [19]. All of the above IB-Signcryption schemes make use of the key extraction algorithm Extract 1 as described in Section 4.2, and their security relies on the BDH assumption.

Barreto et $al.$ [6] proposed another IB-Signcryption scheme based on the key extraction algorithm Extract 2 as described in Section 4.2. The security of this scheme relies on the hardness of the k-BDHI problem. This scheme has been submitted to IEEE P1363.3 [7].

In all the above IB-Signcryption schemes, it was assumed that both encrypter A and decrypter B must obtain their identity-based private keys from the same KGC. This condition might not be held in some real applications. Chen, Harrison and Malone-Lee [26] proposed a scheme where A and B obtain their keys from two key generation centers, KGC_1 and KGC_2, respectively. The scheme is a modification of the scheme from [30].

The Chen, Harrison and Malone-Lee scheme has two versions. In the first one, KGC_1 and KGC_2 use the same system parameters, such as $(q, \mathbb{G}_1, \mathbb{G}_2, \mathbb{G}_T, P_1, P_2)$. In the second one, they do not have to use the same (P_1, P_2). In both versions, KGC_1 and KGC_2 have their own private keys $s_1 \in_R \mathbb{Z}_q^*$ and $s_2 \in_R \mathbb{Z}_q^*$ respectively. For simplicity, we describe the first version with the symmetric pairing setting (i.e. $\mathbb{G}_1 = \mathbb{G}_2$ and $P_1 = P_2 = P$) in Figure 11. As the same as in the original scheme [30], the security of this modified scheme relies on the hardness of the BGH problem. The scheme make use of three hash functions $H_0 : \{0,1\}^* \to \mathbb{G}_1$,

$H_1 : \mathbb{G}_1 \times \{0,1\}^n \to \mathbb{Z}_q^*$ and $H_2 : \mathbb{G}_T \to \{0,1\}^{k_0+k_1+n}$. Here k_0 is the number of bits required to represent an element of $\mathbb{G}_1$; k_1 is the number of bits required to represent an identity; and n is the number of bits of a message to be signed and encrypted. Let A have identity ID_A and B have identity ID_B, $Q_A = H_0(ID_A)$ and $Q_B = H_0(ID_B)$ present A and B's public keys respectively.

Players: A - sender, B - receiver, and T_1 and T_2 - two key generation centers.

System setup: Public parameters are $(q, \mathbb{G}_1, \mathbb{G}_T, P, n, H_0, H_1, H_2)$, and T_1 and T_2's private and public keys are (s_1, s_1P) and (s_2, s_2P) respectively.

Key extract: A's private key is generated by T_1 as $d_A = s_1 Q_A$ and B's private key is generated by T_2 as $d_B = s_2 Q_B$.

Sign-encrypt: To sign $m \in \{0,1\}^n$ and to encrypt it for B, A performs the following steps.

- Choose $r \in_R \mathbb{Z}_q^*$, and compute $X = rP$, $h_1 = H_1(X\|m)$ and $Z = rs_1P + h_1 d_A$.
- Compute $Q_B = H_0(ID_B)$, $w = \hat{e}(Q_B, rs_2P)$ and $y = H_2(w) \oplus (Z\|ID_A\|m)$.
- Return (X, y).

Decrypt-verify: To decrypt m and A's signature from (X, y) and to verify the signature, B performs the following steps.

- Compute $w = \hat{e}(d_B, X)$ and $Z\|ID_A\|m = y \oplus H_2(w)$.
- Compute $Q_A = H_0(ID_A)$ and $h_1 = H_1(X\|m)$.
- If $\hat{e}(P, Z) \equiv \hat{e}(s_1P, X + h_1 Q_A)$, return m and "valid". Else, return "invalid".

Fig. 11. The Chen, Harrison & Malone-Lee IB-Signcryption scheme

9 Identity-Based Cryptography Without Key Escrow

As it has been mentioned before, an ordinary IBC mechanism holds a key escrow property, because it allows a single KGC to issue an identity-based private key for a user. Therefore, this KGC can impersonate any of his users if he wants to. Even if he has never abused any user's key, a malicious user may still be able to deny that he has used his key, e.g. for signing a message. The key escrow property makes difficulty to use an IBC system in many applications, for example, non-repudiation seems impossible.

To solve the problem of key escrow in IBC, researchers have proposed two types of results: **Result 1.** Split a user's private key into two parts. The KGC is allowed to escrow one part only. **Result 2.** Split a KGC into multiple KGCs. Each of them is allowed to escrow part of the user's private key and multiple KGCs' contributions are used to create the user's private key.

9.1 Result 1: Using Multiple Key Pairs

Two solutions for this result were published in 2003.

Gentry [40] proposed a solution for Result 1, which is called certificate-based public key cryptography. In the key construction of this solution, a user's key includes two asymmetric key pairs, $(pk_1, sk_1; pk_2, sk_2)$. pk_1 and sk_1 are created by the user like an ordinary public and private key pair. pk_2 presents the user's identity ID along with pk_1. A KGC is asked to generate sk_2 by combining $pk_2 = ID\|pk_1$ with its own private key.

Al-Riyami and Paterson [1, 2] proposed another solution for Result 1, which they called certificateless public key cryptography. In the key construction of this solution, again, a user has two key pairs, $(pk_1, sk_1; pk_2, sk_2)$. (pk_1, sk_1) is created by the user like an ordinary public and private key pair. (pk_2, sk_2) is generated like an ordinary identity-based key pair, i.e. sk_2 is created by a KGC based on the user's identity presented in pk_2. However, the user is required to generate a link between the two key pairs. The link demonstrates that someone knows both sk_1 and sk_2. The user's whole key includes the two key pairs plus the link.

Obviously the above two solutions do not hold the property of non-pre-interaction between two communication players, such as an encrypter and a decrypter, because the encrypter cannot choose a public key for the decrypter. But, it can be argued that both the two solutions have kept the major advantage of IBC, i.e. one does not have to verify whether the given public key of his communication partner has already been authenticated by the KGC or not.

9.2   Result 2: Using Multiple Key Generation Centers

The second result also has two solutions: a secret sharing solution and a secret aggregating solution. The discussion on this result below is a recall of Chen and Harrison's work [25] a few years ago.

The secret sharing solution. A number of researchers proposed some approaches of splitting the single KGC into two or more co-operating KGCs. For example, Cocks [35] proposed a secret sharing protocol for his IBE scheme, in which more than one KGC can work together to establish an RSA type key. The protocol ensures that no individual KGC knows the factorization of the key. Boneh and Franklin [16] proposed another secret sharing protocol for their IBE scheme, based on a t-out-of-n threshold scheme [68], in which n KGCs each has a share of a master secret, any t of them are able to recover the master secret, but less than t KGCs cannot get any information about the secret.

This solution avoids a single KGC escrowing a user's private key and is a nice usage of the two well-known secret sharing methods. However, one might argue that letting a group of KGCs share a master secret has the following disadvantages regarding flexibility and reliability of using key generation centers:

1. It requires co-operation between these KGCs either in the master key generation process or in the user private key generation process or in both. Particularly, the two secret sharing methods cost expensively when dealing with dynamic changes of the share holder constructions, which, most likely, is necessary for many IBC applications.

2. It requires an individual KGC to have multiple shares if it is involved in multiple share holder groups for different applications, which, again most likely, is necessary for many IBC applications. A potential problem is that a user might find it difficult to trust a KGC since it has many different "faces" (namely public keys or shares). On the other hand, the users have to access multiple public keys from a single KGC, each for a specific application.

3. More importantly, in some real applications, it may not be desirable to organise a group of KGCs to run such a secret sharing protocol, since, for various reasons, some KGCs may not be interested in co-operating with the others, and also since a user may not want these KGCs to communicate to each other any time for the user privacy reason.

As a result, it is almost impossible for an encrypter freely choosing her favorite KGCs for a decrypter, although it is an very attractive feature for identity-based encryption.

The secret aggregating solution. Based on the above consideration, Chen and Harrison [25] introduced a solution for aggregation of the master secret. The goal of this work was to keep the "natural" combination between the KGC's key and the user's key, but to avoid a single KGC escrowing the user key. In this solution, a user can choose an arbitrary set of KGCs without telling them the fact whom they actually share a secret with. The selected KGCs do not have to know each other, to communicate to each other or to trust each other. A set of secret aggregation algorithms were discussed in [25] to cover different cases dependent on whether the multiple KGCs make use of the same system parameters or not and whether a user has multiple identities or not. Some cases were also introduced by Chen *et al.* in [27,28].

We describe one of these cases in Figure 12, in which we use the Boneh-Franklin (BF) IBE scheme [16] as an example by extending a single KGC in the original scheme to multiple KGCs. As the same as the original BF scheme, the security of this extended scheme relies on the hardness of the BDH problem, that can been proved under the Boneh-Franklin model [16]. The set of KGCs make use of the same system parameters $(q, \mathbb{G}_1, \mathbb{G}_T, \hat{e}, n, P, H_1, H_2, H_3, H_4)$, but each has their own private key $s_i \in_R \mathbb{Z}_q^*$ and public key $s_i P$. Four hash-functions are used, $H_1 : \{0,1\}^* \to \mathbb{G}_1$, $H_2 : \mathbb{G}_T \to \{0,1\}^n$, $H_3 : \{0,1\}^n \times \{0,1\}^n \to \mathbb{Z}_q^*$ and $H_4 : \{0,1\}^n \to \{0,1\}^n$.

Note that in the scheme specification of Figure 12, we assume that each part of B's identity, ID_i, is associated to an individual KGC, T_i. For the association between ID_i and T_i, we mean that T_i is required to authenticate the ownership of ID_i and to issue the identity-based private key corresponding to ID_i. In the real usage, one part of the B's identity might be associated to multiple KGCs, and multiple identity parts might be associated to an individual KGC. The scheme can cover the different cases, for example, if ID_i is associated to two KGCs, say T_i and T_{i+1}, thus we let $ID_{i+1} = ID_i$ in the scheme; if both ID_i and ID_{i+1} are associated to a single KGC, T_i, thus we let $T_{i+1} = T_i$ in the scheme.

Players: A - encryptor and B - decryptor, and T_i ($i = 1, 2, ..., w$) - a set of key generation centers.

System setup: Common system parameters are ($q, \mathbb{G}_1$, $\mathbb{G}_T$, $\hat{e}$, n, P, H_1, H_2, H_3, H_4), and each T_i has its own private key s_i and public key s_iP.

Encryption: To encrypt $m \in \{0, 1\}^n$ for B, A performs the following steps:

1. Choose a set of B's identities as ID_i ($i = 1, 2, ..., w$) $\in \{0, 1\}^*$ and the associated set of T_i.
2. Pick $\sigma \in_R \{0, 1\}^n$ and compute $Q_i = H_1(ID_i)$.
3. Compute $r = H_3(\sigma\|m)$ and $g_B = \prod_{1 \le i \le w} \hat{e}(Q_i, s_iP)$.
4. Output the T_i and ID_i list along with the ciphertext C as $C = (U, V, W) = (rP, \sigma \oplus H_2(g_B^r), m \oplus H_4(\sigma))$.

Key extract: B's i-th partial private key d_i ($i = 1, 2, ..., w$) corresponding to ID_i is generated by T_i as $d_i = s_iQ_i$.

Decryption: To recover m from (U, V, W), B performs the following steps:

1. Run **Key extract** to get each part of his private key, d_i ($i = 1, 2, ..., w$).
2. Compute $d_B = \Sigma_{1 \le i \le w} d_i$.
3. Compute $\sigma = V \oplus H_2(\hat{e}(d_B, U))$, $m = W \oplus H_4(\sigma)$ and $r = H_3(\sigma\|m)$.
4. If $U \equiv rP$, return m; else return "invalid".

Fig. 12. The BF IBE scheme with multiple KGCs

Note also that the value $g_B = \prod_{1 \le i \le w} \hat{e}(Q_i, s_iP)$ in the scheme could be pre-computed and used for multiple times. In this case, the cost of on-line computation required for the extended scheme is similar to the cost of the original BF IBE scheme described in Section 5.1.

10   Security Models and Formal Proof

In modern cryptography, security analysis is required for any cryptographic mechanism. A well-known method to achieve the analysis is a carefully scrutinized security reduction in a formal security model to an assumption on hardness of a well-explored number theory problem, such as an integer factorization based problem or a discrete logarithm based problem. A number of security models for various IBC primitives have been developed.

The readers, who would like to find out what kinds of security models have been defined and how they have been used to prove IBC mechanisms, are recommended checking the following works: the Boneh and Franklin IBE security model [16], the Bellare, Namprempre and Neven IBS security proof and identity-based identification proof [8], the Chen, Cheng and Smart IBKA security analysis [24], which make use of the Bellare-Rogaway key agreement security model [10, 13], and the Boyen IB-Signcryption security model [19].

Most of the security proofs in the above works are based on the random oracle model [9]. Recently, many researchers have developed a number of new IBC mechanisms, and the security of these mechanisms have been analyzed without random oracles, e.g. [3, 14, 15, 20, 77, 78, 82].

11   Conclusions

In this paper, we have introduced the basic concept of identity-based cryptography (IBC) and a number of IBC mechanisms in the cryptographic primitives, including identity-based encryption, identity-based signatures, identity-based key agreement and identity-based signcryption. We have also discussed the key escrow issue in IBC and a number of existing solutions.

IBC has attracted a great deal of interest over the last twenty years. Recently, many new research topics have been developed. In particular, the following areas have received a lot of attention:

- a variety of IBC mechanisms from pairings,
- formal security proof of IBC mechanisms, and
- IBC mechanisms without random oracles.

We expect that this will continue to be the case in the near future.

Acknowledgement. The author would like to thank the organizer of the 6th International School on Foundations of Security Analysis and Design (FOSAD 2006) for inviting her to give the lecture and for providing an enjoyable environment for the summer school. The author would also like to thank participants of the lecture for many interesting discussions and comments on this research area.

References

1. Al-Riyami, S., Paterson, K.: Certifficateless Public Key Cryptography. In: Laih, C.-S. (ed.) ASIACRYPT 2003. LNCS, vol. 2894, pp. 452–473. Springer, Heidelberg (2003)
2. Al-Riyami, S., Paterson, K.: CBE from CL-PKE: a generic construction and efficient schemes. In: Vaudenay, S. (ed.) PKC 2005. LNCS, vol. 3386, pp. 398–415. Springer, Heidelberg (2005)
3. Au, M., Liu, J., Yuen, T., Wong, D.: Practical hierarchical identity based encryption and signature schemes without random oracles. Cryptology ePrint Archive, Report 2006/368
4. Barbosa, M., Chen, L., Cheng, Z., Chimley, M., Dent, A., Farshim, P., Harrison, K., Malone-Lee, J., Smart, N.P., Vercauteren, F.: SK-KEM: an identity-based KEM. Submitted to IEEE P 1363.3, available at
http://grouper.ieee.org/groups/1363/IBC/submissions/index.html
5. Barreto, P.: The pairing-based crypto lounge,
http://paginas.terra.com.br/informatica/paulobarreto/pblounge.html

6. Barreto, P., Libert, B., McCullagh, N., Quisquater, J.: Efficient and provably-secure identity-based signatures and signcryption from bilinear maps. In: Roy, B. (ed.) ASIACRYPT 2005. LNCS, vol. 3788, pp. 515–532. Springer, Heidelberg (2005)

7. Barreto, P., Libert, B., McCullagh, N., Quisquater, J.: Efficient and secure identity-based signatures and signcryption from bilinear maps. Submitted to IEEE P.3 1363 available at
   `http://grouper.ieee.org/groups/1363/IBC/submissions/index.html`

8. Bellare, M., Namprempre, C., Neven, G.: Security proofs for identity-based identification and signature schemes. In: Cachin, C., Camenisch, J.L. (eds.) EUROCRYPT 2004. LNCS, vol. 3027, pp. 268–286. Springer, Heidelberg (2004)

9. Bellare, M., Rogaway, P.: Random oracles are practical: a paradigm for designing efficient protocols. In: Proceedings of the First Annual Conference on Computer and Communications Security, pp. 62–73. ACM Press, New York (1993)

10. Bellare, M., Rogaway, P.: Entity authentication and key distribution. In: Stinson, D.R. (ed.) CRYPTO 1993. LNCS, vol. 773, pp. 232–249. Springer, Heidelberg (1994)

11. Bellare, M., Canetti, R., Krawczyk, H.: Keying hash functions for message authentication. In: Koblitz, N. (ed.) CRYPTO 1996. LNCS, vol. 1109, pp. 1–15. Springer, Heidelberg (1996)

12. Bentahar, K., Farshim, P., Malone-Lee, J., Smart, N.P.: Generic constructions of identity-based and certificateless KEMs. Cryptology ePrint Archive, Report 2005/058

13. Blake-Wilson, S., Johnson, D., Menezes, A.: Key agreement protocols and their security analysis. In: Darnell, M. (ed.) Cryptography and Coding. LNCS, vol. 1355, pp. 30–45. Springer, Heidelberg (1997)

14. Boneh, D., Boyen, X.: Efficient selective-ID secure identity-based encryption without random oracles. In: Cachin, C., Camenisch, J.L. (eds.) EUROCRYPT 2004. LNCS, vol. 3027, pp. 223–238. Springer, Heidelberg (2004)

15. Boneh, D., Boyen, X.: Secure identity-based encryption without random oracles. In: Franklin, M. (ed.) CRYPTO 2004. LNCS, vol. 3152, pp. 443–459. Springer, Heidelberg (2004)

16. Boneh, D., Franklin, M.: Identity based encryption from the Weil pairing. In: Kilian, J. (ed.) CRYPTO 2001. LNCS, vol. 2139, pp. 213–229. Springer, Heidelberg (2001)

17. Boneh, D., Gentry, C., Hamburg, M.: Space-efficient identity basd encryption without pairings. Cryptology ePrint Archive, Report 2007/177

18. Boyd, C., Mao, W., Paterson, K.: Key agreement using statically keyed authenticators. In: Jakobsson, M., Yung, M., Zhou, J. (eds.) ACNS 2004. LNCS, vol. 3089, pp. 248–262. Springer, Heidelberg (2004)

19. Boyen, X.: Multipurpose identity-based signcryption: a swiss army knife for identity-based cryptography. In: Boneh, D. (ed.) CRYPTO 2003. LNCS, vol. 2729, pp. 382–398. Springer, Heidelberg (2003)

20. Boyen, X., Waters, B.: Anonymous hierarchical identity-based encryption (without random oracles). In: Dwork, C. (ed.) CRYPTO 2006. LNCS, vol. 4117, Springer, Heidelberg (2006)

21. Cha, J.C., Cheon, J.H.: An identity-based signature from gap Diffie-Hellman groups. In: Desmedt, Y.G. (ed.) PKC 2003. LNCS, vol. 2567, pp. 18–30. Springer, Heidelberg (2002)

22. Chen, L., Cheng, Z.: Security proof of Sakai-Kasahar's identity-based encryption scheme. In: Smart, N.P. (ed.) Cryptography and Coding. LNCS, vol. 3796, pp. 442–459. Springer, Heidelberg (2005)

23. Chen, L., Cheng, Z., Malone-Lee, J., Smart, N.: An efficient ID-KEM based on the Sakai-Kasahara key construction. IEE Proceedings Information Security 153(1), 19–26 (2006)
24. Chen, L., Cheng, Z., Smart, N.: Identity-based key agreement protocols from pairings. International Journal of Information Security. This paper has been submitted to IEEE P 1363.3 (to appear), and is available at `http://grouper.ieee.org/groups/1363/IBC/submissions/index.html`
25. Chen, L., Harrison, K.: Multiple trusted authorities in identifier based cryptography from pairings on elliptic curves. HP Technical Report, HPL-2003-48, Available at `http://www.hpl.hp.com/techreports/2003/HPL-2003-48.html`
26. Chen, L., Harrison, K., Malone-Lee, J. (as co-inventors): Identifier-based signcryption with two trusted authorities. GB patent GB2416282 A: Application No. GB200415774A, filed on July 15, 2004 and (published on January 18, 2006)
27. Chen, L., Harrison, K., Moss, A., Smart, N., Soldera, D.: Certification of public keys within an identity based system. In: Chan, A.H., Gligor, V.D. (eds.) ISC 2002. LNCS, vol. 2433, pp. 322–333. Springer, Heidelberg (2002)
28. Chen, L., Harrison, K., Smart, N., Soldera, D.: Applications of multiple trust authorities in pairing based cryptosystems. In: Davida, G.I., Frankel, Y., Rees, O. (eds.) InfraSec 2002. LNCS, vol. 2437, pp. 260–275. Springer, Heidelberg (2002)
29. Chen, L., Kudla, C.: Identity-based authenticated key agreement from pairings. In: Proceedings of the 16th IEEE Computer Security Foundations Workshop, pp. 219–233. IEEE, Los Alamitos (2003)
30. Chen, L., Malone-Lee, J.: Improved identity-based signcryption. In: Vaudenay, S. (ed.) PKC 2005. LNCS, vol. 3386, pp. 362–379. Springer, Heidelberg (2005)
31. Cheng, Z., Chen, L.: On security proof of McCullagh-Barreto's key agreement protocol and its variants. International Journal of Security and Networks 2(3/4), 251–259 (2007)
32. Cramer, R., Shoup, V.: Design and analysis of practical public-key encryption schemes secure against adaptive chosen ciphertext attack. SIAM Journal on Computing 33, 167–226 (2003)
33. Choie, Y., Jeong, E., Lee, E.: Efficient identity-based authenticated key agreement protocol from pairings. Applied Mathematics and Computation 162, 179–188 (2005)
34. Choudary Gorantla, M., Gangishetti, R., Saxena, A.: A survey on ID-based cryptographic primitives. Cryptology ePrint Archive, Report 2005/094
35. Cocks, C.: An identity-based encryption scheme based on quadratic residues. In: Honary, B. (ed.) Cryptography and Coding. LNCS, vol. 2260, pp. 360–363. Springer, Heidelberg (2001)
36. Desmedt, Y., Quisquater, J.: Public-key systems based on the difficulty of tampering (is there a difference between DES and RSA?). In: Odlyzko, A.M. (ed.) CRYPTO 1986. LNCS, vol. 263, pp. 111–117. Springer, Heidelberg (1987)
37. Dutta, R., Barua, R., Sarkar, P.: Pairing-based cryptographic protocols: a survey. Cryptology ePrint Archive, Report 2004/064
38. Fiat, A., Shamir, A.: How to prove yourself: practical solution to identityfication and signature schemes. In: Odlyzko, A.M. (ed.) CRYPTO 1986. LNCS, vol. 263, pp. 186–194. Springer, Heidelberg (1987)
39. Galbraith, S., Paterson, K., Smart, N.P.: Pairings for cryptographers. Cryptology ePrint Archive, Report 2006/165
40. Gentry, C.: Certificate-Based Encryption and the Certificate Revocation Problem. In: Biham, E. (ed.) Advances in Cryptology – EUROCRPYT 2003. LNCS, vol. 2656, pp. 272–293. Springer, Heidelberg (2003)

41. Girault, M., Paillès, J.C.: An identity-based scheme providing zero-knowledge authentication and authenticated key exchange. In: Proceeedings of First European Symposium on Research in Computer Security – ESORICS '90, AFCET, pp. 173–184 (1990)
42. Girault, M., Stern, J.: On the length of cryptographic hash-values used in identification schemes. In: Günther, C.G. (ed.) EUROCRYPT 1988. LNCS, vol. 330, pp. 202–215. Springer, Heidelberg (1988)
43. Guillou, L., Quisquater, J.: A paradoxical identity-based signature scheme resulting from zeroknowledge. In: Goldwasser, S. (ed.) CRYPTO 1988. LNCS, vol. 403, pp. 216–231. Springer, Heidelberg (1990)
44. Hess, F.: Efficient identity based signature schemes based on pairings. In: Nyberg, K., Heys, H.M. (eds.) SAC 2002. LNCS, vol. 2595, pp. 310–324. Springer, Heidelberg (2003)
45. ISO/IEC 9594-8:2001(the 4th edn.): Information technology – Open Systems Interconnection – The Directory: Public-key and attribute certificate frameworks. International Organization for Standardization, Geneva, Switzerland (2001)
46. ISO/IEC 11770-3:1999: Information technology – Security techniques – Key management – Part 3: Mechanisms using asymmetric techniques. International Organization for Standardization, Geneva, Switzerland (1999)
47. ISO/IEC 14888-2:1998: Information technology – Security techniques – Digital signatures with appendix – Part 2: Identity-based mechanisms. International Organization for Standardization, Geneva, Switzerland (1998)
48. ISO/IEC 14888-3:2006: Information technology – Security techniques – Digital signatures with appendix – Part 3: Discrete logarithm based mechanisms. International Organization for Standardization, Geneva, Switzerland (2006)
49. IEEE P 1363.3, http://grouper.ieee.org/groups/1363/IBC/index.html
50. Li, S., Yuan, Q., Li, J.: Towards security two-part authenticated key agreement protocols. Cryptology ePrint Archive, Report 2005/300
51. Libert, B., Quisquater, J.: New identity based signcryption schemes from pairings. In: Proceedings of IEEE Information Theory Workshop 2003, IEEE Computer Society Press, Los Alamitos (2003)
52. McCullagh, N., Barreto, P.: Efficient and forward-secure identity-based signcryption. Cryptology ePrint Archive, Report 2004/117
53. McCullagh, N., Barreto, P.: A new two-party identity-based authenticated key agreement. In: Menezes, A.J. (ed.) CT-RSA 2005. LNCS, vol. 3376, pp. 262–274. Springer, Heidelberg (2005)
54. Mitsunari, S., Sakai, R., Kasahara, M.: A new traitor tracing. IEICE Trans. Fundamentals E85-A(2), 481–484 (2002)
55. Malone-Lee, J.: Identity-Based Signcryption. Cryptology ePrint Archive, Report 2002/098
56. Maurer, U.M., Yacobi, Y.: Non-interactive public key cryptography. In: Davies, D.W. (ed.) EUROCRYPT 1991. LNCS, vol. 547, pp. 498–507. Springer, Heidelberg (1991)
57. Okamoto, E.: Proposal for identity-based key distribution system. Electronics Letters 22, 1283–1284 (1986)
58. Okamoto, E.: Key distribution system based on identification information. In: Pomerance, C. (ed.) CRYPTO 1987. LNCS, vol. 293, pp. 194–202. Springer, Heidelberg (1988)
59. Paterson, K.: ID-based signatures from pairings on elliptic curves. Electronic Letters 38(18), 1025–1026 (2002)

60. Pointcheval, D., Stern, J.: Security proofs for signature schemes. In: Maurer, U.M. (ed.) EUROCRYPT 1996. LNCS, vol. 1070, pp. 387–398. Springer, Heidelberg (1996)
61. Pointcheval, D., Stern, J.: Security arguments for digital signatures and blind signatures. Journal of Cryptology 13, 361–396 (2000)
62. Ryu, E., Yoon, E., Yoo, K.: An efficient ID-based authenticated key agreement protocol from pairings. In: Mitrou, N.M., Kontovasilis, K., Rouskas, G.N., Iliadis, I., Merakos, L. (eds.) NETWORKING 2004. LNCS, vol. 3042, pp. 1458–1463. Springer, Heidelberg (2004)
63. Sakai, R., Kasahara, M.: ID based cryptosystems with pairing on elliptic curve. Cryptology ePrint Archive, Report 2003/054
64. Sakai, R., Ohgishi, K., Kasahara, M.: Cryptosystems based on pairing. In: The 2000 Symposium on Cryptography and Information Security, Okinawa, Japan (January 2000)
65. Sakai, R., Ohgishi, K., Kasahara, M.: Cryptosystems based on pairing over elliptic curve (in Japanese). In: The 2001 Symposium on Cryptography and Information Security, Oiso, Japan (January 2001)
66. Scott, M.: Authenticated ID-based key exchange and remote log-in with insecure token and PIN number. Cryptology ePrint Archive, Report 2002/164
67. Shacham, H.: New Paradigms in Signature Schemes. PhD Thesis, U. Stanford (2005)
68. Shamir, A.: How to share a secret. Communications of the ACM 22, 612–613 (1979)
69. Shamir, A.: Identity-based cryptosystems and signature schemes. In: Blakely, G.R., Chaum, D. (eds.) CRYPTO 1984. LNCS, vol. 196, pp. 47–53. Springer, Heidelberg (1985)
70. Shim, K.: Efficient ID-based authenticated key agreement protocol based on the Weil pairing. Electronics Letters 39, 653–654 (2003)
71. Silverman, J.: The arithmetic of elliptic curve. Springer, Heidelberg (1986)
72. Smart, N.: An identity based authenticated key agreement protocol based on the Weil pairing. Electronics Letters 38(13), 630–632 (2002)
73. Tanaka, H.: A realization scheme for the identity-based cryptosystem. In: Pomerance, C. (ed.) CRYPTO 1987. LNCS, vol. 293, pp. 340–349. Springer, Heidelberg (1988)
74. Tanaka, K., Okamoto, E.: Key distribution system for mail systems using ID-related information directory. Computers & Security 10, 25–33 (1991)
75. Vanstone, S., Zuccherato, R.: Elliptic curve cryptosystems using curves of smooth order over the ring Z_n. IEEE Transactions on Information Theory 43(4), 1231–1237 (1997)
76. Wang, Y.: Efficient identity-based and authenticated key agreement protocol. Cryptology ePrint Archive, Report 2005/108
77. Wang, S., Cao, Z., Choo, K.: New identity-based authenticated key agreement protocols from pairings (without random oracles). Cryptology ePrint Archive, Report 2006/446
78. Waters, B.: Efficient identity-based encryption without random oracles. In: Cramer, R.J.F. (ed.) EUROCRYPT 2005. LNCS, vol. 3494, pp. 114–127. Springer, Heidelberg (2005)
79. Xie, G.: An ID-based key agreement scheme from pairing. Cryptology ePrint Archive, Report 2005/093
80. Yuan, Q., Li, S.: A new efficient ID-based authenticated key agreement protocol. Cryptology ePrint Archive, Report 2005/309

81. Yi, X.: An identity-based signature scheme from the Weil pairing. IEEE Communications Letters 7(2), 76–78 (2003)
82. Yuen, T., Wei, V.: Constant-size hierarchical identity-based signature/signcryption without random oracles. Cryptology ePrint Archive, Report 2005/412
83. Zheng, Y.: Digital signcryption or how to achieve cost (signature & encryption) << cost (signature) + cost (encryption). In: Kaliski, Jr., B.S. (ed.) CRYPTO 1997. LNCS, vol. 1294, pp. 165–179. Springer, Heidelberg (1997)

Trust and Reputation Systems

Audun Jøsang

QUT, Brisbane, Australia
a.josang@qut.edu.au
http://www.fit.qut.edu.au/~josang/

Abstract. There are currently very few practical methods for assessing the quality of resources or the reliability of other entities in the online environment. This makes it difficult to make decisions about which resources can be relied upon and which entities it is safe to interact with. Trust and reputation systems are aimed at solving this problem by enabling service consumers to reliably assess the quality of services and the reliability of entities before they decide to use a particular service or to interact with or depend on a given entity. Such systems should also allow serious service providers and online players to correctly represent the reliability of themselves and the quality of their services. In the case of reputation systems, the basic idea is to let parties rate each other, for example after the completion of a transaction, and use the aggregated ratings about a given party to derive its reputation score. In the case of trust systems, the basic idea is to analyse and combine paths and networks of trust relationships in order to derive measures of trustworthiness of specific nodes. Reputation scores and trust measures can assist other parties in deciding whether or not to transact with a given party in the future, and whether it is safe to depend on a given resource or entity. This represents an incentive for good behaviour and for offering reliable resources, which thereby tends to have a positive effect on the quality of online markets and communities. This chapter describes the background, current status and future trend of online trust and reputation systems.

1 Introduction

In the early years of the Internet and the Web, determining whether something or somebody online could be trusted was not thought of as a problem because the Internet community consisted of groups and users motivated by common goals, and with strong trust in each other. The early adopters typically had good intentions because they were motivated by the desire to make the new technology successful. Deceptive and fraudulent behaviour only emerged after the new technology was opened up to the general public and started being used for commercial purposes. The legacy technical architecture and the governance structure of the Internet are clearly inspired by the assumption of well intentioned participants. However, people and organisations currently engaging in Internet activities are not uniformly well intentioned, because they are increasingly motivated by financial profit and personal gain which can lead to unethical and criminal behaviour. The current Internet technology makes us poorly prepared for controlling and sanctioning the substantial and increasing number of users and service providers

A. Aldini and R. Gorrieri (Eds.): FOSAD 2006/2007, LNCS 4677, pp. 209–245, 2007.
© Springer-Verlag Berlin Heidelberg 2007

with unethical, malicious and criminal intentions. As a result, the early optimism associated with the Internet has been replaced by cynicism and diminishing trust in the Internet as a reliable platform for building markets and communities.

As a consequence of this development, the topic of trust in open computer networks is receiving considerable attention in the academic community and the Internet industry. One approach to the problem is to deploy traditional IT security solutions. However, this chapter describes a complementary approach that can be described as *soft security*. The difference between IT security and soft security is explained next.

It is normally assumed that information security technologies, when properly designed, can provide protection against viruses, worms, Trojans, spam email and any other threats that users can be exposed to through the Internet. Unfortunately, traditional IT security technology can only provide protection against some, but not all online security threats. To better understand why, it is useful to look at the definitions of security and of information security separately.

Security can generally be defined as *"the quality or state of being secure - to be free from danger"* [38]. This definition is very broad and covers the protection of life and assets from intentional and unintentional human actions, as well as from natural threats such as storms and earthquakes. In case of protection of information assets, the term information security is normally assumed. Information security is commonly defined as *"the preservation of confidentiality, integrity and availability of Information"* [21], commonly known as the CIA properties. It is here assumed that it is the owner of information assets who has an interest in keeping those assets free from danger, and in preserving their CIA properties. However, in many situations we have to protect ourselves from harmful information assets and from those who offer online resources, so that the problem in fact is reversed. Traditional IT security solutions are totally inadequate for protecting against for example deceitful service providers that provide false or misleading information. We are thus in a situation where we are faced with serious threats, against which there is no established and effective protection. The extended view of online security was first described by Rasmussen & Jansson (1996) [44] who used the term "hard security" for traditional IT security mechanisms like authentication and access control, and "soft security" for what they called social control mechanisms.

In case of traditional IT security, the existence of a security policy is always assumed, whereby the owner of information resources authorises certain parties to perform specific actions. White Hats (i.e. the good guys) and Black Hats (i.e. the bad guys) are easily identified depending on whether they act according to, or against the security policy. In the case of soft security however, this distinction becomes blurred, because there is generally no formally defined or generally accepted policy that defines what constitutes acceptable behaviour. For example, misrepresentation of online services might not even be illegal in the jurisdiction of the service provider, yet a consumer who feels deceived by an online service would most likely define the service provider as a Black Hat. Soft security mechanisms that can provide protection against this type of online threats are typically collaborative and based on input from the whole community. In contrast to traditional IT security where security policies are clearcut and often explicitly defined for a specific security domain by a security manager, soft security is based on an implicit security policy collaboratively emerging from the whole community. On this background we define soft security as follows.

Definition 1 (Soft Security). *Soft security is the collaborative enforcement of, and adherence to common ethical norms by participants in a community.*

While the goal of traditional (hard) information security is to preserve the CIA properties (Confidentiality, Integrity and Availability) of assets within a specific domain, the goal of soft security mechanisms is to stimulate the quality of a specific community in terms of the ethical behaviour and the integrity of its members. What constitutes ethical norms within a community will in general not be precisely defined. Instead it will be dynamically defined by certain key players in conjunction with the average user.

Soft security mechanisms use collaborative methods for assessing the behaviour of members in the community against the ethical norms, making it possible to identify and sanction those participants who breach the norms, and to recognise and reward members who adhere to the norms. A natural side effect is to provide an incentive for good behaviour which in turn has a positive effect on market quality. Reputation systems can be called collaborative praise and sanctioning systems to reflect their collaborative nature. Reputation systems are already being used in successful commercial online applications. There is a rapidly growing literature on the theory and applications of trust and reputation systems. A general observation is that the proposals from the academic community so far lack coherence. The systems being proposed are usually designed from scratch, and only in very few cases are authors building on proposals by other authors.

A survey on trust and reputation systems has been published by Jøsang *et al.* [27]. The purpose of this chapter is to complement that survey and to present the background, current status and the future trend of trust and reputation systems.

Section 2 attempts to define the concepts of trust and reputation, and the objectives of trust management in general. Sections 3 and 4 describe some of the main models and architectures for trust and reputation systems. Sec.5 describes some prominent applications and related issues. The study is rounded off with a discussion in Sec.6.

2   Context and Fundamental Concepts

2.1   The Notion of Trust

Trust is a directional relationship between two parties that can be called *trustor* and *trustee*. One must assume the trustor to be a "thinking entity" in some form meaning that it has the ability to make assessments and decisions based on received information and past experience. The trustee can be anything from a person, organisation or physical entity, to abstract notions such as information or a cryptographic key [22].

A trust relationship has a *scope*, meaning that it applies to a specific purpose or domain of action, such as "being authentic" in the case of a an agent's trust in a cryptographic key, or "providing reliable information" in case of a person's trust in the correctness of an entry in Wikipedia[1]. Mutual trust is when both parties trust each other

---

[1] http://www.wikipedia.org/

with the same scope, but this is obviously only possible when both parties are thinking entities. Trust influences the trustor's attitudes and actions, but can also have effects on the trustee and other elements in the environment, for example, by stimulating recipro-cal trust [13]. The literature uses the term trust with a variety of meanings [37]. Two main interpretations are to view trust as the perceived reliability of something or some-body, called *"reliability trust"*, and to view trust as a decision to enter into a situation of dependence, called *"decision trust"*.

As the name suggest, reliability trust can be interpreted as the reliability of something or somebody independently of any actual commitment, and the definition by Gambetta (1988) [16] provides an example of how this can be formulated:

Definition 2 (Reliability). Trust is the subjective probability by which an individual, A, expects that another individual, B, performs a given action on which its welfare depends.

In Def.2, trust is primarily defined as the trustor's estimate of the trustee's reliability (e.g. expressed as probability) in the context of *dependence* on the trustee.

However, trust can be more complex than Gambetta's definition suggests. For exam-ple, Falcone & Castelfranchi (2001) [14] note that having high (reliability) trust in a person is not necessarily sufficient for deciding to enter into a situation of dependence on that person. In [14] they write: *"For example it is possible that the value of the dam-age per se (in case of failure) is too high to choose a given decision branch, and this independently either from the probability of the failure (even if it is very low) or from the possible payoff (even if it is very high). In other words, that danger might seem to the agent an intolerable risk"*.

To illustrate the difference between reliability trust and decision trust with a practi-cal example, consider a fire drill where participants are asked to abseil from the third floor window of a house using a rope that looks old and appears to be in a state of de-terioration. In this situation, the participants would assess the probability that the rope will hold him while abseiling. A person who thinks that the rope could rupture would distrust the rope and refuse to use it. This is illustrated on the left side in Fig.1.

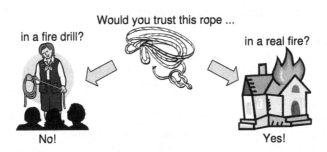

Fig. 1. Same reliability trust, but different decision trust

Imagine now that the same person is trapped in a real fire, and that the only escape is to descend from the third floor window using the same old rope. In this situation it is likely that the person would trust the rope, even if he thinks it is possible that it could rupture. This change in trust decision is perfectly rational because the likelihood of injury or death while abseiling is assessed against the likelihood of smoke suffocation and death by fire. Although the *reliability trust* in the rope is the same in both situations, the *decision trust* changes as a function of the comparatively different utility values associated with the different courses of action in the two situations. The following definition captures the concept of decision trust.

Definition 3 (Decision). Trust is the extent to which a given party is willing to depend on something or somebody in a given situation with a feeling of relative security, even though negative consequences are possible.

In Def.3, trust is primarily defined as the willingness to rely on a given object, and specifically includes the notions of *dependence* on the trustee, and its *reliability*. In addition, Def.3 implicitly also covers situational elements such as *utility* (of possible outcomes), *environmental factors* (law enforcement, contracts, security mechanisms etc.) and *risk attitude* (risk taking, risk averse, etc.).

Both reliability trust and decision trust reflect a positive belief about something on which trustor depends for his welfare. Reliability trust is most naturally measured as a discrete or continuous degree of reliability, whereas decision trust is most naturally measured in terms of a binary decision. While most trust and reputation models assume reliability trust, decision trust can also modelled. Systems based on decision trust models should be considered as decision making tools.

The difficulty of capturing the notion of trust in formal models in a meaningful way has led some economists to reject it as a computational concept. The strongest expression for this view has been given by Williamson (1993) [52] who argues that the notion of trust should be avoided when modelling economic interactions, because it adds nothing new, and that well studied notions such as reliability, utility and risk are adequate and sufficient for that purpose. Personal trust is the only type of trust that can be meaningful for describing interactions, according to Williamson. He argues that personal trust applies to emotional and personal interactions such as love relationships where mutual performance is not always monitored and where failures are forgiven rather than sanctioned. In that sense, traditional computational models would be inadequate e.g. because of insufficient data and inadequate sanctioning, but also because it would be detrimental to the relationships if the involved parties were to take a computational approach. Non-computation models for trust can be meaningful for studying such relationships according to Williamson, but developing such models should be done within the domains of sociology and psychology, rather than in economy.

In the light of Williamson's view on modelling trust it becomes important to judge the purpose and merit of trust management itself. Can trust management add anything new and valuable to the Internet technology and economy? The answer, in our opinion, is definitely yes. The value of trust management lies in the architectures and mechanisms for collecting trust relevant information, for efficient, reliable and secure processing, for distribution of derived trust and reputation scores, and for taking this information into account when navigating the Internet and making decisions about online activities and transactions. Economic models for risk taking and decision making are abstract and do not address how to build trust networks and reputation systems. Trust management specifically addresses how to build such systems, and can in addition include aspects of economic modelling whenever relevant and useful.

It can be noted that the traditional cues of trust and reputation that we are used to observe and depend on in the physical world are missing in online environments. Electronic substitutes are therefore needed when designing online trust and reputation systems. Furthermore, communicating and sharing information related to trust and reputation is relatively difficult, and normally constrained to local communities in the physical world, whereas IT systems combined with the Internet can be leveraged to design extremely efficient systems for exchanging and collecting such information on a global scale. Motivated by these basic observations, the design of trust and reputation systems should focus on:

a. Finding adequate online substitutes for the traditional cues to trust and reputation that we are used to in the physical world, and identifying new information elements (specific to a particular online application) which are suitable for deriving measures of trust and reputation.
b. Taking advantage of IT and the Internet to create efficient systems for collecting that information, and for deriving measures of trust and reputation, in order to support decision making and to improve the quality of online markets.

These simple principles invite rigorous research in order to answer some fundamental questions: What information elements are most suitable for deriving measures of trust and reputation in a given application? How can these information elements be captured and collected? What are the best principles for designing such systems from a theoretic and from a usability point of view? Can they be made resistant to attacks of manipulation by strategic agents? How should users include the information provided by such systems into their decision process? What role can these systems play in the business model of commercial companies? Do these systems truly improve the quality of online trade and interactions? These are important questions that need good answers and corresponding solutions in order for trust and reputation systems to reach their full potential in online environments.

2.2   Reputation and Trust

The concept of reputation is closely linked to that of trustworthiness, but it is evident that there is a clear and important difference. For the purpose of this study, we will define reputation according to Merriam-Webster's online dictionary [38].

Definition 4 (Reputation). *The overall quality or character as seen or judged by people in general.*

This definition corresponds well with the view of social network researchers [15,36] that reputation is a quantity derived from the underlying social network which is globally visible to all members of the network. The difference between trust and reputation can be illustrated by the following perfectly normal and plausible statements:

a. *"I trust you because of your good reputation."*
b. *"I trust you despite your bad reputation."*

Assuming that the two sentences relate to the same trust scope, statement a) reflects that the relying party is aware of the trustee's reputation, and bases his trust on that. Statement b) reflects that the relying party has some private knowledge about the trustee, e.g. through direct experience or intimate relationship, and that these factors overrule any (negative) reputation that a person might have. This observation reflects that trust ultimately is a personal and subjective phenomenon that that is based on various factors or evidence, and that some of those carry more weight than others. Personal experience typically carries more weight than second hand trust referrals or reputation, but in the absence of personal experience, trust often has to be based on referrals from others.

Reputation can be considered as a collective measure of trustworthiness (in the sense of reliability) based on the referrals or ratings from members in a community. An individual's subjective trust can be derived from a combination of received referrals and personal experience. In order to avoid dependence and loops it is required that referrals be based on first hand experience only, and not on other referrals. As a consequence, an individual should only give subjective trust referral when it is based on first hand evidence or when second hand input has been removed from its derivation base [30]. It is possible to abandon this principle for example when the weight of the trust referral is normalised or divided by the total number of referrals given by a single entity, and the latter principle is e.g. applied in Google's PageRank algorithm [43] described in more detail in Sec.5.2 below.

Reputation can relate to a group or to an individual. A group's reputation can for example be modelled as the average of all its members' individual reputations, or as the average of how the group is perceived as a whole by external parties. Tadelis' (2001) [51] study shows that an individual belonging to to a given group will inherit an *a priori* reputation based on that group's reputation. If the group is reputable all its individual members will *a priori* be perceived as reputable and vice versa.

2.3   Trust Transitivity

Trust transitivity means, for example, that if Alice trusts Bob who trusts Eric, then Alice will also trust Eric. This assumes that Bob actually tells Alice that he trusts Eric, which is called a *recommendation*. This is illustrated in Fig.2, where the indexes indicate the order in which the trust relationships and recommendations are formed.

Trust is only conditionally transitive [8]. For example the fact that Alice trusts Bob to look after her child, and Bob trusts Eric to fix his car, does not imply that Alice trusts Eric for looking after her child, nor for fixing her car. However, under certain semantic constraints [30], trust can be transitive, and a trust system can be used to derive trust. In the last example, trust transitivity collapses because the scopes of Alice's and Bob's trust are different.

Based on the situation of Fig.2, let us assume that Alice needs to have her car serviced, so she asks Bob for his advice about where to find a good car mechanic in town. Bob is thus trusted by Alice to know about a good car mechanic and to tell his honest opinion about that. Bob in turn trusts Eric to be a good car mechanic.

It is important to separate between trust in the ability to recommend a good car mechanic which represents *referral trust*, and trust in actually being a good car mechanic which represents *functional trust*. The scope of the trust is nevertheless the same,

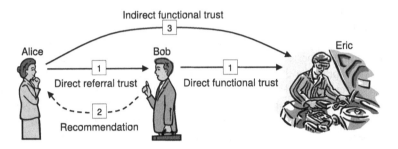

Fig. 2. Transitive trust principle

namely to be a good car mechanic. Assuming that, on several occasions, Bob has proven to Alice that he is knowledgeable in matters relating to car maintenance, Alice's referral trust in Bob for the purpose of recommending a good car mechanic can be considered to be *direct*. Assuming that Eric on several occasions has proven to Bob that he is a good mechanic, Bob's functional trust in Eric can also be considered to be direct. Thanks to Bob's advice, Alice also trusts Eric to actually be a good mechanic. However, this functional trust must be considered to be *indirect*, because Alice has not directly observed or experienced Eric's skills in servicing and repairing cars.

Let us slightly extend the example, wherein Bob does not actually know any car mechanics himself, but he trusts Claire, whom he believes knows a good car mechanic. As it happens, Claire is happy to recommend the car mechanic named Eric. As a result of transitivity, Alice is able to derive trust in Eric, as illustrated in Fig.3, where dr-trust denotes direct referral trust, df-trust denotes direct functional trust, and if-trust denotes indirect functional trust.

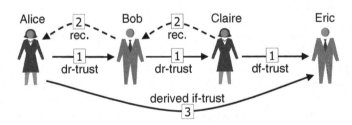

Fig. 3. Trust derived through transitivity

Defining the exact scope of Alice's trust in Bob is more complicated in this extended example. It seems that Alice trusts Bob to recommend somebody (who can recommend somebody etc.) who can recommend a good car mechanic. The problem with this type of formulation is that the length of the trust scope expression becomes proportional with the length of the transitive path, so that the trust scope expression rapidly becomes unmanageable. It can be observed that this type of trust scope has a recursive structure that can be exploited to define a more compact expression for the trust scope. As already mentioned, trust in the ability to recommend represents referral trust, and is precisely what allows trust to become transitive. At the same time, referral trust always assumes the existence of a functional trust scope at the end of the transitive path, which in this example is about being a good car mechanic.

The "referral" variant of a trust scope can be considered to be recursive, so that any transitive trust chain, with arbitrary length, can be expressed using only one trust scope with two variants. This principle is captured by the following criterion.

Definition 5 (Functional Trust Derivation Criterion). *Derivation of functional trust through referral trust, requires that the last trust arc represents functional trust, and all previous trust arcs represents referral trust.*

In practical situations, a trust scope can be characterised by being general or specific. For example, knowing how to change wheels on a car is more specific than to be a good car mechanic, where the former scope is a subset of the latter. Whenever the functional trust scope is equal to, or a subset of the referral trust scopes, it is possible to form transitive paths. This can be expressed with the following consistency criterion.

Definition 6 (Trust Scope Consistency Criterion). *A valid transitive trust path requires that the trust scope of the functional/last arc in the path be a subset of all previous arcs in the path.*

Trivially, every arc can have the same trust scope. Transitive trust propagation is thus possible with two variants (i.e. functional and referral) of a single trust scope.

A transitive trust path stops at the first functional trust arc encountered. It is, of course, possible for a principal to have both functional and referral trust in another principal, but that should be expressed as two separate trust arcs. The existence of both a functional and a referral trust arc, e.g. from Claire to Eric, should be interpreted as Claire having trust in Eric not only to be a good car mechanic, but also to recommend other car mechanics.

The examples above assume some sort of absolute trust between the agents in the transitive chain. In reality trust is never absolute, and many researchers have proposed to express trust as discrete verbal statements, as probabilities or other continuous measures. When applying computation to such trust measures, intuition dictates that trust should be weakened or diluted through transitivity. Revisiting the above example, this means that Alice's derived trust in the car mechanic Eric through the recommenders Bob and Claire can be at most as strong or confident as Claire's trust in Eric. How trust strength and confidence should be formally represented depends on the particular formalism used.

It could be argued that negative trust in a transitive chain can have the paradoxical effect of strengthening the derived trust. Take for example the case where Alice distrusts Bob, and Bob distrusts Eric. In this situation, it might be reasonable for Alice to derive positive trust in Eric, since she thinks "Bob is trying to trick me, I will not rely on him". When using the principle that the enemy of my enemy is my friend, the fact that Bob recommends distrust in Eric should count as a pro-Eric argument from Alice's perspective. The question of how transitivity of distrust should be interpreted can quickly become very complex because it can involve multiple levels of deception. Models based on this type of reasoning have received minimal attention in the trust and reputation systems literature, and it might be argued that the study of such models belongs to the intelligence analysis discipline, rather than online trust management. However, the fundamental issues and problems are the same in both disciplines.

The analysis of transitive trust relating to the example of Fig.3 uses a rich set of semantic elements. In practical systems and implementations it might be necessary to use simplified models, e.g. by not making any distinction between referral and functional trust, or between direct and indirect trust, and by not specifying trust scopes. This is because it might not be possible to obtain detailed information for making distinctions between trust semantics, and because it would require overly complex mathematical models to take the rich set of aspects into account.

2.4   IT Security and Trust

The term trust is being used extensively in the context if IT security where it can take various meanings. The concepts of Trusted Systems and TCB (Trusted Computing Base) are among the earliest examples of this (see e.g. Abrams 1995 [3]). A trusted system can simply be interpreted as a system designed with strong security as a major goal, and the TCB as the set of hardware and software components that contribute to the security. The concept of evaluation assurance level is a standardised measure of security for trusted systems[2]. Some organisations require systems with high assurance levels for high risk applications or for processing sensitive information. In an informal sense, the assurance level expresses a level of (reliability) trustworthiness of given system. However, it is evident that additional information, such as warnings about newly discovered security flaws, can carry more weight than the evaluation assurance level when users form their own subjective opinion about a trusted system.

More recently, the concept of TC (Trusted Computing) has been introduced by the industry. In general, TC can be defined as information processing on a platform with specialised security hardware. More specifically, TC can mean information processing on a platform equipped with a TPM (Trusted Platform Module) hardware chip that provides specific functionality as standardised by the TCG (Trusted Computing Group)[3].

The term Trust Management has been, and still is used with the relatively narrow meaning of distributed access control, which was in fact the first usage of the term [5]. According to this interpretation, the owner of a resource can determine whether a third party can be trusted to access resources based on attribute certificates that can be chained in a transitive fashion. The related concept of Trust Negotiation is used to describe the process of exchanging access credentials and certificates between a requestor and the resource owner with the purpose of determining whether the requestor is authorised to access the resources.

In identity management, the term Circle of Trust is defined by the Liberty Alliance[4] to denote a group of organisations that have entered into an agreement of mutual acceptance of security and authentication assertions for authentication and access control of

---

[2] See e.g. the UK CESG at http://www.cesg.gov.uk/ or the Common Criteria Project at http://www.commoncriteriaportal.org/

[3] https://www.trustedcomputinggroup.org/home

[4] http://www.projectliberty.org/

users. The Liberty alliance has adopted SAML2.0 [42] as the standard for specifying such security assertions. The WS-Trust standard [5] which has been developed mainly by IBM and Microsoft specifies how to define security assertions that can be exchanged with the WS-Security protocol. WS-Trust and WS-Security have the same purpose as, but are incompatible with SAML2.0. It remains to be seen which of these standards will survive in the long run. Other trust related IT terms are for example

- TTP (Trusted Third Party), which normally denotes an entity that can keep secrets
- Trusted Code, which means a program that runs with system or root privileges
- Trust Provider, which can mean a CA (Certificate Authority) in a PKI.

In cryptography and security protocol design, trust is often used to denote the beliefs in the initial assumptions and in the derived conclusions. In that sense, security protocols represent mechanisms for propagating trust from where it exists (i.e. the initial assumptions) to where it is needed (i.e. the conclusions). Analysing this form of trust propagation can be done with formal logics and formal methods [50].

The meanings of the various trust related terms used by the IT security community can in general not be intuitively derived and understood solely from the terms themselves. Instead they often have a complex meaning that must be explained in order to be properly understood. The purpose of using trust related terms is twofold: they provide a short and practical metaphor for something that would be tedious to explain each time, and they can also represent marketing slogans to promote particular solutions or interests. The TPM is for example criticised for representing DRM (Digital Rights Management) technology that creates unnecessary complexity and increased cost in PCs and media devices and that can be used to lock users to specific vendors[6]. Applying the term "trusted computing" to this technology has the deceptive marketing effect of defusing public criticism because it sounds like it protects the users whereas in reality it does not[7].

In general, security mechanisms protect systems and data from being adversely affected by malicious and non-authorised parties. The effect of this is that those systems and data can be considered more reliable, and thus more trustworthy. A side effect of implementing strong security is that the functionality and flexibility suffer, so that there is a trade-off between security on the one hand and functionality/flexibility on the other. It is therefore clear that the potential for business applications can suffer with increased real security. On the other hand, users and organisations will tend to use systems that they trust, and increased perceived security is a contributing factor for increased trust, which in turn is a catalyst for the uptake of online activity and business. Because real and perceived security seems to have opposite effects on e-business it is interesting to look at their combined effect, as illustrated in Fig.4.

The shaded triangle on the right hand side graph represents the potential for e-business which is bounded by the effect of decreased functionality as a result of real security, and by the effect of distrust as a result of perceived insecurity. Assuming that

---

[5] http://www.ibm.com/developerworks/library/specification/ws-trust/

[6] See e.g. the TC FAQ at http://www.cl.cam.ac.uk/~rja14/tcpa-faq.html and the Content Protection Cost Analysis at http://www.cs.auckland.ac.nz/~pgut001/pubs/vista_cost.html

[7] See e.g. the animation about TC at http://www.lafkon.net/tc/

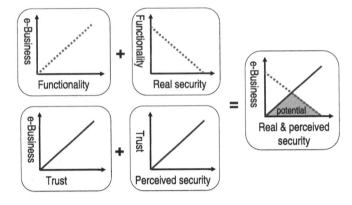

Fig. 4. Combining the effects of real and perceived security on e-business

the levels of perceived and real security are equal, the optimal situation would be to have a moderate level of real security which results in a moderate level of trust. If it were possible to separate perceived security from real security, it could be optimal to decrease the level of real security and artificially boost the level of perceived security. There is evidence of this happening in the e-commerce industry. For example, online banks used to instruct their customers to look for the locked padlock in the corner of the Web browser as an indicator for transaction security in the form of SSL-based encryption and authentication. That was until phishing attacks emerged. In contradiction to what was claimed, SSL does not provide any practical authentication. The padlock gives a false impression of security because Web browsers display it even when connected to phishing Websites. However, the padlock initially had the effect of making customers trust and start using the Internet as a medium for conducting bank transactions. With the realisation that SSL does not provide any practical authentication, perceived Web security has subsequently been adjusted to correspond better with real Web security.

2.5   Collaborative Filtering and Collaborative Sanctioning

Collaborative filtering systems (CF) have similarities with reputation systems in the sense that both types of systems collect ratings from members in a community. However they also have fundamental differences. The assumptions behind CF systems is that different people have different tastes, and rate things differently according to subjective taste. If two users rate a set of items similarly, they share similar tastes, and are grouped in the same cluster. This information can be used to recommend items that one participant likes, to other members of the same cluster. Implementations of this technique represent a form of *recommender systems* which is commonly used for targeted marketing. This must not be confused with reputation systems which are based on the seemingly opposite assumption, namely that all members in a community should judge a product or service consistently. In this sense the term *"collaborative sanctioning"* (CS) [39] has been used to describe reputation systems, because the purpose is to sanction poor service providers, with the aim of giving an incentive for them to provide quality services.

CF takes ratings subject to taste as input, whereas reputation systems take ratings assumed insensitive to taste as input. People will for example judge data files containing film and music differently depending on their taste, but all users will judge files containing viruses to be bad. CF systems can be used to select the preferred files in the former case, and reputation systems can be used to avoid the bad files in the latter case. There will of course be cases where CF systems identify items that are invariant to taste, which simply indicates low usefulness of that result for recommendation purposes. Inversely, there will be cases where ratings that are subject to personal taste are being fed into reputation systems. The latter can cause problems, because a reputation system would normally interpret difference in taste as difference in service provider reliability, potentially leading to misleading reputation scores.

There is a great potential for combining CF and reputation systems, e.g. by filtering reputation scores to reflect ratings from users with a common taste. This could result in more reliable reputation scores. Theoretic schemes include Damiani *et al.*'s (2002) proposal to separate between provider reputation and resource reputation in P2P networks [11].

3   Trust Models and Systems

The main differences between trust and reputation systems can be described as follows: Trust systems produce a score that reflects the relying party's subjective view of an entity's trustworthiness, whereas reputation systems produce an entity's (public) reputation score as seen by the whole community. Secondly, transitivity of trust paths and networks is an explicit component in trust systems, whereas reputation systems usually do not take transitivity into account, or only in an implicit way. Finally, trust systems take subjective expressions of (reliability) trust about other entities as input, whereas reputation systems take ratings about specific (and objective) events as input.

There can of course be trust systems that incorporate elements of reputation systems and vice versa, so that it is not always clear how a given systems should be classified. The descriptions of the various trust and reputation systems below must therefor be seen in this light.

Interpreting trust or trustworthiness as a measure of reliability allows a whole range of metrics to be applied, from discrete to continuous and normalised metrics. This section gives a brief overview of these approaches.

3.1   Discrete Trust Models

Humans are often better able to rate performance in the form of discrete verbal statements, than in the form of continuous measures. A system that allows trust to be expressed in the form of a discrete statement like *"usually trusted"* provides better usability than in the form of a probability value. This is because the meaning of discrete verbal statements comes to mind immediately, whereas probability values require more cognitive effort to be interpreted. Some systems, including [1,6,7,35,55] are based on discrete trust models.

Discrete measures do not easily lend themselves to sound computational principles. Instead, heuristic methods such as look-up tables must be used. The software encryption tool PGP uses discrete measures for expressing and analysing trust in public keys. PGP implements a very pragmatic approach to the complex issue of deriving trust from a trust network, and is described in more detail in Sec.5.1.

3.2 Probabilistic Trust Models

The advantage of probabilistic models is that the rich body of probabilistic methods can be directly applied. This provides a great variety of possible derivation methods, from simple models based on probability calculus to models using advanced statistical methods. An overview of Bayesian approaches is provided in [32].

Certain models require normalisation in order to produce consistent results. This is for example the case for Google's PageRank algorithm [43]. This is because PageRank requires additivity (i.e. that the sum of probabilities equals one) over the whole population of Web pages. This means that a Web page can only increase its rank at the cost of others. PageRank can also be described as a flow models because it computes trust or reputation by transitive iteration through looped or arbitrarily long chains. PageRank is described in more detail in Sec.8.

Other flow models are the Appleseed algorithm [54], Advogato's reputation scheme [33], and the EigenTrust model [31]. The latter computes agent trust scores in P2P networks through repeated and iterative multiplication and aggregation of trust scores along transitive chains until the trust scores for all agent members of the P2P community converge to stable values.

3.3 Belief Models

Belief theory is a framework related to probability theory, but where the sum of probabilities over all possible outcomes not necessarily add up to 1, and the remaining probability is interpreted as uncertainty.

Jøsang (1999,2001) [23,24] has proposed a belief/trust metric called *opinion* denoted by $\omega_x^A = (b, d, u, a)$, which expresses the relying party A's belief in the truth of statement x. Here b, d, and u represent belief, disbelief and uncertainty respectively where $b, d, u \in [0, 1]$ and $b + d + u = 1$. The parameter $a \in [0, 1]$ represents the base rate in the absence of evidence, and is used for computing an opinion's probability expectation value $E(\omega_x^A) = b + au$, meaning that a determines how uncertainty shall contribute to $E(\omega_x^A)$. When the statement x for example says *"David is honest and reliable"*, then the opinion can be interpreted as reliability trust in David. As an example, let us assume that Alice needs to get her car serviced, and that she asks Bob to recommend a good car mechanic. When Bob recommends David, Alice would like to get a second opinion, so she asks Claire for her opinion about David. This situation is illustrated in fig. 5 below.

When trust and trust referrals are expressed as opinions, each transitive trust path Alice→Bob→David, and Alice→Claire→David can be computed with the *discounting operator*, where the idea is that the referrals from Bob and Claire are discounted as a function Alice's trust in Bob and Claire respectively. Finally the two paths can be combined using the cumulative *consensus operator* or by the averaging operator. These operators form part of *Subjective Logic* [24,25], and semantic constraints must be satisfied in order for the transitive trust derivation to be meaningful [30]. Opinions can be

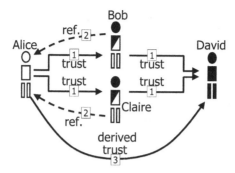

Fig. 5. Deriving trust from parallel transitive chains

uniquely mapped to beta PDFs, and this sense the consensus operator is equivalent to the Bayesian updating described in Sec.4.3. This model is thus both belief-based and Bayesian.

By assuming Alice's trust in Bob and Bob's trust in Claire to be positive but not absolute, Alice's derived trust in Eric is intuitively weaker than Claire's trust in Eric.

Claire obviously recommends to Bob her opinion about Eric as a car mechanic, but Bob's recommendation to Alice is ambiguous. It can either be that Bob passes Claire's recommendation unaltered on to Alice, or that Bob derives indirect trust in Eric which he recommends to Alice. The latter way of passing recommendations can create problems, and it is better when Alice receives Claire's recommendation unaltered.

3.4 Fuzzy Models

Trust and reputation can be represented as linguistically fuzzy concepts, where membership functions describe to what degree an agent can be described as e.g. trustworthy or not trustworthy. Fuzzy logic provides rules for reasoning with fuzzy measures of this type. The scheme proposed by Manchala (1988) [35] described in Sec.2 as well as the REGRET reputation system proposed by Sabater & Sierra (2001,2002) [46,47,48] fall in this category. In Sabater & Sierra's scheme, what they call *individual reputation* is derived from private information about a given agent, what they call *social reputation* is derived from public information about an agent, and what they call *context dependent reputation* is derived from contextual information.

3.5 Modelling Decision Trust

There are only a few computational trust models that explicitly take risk into account [17]. Studies that combine risk and trust include Manchala (1998) [35] and Jøsang & Lo Presti (2004) [29]. The system described by Manchala (1998) [35] avoids expressing measures of trust directly, and instead develops a model based on trust-related variables such as the cost of the transaction and its history, and defines risk-trust decision matrices as illustrated in Figure 6. The risk-trust matrices are then used together with fuzzy logic inference rules to determine whether or not to transact with a particular party.

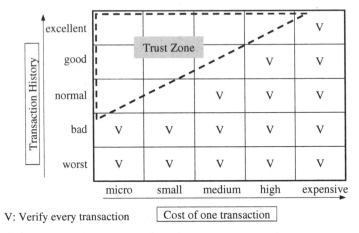

Fig. 6. Risk-trust matrix (from Manchala (1998) [35])

Manchala's risk-trust matrix is intuitive and simple to apply. The higher the value at stake, the more positive experiences are required to decide to trust.

Jøsang and Lo Presti use simple economic modelling, taking into account probability of success, gain, risk attitude and asset value at stake. Let F_C express the fraction of capital at stake, meaning that the relying party is investing fraction F_C of its total capital in the transaction. Let G_s express the gain factor and let p express the probability of success of the transaction. Intuitively F_C increases with G_s when p is fixed, and similarly F_C increases with p when G_s fixed. In order to illustrate this general behaviour let a given agent's risk attitude for example be determined by the function:

$$F_C(p, G_s) = p^{\frac{\lambda}{G_s}} \tag{1}$$

where $\lambda \in [1, \infty]$ is a factor moderating the influence of the transaction gain G_s on the fraction of total capital that the relying party is willing to put at risk. The term *decision surface* describes the type of surface illustrated in Figure 7.

λ is interpreted as a factor of the relying party's risk attitude in the given transaction context, and in the graph of Fig.7 we have set $\lambda = 10000$. A low λ value is representative of a risk-taking behaviour because it increases the volume under the surface delimited by F_C (pushes the decision surface upwards in Figure 7), whereas a high λ value represents risk aversion because it reduces the volume under the surface (pushes the decision surface down).

Risk attitudes are relative to each individual, so the shape of the surface in Figure 7 only represents an example and will of course differ for each agent.

A particular transaction will be represented by a point in the 3D space of Figure 7 with coordinates (G_s, p, F_C). Because the surface represents an agent's risk attitude the agent will per definition accept a transaction for which the point is located underneath the decision surface, and will reject a transaction for which the point is located above the decision surface.

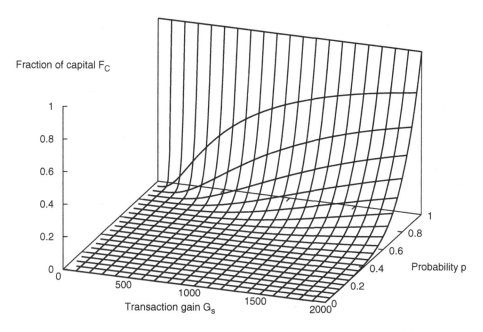

Fig. 7. Example of an agent's risk attitude expressed as a decision surface

4 Reputation Models and Systems

Seen from the relying party's point of view, reputation scores can be computed based on own experience, on second hand referrals, or on a combination of both. In the jargon of economic theory, the term *private information* is used to describe first hand information resulting from own experience, and *public information* is used to describe publicly available second hand information, i.e. information that can be obtained from third parties.

Reputation systems are typically based on public information in order to reflect the community's opinion in general, which is in line with Def.4 of reputation. Private information that is submitted to a public reputation center is here considered as public information. An entity who relies on the reputation score of some remote party, is in fact trusting that party by implicitly trusting those who have rated that party, which in principle is *trust transitivity* as described in Sec.2.3.

This section describes reputation system architectures and various principles for computing reputation and trust measures. Some of the principles are used in commercial applications, whereas others have been proposed by the academic community.

4.1 Reputation Network Architectures

The technical principles for building reputation systems are described in this and the following section. The network architecture determines how ratings and reputation scores are communicated between participants in a reputation systems. The two main types are centralised and distributed architectures.

Centralised Reputation Systems. In centralised reputation systems, information about the performance of a given participant is collected as ratings from other members in the community who have had direct experience with that participant. The central authority (reputation centre) that collects all the ratings typically derives a reputation score for every participant, and makes all scores publicly available. Participants can then use each other's scores, for example, when deciding whether or not to transact with a particular party. The idea is that transactions with reputable participants are likely to result in more favourable outcomes than transactions with disreputable participants.

Fig.8 below shows a typical centralised reputation framework, where A and B denote transaction partners with a history of transactions in the past, and who consider transacting with each other in the present.

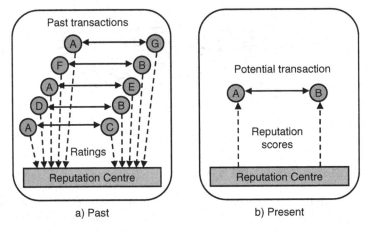

Fig. 8. General framework for a centralised reputation system

After each transaction, the agents provide ratings about each other's performance in the transaction. The reputation centre collects ratings from all the agents, and continuously updates each agent's reputation score as a function of the received ratings. Updated reputation scores are provided online for all the agents to see, and can be used by the agents to decide whether or not to transact with a particular agent. The two fundamental aspects of centralised reputation systems are:

a. *Centralised communication protocols* that allow participants to provide ratings about transaction partners to the central authority, as well as to obtain reputation scores of potential transaction partners from the central authority.
b. *A reputation computation engine* used by the central authority to derive reputation scores for each participant, based on received ratings, and possibly also on other information.

Distributed Reputation Systems. There are environments where a distributed reputation system, i.e. without any centralised functions, is better suited than a centralised system. In a distributed system there is no central location for submitting ratings or obtaining reputation scores of others. Instead, there can be distributed stores where ratings can be submitted, or each participant simply records the opinion about each experience with other parties, and provides this information on request from relying parties. A relying party, who considers transacting with a given target party, must find the distributed stores, or try to obtain ratings from as many community members as possible who have had direct experience with that target party. This is illustrated in fig.9 below.

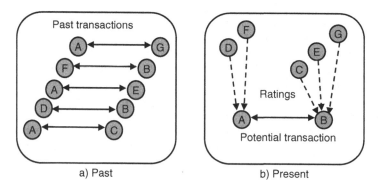

Fig. 9. General framework for a distributed reputation system

The relying party computes the reputation score based on the received ratings. In case the relying party has had direct experience with the target party, the experience from that encounter can be taken into account as private information, possibly carrying a higher weight than the received ratings. The two fundamental aspects of distributed reputation systems are:

a. A *distributed communication protocol* that allows participants to obtain ratings from other members in the community.
b. A *reputation computation method* used by each individual agent to derive reputation scores of target parties based on received ratings, and possibly on other information.

Peer-to-Peer (P2P) networks represent a environment well suited for distributed reputation management. In P2P networks, every node plays the role of both client and server, and is therefore sometimes called a *servent*. This allows the users to overcome their passive role typical of web navigation, and to engage in an active role by providing their own resources. There are two phases in the use of P2P networks. The first is the *search* phase, which consists of locating the servent where the requested resource resides. In some P2P networks, the search phase can rely on centralised functions. One such example is Napster[8] which has a resource directory server. In pure P2P networks like Gnutella[9] and Freenet[10], also the search phase is distributed. Intermediate architectures also exist, e.g. the FastTrack architecture which is used in P2P networks like

---

[8] http://www.napster.com/
[9] http://www.gnutella.com
[10] http://www.zeropaid.com/freenet

KaZaA[11], grokster[12] and iMesh[13]. In FastTrack based P2P networks, there are nodes and supernodes, where the latter keep tracks of other nodes and supernodes that are logged onto the network, and thus act as directory servers during the search phase.

After the search phase, where the requested resource has been located, comes the *download phase*, which consists of transferring the resource from the exporting to the requesting servent.

P2P networks introduce a range of security threats, as they can be used to spread malicious software, such as viruses and Trojan horses, and easily bypass firewalls. There is also evidence that P2P networks suffer from free riding [4]. Reputation systems are well suited to fight these problems, e.g. by sharing information about rogue, unreliable or selfish participants. P2P networks are controversial because they have been used to distribute copyrighted material such as MP3 music files, and it has been claimed that content poisoning[14] has been used by the music industry to fight this problem. We do not defend using P2P networks for illegal file sharing, but it is obvious that reputation systems could be used by distributors of illegal copyrighted material to protect themselves from poisoning. Many authors have proposed reputation systems for P2P networks [2,10,11,12,18,31,34]. The purpose of a reputation system in P2P networks is to determine:

a. which servents are most reliable at offering the best quality resources, and
b. which servents provide the most reliable information with regard to (1).

In a distributed environment, each participant is responsible for collecting and combining ratings from other participants. Because of the distributed environment, it is often impossible or too costly to obtain ratings resulting from all interactions with a given agent. Instead the reputation score is based on a subset of ratings, usually from the relying party's "neighbourhood".

4.2 Simple Summation or Average of Reputation Ratings

The simplest form of computing reputation scores is simply to sum the number of positive ratings and negative ratings separately, and to keep a total score as the positive score minus the negative score. This is the principle used in eBay's reputation forum which is described in detail in [45]. The advantage is that anyone can understand the principle behind the reputation score, the disadvantage that it is primitive and therefore gives a poor picture participants' reputation score although this is also due to the way rating is provided.

A slightly more advanced scheme proposed in e.g. [49] is to compute the reputation score as the average of all ratings, and this principle is used in the reputation systems of numerous commercial web sites, such as Epinions, and Amazon.

---

[11] http://www.kazaa.com

[12] http://www.grokster.com/

[13] http://imesh.com

[14] Poisoning music file sharing networks consists of distributing files with legitimate titles - and put inside them silence or random noise.

Advanced models in this category compute a weighted average of all the ratings, where the rating weight can be determined by factors such as rater trustworthiness/reputation, age of the rating, distance between rating and current score etc.

4.3 Bayesian Reputation Systems

Bayesian systems have a solid mathematical foundation, and are based on computing reputation scores by statistical updating of binomial Beta or multinomial Dirichlet probability density functions (PDF). The *a posteriori* (i.e. the updated) reputation score is computed by combining the *a priori* (i.e. previous) reputation score with the new rating [26,39,40,41,53,28]. Binomial reputation systems allow ratings to be expressed with two values, as either positive (e.g. *good*) or negative (e.g. *bad*). Multinomial reputation systems allow the possibility of providing ratings with graded levels such as e.g. *mediocre - bad - average - good - excellent.* In addition, multinomial models are able to distinguish between the case of polarised ratings (i.e. a combination of strictly good and bad ratings) and the case of only average ratings. The ability to indicate when ratings are polarised can provide valuable clues to the user in many situations. Multinomial reputation systems therefore provide great flexibility when collecting ratings and providing reputation scores.

Multinomial Bayesian reputation systems allow ratings to be provided over k different levels which can be considered as a set of k disjoint elements. Let this set be denoted as $\Lambda = \{L_1, \ldots L_k\}$, and assume that ratings are provided as votes on the elements of Λ. This leads to a Dirichlet probability density function over the k-component random probability variable $p(L_i)$, $i = 1 \ldots k$ with sample space $[0, 1]^k$, subject to the simple additivity requirement $\sum_{i=1}^{k} p(L_i) = 1$.

The Dirichlet distribution with prior captures a sequence of observations of the k possible outcomes with k positive real rating parameters $r(L_i)$, $i = 1 \ldots k$, each corresponding to one of the possible levels. In order to have a compact notation we define a vector $\vec{p} = \{p(L_i) \mid 1 \le i \le k\}$ to denote the k-component probability variable, and a vector $\vec{r} = \{r_i \mid 1 \le i \le k\}$ to denote the k-component rating variable.

In order to distinguish between the *a priori* default base rate, and the *a posteriori* ratings, the Dirichlet distribution must be expressed with prior information represented as a base rate vector $\vec{a}$ over the state space.

Let $\Lambda = \{L_1, \ldots L_k\}$ be a state space consisting of k mutually disjoint elements which can be rating levels. Let $\vec{r}$ represent the rating vector over the elements of Λ and let $\vec{a}$ represent the base rate vector over the same elements. The reputation score is defined in terms of the expectation value of each random probability variable corresponding to the rating levels. This provides a sound mathematical basis for combining ratings and for expressing reputation scores. The probability expectation of any of the k random probability variables can be written as:

$$\mathrm{E}(p(L_i) \mid \vec{r}, \vec{a}) = \frac{r(L_i) + Ca(L_i)}{C + \sum_{i=1}^{k} r(L_i)} \, . \tag{2}$$

The *a priori* weight C will normally be set to $C = 2$ when a uniform distribution over binary state spaces is assumed. Selecting a larger value for C will result in new observations having less influence over the Dirichlet distribution. The combination of the base rate vector $\vec{a}$ and the *a priori* weight C can in fact represent specific *a priori* information provided by a domain expert or by another reputation system. It can be noted that it would be unnatural to require a uniform distribution over arbitrary large state spaces because it would make the sensitivity to new evidence arbitrarily small. The value of C determines the approximate number of votes needed for a particular level to influence the probability expectation value of that level from 0 to 0.5.

A general reputation system allows for an agent to rate another agent or service, with any level from a set of predefined rating levels. Some form of control over what and when ratings can be given is normally required, such as e.g. after a transaction has taken place, but this issue will not be discussed here. Let there be k different discrete rating levels. This translates into having a state space of cardinality k for the Dirichlet distribution. Let the rating level be indexed by i. The aggregate ratings for a particular agent y are stored as a cumulative vector, expressed as:

$$\vec{R}_y = (R_y(L_i) \mid i = 1 \ldots k). \tag{3}$$

Each new discrete rating of agent y by an agent x takes the form of a trivial vector $\vec{r}_y^x$ where only one element has value 1, and all other vector elements have value 0. The index i of the vector element with value 1 refers to the specific rating level. The previously stored vector $\vec{R}$ is updating by adding the newly received rating vector $\vec{r}$.

Agents (and in particular human agents) may change their behaviour over time, so it is desirable to give relatively greater weight to more recent ratings. This can be achieved by introducing a longevity factor $\lambda \in [0, 1]$, which controls the rapidity with which old ratings are aged and discounted as a function of time. With $\lambda = 0$, ratings are completely forgotten after a single time period. With $\lambda = 1$, ratings are never forgotten.

Let new ratings be collected in discrete time periods. Let the sum of the ratings of a particular agent y in period t be denoted by the vector $\vec{r}_{y,t}$. More specifically, it is the sum of all ratings $\vec{r}_y^x$ of agent y by other agents x during that period, expressed by:

$$\vec{r}_{y,t} = \sum_{x \in M_{y,t}} \vec{r}_y^x \tag{4}$$

where $M_{y,t}$ is the set of all agents who rated agent y during period t.

Let the total accumulated ratings (with aging) of agent y after the time period t be denoted by $\vec{R}_{y,t}$. The new accumulated rating after time period $t + 1$ is expressed as:

$$\vec{R}_{y,(t+1)} = \lambda \cdot \vec{R}_{y,t} + \vec{r}_{y,(t+1)}, \text{ where } 0 \leq \lambda \leq 1. \tag{5}$$

Eq.(5) represents a recursive updating algorithm that can be executed every period for all agents. A reputation score applies to member agents in a community M. Before any evidence is known about a particular agent y, its reputation is defined by the base rate reputation which is the same for all agents. As evidence about a particular agent is gathered, its reputation will change accordingly.

The most natural representation of reputation scores is in the form of the probability expectation values of each element in the state space. The expectation value for each rating level can be computed with Eq.(2). Let $\vec{R}$ represent a target agent's aggregate ratings. The vector $\vec{S}$ defined by:

$$\vec{S}_y : \left(S_y(L_i) = \frac{R_y(L_i) + Ca(L_i)}{C + \sum_{j=1}^{k} R_y(L_j)}; \mid i = 1 \ldots k \right). \tag{6}$$

is the corresponding multinomial probability reputation score. As already stated, $C = 2$ is the value of choice, but larger value for the weight C can be chosen if a reduce influence of new evidence over the base rate is required.

The reputation score $\vec{S}$ can be interpreted as a multinomial probability measure expressing how a particular agent is expected to behave in future transactions. It can easily be verified that

$$\sum_{i=1}^{k} S(L_i) = 1. \tag{7}$$

The multinomial reputation score can for example be visualised as columns, which would clearly indicate if ratings are polarised. Assume for example 5 levels:

$$L_1 : \text{Mediocre}, \quad L_2 : \text{Bad}, \quad L_3 : \text{Average}, \quad L_4 : \text{Good}, \quad L_5 : \text{Excellent}. \tag{8}$$

We assume a default base rate distribution. Before any ratings have been received, the multinomial probability reputation score will be equal to $1/5$ for all levels. We consider two different cases where 10 ratings are received. In the first case, 10 *average* ratings are received, which translates into the concentric probability reputation score of Fig.10.a. In the second case, 5 mediocre and 5 excellent ratings are received, which translates into the polarized probability reputation score of Fig.10.b.

While informative, the multinomial probability representation can require considerable space to be displayed on a computer screen. A more compact form can be to express the reputation score as a single value in some predefined interval. This can be done by assigning a point value ν to each rating level i, and computing the normalised weighted point estimate score σ.

Assume e.g. k different rating levels with point values evenly distributed in the range $[0,1]$, so that $\nu(L_i) = \frac{i-1}{k-1}$. The point estimate reputation is then computed as:

$$\sigma = \sum_{i=1}^{k} \nu(L_i)S(L_i). \tag{9}$$

However, this point estimate removes information, so that for example the difference between the average ratings and the polarised ratings of Fig.10.a and Fig.10.b is no longer visible. The point estimates of the reputation scores of Fig.10.a and Fig.10.b are both 0.5, although the ratings in fact are quite different. A point estimate in the range $[0,1]$ can be mapped to any range, such as 1-5 stars, a percentage or a probability.

Bootstrapping a reputation system to a stable and conservative state is important. In the framework described above, the base rate distribution $\vec{a}$ will define initial default reputation for all agents. The base rate can for example be evenly distributed, or biased

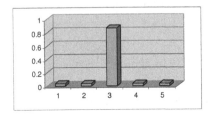

(a) After 10 average ratings

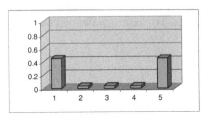

(b) After 5 mediocre and 5 excellent ratings (polarised case)

Fig. 10. Reputation scores resulting from average and from polarised ratings

towards either a negative or a positive reputation. This must be defined by those who set up the reputation system in a specific market or community.

Agents will come and go during the lifetime of a market, and it is important to be able to assign new members a reasonable base rate reputation. In the simplest case, this can be the same as the initial default reputation that was given to all agents during bootstrap.

However, it is possible to track the average reputation score of the whole community, and this can be used to set the base rate for new agents, either directly or with a certain additional bias.

Not only new agents, but also existing agents with a standing track record can get the dynamic base rate. After all, a dynamic community base rate reflects the whole community, and should therefore be applied to all the members of that community.

The aggregate reputation vector for the whole community at time t is computed as:

$$\vec{R}_{M,t} = \sum_{y_j \in M} \vec{R}_{y,t} \tag{10}$$

This vector then needs to be normalised to a base rate vector as follows:

Definition 7 (Community Base Rate). *Let $\vec{R}_{M,t}$ be an aggregate reputation vector for a whole community, and let $S_{M,t}$ be the corresponding multinomial probability reputation vector which can be computed with Eq.(6). The community base rate as a function of existing reputations at time $t + 1$ is then simply expressed as the community score at time t:*

$$\vec{a}_{M,(t+1)} = \vec{S}_{M,t}. \tag{11}$$

The base rate vector of Eq.(11) can be given to every new agent that joins the community. In addition, the community base rate vector can be used for every agent every time their reputation score is computed. In this way, the base rate will dynamically reflect the quality of the market at any one time.

If desirable, the base rate for new agents can be biased in either negative or positive direction in order to make it harder or easier to enter the market.

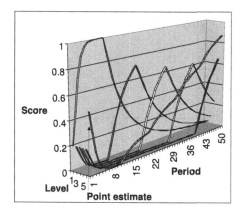

Fig. 11. Scores and point estimate during sequence of varying ratings

As an example we consider the following sequence of varying ratings:

Periods 1 - 10: L1 Mediocre
Periods 11 - 20: L2 Bad
Periods 21 - 30: L3 Average
Periods 31 - 40: L4 Good
Periods 41 - 50: L5 Excellent

The longevity factor is $\lambda = 0.9$ as before, and the base rate is dynamic. The evolution of the scores of each level as well as the point estimate are illustrated in Fig.11.

In Fig.11 the multinomial reputation scores change abruptly between each sequence of 10 periods. The point estimate first drops as the score for L1 increase during the first 10 periods. After that the point estimate increases relatively smoothly during the subsequent 40 periods. Because of the dynamic base rate, the point estimate will eventually converge to 1.

5   Applications and Examples

5.1   The PGP Trust Model

The software encryption tool PGP (Pretty Good Privacy) [55] provides support for managing public keys and public-key certificates. The trustworthiness of imported keys and their owners is derived using PGP's particular trust model.

Trust is is applied to three different aspects which are *"Owner Trust"* which corresponds to trust in the owner of a public key, *"Signature Trust"* which corresponds to trust in received certificates, and *"Key Validity"* which corresponds to trust in a public key, where each trust type can take discrete trust values, as indicated below.

Owner Trust
Signature Trust $\begin{cases} \textit{always trusted} \\ \textit{usually trusted} \\ \textit{not trusted} \\ \textit{unknown trust} \end{cases}$ Key Validity $\begin{cases} \textit{complete} \\ \textit{marginal} \\ \textit{undefined} \end{cases}$

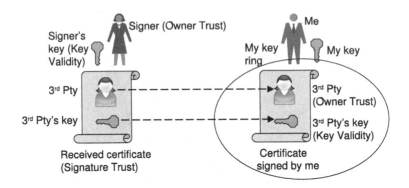

Fig. 12. The PGP trust model

A user's private key(s) is/are stored in a table called the 'Secret Key Ring'. Keys stored here are used for signing messages and to decrypt received encrypted messages. A table called the 'Public Key Ring' is used to store other users' public keys together with the trust parameters Key Validity and Owner trust for each key. Keys stored here are used for encrypting messages sent to other users and to verify signed messages received from them.

When a new public key is received and introduced through a certificate PGP first checks that the Key Validity of the key used for signing the certificate is *complete*, otherwise the certificate is ignored. After having accepted a certificate its Signature Trust gets the Owner Trust value of the user who signed it. When a key has one or more certificates, the accumulated Signature Trust values determine the Key Validity of the key according to the skepticism level. By default PGP requires one *always trusted* or two *usually trusted* signatures in order to assign *complete* Key Validity to the received public key, but these parameters can be tuned by the user according to his or her trust attitude. An insufficient number of *always trusted* or *usually trusted* signatures results in *marginal* Key Validity, and a key received without even a *usually trusted* signature gets *undefined* Key Validity.

Only the Key Validity is automatically computed by PGP, not the Owner Trust. PGP therefore asks the user how much he or she trusts the owner for introducing new keys, and this decision is purely subjective. The Key Validity and the Owner Trust parameters represent confidential information that is not communicated to other users.

After having defined the Key Validity and Owner Trust for a particular key, PGP allows the user to sign and add it to the Public Key Ring. The user can now introduce it to others who will evaluate this key in exactly the same way as describe above. The various elements (with their corresponding discrete trust parameters in brackets) are illustrated in Fig.12.

Because trust parameters are subjective it is not meaningful to share the Public Key Ring with others. Furthermore it is only meaningful to express trust in someone you know, theoretically limiting the number of keys that anyone can store on the Public Key Ring to the number of people he or she actually knows. Current usage however shows that this design assumption is wrong; many people fill their Public Key Rings with keys of people whom they have never met and with whom they have never communicated. Unfortunately this practice destroys PGP's trust management and reduces PGP to a purely mechanical encryption tool.

PGP users can in principle follow whatever certification practice they want but they are of course expected to be convinced that the key is authentic, or in PGP terms that the Key Validity is considered to be *complete*, before issuing a certificate and this can be considered as an informal certificate policy. PGP was primarily built as an e-mail encryption tool for creating a secure channel between people who know each other or who can establish an indirect trust path between each other, and for that purpose it has been extremely successful.

5.2 Web Page Ranking

The early web search engines such as Altavista simply presented every web page that matched the key words entered by the user, which often resulted in too many and irrelevant pages being listed in the search results. Altavista's proposal for handling this problem was to offer advanced ways to combine keywords based on binary logic. This was too complex for users, and therefore did not provide a good solution.

PageRank proposed by Page *et al.* (1998) [43] represents a way of ranking the best search results based on a page's score according to a specific metric. Roughly speaking, PageRank computes the score for any Web page as the sum of the normalised weights of hyperlinks pointing to it, where a normalised hyperlink weight is determined by the score of the page containing the hyperlink, divided by the total number of hyperlinks from that page. This can be described as a trust system, because the total set of hyperlinks form transitive trust chains that can be used as a basis for deriving a relative trust measures for each page. A single hyperlink to a given web page can be seen as a unidirectional trust relationship between the source and the target page. Google's search engine[15] is based on the PageRank algorithm, and the rapidly rising popularity of Google at the cost of Altavista was obviously caused by the superior search results that the PageRank algorithm delivered. The definition of the PageRank algorithm from Page *et al.* (1998) [43] is given below:

Definition 8 (PageRank). Let P be a set of hyperlinked web pages and let u and v denote web pages in P. Let $N^-(u)$ denote the set of web pages pointing to u and let $N^+(v)$ denote the set of web pages that v points to. Let s be some vector over P corresponding to a distribution of initial score such that $\sum_{u \in P} s(u) = 1$. Then, the rank of a web page u is:

$$r(u) = d\,s(u) \ + \ (1-d) \sum_{v \in N^-(u)} \frac{r(v)}{|N^+(v)|}\,, \tag{12}$$

In [43] it is recommended that d be chosen such that $d = 0.15$. The first term in Eq.(12) gives rank value based on initial score. The second term gives rank value as a function

---

[15] http://www.google.com/

of normalised weights of hyperlinks pointing at u. The algorithm of Def.8 must be iterated over the whole Web until the scores for all Web pages stabilise.

The PageRank algorithm provides an algorithmic representation of the *"random surfer model"*, i.e. the value $r(u)$ represents the probability of arriving at Web page u by randomly surfing the Web. Intuitively, because of the very large total number of hyperlinked Web pages in the Internet, this probability value is very close to zero for any random web page.

According to Def.8, $r(u) \in [0, 1]$, but the PageRank values that Google provides to the public are scaled to the range [0,10]. We will denote the public PageRank of a page u as $PR(u)$. This public PageRank measure can be viewed for any web page using Google's toolbar which is a plug-in to the MS Internet Explorer. Although Google do not specify exactly how the public PageRank is computed, it is widely conjectured that it measured on a logarithmic scale with base close to 10. An approximate expression for computing the public PageRank could for example be:

$$PR(u) = l + \log_{10} r(u) \qquad (13)$$

where l is a constant that defines the cut-off value, so that only pages with $r(u) > 10^{-l}$ will be listed by Google. A typical value is $l = 11$.

It is not publicly known how the source rank vector s is defined, but it would be natural to distribute it over the root web pages of all domains weighted by the cost of buying each domain name. Assuming that the only way to improve a page's PageRank is to buy domain names, Clausen (2004) [9] shows that there is a lower bound to the cost of obtaining an arbitrarily good $PR(u)$ for a Web page u.

Without specifying many details, Google state that the PageRank algorithm they are using also takes other elements into account, with the purpose of making it difficult or expensive to deliberately influence PageRank.

In order to provide a semantic interpretation of a PageRank value, a hyperlink can be seen as a positive rating of the page it points to. Negative ratings do not exist in PageRank so that it is impossible to blacklist web pages with the PageRank algorithm of Eq.(12) alone. Before Google with it's PageRank algorithm entered the search engine arena, some webmasters would promote web sites by filling web pages with large amounts of commonly used search key words as invisible text or metadata in order for the page to have a high probability of being listed by a search engine no matter what the user searched for. The PageRank algorithm compensates for problem because a high R is also needed in addition to matching key words in order for a page to be presented to the user.

The growing importance of having a high score in search engines has made many owners of Web sites very restrictive with placing hyperlinks to other websites, because outgoing hyperlinks normally result in decreased scores for Web pages on the own Web site. The very existence of search engines thus had the inevitable effect of interfering with the structure of the Web.

The increasing popularity and economic importance of search engines has also lead to more damaging methods for artificially boosting the score of Web pages. One such example is the phenomenon called *link spam* which consists of placing many hyperlinks to the same Web page on open Web fora such as online discussion boards, guest books, weblogs and wikis. The motivation behind this attack is that search engines will give an increased score for the Web page that these hyperlinks point to.

In order to counter the link spam attacks Google announced in early 2005 that hyperlinks marked with the attribute `rel="nofollow"` would not influence the hyperlink target's score in the search engine's index. This is implemented as follows:

```
<a href="http://some-spammer-website.com"
rel="nofollow" >Click here!</a>
```

Most open Web fora now mark user-submitted hyperlinks this way by default, with no option to disable it by the users, and most search engines take it into account when computing scores. This is an example where a simple technical solution was able to solve a growing problem. However, it has negative side effects.

The increasing usage of `rel="nofollow"` in Web pages will have the effect that scores computed by Google and search engines no longer reflect the real structure of the Web, and removes the model more and more from the random surfer model. The random surfer follows any link, whereas search engines only follow those that are not marked by `rel="nofollow"`. A likely development is that most outgoing hyperlinks will be marked in this way in a selfish manner in order not to suffer decreased scores. The search engines will then face the problem of scarcity of cross links between Web sites, making the computed scores increasingly unreliable.

As a substitute for the hyperlinks, search engines need to use other types of evidence. An obvious source of information is the links that users actually select after a specific search. algorithms can for example be designed that increase the rank of a specific Web page when many people select the link to that page after a Web search. However, the value of this information is limited, because it only becomes available during searches, and does not reflect which Web pages people go to when not using search engines.

It would be more valuable for search engines to know the link to every page that people visit. By encouraging people to use toolbars, search engines can get precisely that information. A toolbar provides some value-added functionality to users, such as displaying the PageRank of every page the user visits. In return for this functionality, the engine is informed about every single Web page that the user visits. This architecture is illustrated in Fig.13 below.

Users often ignored that the toolbar provides this information. Constantly providing the search engine with information about Web pages visited by the user can be considered quite intrusive, and this functionality is usually also found in so-called spyware.

On the basis of information provided by toolbars, search engines are able to compute the probability that an intentional surfer will go to any particular Web page. This can be called the *intentional surfer model*, which represents an improvement over the random surfer model of the original PageRank algorithm.

However, it is likely that the current model is already under attack with the purpose of artificially increasing the ranking of certain Web pages. An obvious attack method is e.g. to install search engine toolbars on a large number of computers, and let programs automatically browse specific Websites. Google and other toolbar providers are aware of this potential problem, and usually registers each individual toolbar installation in order to identify possible "click spamming". It is still unclear to what degree

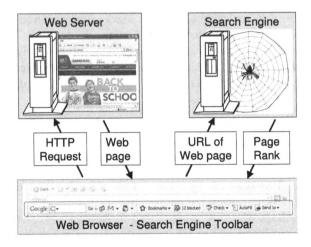

Fig. 13. Network architecture for search engine toolbars

click spamming already is or will be a problem in the near future. The "pay per click" business model is being abused through click spamming, and it is therefore to be expected that the intentional surfer model that bases rank on the number of clicks to Web pages already is under attack as well.

In general it can be observed that any new method for improving rank computation becomes the subject of new attacks as soon as it is implemented. The robustness and reliability of searching and Web navigation has become a cat-and-mouse game, similarly to that of traditional information security.

As a simple example of how a reputation system can be implemented in a general level we describe a simple reputation toolbar which can be installed on any browser. This allows the reputation score of any Web page to be visualised to the user, as well as the user to rate Web sites and Web pages. The toolbar communicates with a centralised server which keeps the reputation vectors of all Web pages. A Web page can be rated by the user with a discrete set of different levels, as described above. This architecture is illustrated in Fig.14.

While the browser is fetching a Web page, the reputation toolbar will query the reputation server about the reputation score of that Web page or Web site. The user is also invited to rate the same Web site through the toolbar. This rating is sent to the reputation server, and taken into account when computing the reputation score in the future.

The functionality of the reputation toolbar of Fig.14 can very well be integrated with a traditional search engine toolbar. The reputation scores can be taken into account for computing rank when presenting Web search results, or can be presented as a separate score for each search query result. In the latter case, the reputation server and the search engine do not need to be co-located. The reputation score can simply be fetched as part of a search query, either by the search engine itself, or by a shell on the client machine. The addition of a reputation system to the traditional search engine will allow the implementation of the *critical surfer model*, which represents an improvement over the current *random surfer* and the *intentional surfer* models, as illustrated in Fig.15.

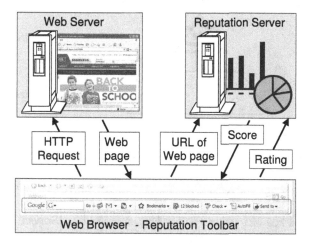

Fig. 14. Network architecture for reputation toolbars

Fig. 15. Past, present and future Web ranking models

While the introduction of the PageRank algorithm represented a revolution in the quality of Web searches, there is still an untapped potential for improvement by integrating reputation systems with search engines.

5.3   The Slashdot Model and Hierarchic Reputation Systems

An approach that seems to work relatively well is that of meta-moderation used on Slashdot[16] which is a *"news for nerds"* message board started in 1997. More precisely it is a forum for posting articles and comments to articles. In the early days when the community was small, the signal to noise ratio was very high. As is the case with all mailing lists and discussion fora where the number of members grow rapidly, spam and low quality postings emerged to become a major problem, and this forced Slashdot to introduce moderation. To start with there was a team of 25 moderators which after a while grew to 400 moderators to keep pace with the growing number of users and the amount of spam that followed. In order to create a more democratic and healthy moderation scheme, automated moderator selection was introduced.

---

[16] http://slashdot.org/

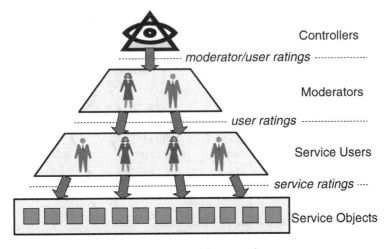

Fig. 16. Hierarchic model for reputation systems

The moderation scheme actually consists of two moderation layers where M1 is for moderating comments to articles, and M2 is for moderating M1 moderators. The purpose of M1 is to be able to filter the good comments from the bad. The purpose of M2 is to address the issue of unfair moderations, or more precisely to sanction M1 moderators. Above M2 in the hierarchy are the staff of Slashdot with omnipotent powers to sanction any M1 or M2 moderator who is detected in abusing the system. Details of the Slashdot reputation systems are described in [27].

Slashdot implements a hierarchic reputation system that directs and stimulates the massive collaborative effort of moderating thousands of postings every day. The system is constantly being tuned and modified and can be described as an ongoing experiment in search for the best practical way to promote quality postings, discourage noise and to make Slashdot as readable and useful as possible for a large community.

In a hierarchical reputation system, ratings occur at different levels, and scores can be computed for elements on each level. Here we describe a general approach to designing hierarchical reputation systems.

Service objects can have a reputation score based on ratings from service users. Users who provide ratings have a credit score based ratings from moderators. Moderators have a credit score based on ratings from Controllers who represent the top of the hierarchy. Users rate service objects positively or negatively based on direct experience with those services. A reputation score can be computed for each object as a function of those ratings. Moderators can rate users depending on whether they provide fair or unfair service ratings. A credit score can be computed for each user based on the user's fairness in rating services. The idea is that service ratings provided by discredited users will carry relatively less weight than service ratings provided by credited users, when the reputation scores for service objects are derived. Controllers, who for example can be representatives from the reputation centre, can rate moderators, and depending on the design, can also rate users. This model is illustrated in Fig. 16.

The idea being this design is to spread the workload of providing ratings over all the service users, and provide a mechanisms for stabilising the system and sanctioning unfair raters. Design issues are for example the determination of the optimal Moderator/User and Controller/Moderator ratios, and defining adequate incentives for participants to contribute to the collaborative effort. From a purely rational viewpoint, a participant has little incentive to rate a service after the fact, because providing ratings benefits others, not oneself. A study from eBay [45] shows that 60.7% of the buyers and 51.7% of the sellers on eBay provided ratings about each other. Possible explanations for these relatively high values can for example be that providing reciprocal ratings simply is an expression of politeness. However lack of incentives for providing ratings is a general problem that needs special attention when designing reputation systems.

6   Discussion and Conclusion

The robustness of trust and reputation systems for resisting attacks and strategic manipulation is the critical factor for the success of this technology, and which currently is not being sufficiently addressed. Traditional security mechanisms can be used to achieve goals such as anonymity and integrity of ratings [19]. Identity and credentials management can be used to control when and by whom ratings can be provided, e.g. to prevent ballot stuffing [20]. The robustness of soft security mechanisms will thus depend on hard security mechanisms.

Social acceptance of trust and reputation systems is another critical factor, which many commercial systems have addressed and solved quite well. However, for the more widespread and general usage of these systems, social acceptance by all parties is an issue that needs to be considered.

Given that reputation systems used in commercial and online applications have serious vulnerabilities, it is obvious that the reliability of these systems sometimes is questionable. Assuming that reputation systems give unreliable scores, why then are they used? A possible answer to this question is that in many situations the reputation systems do not need to be robust because their value lies elsewhere. Resnick & Zeckhauser (2002) [45] consider two explanations in relation to eBays reputation system: (a) Even though a reputation system is not robust it might serve its purpose of providing an incentive for good behaviour if the participants think it works, and (b) even though the system might not work well in the statistical normative sense, it may function successfully if it swiftly reacts against bad behaviour (called *"stoning"*) and if it imposes costs for a participant to get established (called *"label initiation dues"*).

Given that some online reputation systems are far from being robust, it is obvious that the organisations that run them have a business model that is relatively insensitive to their robustness. It might be that the reputation system serves as a kind of social network to attract more people to a web site, and if that is the case, then having simple rules for participating is more important than having strict rules for controlling participants' behaviour. Any reputation system with user participation will depend on how people respond to it, and must therefore be designed with that in mind. Another explanation is that, from a business perspective, having a reputation system that is not robust can be desirable if it generally gives a positive bias. After all, commercial web stores are in the business of selling, and positively biased ratings are more likely to promote sales than negative ratings.

Whenever the robustness of a reputation system is crucial, the organisation that runs it should take measures to protect the stability of the system and robustness against attacks. This can for example be by including routine manual control as part of the scheme, such as in Epinions' case when selecting Category Lead reviewers, or in Slashdot's case where Slashdot staff are omnipotent moderators. Exceptional manual control will probably always be needed, should the system come under heavy attack. Another important element is to keep the exact details of the computation algorithm and how the system is implemented confidential (called *"security by obscurity"*), such as in the case of Epinions, Slashdot and Google. Ratings are usually based on subjective judgement, which opens up the Pandora's box of unfair ratings, but if ratings can be based on objective criteria it would be much simpler to achieve high robustness.

The rich literature growing around trust and reputation systems for Internet transactions, as well as the implementation of reputation systems in successful commercial application, give a strong indication that this is an important technology. The early commercial and live implementations were, and still are, based on relatively simple schemes, whereas a multitude of different systems with advanced features are continuously being proposed by the academic community. Some of the advanced schemes are slowly finding their way into real implementations as more experience is gained with this type of technology.

Designing and implementing robust trust and reputation systems represents a formidable challenge, and the long term acceptance of the Internet as a reliable platform for supporting open markets and communities depends on the success of this endeavour. To have effective and pervasive trust management on the Internet is like finding the holy grail because the value of the Internet would increase manifold. How to make it happen is therefore an extremely important research problem for the global Internet community.

References

1. Abdul-Rahman, A., Hailes, S.: Supporting Trust in Virtual Communities. In: Proceedings of the Hawaii International Conference on System Sciences, Maui, Hawaii, January 4-7, 2000 (2000)
2. Aberer, K., Despotovic, Z.: Managing trust in a peer-2-peer information system. In: Paques, H., Liu, L., Grossman, D. (eds.) Proceedings of the Tenth International Conference on Information and Knowledge Management (CIKM01), pp. 10–317. ACM Press, New York (2001)
3. Abrams, M.D.: Trusted System Concepts. Computers and Security 14(1), 45–56 (1995)
4. Adar, E., Huberman, B.A.: Free Riding on Gnutella. First Monday (Peer-reviewed Journal on the Internet) 5(10), 8 (2000)
5. Blaze, M., Feigenbaum, J., Lacy, J.: Decentralized trust management. In: Proceedings of the 1996 IEEE Conference on Security and Privacy, Oakland, CA (1996)
6. Cahill, V., Shand, B., Gray, E., et al.: Using Trust for Secure Collaboration in Uncertain Environments. Pervasive Computing 2(3), 52–61 (2003)
7. Carbone, M., Nielsen, M., Sassone, V.: A Formal Model for Trust in Dynamic Networks. In: Proc. of International Conference on Software Engineering and Formal Methods (SEFM'03), Brisbane (September 2003)

8. Christianson, B., Harbison, W.S.: Why Isn't Trust Transitive? In: Proceedings of the Security Protocols International Workshop, University of Cambridge, Cambridge (1996)
9. Clausen, A.: The Cost of Attack of PageRank. In: Proceedings of The International Conference on Agents, Web Technologies and Internet Commerce (IAWTIC'2004), Gold Coast (July 2004)
10. Cornelli, F., et al.: Choosing Reputable Servents in a P2P Network. In: Proceedings of the eleventh international conference on World Wide Web (WWW'02), ACM, New York (2002)
11. Damiani, E., et al.: A Reputation-Based Approach for Choosing Reliable Resources in Peer-to-Peer Networks. In: Proceedings of the 9th ACM conference on Computer and Communications Security (CCS'02), pp. 207–216. ACM, New York (2002)
12. Fahrenholtz, D., Lamesdorf, W.: Transactional Security for a Distributed Reputation Management System. In: Bauknecht, K., Tjoa, A.M., Quirchmayr, G. (eds.) EC-Web 2002. LNCS, vol. 2455, pp. 214–223. Springer, Heidelberg (2002)
13. Falcone, R., Castelfranchi, C.: How trust enhances and spread trust. In: Proceedings of the 4th Int. Workshop on Deception Fraud and Trust in Agent Societies, in the 5th International Conference on Autonomous Agents (AGENTS'01) (May 2001)
14. Falcone, R., Castelfranchi, C.: Social Trust: A Cognitive Approach. In: Castelfranchi, C., Tan, Y.H. (eds.) Trust and Deception in Virtual Societies, pp. 55–99. Kluwer, Dordrecht (2001)
15. Freeman, L.C.: Centrality on Social Networks. Social Networks 1, 215–239 (1979)
16. Gambetta, D.: Can We Trust Trust? In: Gambetta, D. (ed.) Trust: Making and Breaking Co-operative Relations, pp. 213–238. Basil Blackwell, Oxford (1990)
17. Grandison, T., Sloman, M.: A Survey of Trust in Internet Applications. IEEE Communications Surveys and Tutorials, 3 (2000)
18. Gupta, M., Judge, P., Ammar, M.: A reputation system for peer-to-peer networks. In: Proceedings of the 13th international workshop on Network and operating systems support for digital audio and video (NOSSDAV) (2003)
19. Ismail, R., Boyd, C., Jøsang, A., Russel, S.: Strong Privacy in Reputation Systems. In: Proceedings of the 4th International Workshop on Information Security Applications (WISA), Jeju Island, Korea (August 2003)
20. Ismail, R., Boyd, C., Jøsang, A., Russel, S.: An Efficient Off-Line Reputation Scheme Using Articulated Certificates. In: Proceedings of the Second International Workshop on Security in Information Systems (WOSIS-2004) (2004)
21. ISO: ISO/IEC IS 17799 - Information technology – Code of practice for information security management. ISO/IEC (2005)
22. Jøsang, A.: The right type of trust for distributed systems. In: Meadows, C. (ed.) Proc. of the 1996 New Security Paradigms Workshop, ACM, New York (1996)
23. Jøsang, A.: Trust-Based Decision Making for Electronic Transactions. In: Yngström, L., Svensson, T. (eds.) Proceedings of the 4th Nordic Workshop on Secure Computer Systems (NORDSEC'99). Stockholm University, Sweden (1999)
24. Jøsang, A.: A Logic for Uncertain Probabilities. International Journal of Uncertainty, Fuzziness and Knowledge-Based Systems 9(3), 279–311 (2001)
25. Jøsang, A.: Probabilistic Logic Under Uncertainty. In: Proceedings of Computing: The Australian Theory Symposium (CATS2007), CRPIT Ballarat, Australia, vol. 65 (January 2007)
26. Jøsang, A., Ismail, R.: The Beta Reputation System. In: Proceedings of the 15th Bled Electronic Commerce Conference (June 2002)
27. Jøsang, A., Ismail, R., Boyd, C.: A Survey of Trust and Reputation Systems for Online Service Provision. Decision Support Systems 43(2), 618–644 (2007)
28. Jøsang, A., Haller, J.: Dirichlet Reputation Systems. In: Proceedings of the International Conference on Availability, Reliability and Security (ARES 2007), Vienna, Austria (April 2007)

29. Jøsang, A., Lo Presti, S.: Analysing the Relationship Between Risk and Trust. In: Jensen, C., Poslad, S., Dimitrakos, T. (eds.) iTrust 2004. LNCS, vol. 2995, Springer, Heidelberg (2004)
30. Jøsang, A., Pope, S.: Semantic Constraints for Trust Tansitivity. In: Hartmann, S., Stumptner, M. (eds.) Proceedings of the Asia-Pacific Conference of Conceptual Modelling (APCCM) (Conferences in Research and Practice in Information Technology), Newcastle, Australia, vol. 43 (February 2005)
31. Kamvar, S.D., Schlosser, M.T., Garcia-Molina, H.: The EigenTrust Algorithm for Reputation Management in P2P Networks. In: Proceedings of the Twelfth International World Wide Web Conference, Budapest (May 2003)
32. Krukow, K., Nielsen, M.: From Simulations to Theorems: A Position Paper on Research in the Field of Computational Trust. In: Proceedings of the Workshop of Formal Aspects of Security and Trust (FAST 2006), Ontario, Canada (August 2006)
33. Levien, R.: Attack Resistant Trust Metrics. PhD thesis, University of California at Berkeley (2004)
34. Liau, C.Y., et al.: Efficient Distributed Reputation Scheme for Peer-to-Peer Systems. In: Chung, C.-W., Kim, C.-k., Kim, W., Ling, T.-W., Song, K.-H. (eds.) HSI 2003. LNCS, vol. 2713, pp. 54–63. Springer, Heidelberg (2003)
35. Manchala, D.W.: Trust Metrics, Models and Protocols for Electronic Commerce Transactions. In: Proceedings of the 18th International Conference on Distributed Computing Systems (1998)
36. Marsden, P.V., Lin, N. (eds.): Social Structure and Network Analysis. Sage Publications, Beverly Hills (1982)
37. McKnight, D.H., Chervany, N.L.: The Meanings of Trust. Technical Report MISRC Working Paper Series 96-04, University of Minnesota, Management Information Systems Reseach Center (1996)
38. Merriam-Webster: Merriam-Webster Online (accessed June 2007), Available from http://www.m-w.com/
39. Mui, L., Mohtashemi, M., Ang, C.: A Probabilistic Rating Framework for Pervasive Computing Environments. In: Proceedings of the MIT Student Oxygen Workshop (SOW'2001) (2001)
40. Mui, L., Mohtashemi, M., Ang, C., Szolovits, P., Halberstadt, A.: Ratings in Distributed Systems: A Bayesian Approach. In: Proceedings of the Workshop on Information Technologies and Systems (WITS) (2001)
41. Mui, L., Mohtashemi, M., Halberstadt, A.: A Computational Model of Trust and Reputation. In: Proceedings of the 35th Hawaii International Conference on System Science (HICSS) (2002)
42. OASIS: Conformance Requirements for the OASIS Security Assertion Markup Language (SAML) V2.0, Committee Draft. Organization for the Advancement of Structured Information Standards (January 15, 2005)
43. Page, L., Brin, S., Motwani, R., Winograd, T.: The PageRank Citation Ranking: Bringing Order to the Web. Technical report, Stanford Digital Library Technologies Project (1998)
44. Rasmusson, L., Janssen, S.: Simulated Social Control for Secure Internet Commerce. In: Meadows, C. (ed.) Proceedings of the 1996 New Security Paradigms Workshop, ACM, New York (1996)
45. Resnick, P., Zeckhauser, R.: Trust Among Strangers in Internet Transactions: Empirical Analysis of eBay's Reputation System. In: Baye, M.R. (ed.) The Economics of the Internet and E-Commerce. Advances in Applied Microeconomics, vol. 11, Elsevier Science, Amsterdam (2002)
46. Sabater, J., Sierra, C.: REGRET: A reputation model for gregarious societies. In: Proceedings of the 4th Int. Workshop on Deception, Fraud and Trust in Agent Societies, in the 5th Int. Conference on Autonomous Agents (AGENTS'01), Montreal, Canada, pp. 61–69 (2001)

47. Sabater, J., Sierra, C.: Reputation and Social Network Analysis in Multi-Agent Systems. In: Alonso, E., Kudenko, D., Kazakov, D. (eds.) Adaptive Agents and Multi-Agent Systems. LNCS (LNAI), vol. 2636, Springer, Heidelberg (2003)
48. Sabater, J., Sierra, C.: Social ReGreT, a reputation model based on social relations. SIGecom Exchanges 3(1), 44–56 (2002)
49. Schneider, J., et al.: Disseminating Trust Information in Wearable Communities. In: Proceedings of the 2nd International Symposium on Handheld and Ubiquitous Computing (HUC2K) (September 2000)
50. Simmons, G.J.: An introduction to the mathematics of trust in security protocols. In: Proceedings of the 1993 Computer Security Foundations Workshop, pp. 121–127. IEEE Computer Society Press, Los Alamitos, CA (1993)
51. Tadelis, S.: Firm Reputation with Hidden Information. Economic Theory 21(2), 635–651 (2003)
52. Williamson, O.E.: Calculativeness, Trust and Economic Organization. Journal of Law and Economics 36, 453–486 (1993)
53. Withby, A., Jøsang, A., Indulska, J.: Filtering Out Unfair Ratings in Bayesian Reputation Systems. The Icfain Journal of Management Research 4(2), 48–64 (2005)
54. Ziegler, C.-N., Lausen, G.: Spreading Activation Models for Trust Propagation. In: Proceedings of the IEEE International Conference on e-Technology, e-Commerce, and e-Service (EEE '04), Taipei (March 2004)
55. Zimmermann, P.R.: The Official PGP User's Guide. MIT Press, Cambridge (1995)

An Introduction to the Role Based Trust Management Framework RT

Marcin Czenko[1], Sandro Etalle[1,2], Dongyi Li[3], and William H. Winsborough[3]

[1] Department of Computer Science
University of Twente, The Netherlands
[2] University of Trento, Italy
{marcin.czenko,sandro.etalle}@utwente.nl
[3] Department of Computer Science
University of Texas
San Antonio, USA
wwinsborough@acm.org,
dli@cs.utsa.edu

Abstract. Trust Management (TM) is a novel flexible approach to access control in distributed systems, where the access control decisions are based on the policy statements, called credentials, made by different principals and stored in a distributed manner. In this chapter we present an introduction to TM focusing on the role-based trust-management framework RT. In particular, we focus on RT_0, the simplest representative of the RT family, and we describe in detail its syntax and semantics. We also present the solutions to the problem of credential discovery in distributed environments.

1 Introduction

The problem of guaranteeing that confidential data is not disclosed to unauthorized users is paramount in our IT-dominated world, and is usually tackled by implementing access control techniques. Traditional access control schemes make authorization decisions based on the identity, or the role of the requester. However, in decentralized environments, the resource owner and the requester often are unknown to one another, making access control based on identity ineffective. To give a simple example, consider the situation in which a bookstore adopts the policy of giving 10% discount to students of accredited universities. Although a certificate authority may assert that the requester's name is John Q. Smith, if this name is unknown to the bookstore, the name itself does not aid in making a decision whether he is entitled to a discount or not. What is needed is information about the rights, qualifications, and other characteristics assigned to John Q. Smith by one or more authorities (in our example, the university he attends), as well as trust information about the authority itself (e.g. is it accredited?).

Trust management [10,8,29,14,16,19,24,31] is an approach to access control in decentralized distributed systems with access control decisions based on policy statements made by multiple principals. In trust management systems, statements that are maintained in a distributed manner are often digitally signed to ensure their authenticity and integrity; such statements are called credentials or certificates. A key aspect of trust

A. Aldini and R. Gorrieri (Eds.): FOSAD 2006/2007, LNCS 4677, pp. 246–281, 2007.

management is delegation: a principal may transfer limited authority over one or more resources to other principals.

RT [24,25,23] is a family of Role-based Trust management languages introduced by Li, Winsborough and Mitchell. At its most abstract, the notion of role used is simply a set of principals. The primary application of RT is intended to be authorization and access control, and the main purpose of roles is to confer to their members access to specific resources. Nevertheless, roles can also be used in more general terms. For instance, membership in the role of student at the University of Texas may entail certain privileges, but serves to characterize the status of its members more generally. Such characterizations greatly facilitate granting new privileges to entire classes of users.

This tutorial is meant as an introduction to the RT family of trust management languages. It contains a thorough description of RT_0 which is the core language of the family, and some examples of the more complex members: RT_1, RT_2, RT^T, RT^D [24], and the later $RT_\ominus$, introduced by Czenko et al. [26]. Concerning RT_0, this chapter describes in detail, syntax, semantics, decentralized storage and credential chain discovery. Technically, the content of this chapter derives directly from the original papers [24,25], with some changes which simplify the exposition while maintaining generality: in particular a restriction, we employ a restriction on queries that simplifies the definition of credential graph (see Remark 1). We also introduce new pseudo-code versions of the credential chain discovery algorithms.

2 RT_0

The RT framework encompasses a number of languages which have the same basic structure, while offering different features. The main members of the RT family are RT_0, RT_1, RT^T, and RT^D. Here we focus on the core member of RT: RT_0. Later, in Sect. 5, we are going to see examples of the features of RT_1, RT^T, and RT^D.

2.1 Syntax

The basic constructs of RT_0 are *entities*, *role names* and *roles*. *Entities* are also often called principals. They can define roles, issue credentials, and make requests. In general, an entity may be identified by a public key, or by a user account; following Li et al. [25], we abstract away from the mechanism used for identifying entities. We denote them by names starting with an uppercase letter (possibly with a subscript), e.g. A, B, B_1, and *Alice* are all entities. *Role names*, on the other hand, are denoted by strings starting with a lowercase letter (possibly with a subscript), like r, r_1, and *student*.

Finally, *roles* have the form of an entity followed by a role name, separated by a dot. For example, $A.r$, $B.r_1$, and *University.student* are valid roles. The notion of a role is central to RT_0. A role $A.r$ denotes the set of entities that are members of it – a set that we refer to informally by *members*$(A.r)$. A is called the *owner* of the role $A.r$, and is the only authority that can directly determine which are the members of $A.r$.

Permissions in RT_0 are represented by roles. For example, the permission to read confidential document on a corporate network of a company C can be represented by role *C.readConfidential*: in this case, an entity has the read permission if and only if it belongs to *members*(*C.readConfidential*). Other roles are used to represent other properties, sometimes called *attributes*, that characterize the members or their relationship to the role owner. For example, membership in *C.employee* might indicate an employment relationship with C. This example illustrates one aspect of how RT supports decentralization by making the entity with which one has an employment relationship explicit. In RT there is no notion of simply being employed without mentioning the entity whose judgement is being asserted or whose consent makes it so.

There are four types of credentials in RT_0 that an entity A can issue, each corresponding to a different way of defining the membership of one of A's roles, $A.r$.

- *Simple Member*: $A.r \longleftarrow D$.
  With this credential A asserts that D is a member of $A.r$.
- *Simple Inclusion*: $A.r \longleftarrow B.r_1$.
  With this credential A asserts that $A.r$ includes (all members of) $B.r_1$. This represents a delegation from A to B, as B may cause new entities to become members of the role $A.r$ by issuing credentials defining (and extending) $B.r_1$.
- *Linking Inclusion*: $A.r \longleftarrow A.r_1.r_2$.
  $A.r_1.r_2$ is called a *linked role*. With this credential A asserts that $A.r$ includes $B.r_2$ for every B that is a member of $A.r_1$. This represents a delegation from A to all the members of the role $A.r_1$.
- *Intersection Inclusion*: $A.r \longleftarrow B_1.r_1 \cap B_2.r_2$.
  $B_1.r_1 \cap B_2.r_2$ is called an *intersection*. With this credential A asserts that $A.r$ includes every principal who is a member of both $B_1.r_1$ and $B_2.r_2$. This represents partial delegations from A to B_1 and to B_2.

In the original paper introducing RT_0 [25], the number of intersection elements in the intersection inclusion credentials is unlimited. Also, each intersection element can be either a role or a linked role. Here we restrict the number of intersection elements to two and require that each intersection element be a role. This makes the description easier to follow and simplifies some definitions. However it imposes no restriction on the expressive power of the language. A credential of the more general form can be replaced by several of the more restricted credentials presented above by introducing auxiliary roles, splitting longer intersections into several intersection inclusions, and introducing a linking inclusion for each linked role.

A *policy* is a finite set of credentials. We use the term *role expression* for any entity, role, linked role, or intersection; thus each RT_0 credential has the form $A.r \longleftarrow e$, where e is a role expression. Such a credential means that $members(e) \subseteq members(A.r)$. We say that this credential *defines* the role $A.r$. Further, we call A the *issuer*, e the *body* and each entity occurring syntactically in e a *subject* of this credential. To be precise, the set $base(e)$ of subjects of $A.r \longleftarrow e$ is defined as follows: $base(A) = \{A\}$, $base(A.r) = \{A\}$, $base(A.r_1.r_2) = \{A\}$, and $base(B_1.r_1 \cap B_2.r_2) = base(B_1.r_1) \cup base(B_2.r_2) = \{B_1, B_2\}$.

2.2 Semantics

In this section, we present declarative semantics of RT_0. We follow Li et al. [24] and do this in terms of the semantics for logic programs by providing a translation of a policy $\mathcal{C}$

to a Datalog program, which we call the *semantic program*. The set-theoretic semantics for RT_0 can be found in [25].

Given a set $\mathcal{C}$ of RT_0 credentials (i.e. a policy) the corresponding *semantic program*, $SP(\mathcal{C})$, is a Datalog program with one ternary predicate m. Intuitively, $m(A, r, D)$ indicates that D is a member of the role $A.r$. Given an RT statement c, the *semantic program* of c, $SP(c)$, is defined as follows (identifiers starting with "?" are logical variables):

$$SP(A.r \longleftarrow D) = m(A, r, D).$$
$$SP(A.r \longleftarrow B.r_1) = m(A, r, ?X) :- m(B, r_1, ?X).$$
$$SP(A.r \longleftarrow A.r_1.r_2) = m(A, r, ?X) :- m(A, r_1, ?Y), m(?Y, r_2, ?X).$$
$$SP(A.r \longleftarrow B_1.r_1 \cap B_2.r_2) = m(A, r, ?X) :- m(B_1, r_1, ?X), m(B_2, r_2, ?X).$$

SP extends to a set of statements as expected: $SP(\mathcal{C}) = \{SP(c) \mid c \in \mathcal{C}\}$. Finally, given a policy $\mathcal{C}$, the semantics of a role $A.r \in \mathcal{C}$ is defined in terms of atoms entailed by the semantic program.

Definition 1 (Semantics of a Role). *Let $\mathcal{C}$ be an RT_0 policy, and let $SP(\mathcal{C})$ be the corresponding semantic program. The semantics of a role is defined as follows:*

$$[\![A.r]\!]_{SP(\mathcal{C})} = \{D \mid SP(\mathcal{C}) \models m(A, r, D)\}.$$

2.3 Examples

We now present some examples presenting how RT_0 can be used in different application areas. We begin with an example from [25], showing a typical scenario from the area of electronic commerce.

Example 1. EPub is an electronic publishing company that offers a special discount to anyone who is both a preferred customer of the sister organization, *EOrg*, and an *ACM* member. *Alice* is both. We have the following set $\mathcal{C}$ of credentials:

$$EPub.spdiscount \longleftarrow EOrg.preferred \cap ACM.member \tag{1}$$
$$EOrg.preferred \longleftarrow EOrg.university.student \tag{2}$$
$$EOrg.university \longleftarrow ABU.accredited \tag{3}$$
$$ABU.accredited \longleftarrow StateU \tag{4}$$
$$StateU.student \longleftarrow RegistrarB.student \tag{5}$$
$$RegistrarB.student \longleftarrow Alice \tag{6}$$
$$ACM.member \longleftarrow Alice \tag{7}$$
$$ACM.member \longleftarrow Bob \tag{8}$$

The semantic program, $SP(\mathcal{C})$, corresponding to the above policy is:

$$m(EPub, spdiscount, ?X) :- m(EOrg, preferred, ?X), m(ACM, member, ?X). \tag{1}$$
$$m(EOrg, preferred, ?X) :- m(EOrg, university, ?Y), m(?Y, student, ?X). \tag{2}$$
$$m(EOrg, university, ?X) :- m(ABU, accredited, ?X). \tag{3}$$
$$m(ABU, accredited, StateU). \tag{4}$$

$$m(StateU, student, ?X) :- m(RegistrarB, student, ?X). \tag{5}$$
$$m(RegistrarB, student, Alice). \tag{6}$$
$$m(ACM, member, Alice). \tag{7}$$
$$m(ACM, member, Bob). \tag{8}$$

The semantics of the roles defined by the set of credentials above is then the following:

$$[\![EPub.spdiscount]\!]_{SP(\mathcal{C})} = \{Alice\}$$
$$[\![EOrg.preferred]\!]_{SP(\mathcal{C})} = \{Alice\}$$
$$[\![ACM.member]\!]_{SP(\mathcal{C})} = \{Alice, Bob\}$$
$$[\![EOrg.university]\!]_{SP(\mathcal{C})} = \{StateU\}$$
$$[\![ABU.accredited]\!]_{SP(\mathcal{C})} = \{StateU\}$$
$$[\![StateU.student]\!]_{SP(\mathcal{C})} = \{Alice\}$$
$$[\![RegistrarB.student]\!]_{SP(\mathcal{C})} = \{Alice\}$$

We see then that only *Alice* is eligible for a discount as *Bob*, though being a member of *ACM*, is not a student of an accredited university.

The next example presents the use of RT_0 in collaborating organizations. This example originally appeared in [15].

Example 2. Consider the situation in which two companies: *CITA* (in Italy) and *CUS* (in the US), work on a joint project. *CITA* and *CUS*, have different management structures:

CITA.partner ⟵ Antonio	CUS.ceo ⟵ Bob
CITA.manager ⟵ Luca	CUS.employee ⟵ John
CITA.programmer ⟵ Sandro	CUS.employee ⟵ David
CITA.all ⟵ CITA.partner	CUS.all ⟵ CUS.ceo
CITA.all ⟵ CITA.manager	CUS.all ⟵ CUS.employee
CITA.all ⟵ CITA.programmer	

In both companies there is an agreement that employees may trust all the sources that are trusted by the *partner* (resp. *ceo*). They can – of course – trust other sources as well.

Luca.partner ⟵ CITA.partner	John.ceo ⟵ CUS.ceo
Luca.trusted ⟵ Luca.partner.trusted	John.trusted ⟵ John.ceo.trusted
Sandro.partner ⟵ CITA.partner	David.ceo ⟵ CUS.ceo
Sandro.trusted ⟵ Sandro.partner.trusted	David.trusted ⟵ David.ceo.trusted

CITA and *CUS* decide to join forces on *projX*, and they agree that most of the documents developed in *projX* should be accessible only to people working on the project, and that some particularly confidential documents should circulate only among the senior personnel. To implement this, the two companies agree to employ the role names *projX* and *seniorprojX*. In *CITA*, the partner decides who participates in projectX, and decides (in agreement with *CUS*) that the managers of *CITA* should be considered senior people, while in *CUS*, the ceo delegates to *John* the definition of the projectX team as well as of the senior people in it. Finally, *CITA* and *CUS* trust each other's definitions of (senior) people working on projectX. This policy is described and implemented by the following set of credentials.

$$CITA.projX \longleftarrow Antonio.projX$$

$$CITA.seniorprojX \longleftarrow CITA.partner$$

$$CITA.seniorprojX \longleftarrow CITA.projX \cap CITA.manager$$

$$Antonio.projX \longleftarrow Luca$$

$$Antonio.projX \longleftarrow Sandro$$

$$CITA.projX \longleftarrow CUS.projX$$

$$CITA.seniorprojX \longleftarrow CUS.seniorprojX$$

$$CUS.projX \longleftarrow John.projX$$

$$CUS.seniorprojX \longleftarrow CUS.ceo$$

$$CUS.seniorprojX \longleftarrow John.seniorprojX$$

$$John.seniorprojX \longleftarrow John$$

$$John.projX \longleftarrow John$$

$$John.projX \longleftarrow David$$

$$CUS.projX \longleftarrow CITA.projX$$

$$CUS.seniorprojX \longleftarrow CITA.seniorprojX$$

The following two examples were initially presented by Winsborough and Li in [32]. The first of them shows an example of a co-operation between banking institutions and universities when providing financial support for students. Then, we show an example of policies that can be used by medical suppliers and charity organizations when handling natural disasters.

Example 3. A bank wants to know whether an entity is a full time student in order to determine whether the entity is eligible to defer repayment on a guaranteed student loan (GLS). (The US government insures banks against default of GLSs and requires participating banks to allow full-time students to defer repayments.) The *StateU* university may define its full-time student attribute by the following two credentials:

$$StateU.fullTimeStudent \longleftarrow RegistrarB.fullTimeStudent$$

$$StateU.fullTimeStudent \longleftarrow StateU.phdCandidate \cap RegistrarB.partTimeStudent$$

We see that *StateU* says that one is a full-time student if either *RegistrarB* says so, or if one is registered as a Ph.D. candidate at *StateU* and considered part-time student by *RegistrarB*. The following credentials, together with the above ones, show that *Bob* is a full-time student, i.e. $Bob \in \llbracket StateU.fullTimeStudent \rrbracket_{SP(\mathcal{C})}$:

$$StateU.phdCandidate \longleftarrow StateU.gradOfficer.phdCandidate$$

$$StateU.gradOfficer \longleftarrow Carol$$

$$Carol.phdCandidate \longleftarrow Bob$$
$$RegistrarB.partTimeStudent \longleftarrow Bob$$

Now, assume that $StateU$ is certified by accreditation board ABU.

$$ABU.accredited \longleftarrow StateU$$

If universities define *fullTimeStudent* appropriately (for example, as done by $StateU$ above), *BankWon* can issue credentials like those bellow to grant loan-deferment permission (denoted by *BankWon.deferGLS*) to students like Bob.

$$BankWon.deferGLS \longleftarrow BankWon.university.fullTimeStudent$$
$$BankWon.university \longleftarrow ABU.accredited$$

Clearly, $Bob \in [\![BankWon.deferGLS]\!]_{SP(\mathcal{C})}$.

Example 4. In the aftermath of a large natural disaster, *MedSup*, a medical supply merchant, offers to sell at a discount medical supplies to be used in the official clean up, which is being organized by a coalition called *ReliefNet*. *Alice* works for *MedixFund*, one of several charity organizations that use private contributions to obtain emergency medical supplies for emergency teams working at the disaster site. The following four credentials show that *Alice* is authorized for the discount.

$$MedixFund.pA \longleftarrow Alice \qquad (1)$$
$$ReliefNet.coaMember \longleftarrow MedixFund \qquad (2)$$
$$MedSup.partner \longleftarrow ReliefNet.coaMember \qquad (3)$$
$$MedSup.discount \longleftarrow MedSup.partner.pA \qquad (4)$$

Prior to joining the coalition, *MedixFund* issued credential (1), which states that *Alice* is a purchasing agent for the fund. One of *ReliefNet*'s responsibilities is to identify coalition-member organizations, as it does in credential (2). *MedSup* recognizes these organizations as its coalition partners, as in credential (3), and offers discounted sales to the purchasing agents of those partners, as stated in credential (4). In this example, the judgments of *MedixFund*, *ReliefNet*, and *MedSup* are combined to authorize *Alice*'s receiving a discount from *MedSup*. When *MedSup* enters into other coalition, it can add an additional credential defining *MedSup.partner* to give the discount to the purchasing agents of its new partners.

With the increasing popularity of the P2P networks and their excellent support for sharing of private content, a high demand for flexible user-oriented policies can be observed. Below, we show an example of how RT_0 facilitates the use of personal policies in heterogeneous P2P environment.

Example 5. Charles wants to share his pictures using a P2P file sharing system. He restricts the access to his gallery to his friends and friends of his friends. For his movie collection, Charles applies a somewhat stronger policy: to access it, one has to be a member of Charles's *friend* role, and a member of the film club Charles is also a member of. The set of credentials, $\mathcal{C}$, modelling this scenario is shown below:

$$Charles.accessMovies \longleftarrow Charles.friend \cap Charles.filmClub$$
$$Charles.accessPictures \longleftarrow Charles.friend$$
$$Charles.friend \longleftarrow Charles.friend.friend$$
$$Charles.friend \longleftarrow Alice$$
$$Charles.friend \longleftarrow Bob$$
$$Charles.filmClub \longleftarrow Johan$$
$$Alice.friend \longleftarrow Jeffrey$$
$$Bob.friend \longleftarrow Johan$$
$$Johan.friend \longleftarrow Sandro$$

Notice that the delegation depth in RT_0 is unlimited. It means that Charles's role *friend* contains not only friends of his friends, but also friends of friends of his friends and so on (*friends* is a transitive closure of the set of Charles's friends). Therefore, for the given set of credentials, we have the following semantics:

$$[\![Charles.accessMovies]\!]_{SP(\mathcal{C})} = \{Johan\}$$
$$[\![Charles.accessPictures]\!]_{SP(\mathcal{C})} = \{Alice, Bob, Jeffrey, Johan, Sandro\}$$

3 RT_0: The Credential Chain Discovery Algorithm

We have seen how RT_0 can be used to define roles and how roles can represent permissions or attributes. We now illustrate the mechanisms needed to answer the *queries* in the RT system. To set the stage, let us first enumerate the three *sorts of queries* we need to cope with. Let $\mathcal{C}$ be a set of credentials.

Sort 1. Given a role $A.r$ and an entity D, determine whether $D \in [\![A.r]\!]_{SP(\mathcal{C})}$.
Sort 2. Given a role $A.r$, determine its member set, $[\![A.r]\!]_{SP(\mathcal{C})}$.
Sort 3. Given an entity D, determine all the roles it is a member of, i.e. generate the set $\{A.r \mid D \in [\![A.r]\!]_{SP(\mathcal{C})}\}$.

Notice that while queries of Sort 1 simply require a yes/no answer, the other two sorts require to generate a whole set. Also, notice that queries of Sort 2 and 3 are strictly more expressive than queries of Sort 1: if we are able to answer a query of Sort 2 or 3 we are certainly able to answer a query of Sort 1, while the opposite is not true. At this stage, one might wonder if Sort 3 queries are actually needed. This will become clear in the sequel.

Remark 1. Technically, this section is based on [25] with the additional simplifying assumption that queries may refer only to roles and principals (and not to role expressions, e.g. we do not allow queries such as "given a role expression $A.r_1.r_2$, determine its member set $[\![A.r_1.r_2]\!]_{SP(\mathcal{C})}$"). This assumption allows us to simplify the notation by a great deal, and does not limit the expressiveness of the framework, as one can always introduce a new role to take the meaning of a role expression.

The algorithms we present in this section operate on a *credential graph*, which is a directed graph representing a set $\mathcal{C}$ of credentials and is built as follows: each node $[e]$ represents a role expression e; every credential $A.r \longleftarrow e$ in $\mathcal{C}$ contributes to the graph an edge from $[e]$ (the node representing e) to $[A.r]$ (the node representing $A.r$), which is denoted by $[A.r] \Leftarrow [e]$, and is called a credential edge. A path in the graph from the node $[e_1]$ to the node $[e_2]$ consists of zero or more edges and is denoted $[e_2] \overset{*}{\Leftarrow} [e_1]$. Additional edges, called *derived edges*, are added to handle linked roles and intersections. These edges are called derived edges because their inclusion in the credential graph comes from the existence of other, semantically related, paths in the graph.

Given a set $\mathcal{C}$ of credentials, we define the following finite structures: Entities($\mathcal{C}$) is the set of entities in $\mathcal{C}$, Names($\mathcal{C}$) is the set of role names in $\mathcal{C}$, and RoleExpressions($\mathcal{C}$) is the set of role expressions that can be constructed using Entities($\mathcal{C}$) and Names($\mathcal{C}$), i.e.:

$$\text{RoleExpressions}(\mathcal{C}) = \begin{cases} A, \\ A.r_1, \\ A.r_1.r_2, \\ B_1.r_1 \cap B_2.r_2 \end{cases} \quad \text{where } A, B_1, B_2 \in \text{Entities}(\mathcal{C}), \\ r_1, r_2 \in \text{Names}(\mathcal{C})$$

The following definition is a simplified version of Definition 2 in [25] (see Remark 1). Thanks to this simplification we can restrict our attention to the *basic* credential graph and avoid some complexities from the original presentation.

Definition 2 (Basic Credential Graphs). *Let $\mathcal{C}$ be a set of RT_0 credentials. The basic credential graph $G_{\mathcal{C}}$ relative to $\mathcal{C}$ is defined as follows: the set of nodes $N_{\mathcal{C}} = RoleExpressions(\mathcal{C})$ and the set of edges $E_{\mathcal{C}}$ is the least set of edges over $N_{\mathcal{C}}$ that satisfies the following three closure properties:*

- *Closure property 1: If $A.r \longleftarrow e \in \mathcal{C}$, then $[A.r] \Leftarrow [e] \in E_{\mathcal{C}}$. $[A.r] \Leftarrow [e]$ is called a credential edge.*
- *Closure property 2: If there exists a path $[A.r_1] \overset{*}{\Leftarrow} [B]$ in $G_{\mathcal{C}}$, then $[A.r_1.r_2] \Leftarrow [B.r_2] \in E_{\mathcal{C}}$. We call $[A.r_1.r_2] \Leftarrow [B.r_2]$ a derived link edge, and call the path $[A.r_1] \overset{*}{\Leftarrow} [B]$ a support set for this edge.*
- *Closure property 3: If $D, B_1.r_1 \cap B_2.r_2 \in N_{\mathcal{C}}$, and there exist paths $[B_1.r_1] \overset{*}{\Leftarrow} [D]$ and $[B_2.r_2] \overset{*}{\Leftarrow} [D]$ in $G_{\mathcal{C}}$, then $[B_1.r_1 \cap B_2.r_2] \Leftarrow [D] \in E_{\mathcal{C}}$. This is called a derived intersection edge, and $\{[B_1.r_1] \overset{*}{\Leftarrow} [D], [B_2.r_2] \overset{*}{\Leftarrow} [D]\}$ is a support set for this edge.*

The set of edges $E_{\mathcal{C}}$ can be constructed inductively as follows. We start with the set $E_{\mathcal{C}}^0 = \{[A.r] \Leftarrow [e] \mid A.r \longleftarrow e \in \mathcal{C}\}$ and then construct $E_{\mathcal{C}}^{i+1}$ from $E_{\mathcal{C}}^i$ by adding one edge according to either closure property 2 or 3. Since $N_{\mathcal{C}}$ is finite, the order in which edges are added is not important, and the sequence $\{E_{\mathcal{C}}^i\}_{i \in \mathcal{N}}$ converges to $E_{\mathcal{C}}$.

Example 6. Figure 1 shows a subset of the basic credential graph for the set of credentials in Example 1. Edges labelled with numbers are credential edges, and the numbers correspond to the ones marking credentials in Example 1. The two edges without labels are derived edges: one added by the closure property 2 ($[EOrg.university.student] \Leftarrow [StateU.student]$), and one by the closure property 3 ($[EOrg.preferred \cap ACM.member] \Leftarrow [Alice]$).

In [25] it is proven that the credential graphs are sound and complete w.r.t. to the set-theoretic semantics: if there is a path $[e_2] \overset{*}{\Leftarrow} [e_1]$ in any $G_{\mathcal{C}}$, then $expr[\mathcal{S}_{\mathcal{C}}](e_2) \supseteq expr[\mathcal{S}_{\mathcal{C}}](e_1)$, and if $D \in expr[\mathcal{S}_{\mathcal{C}}](e_0)$, then there exists path $[e_0] \overset{*}{\Leftarrow} [D]$ in $G_{\mathcal{C}}$. Here $expr[\mathcal{S}_{\mathcal{C}}](e)$ is the set-theoretic semantics of a role expression e, which can be proven in a straightforward way to be equivalent to the LP based semantics we have introduced in Sect. 2.2.

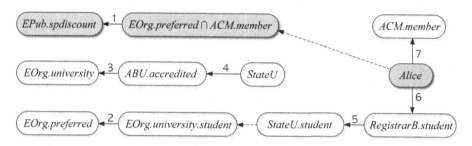

Fig. 1. The subset of the credential graph for the set of credentials in Example 1 containing path from *EPub.spdiscount* to *Alice*

Therefore, given a set $\mathcal{C}$ of credentials, we can answer each of the queries enumerated at the beginning of this section by consulting a basic credential graph of $\mathcal{C}$. Constructing the path $[A.r] \overset{*}{\Leftarrow} [D]$ alone proves that $D \in [\![A.r]\!]_{SP(\mathcal{C})}$, provided that each derived edge has at least one support set. The portion of the credential graph that must be constructed for it is what we call a *credential chain*.

Definition 3 (Credential Chains). *Given a set $\mathcal{C}$ of credentials, a role $A.r$, and an entity D, a credential chain from D to $A.r$, denoted $\langle A.r \leftarrow D \rangle$, is a minimal subset of $E_{\mathcal{C}}$ containing a path $[A.r] \overset{*}{\Leftarrow} [D]$ and also containing a support set for each derived edge in the subset.*

The chain discovery starts at the node representing the requester, or at the node representing the role (permission) to be proven, or both, and then traversing paths in the graph trying to build an appropriate chain. In addition to being goal-directed, this approach allows the elaboration of the graph to be scheduled flexibly. Also, the graphical representation of the evaluation state makes it relatively straightforward to manage cyclic dependencies.

In the rest of this section we illustrate the three algorithms originally defined in [25] to answer the three sorts of queries, listed at the top of this section (with the simplifying assumption illustrated in Remark 1). The backward search algorithm (also called the top-down algorithm) (Sect. 3.1) answers the second sort of queries, i.e. it determines all members of a role expression. The forward search algorithm (also called the bottom-up algorithm) in Sect. 3.2 answers the third sort of queries, i.e. it determines all roles that an entity is a member of. The bidirectional search algorithm (Sect. 3.3) answers the first sort of queries, i.e. it determines whether an entity is a member of a role expression. Note that in this section we assume that credentials are stored in such a way that we can list them all at any time. In practice, this is not always the case. We address the problem of distributed storage in the next section.

3.1 The Backward Search Algorithm

The backward search algorithm can determine all the members of a given role $A.r$. In terms of the credential graph, it finds all the entity nodes that can reach the node $A.r$, and for each such entity D, it constructs a chain $\langle A.r \leftarrow D \rangle$. It is called backward because it follows edges in the reverse direction. The algorithm works by constructing a *proof graph*, which is a data structure that represents a credential graph and maintains certain information on the nodes. Listing 1.1 shows the algorithm in pseudo-code using a Python-like syntax. We have four classes: *ProofGraph* representing the proof graph, *ProofNode* representing proof graph nodes, *BLinkingMonitor* and *BIntersectionMonitor* used to handle linked and intersection roles respectively.

The ProofGraph class stores the set of nodes and the set of edges corresponding to the set of nodes and the set of edges in the basic credential graph in its instance variables: *nodes* and *edges* respectively. Adding nodes and edges is handled by the *addNode()* and *addEdge()* methods. The main processing is handled by the *bProcess()* method of the ProofGraph class. The nodes to be processed are stored in the backward processing queue (*bQueue*).

Each node in the graph is represented by an instance of the ProofNode class. Each ProofNode object stores the set of backward solutions in the *bSolutions* attribute. A *solution* in the backward search algorithm is an entity. Thus, the *solution* attribute of the ProofNode class stores all the entities which are known to be members of the corresponding role expression. When a new solution D is discovered, every node e such that there is a path $[e] \overset{*}{\Leftarrow} [D]$ in the proof graph must be notified about this solution. This is realized using a well-know *observer* design pattern. Every instance of the ProofNode class maintains a list of observers, called *backward solution monitors* in the text. When a node is notified about one or more new solutions – by invoking node's *notify()* operation – it immediately notifies all the monitors (observers) of the node using node's *notifyAll()* operation. Every node which is not an entity node (entities do not have any solutions other than themselves) can be *registered* as a backward monitor of a node using node's *bAttach()* operation. There are two special backward monitors that are not instances of the ProofNode class: backward linking and intersection monitors. In Listing 1.1 they are represented by two classes: *BLinkingMonitor* and *BIntersection-Monitor*. Linking and intersection monitors realize the basic credential graph closure properties 2 and 3 respectively.

When processing a linked role $A.r_1.r_2$, the algorithm first creates a new node for the role $A.r_1$, then it creates a backward linking monitor and attaches this monitor to $[A.r_1]$. The backward linking monitor works as follows: when the backward linking monitor corresponding to a linked role $A.r_1.r_2$ is notified about a new solution B, it means that B became a member of $A.r_1$. By the closure property 2 in Definition 2 this implies that the basic credential graph contains the edge $[A.r_1.r_2] \Leftarrow [B.r_2]$. The backward linking monitor realizes this by creating new node corresponding to role $B.r_2$ and by adding the edge $[A.r_1.r_2] \Leftarrow [B.r_2]$ to the proof graph (lines (42–45)).

When processing an intersection node $[B_1.r_1 \cap B_2.r_2]$, the algorithm first creates two new nodes $[B_1.r_1]$ and $[B_2.r_2]$, then it creates a backward intersection monitor and attaches this monitor to these two newly created nodes. When any of these two nodes receives a new solution D, it notifies all of its backward solution monitors, including the monitor associated to $B_1.r_1 \cap B_2.r_2$. When this monitor is notified about solution D it checks how many times it observed the addition of entity D. When the counter reaches 2, it adds edge $[B_1.r_1 \cap B_2.r_2] \Leftarrow [D]$ to the proof graph (lines (47–51)).

In order to find all members of a role $A.r$ the algorithm is initialized using the following sequence:

```
proofGraph = new ProofGraph()
proofGraph.addNode(A.r)
proofGraph.bProcess()
```

Listing 1.1. Backward Search Algorithm

```
 1  class ProofGraph:
      def bProcess():
 3      while not bQueue.empty():
          n = bQueue.dequeue()
 5        if n is an entity D:
            n.bSolutions.add(D)
 7          n.notifyAll(D)
            continue
 9        if n is a role A.r:
            foreach A.r ⟵ e ∈ C:
11            addNode(e)
              addEdge([A.r] ⟸ [e])
13          continue
          if n is a linked role A.r_1.r_2:
15            n_1 = addNode(A.r_1)
              n_1.bAttach(new BLinkingMonitor(A.r_1.r_2))
17          continue
          if n is an intersection B_1.r_1 ∩ B_2.r_2:
19            n_1 = addNode(B_1.r_1)
              n_2 = addNode(B_2.r_2)
21            m = new BIntersectionMonitor(B_1.r_1 ∩ B_2.r_2)
              n_1.bAttach(m)
23            n_2.bAttach(m)
            continue
25    def addNode(e):
        if nodes.contains(e): return getNode(e)
27      n = new ProofNode(e)
        nodes.add(n)
29      bQueue.enqueue(n)
        return n
```

```
31      def addEdge([e₂] ⇐ [e₁]):
           n₁ = getNode(e₁)
33         n₂ = getNode(e₂)
           if not edges. contains ([n₂] ⇐ [n₁]):
35            edges. add([n₂] ⇐ [n₁])
           if n₁.hasSolutions():
37            s = n₁.getSolutions()
              n₂.bSolutions.add(s)
39            n₂.notifyAll(s)
           n₁.bAttach(n₂)
41
        class BLinkingMonitor(A.r₁.r₂):
43        def notify (B):
            n = proofGraph.addNode(B.r₂)
45          proofGraph.addEdge([A.r₁.r₂] ⇐ [B.r₂])

47      class BIntersectionMonitor (B₁.r₁ ∩ B₂.r₂):(A.r₁.r₂):
          def notify (D):
49          solutions . add(D)
            if solutions . count(D) == 2:
51            proofGraph.addEdge([B₁.r₁ ∩ B₂.r₂] ⇐ [D])

53      class ProofNode:
          def bAttach(m):
55          bMonitors.add(m)
          def notify (solutions ):
57          bSolutions . add(solutions )
            notifyAll (solutions )
59        def notifyAll (solutions ):
            foreach m in bMonitors:
61            m.notify (solutions )
```

Example 7. Figures 2(a)-(d) illustrate the process of constructing the proof graph by doing backward search from *EPub.discount* for the following set of credentials $\mathcal{C}$ (a subset of Example 1). This corresponds to the query of Sort 1: determine the set of members of *EPub.spdiscount*, $[\![EPub.spdiscount]\!]_{SP(\mathcal{C})}$.

$$EPub.spdiscount \longleftarrow EOrg.preferred \cap ACM.member \qquad (1)$$

$$EOrg.preferred \longleftarrow EOrg.university.student \qquad (2)$$

$$EOrg.university \longleftarrow ABU.accredited \qquad (3)$$

$$ABU.accredited \longleftarrow StateU \qquad (4)$$

$$StateU.student \longleftarrow RegistrarB.student \qquad (5)$$

$$RegistrarB.student \longleftarrow Alice \qquad (6)$$

$$ACM.member \longleftarrow Alice \qquad (7)$$

In Figs. 2(a)-(d), the first line of each node gives the node number (following the order of creation) and the role expression represented by the node. The second line lists the solutions associated to the node. To simplify the reading, we have labelled each solution and each graph edge with the number of the node that was being processed when the solution or edge was added. In each of the figures dashed edges and nodes are the newly processed nodes while the newly added solutions are grey. Below we repeat the process of the construction of this proof graph.

The algorithm starts the search from $EPub.spdiscount$. The only credential defining role $EPub.spdiscount$ is (1). To process it, the algorithm adds the new node $[EOrg.preferred \cap ACM.member]$ to the proof graph, and it inserts it in the queue of nodes $bQueue$ (lines (25–30)). Then the algorithm adds a credential edge from the newly added node to $EPub.spdiscount$ (Fig. 2(a)). We label the edge with number 0 to indicate that this edge was added while processing node $EPub.spdiscount$. The new node is an intersection. To process it, the algorithm first creates two new nodes: $[EOrg.preferred]$ and $[ACM.member]$, and adds them to the processing queue in this order. Next it creates an intersection monitor and it attaches it to both $[EOrg.preferred]$ and $[ACM.member]$ (lines (18–24, and the two edges labelled with 1 in Fig. 2(a)). This monitor guarantees that if the same solution D appears in both $[EOrg.preferred]$ and $[ACM.member]$, a derived edge is added from $[D]$ to $[EOrg.preferred \cap ACM.member]$ (lines (47–51)). The next node to process is $[EOrg.preferred]$. The only credential defining this role is the linking inclusion $EOrg.preferred \longleftarrow EOrg.university.student$. The algorithm adds node $[EOrg.university.student]$ to the graph, and a credential edge from this node to $[EOrg.preferred]$ (Fig. 2(b)). Next, the node $[ACM.member]$ is processed. Giving the presence of the credential $ACM.member \longleftarrow Alice$, the algorithm adds a new node $[Alice]$ to the graph and to the processing queue. This node will be processed *after* the node $[EOrg.university.student]$, so we do not add any solution at this stage.

The next node to process is $[EOrg.university.student]$. As this is a node representing a linked role, the algorithm first adds new node $[EOrg.university]$ to the proof graph (and also to the processing queue) and then it attaches a linking monitor to $[EOrg.university]$ (lines (14–17 and Edge 4 in Fig. 2(b)). This monitor behaves as follows: each time $[EOrg.university]$ receives a new solution B, it creates a node for $B.student$ and adds the derived edge from $[B.student]$ to $[EOrg.university.student]$ (lines (42–45)).

The next node to process is $[Alice]$. As this is an entity node, it immediately receives $Alice$ as solution and it notifies all its backward solution monitors: in our case $[ACM.member]$. The intersection monitor stored by $[ACM.member]$ observes that $Alice$ is the received solution, but takes no action as it has been added only to $[ACM.member]$, and does not appear as a solution at $EOrg.preferred$ yet.

In a similar manner, $[EOrg.university]$ receives the solution $StateU$ when processing node $[StateU]$ (Fig. 2(c)). After this, the linking monitor stored at $[EOrg.university]$ creates the new node $[StateU.student]$.

When $StateU.student$ receives the solution $Alice$ from $[RegistrarB.student]$ (Fig. 2(d)), this solution is propagated upward to $[EOrg.university.student]$ and $[EOrg.preferred]$. The intersection monitor at node $[EOrg.preferred]$ observes that $Alice$ is added for the second time, this time by means of node $[EOrg.preferred]$, and

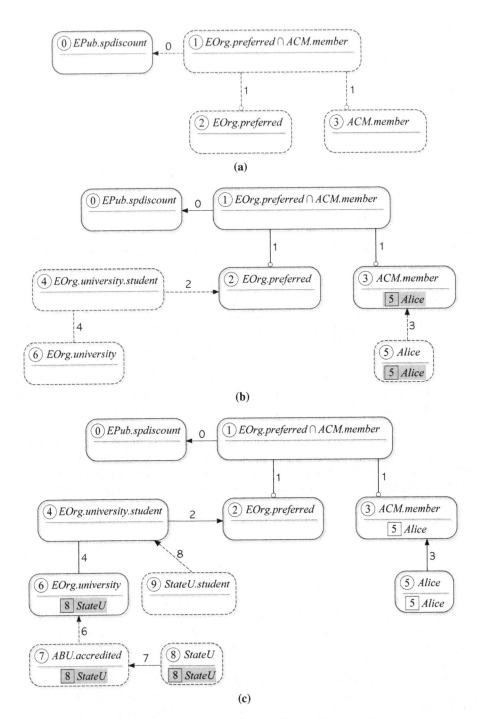

Fig. 2. Backward search from *EPub.spdiscount*

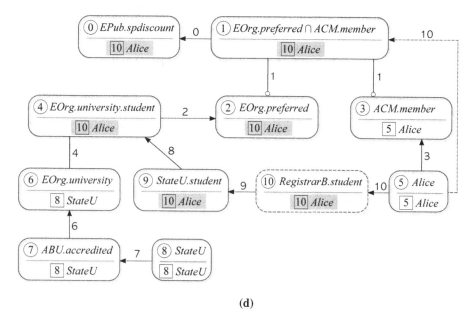

(d)

Fig. 2. (*continued*)

in response it creates a derived edge from [*Alice*] to [*EOrg.preferred* ∩ *ACM.member*]. The solution *Alice* is then immediately copied from [*Alice*] to node [*EOrg.preferred* ∩ *ACM.member*] and then to [*EPub.spdiscount*] (lines (36–39)).

At this point, there are no more nodes to process and the algorithm terminates. Given the set of credentials shown above, *EPub.spdiscount* has only one member: *Alice*.

3.2   The Forward Search Algorithm

The forward search algorithm answers queries of the third sort, i.e. it finds all roles that contain a given entity D_0 as a member. The direction of the search moves from the subject of a credential towards its issuer.

The forward algorithm has the same overall structure as the backward algorithm. It constructs a proof graph, maintaining a queue of nodes to be processed; both contain initially just one node, [D_0]. Nodes are processed one by one until the queue is empty. Listing 1.2 reports the algorithm's pseudo-code.

A solution in the forward search algorithm can be a *full solution* or a so called *partial solution*. A full solution is a role and indicates that the initial node is a member of this role. Partial solutions are necessary to properly handle intersections (see Closure Property 3 in Definition 2). Given an intersection $B_1.r_1 \cap B_2.r_2$ a partial solution has the form $(B_1.r_1 \cap B_2.r_2, i)$ where $i \in \{1, 2\}$. We add the partial solution $(B_1.r_1 \cap B_2.r_2, i)$ to the node [e] when [$B_i.r_i$] is reachable from [e] (lines (8–9)).

Similarly to the backward processing algorithm, when a node receives either a full, or a partial solution, it notifies each of its forward solution monitors. The solutions travel through the edges eventually reaching some other entity node [D]. When [D] is notified about new partial solution $(B_1.r_1 \cap B_2.r_2, i)$, it checks whether it has the two partial solutions $(B_1.r_1 \cap B_2.r_2, 1)$ and $(B_1.r_1 \cap B_2.r_2, 2)$, and, if so, it adds a derived edge $[B_1.r_1 \cap B_2.r_2] \Leftarrow [D]$ to the proof graph (lines (37–37)).

Linking roles are handled using forward linking monitors. A linking monitor is created when processing a role $B.r_2$. A new node $[B]$ is created and a forward linking monitor $FLinkingMonitor(B.r_2)$ is attached to $[B]$ (lines (12–13)). This monitor, when notified by $[B]$ about new solution $A.r_1$, creates new node $[A.r_1.r_2]$ and adds it to the proof graph and to the forward processing queue. Then, it adds new edge $[A.r_1.r_2] \Leftarrow [B.r_2]$ to the proof graph (lines (27–30)).

In order to find all roles $A.r$ an entity D_0 is a member of, the algorithm should be initialized using the following sequence:

```
proofGraph = new ProofGraph()
proofGraph.addNode(D)
proofGraph.fProcess ()
```

Listing 1.2. Forward Search Algorithm

```
class  ProofGraph:
  def  fProcess ():
    s = ∅
    while not fQueue.empty():
      n = fQueue.dequeue()
      if  n is a role B.r₂:
        s. add(B.r₂)
        foreach A.r ⟵ f₁ ∩ f₂ ∈ C s.t. ∃i ∈ {1,2}, fᵢ = B.r₂:
          s. add(( f₁ ∩ f₂, i))
        n. fSolutions . add(s)
        n. notifyAll ( s )
        n₁ = addNode(B)
        n₁.fAttach(new FLinkingMonitor(B.r₂))
      # get the role expression associated with node n
      e = n. roleExpression ()
      foreach A.r ⟵ e ∈ C:
        addNode(A.r)
        addEdge([A.r] ⟸ [e])
  def addNode(e): # see Listing 1.1 line 25 for the definition
  def addEdge([e₂] ⟸ [e₁]):
    n₁ = getNode(e₁)
    n₂ = getNode(e₂)
    if  not edges. contains ( [n₂] ⟸ [n₁]):
      edges. add([n₂] ⟸ [n₁])
    n₂.fAttach(n₁)

class  FLinkingMonitor(B.r₂):
  def  notify ( A.r₁):
```

```
          proofGraph.addNode(A.r₁.r₂)
          proofGraph.addEdge([A.r₁.r₂] ⇐ [B.r₂])

    class ProofNode:
      def fAttach(m):
        fMonitors. add(m)
      def notify (solutions ):
        fSolutions . add(solutions )
        if the node is an entity node D:
          foreach f₁ ∩ f₂ s.t. ∀i ∈ {1,2}∃(f₁ ∩ f₂, i) ∈ fSolutions:
            proofGraph.addNode(f₁ ∩ f₂)
            proofGraph.addEdge([f₁ ∩ f₂] ⇐ [D])
        else : notifyAll (solutions )
      def notifyAll (solutions ):
        foreach m in fMonitors:
          m.notify (solutions )
```

Example 8. Figures 3(a)-(c) depict the process of constructing the proof graph by forward search from $[Alice]$ for the set of credentials from Example 1.

The first line of each node reports the node number in order of creation and the role expression represented by the node. The second part of a node lists the solutions associated to the node. Each solution and each graph edge is labelled with the number of the node that was being processed when the solution or edge was added. In each of the figures the dashed edges and nodes are the new ones and the new solutions are grayed. The process begins from node $[Alice]$ (Fig. 3(a)). As $[Alice]$ is an entity node, the algorithm searches for all credentials having *Alice* as the body. There are two such credentials: *ACM.member* ⟵ *Alice* and *RegistrarB.student* ⟵ *Alice*. Thus, the algorithm creates two nodes: $[ACM.member]$ and $[RegistrarB.student]$ and adds two credential edges from $[Alice]$ to them. The next node to be processed is $[ACM.member]$ (recall that the number in the circle displays the order of the processing). *ACM.member* is a role. Therefore, the algorithm first adds *ACM.member* as a solution to it. Next, it checks if there are any intersection credentials having *ACM.member* in the body. The role *ACM.member* appears as the second component of *EOrg.preferred* ∩ *ACM.member* in credential (1). Thus, the algorithm adds the partial solution (*EOrg.preferred* ∩ *ACM.member*,2) to the solution space of $[ACM.member]$ (lines (8–9)). The node $[ACM.member]$ notifies all its forward solution monitors about the new solutions. So, $[Alice]$ receives *ACM.member* and (*EOrg.preferred* ∩ *ACM.member*,2) as its first solutions. Now, the algorithm creates the node $[ACM]$ and a forward linking monitor (edge with number 1 in Fig. 3(a)), which is then added as a solution monitor to $[ACM]$ (lines (12–13)). This monitor, on observing that $[ACM]$ gets a full solution *A.r*, creates the node $[A.r.member]$ and adds the edge from $[ACM.member]$ to $[A.r.member]$ to the proof graph (lines (27–30)). The node $[RegistrarB]$ is processed in a similar way. There are no credentials having *ACM* or *RegistrarB* as the body, so they do not have any solutions. Figure 3(a) shows the snapshot of the graph after processing of node *RegistrarB*.

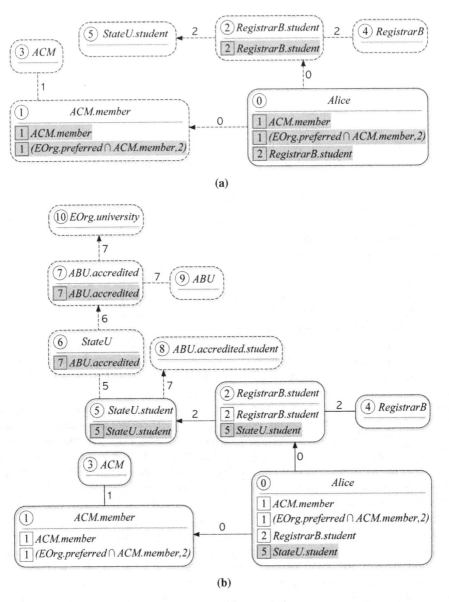

Fig. 3. Forward search from *Alice*

Figure 3(b) shows the graph after processing of node *ABU.accredited*. The nodes [*ABU*] and [*EOrg.university*] are the ones added when processing [*ABU.accredited*] and are next to be processed. When [*StateU*] receives the solution [*ABU.accredited*] its (forward) linking monitor creates node [*ABU.accredited.student*].

Figure 3(c) shows the complete graph. [*EOrg.preferred*] has one full solution, *EOrg.preferred*, and one partial solution (*EOrg.preferred* ∩ *ACM.member*,1), which

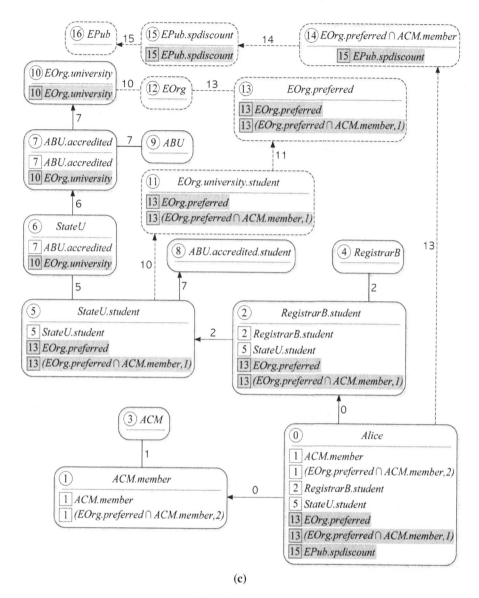

(c)

Fig. 3. (*continued*)

comes from the fact that *EOrg.preferred* is the first component of the intersection in the body of credential (1). [*EOrg.preferred*] notifies its forward solution monitors about these two solutions, which eventually reach [*Alice*]. When [*Alice*] is notified, since it has the two partial solutions corresponding to the intersection *EOrg.preferred* ∩ *ACM.member*, it creates the intersection node [*EOrg.preferred* ∩ *ACM.member*] and the edge from [*Alice*] to it. Finally, [*Alice*] receives the solution from [*EPub.spdiscount*].

3.3 The Bidirectional Search Algorithm

The two algorithms presented in Sect. 3.1 and Sect. 3.2 can also be used to answer the queries of Sort 1 presented at the top of Sect. 3 in which given a role $A.r$ and an entity D, one wants to determine whether $D \in [\![A.r]\!]_{SP(C)}$. This can be done either by using the backward search and starting from $A.r$ or by using forward search and staring from D. It is also possible to perform both searches at the same time. Such an algorithm is called *bidirectional search algorithm*. This may not make too much sense at first – as the bidirectional search algorithm may construct a larger graph than does either backward or forward search – but as we show later in Sect. 4, this may be very useful when the credential storage is distributed. We leave as an exercise for the reader to merge the two algorithms presented in Sects. 3.1 and 3.2 in order to obtain the bidirectional search algorithm.

4   The Storage Type System

Winsborough and Li argue that a trust management language should have some support for the *distributed* credential storage [32]. In our description so far, we assumed that the credential storage is centralized; more precisely, we have assumed that at any time we can list the whole set of credentials. Such an assumption is not realistic in practice, as sometimes we may want to store the credentials by their issuers and sometimes by their subjects (see [25,32] for a discussion). Intuitively, the problem with decentralized storage is that one may not know where to find the credentials needed to build a proof. Let us see an example of this.

Example 9. Assume that the policy contains only two credentials:

$$A.r \longleftarrow B.r_1 \tag{1}$$
$$B.r_1 \longleftarrow D \tag{2}$$

Now, assume that one wants to know whether $D \in [\![A.r]\!]_{SP(C)}$. Each of these two credentials could be stored at either its issuer and/or its subject.

First, let us assume that credential (1) is stored at A and credential (2) at D. Using backward search, we start from node $[A.r]$ by listing all credentials defining $A.r$. The only credential stored at A is $A.r \longleftarrow B.r_1$, so, the only way to proceed from here is to "go to" B, but since B does not store any credentials, the backward search algorithm concludes that $[\![A.r]\!]_{SP(C)}$ is empty. In the forward search algorithm we would start from $[D]$ by searching for all the credentials having D as the body. D stores only one credential: $B.r_1 \longleftarrow D$. The forward search algorithm then "goes to" B and fetches the credentials it stores. However, since B does not store any credentials, the forward search algorithm concludes that the only role D is a member of is $B.r$. Also, the forward search does not allow us to prove that $D \in [\![A.r]\!]_{SP(C)}$. The bidirectional search algorithm, on the other hand, succeeds because when backward search stops at node $B.r_1$ it knows from the forward search that D is a member of $B.r_1$. Therefore, it can conclude that D must be the member of $A.r$ as well.

Second, and perhaps more importantly, suppose that the two credentials above were stored at entity B (i.e. that (1) was stored by the subject and (2) was stored by the issuer). In this case, following the same reasoning, it is easy to see that both forward and backward search algorithms fail again, but, in addition, even the bidirectional search fails.

When both credentials are stored by their issuers (i.e. credential (1) is stored at A and credential (2) is stored at B) the only way to discover that $D \in [\![A.r]\!]_{SP(\mathcal{C})}$ is by using backward search starting from $A.r$.

Finally, when both credentials are stored by their subjects (i.e. (1) is stored at B and (2) is stored at D) only the forward search starting from D can find out that $D \in [\![A.r]\!]_{SP(\mathcal{C})}$.

This example shows that when credential storage is distributed some chain discovery algorithms may or may not work. In particular, if credential storage is not regulated, one may be unable to find the answers to a query.

RT_0 deals with this problem by introducing a *storage type system* limiting the number of possible storage location by introducing the notion of *well-typed* credentials. Each role name r has two types: an issuer-side type and a subject-side type. On the issuer side, each role name can have one of three type values: *issuer-traces-none*, *issuer-traces-def*, and *issuer-traces-all*. On the subject side, each role can have one of two type values: *subject-traces-none* and *subject-traces-all*. The intuition behind these type values is the following: if a role name r has the (issuer-side) type issuer-traces-all then one should be able to answer the queries of Sort 2 and to find all members of any role of the form $A.r$ using solely the backward search algorithm. Similarly, if a role name r has (subject-side) type subject-traces-all then starting from any entity D one should be able to find all roles of the form $A.r$ such that D is a member of $A.r$ (which corresponds to the queries of Sort 3). The type value issuer-traces-def is a weaker version of the issuer-traces-all type value. If a role name r has (issuer-side) type issuer-traces-def, then from any entity A one can find all credentials defining $A.r$. If a role name r has type value issuer-traces-none then for any role $A.r$, the backward search algorithm will not find any member of this role. If a role name r has type value subject-traces-none, then starting from any entity D, the forward search algorithm will not be able to find any role $A.r$ such that D is a member of $A.r$.

Summarizing, we have the following definition:

Definition 4 (Type). *A type is a mapping from role names into two-element sets of the form $\{i, s\}$, such that:*

– $i \in \{$ *issuer-traces-all, issuer-traces-def, issuer-traces-none* $\}$*, and*
– $s \in \{$ *subject-traces-all, subject-traces-none* $\}$*.*

We call i the *issuer-side* type value and s the *subject-side* type value of r, denoted $itype(r)$ and $stype(r)$ respectively, and we let $type(r) = itype(r) \cup stype(r)$.

The type of a role name directly indicates the storage location of the credentials.

Definition 5 (Storage). *Let r be a role name and $A.r \longleftarrow e$ be a credential.*

– *If $itype(r) \in \{$ issuer-traces-all, issuer-traces-def $\}$ then A must store this credential.*
– *If $stype(r) = $ subject-traces-all then every entity $B \in base(e)$ must store credential $A.r \longleftarrow e$.*

Table 1. Well Typed RT_0 credentials

		$A.r \longleftarrow B.r_1$		
	r_1	ITA	ITD	STA
r	ITA	OK		
	ITD	OK	OK	OK
	STA			OK

(a)

		$A.r \longleftarrow A.r_1.r_2$								
	r_1	ITA			ITD			STA		
	r_2	ITA	ITD	STA	ITA	ITD	STA	ITA	ITD	STA
r	ITA	OK								
	ITD	OK	OK	OK			OK			OK
	STA									OK

(b)

		$A.r \longleftarrow B_1.r_1 \cap B_2.r_2$								
	r_1	ITA			ITD			STA		
	r_2	ITA	ITD	STA	ITA	ITD	STA	ITA	ITD	STA
r	ITA	OK	OK	OK	OK			OK		
	ITD	OK	OK	OK	OK	OK	OK	OK	OK	OK
	STA			OK			OK	OK	OK	OK

(c)

Notice that a credential might have to be stored both by the issuer and by the subject (this is the case e.g. when one wants to be able to answer the queries of both Sort 2 and Sort 3). The type value issuer-traces-none (resp. subject-traces-none) indicates that A (resp. any entity $B \in \mathit{base}(e)$) does not store credential $A.r \longleftarrow e$. Notice that if a role name r is issuer-traces-none and subject-traces-none at the same time, nobody would have to store the credential $A.r \longleftarrow e$ (this is an ill-typed combination and will be ruled out in the next definition).

Let us go back to the two clauses in Example 9. We saw that if credential (1) was stored only by its subject and credential (2) was stored only by its issuer then any of the presented algorithms would be able to give a correct answer to the query "is D a member of $[\![A.r]\!]_{SP(\mathcal{C})}$?". In the light of Definition 5 this means that we have to avoid credentials of the form $A.r \longleftarrow B.r_1$, where $\mathit{itype}(r) = \mathit{issuer\text{-}traces\text{-}none}$ and $\mathit{stype}(r) = \mathit{subject\text{-}traces\text{-}none}$. In order to know which combinations are "good", we have the notion of *well-typed* credentials:

Definition 6 (Well-typed Credentials). *An RT_0 credential c is* well-typed *if no role name occurring in c has type {issuer-traces-none, subject-traces-none} and:*

- *if* $c = A.r \longleftarrow B.r_1$ *then* $\forall t \in \mathit{type}(r), \exists t_1 \in \mathit{type}(r_1)$ *s.t. the corresponding entry in Table 1(a) is* OK;
- *if* $c = A.r \longleftarrow A.r_1.r_2$ *then* $\forall t \in \mathit{type}(r), \exists t_1 \in \mathit{type}(r_1)$ *and* $\exists t_2 \in \mathit{type}(r_2)$ *s.t. the corresponding entry in Table 1(b) is* OK;

- if $c = A.r \longleftarrow B_1.r_1 \cap B_2.r_2$ then $\forall t \in type(r), \exists t_1 \in type(r_1)$ and $\exists t_2 \in type(r_2)$ s.t. the corresponding entry in Table 1(c) is OK.

For example, take the credential $c : A.r \longleftarrow A.r_1.r_2$ and assume that $type(r) = type(r_1) = \{issuer\text{-}traces\text{-}def, subject\text{-}traces\text{-}all\}$ and that $type(r_2) = \{issuer\text{-}traces\text{-}none, subject\text{-}traces\text{-}all\}$. Then, we see that for both type values of r, issuer-traces-def and subject-traces-all, one can find a combination of type values for r_1 and r_2 such this combination appears as a valid type assignment in Table 1(b). For the issuer-side type value of r, issuer-traces-def, we have $itype(r_1) = issuer\text{-}traces\text{-}def$ and $stype(r_2) = subject\text{-}traces\text{-}all$; for the subject-side type value of r, subject-traces-all, we have $stype(r_1) = stype(r_2) = subject\text{-}traces\text{-}all$. On the other hand, if we had that $type(r) = type(r_1) = type(r_2) = \{issuer\text{-}traces\text{-}def, subject\text{-}traces\text{-}none\}$, then c would not be well typed as there is no valid entry for this type value assignment in Table 1(b). Note that simple member credentials (of the form $A.r \longleftarrow D$) are always well-typed.

The following theorem summarizes the results given in [25] and shows that using well-typed credentials guarantees that the algorithms presented in Sect. 3 give correct answers to queries even in presence of distributed credentials.

Theorem 1. *Let $\mathcal{C}$ be a set of well typed RT_0 credentials, and r be a role name.*

- *If $itype(r) = issuer\text{-}traces\text{-}all$ then for each entity A, the backward search algorithm correctly computes $[\![A.r]\!]_{SP(\mathcal{C})}$.*
- *If $stype(r) = subject\text{-}traces\text{-}all$ then for each entity D the forward search algorithm finds all the roles $A.r$ such that $D \in [\![A.r]\!]_{SP(\mathcal{C})}$.*
- *For any given entity D, the bidirectional search algorithm can always correctly determine if $D \in [\![A.r]\!]_{SP(\mathcal{C})}$.*

Example 10. Consider again the policy of Example 9, if $type(r) = \{issuer\text{-}traces\text{-}all, subject\text{-}traces\text{-}none\}$ then, according to Table 1, for the credential (1) to be well-typed, the type of role name r_1 must also be $\{issuer\text{-}traces\text{-}all, subject\text{-}traces\text{-}none\}$. By Theorem 1, one can use the backward search algorithm to compute $[\![A.r]\!]_{SP(\mathcal{C})}$. On the other hand, if $type(r) = \{issuer\text{-}traces\text{-}none, subject\text{-}traces\text{-}all\}$ then, for the credential (1) to be well-typed, the type of r_1 must also be $\{issuer\text{-}traces\text{-}none, subject\text{-}traces\text{-}all\}$. For this type assignment, Theorem 1 says that, starting from D, the forward search algorithm will discover that D is a member of $B.r_1$ and $A.r$.

Finally, if $type(r) = \{issuer\text{-}traces\text{-}def, subject\text{-}traces\text{-}none\}$ and $type(r_1) = \{issuer\text{-}traces\text{-}none, subject\text{-}traces\text{-}all\}$ then one can check that $D \in [\![A.r]\!]_{SP(\mathcal{C})}$ using the bidirectional search algorithm.

5   Other Members of the RT Family

As we have already mentioned, RT_0 is only one of the members of the RT family of TM languages. In this section we intend to give a flavour of these extensions and of the reasons why they have been introduced. We do so by presenting significative examples. For a full explanation of their syntax and semantics, we refer to [24] and [23].

5.1 RT$_1$

RT$_1$ extends RT$_0$ with parameterized roles. In RT$_1$ a role name consists of an RT$_0$ role name and zero or more parameters surrounded by parenthesis. A parameter can be a constant or a variable of one of five types: integer, closed enumeration, open enumeration, float, and date and type (see [24] for details).

Example 11. In CITA a project document can always be read and written by its author, no matter which policy applies to it. The remaining project members can read the document only if approved by the document author (identifiers starting with "?" are variables).

$$CITA.accessDoc(rw, ?proj, ?doc) \longleftarrow CITA.owner(?doc) \cap CITA.member(?proj)$$
$$CITA.accessDoc(?access, ?proj, ?doc) \longleftarrow$$
$$CITA.approved(?access, ?doc) \cap CITA.member(?proj)$$
$$CITA.approved(?access, ?doc) \longleftarrow CITA.owner(?doc).approved(?access, ?doc)$$

For each data type one can create a so called *static data set*, which can be used to constrain variables in credentials. Static in this context means that the values in the value set cannot depend on credentials but must be known at the time the value set is being specified.

Example 12. Charles restricts the access to his picture gallery to his friends that are over 18.

$$Charles.accessPictures \longleftarrow Charles.friend(?Age:[18..100])$$

In the example above, the possible values of the variable *?Age* are restricted to be in the range between 18 and 100.

For the linking inclusion credentials, a parameter can also be a special keyword *this*, which refers to a potential member of a linked role.

Example 13. CITA gives an annual salary increase to an employee if the employee's manager says that the performance of the employee is good.

$$CITA.salaryIncrease \longleftarrow CITA.managerOf(this).goodPerformance$$

5.2 RT$_2$

RT$_2$ extends RT$_1$ with *logical objects* that can be used to dynamically restrict possible values of the variables occurring in credentials. A logical object, or *o-set*, is similar to an RT$_1$ credential, but its member set is not restricted to that of entities. For instance, a company can define an o-set containing a selection of company's documents, running projects, and also any other valid RT$_1$ entity.

Example 14. The policy of CITA states that any document of a project in CUS is also a document of this project in CITA.

$$CITA.document(?proj) \longleftarrow CUS.document(?proj)$$

Now, CITA allows members of a project team to read documents of this project:

$$CITA.accessDoc(read, ?D:CITA.documents(?proj)) \longleftarrow CITA.member(?proj)$$

In the example above, $?D:CITA.documents(?proj)$ shows the application of a dynamic value set. A dynamic value set is a generalization of the static value set of which example was given in Example 12. Similarly to the static value set, the dynamic value set can be used to constrain variables occurring in credentials. However, when the values in a static value set are fixed, the set of values a dynamic value set contains is given by the members of an o-set used as a constrain. In the example above, the set of values the variable $?D$ can take is restricted to the members of the o-set $CITA.documents(?proj)$.

5.3 RT^T

RT^T has been introduced to support threshold and separation of duty policies. Consider the following policy taken from [24]: "*A says that an entity is a member of $A.r$ if one member of $A.r_1$ and two *different* members of $A.r_2$ all say so*". This policy cannot be expressed in the RT dialects presented so far, and to express this in RT one needs to use the so-called *manifold roles*. Manifold roles extend the notion of roles by allowing role members to be *collections* of entities (rather than just principals). This is done in RT^T by defining the operators $\odot$ and $\otimes$. A credential of the form $A.r \longleftarrow B_1.r_1 \odot B_2.r_2$ says that $\{s_1 \cup s_2\}$ is a member of $A.r$ if s_1 is a member of $B_1.r_1$ and s_2 is a member of $B_2.r_2$. Notice that both s_1 and s_2 are (possibly singleton) sets of entities. A credential $A.r \longleftarrow B_1.r_1 \otimes B_2.r_2$ has a similar meaning, but it additionally requires that $s_1 \cap s_2 = \emptyset$. With these two additional sorts of credentials one can express the above statement as follows:

$$A.r \longleftarrow A.r_4.r$$
$$A.r_4 \longleftarrow A.r_1 \odot A.r_3$$
$$A.r_3 \longleftarrow A.r_2 \otimes A.r_2$$

Example 15. In CITA, a program must be verified by two *different* testers: one from CITA and one form CUS.

$$CITA.verified \longleftarrow CITA.testTeam.approved$$
$$CITA.testTeam \longleftarrow CITA.tester \otimes CUS.tester$$

5.4 RT^D

The RT framework also supports the so called *delegation of role activations*, which are useful when one needs to delegate authority temporarily to a process or an agent. RT^D provides a *delegation credential* for this reason. As delegation of role activation is a complex matter, here we only present the basic intuition of how it works. The simplest form of delegation credential is $D \xrightarrow{\ D \text{ as } A.r\ } B_0$, which means that D delegates to B_0 the right of acting in D's behalf "as member of $A.r$". We call "D as $A.r$" a *role activation*. In the delegation credential above, B_0 can also represent a request, rather than an entity. Consider for instance the following example:

Example 16. Frank is the general practitioner (GP) of Henk in the hospital of Enschede (Ziekenhuis Enschede – ZE). A general practitioner in ZE can access all medical records of his patients.

$$ZE.gp(Henk) \longleftarrow Frank$$
$$ZE.accessMedRec(?Patient) \longleftarrow ZE.gp(?Patient)$$

During his holiday in Poland, Henk had a serious accident and required immediate surgery in one of the hospitals in Warsaw (WH). Weronika, the operating doctor, needs to access Henk's medical records at ZE.

ZE and WH are members of the European Hospital Alliance (EHA). In case of necessity, a doctor from one of the associated hospitals can access the medical records of a patient of another hospital by activating her *emergency* role (this role is not active by default, and every activation is carefully logged in both the hospital and EHA logs).

$$EHA.member \longleftarrow ZE$$
$$EHA.member \longleftarrow WH$$
$$ZE.accessMedRec(?Patient) \longleftarrow ZE.emergencyGroup.emergency(?Patient)$$
$$ZE.emergencyGroup \longleftarrow EHA.member$$
$$EHA.member \longleftarrow WH$$
$$WH.canActivateEmergency \longleftarrow WH.doctor$$
$$WH.doctor \longleftarrow Weronika$$

Weronika can activate her role *WH.emergency(Henk)* and request Henk's medical records from ZA using the following delegation credential:

$$Weronika \xrightarrow{\text{Weronika as WH.emergency(Henk)}} accessMedRec(ZE,Henk)$$

Here notice that *accessMedRec(ZE,Henk)* is not an entity but represent an explicit request, which is then handled by a dummy entity in RT.

5.5   RT$_\ominus$

The members of the RT family presented so far are monotonic: adding a credential to the system can only result in granting additional privileges. However, banishing negation from a TM language is not a realistic option. In fact, as stated by Li et al. [22]: "many security policies are non-monotonic, or more easily specified as non-monotonic ones". In [26], Czenko et al. argue that many access control decisions in complex distributed systems, like Virtual Communities (VC), are hard to model in a purely monotonic language. They propose RT$_\ominus$, which adds to RT a restricted form of negation called *negation in context*.

RT$_\ominus$ introduces a new operator $\ominus$ and the so called *exclusion* credential $A.r \longleftarrow B_1.r_1 \ominus B_2.r_2$ indicating that all members of $B.r_1$ which are *not* members of $B_2.r_2$ are members of $A.r$.

Example 17. Consider the policy of Example 5. In this policy Charles's role *friends* is defined to be a transitive closure of the set of his direct friends. Now, if for some reason Charles would like to *exclude* some entities from this set, he needs to use the following exclusion credential:

$$Charles.accessPictures \longleftarrow Charles.friend \ominus Charles.blackList$$

Now, an entity is a member of Charles's *accessPicture* role if she is a member of Charles's role *friend* and she is *not* on the Charles's black list. Assume that we have:

$$Charles.blackList \longleftarrow Sandro$$

Then the semantics of the role *Charles.accessPictures* is:

$$[\![Charles.accessPictures]\!]_{SP(\mathcal{C})} = \{Alice, Bob, Jeffrey, Johan\}.$$

5.6 Summary

The table below summarizes the key features of all the members of the RT framework.

The RT family member	Key extensions
RT_1	parameterized roles
RT_2	logical objects
RT^T	manifold roles and role-product operators, which can express threshold and separation of duty policies
RT^D	delegation of role activation, which allows for selective use of credentials
$RT_\ominus$	restricted form of negation

RT^D and RT^T can be used, together or separately, in combination with either RT_0, RT_1, or RT_2. The resulting combinations are written RT_i^D, RT_i^T, and RT_i^{DT} for $i = 0, 1, 2$.

6   Related Work

6.1   Trust Management Systems

PolicyMaker and KeyNote. The notion of trust management was introduced by Blaze et al. [10], as a problem in network security for which the authors proposed an approach based on a small collection of general principals: unified mechanism, flexibility (expressiveness), locality of control (autonomy of system participants), and separation of policy from mechanism. PolicyMaker, also designed and developed by Blaze et al. [9,10], was the first trust management prototype system that "facilitates the development of security features in a wide range of network services." [10]

Unlike RT, PolicyMaker places very few restrictions on the specification of authorizations and delegations. Policies and credentials are fully programmable, and can be arbitrary executable programs, limited only by being strongly "sandboxed." The advantage is that the PolicyMaker approach enables application developers tremendous flexibility to define authorizations and delegations. However, its compliance checking (evaluation) is in general undecidable: no algorithm can, for each possible request, decide whether the request is authorized. There are several variants of PolicyMaker's proof of compliance problem that are proven to be decidable, but NP-hard: globally bounded proof of compliance (GBPOC), locally bounded proof of compliance (LBPOC), and monotonic proof of compliance(MPOC). A polynomial time bound can be achieved for compliance checking by combining the restrictions used in LBPOC with the requirement that assertions be monotonic. However, the constant parameters that limit computational effort expended by a legal proof of compliance are imposed arbitrarily without apparently natural justification.

KeyNote [8] is a direct descendant of PolicyMaker. KeyNote's assertions are written in a concise and human readable assertion language. Evaluation is based on expression evaluation, rather than on the execution of arbitrary programs, and is specified by an informal, implementation-independent semantics that defines authorization decisions based on requested actions. Action requests are represented by a collection of variable bindings, and credentials can contain constraints on these variables that can be used to restrict the actions for which credential owners are authorized.

Credentials, in both PolicyMaker and KeyNote, bind public keys (of the credential subjects) to direct authorizations of security-critical actions. Therefore, similarly to capability-based system, KeyNote's authorization decision procedure is quite straightforward, without necessarily resolving the name or identity of the requester. However, capability-based systems are not as scalable as attribute-based systems. In capability-based systems, managing the delegation of access rights, for instance, to all students at a given university requires issuing a credential to each student for each resource to which they have access (library, cafeteria, gym, etc.). In attribute-based systems, such as RT, by utilizing credentials that characterize their owners as being students, the same student ID credential can be used to authorize a wide range of actions.

SPKI/SDSI. SPKI/SDSI [12] merged the SDSI [29] and the SPKI [14] efforts together to achieve an expressive and powerful trust management system. SDSI (pronounced "sudsy"), short for "a Simple Distributed Security Infrastructure," was proposed as a new public-key infrastructure by Lampson and Rivest. Concurrently, Carl Ellison et al. developed SPKI (pronounced "spooky"), which was an abbreviation for "Simple Public Key Infrastructure."

SDSI's main contribution is its design of linked local names, which solves the problem of determining globally unique names. In SDSI, the owner of each public key can define names local to a name space that is identified by that key. For example, "K_{Alice} friends" represents a SDSI name, where K_{Alice} is a key identifying its name space and "friends" is a name defined locally in that name space by K_{Alice}. SDSI names that start with different keys are different names, so there is no danger that local names in different name spaces will interfere with one another. In this way, global uniqueness of names is achieved without synchronizing and coordinating naming authorities. The way in which RT's roles are defined locally, but can be referenced non-locally, is inherited from SDSI's design of local name spaces.

While SDSI is responsible for binding names to public keys, SPKI is responsible for making authorizations. SPKI's authorization scheme can be regarded as being orthogonal to SDSI's naming scheme. Originally in SPKI, the certificate subject is represented by its public key. However, in SPKI/SDSI, the subject can be represented by its SDSI name. SDSI names provide a method to define *groups* of authorized principals, which simplifies the delegation procedure.

For example, if Bob wants to grant an authorization to Alice's friends, Bob can simply use SDSI's group name "K_{Alice} friends". By contrast, using KeyNote, Bob would have to enumerate the public keys of every friend of Alice's in the "Licensee" field of the assertion. The flexibility obtained by using SDSI names is useful in a decentralized system. On one hand, Bob does not need to have a list of Alice's friends when he is writing the authorization policies. On the other hand, any changes on Alice's friends list will be immediately reflected in the semantics of Bob's authorization policies.

SPKI/SDSI's evaluator uses a bottom-up algorithm to compute a closure set containing all certificates that can be derived from the given set of certificates. A request can be authorized if it can be found in the closure set. This algorithm is proven to be polynomial [12]. However, the evaluation process must be repeated whenever any certificate has been added or revoked, or has expired, so it is not suitable for use with a large and frequently changing credential pool.

Cassandra. Cassandra [6,7] is a role-based trust management system, which was designed with the goal of supporting the access control policies for a national electronic health record (EHR) system.

Like RT^C, Cassandra represents policy statements in Datalog clauses with constraints. Six special predicates are predefined in Cassandra. Firstly, $canActivate(e, r)$ expresses that entity e can activate role r and, as such, that e is a member of r. Secondly, $hasActivated(e, r)$ indicates that entity e has activated role r. The distinction between the predicates $canActivate$ and $hasActivated$ corresponds to the distinction between the role membership and the session activation in traditional RBAC [2]. Thirdly, $canDeactivate(e_1, e_2, r)$ holds if entity e_1 has the power to deactivate e_2's activation of role r. Fourthly, $isDeactivated(e, r)$ becomes true if entity e's role r is deactivated. Therefore, unlike RT that can only support role membership, Cassandra can also express role activations and deactivations. If a role is activated by a principal, a new fact (i.e., an atomic formula) representing this activation, and using predicate $hasActivated$, is put into the policy; similarly, deactivation of roles causes facts with predicate *hasActivated* to be removed from the policy. Fifthly, $permits(e, a)$ says that the entity e is permitted to perform action a. This differs from the standard notion of role-permission assignment in two ways. On one hand, the parameter e allows constraints to refer directly to the subject of the activation. On the other hand, *permits* has no parameter for a role associated with the action, thus allowing more flexible permission specifications, e.g., a permission that is conditioned on the activation or (or perhaps merely membership in) more than one single role. Finally, $canReqCred(e_1, e_2.p(\overrightarrow{e}))$ says that the entity e_1 is allowed to request credentials issued by the entity e_2 and asserting the predicate $p(\overrightarrow{e})$. Besides these six special predicates, application developers can also define their own customized predicates.

TPL. TPL (Trust Policy Language) [17], designed at IBM Haifa Research Lab, was proposed specifically for trust establishment between e-strangers. TPL is based on

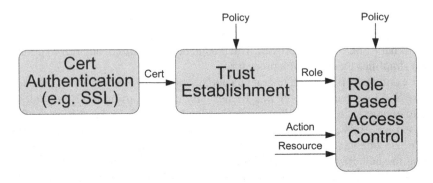

Fig. 4. TCP

RBAC [2] and extends it by being able to map strangers to roles. Unlike RT and Cassandra, TPL's efforts are claimed to be put only into mapping users to roles, but not into mapping roles to privileges, which simplifies the design. Figure 4 shows the relations between TPL and RBAC that TPL works in the Trust Establishment module and transfers the resolved role names to RBAC module.

TPL uses XML for application developers to write security rules, which will be translated in TPL to a standard logic programming language, e.g. Prolog. Unlike RT, which is monotonic, TPL is non-monotonic, since it includes negative rules. A negative rule indicates that learning a new piece of knowledge (e.g., a credential) will reduce the requester's privileges. For example, a negative rule represented in Prolog statement can be "$group(X, \text{Discount}) :- \backslash+ group(X, \text{Felon})$," in which "$\backslash+$" represents the *negation of failure*. It means that if the credential of being a felon is failed to be derived, then the requester is allowed to have the discount. However, the completeness and soundness of TPL are not specified in the original work. The example below [17] shows a rule written in XML and its Prolog translation.

XML:
```
<GROUP NAME="Hospitals">
    <RULE>
        <INCLUSION ID="reco" TYPE="Recommendation" FROM="self"/>
    </RULE>
</GROUP>
```

Prolog:
$$group(?X, Hospitals) :- cert(?Y, ?X, Recommendation, \_RecFields),$$
$$group(?Y, self).$$

PCA. PCA (Proof Carrying Authorization) [3,5,4] was mainly designed for the access control on server's web page resources. Figure 5 shows the components of PCA system working in a web browsing environment. $HTTP\ proxy$ is used to make the whole process of accessing a web page transparent to the web browser. The web browser only knows the final result: either the requested web page or a denial message is displayed.

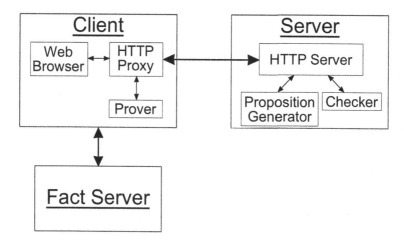

Fig. 5. PCA system

The proxy is designed to be portable and easily integrated into the client system without changing anything inside the original web browser. Therefore, it facilitates the client who is not knowledgeable in collecting relevant credentials and negotiating with the resource owner.

PCA uses higher-order logic to specify policies and credentials, so that it can be very expressive. However, its evaluation is thus undecidable. In their design, undecidability is resolved in two phases. Firstly, in order to reduce the computation burden on the server's PCA evaluator, it is required that the requesting client constructs the proof. The server's evaluator only needs to check the proof, which is not only decidable, but can be done quite efficiently. Secondly, on the client side, the proxy is responsible for navigating and retrieving credentials, computing proofs and communicating with the server. In order to avoid undecidable computation at the client side, the client proxy does not use the full logic, but use an application-specific limited logic, which should be tractable.

QCM. QCM [16], short for "Query Certificate Manager", was designed at the University of Pennsylvania as a part of the SwitchWare project on active networks to support secure maintenance of distributed data sets. For example, QCM can be used to support decentralized administration of distributed repositories housing public key certificates that map names to public keys. For the purposes of access control, QCM provides security support for ACL's query and retrieval.

QCM's policy is specified in relational calculus. One of the main contributions of QCM is its design of a policy directed certificate retrieval mechanism [16], which enables the TM evaluator automatically to detect and identify missing but needed certificates, and to retrieve them from remote certificate repositories. It uses query decomposition and optimization techniques, and its novel solutions are discussed in terms of network security, such as private key protection methods. However, unlike RT credentials, which can be stored with their either their subjects or their issuers, and can then

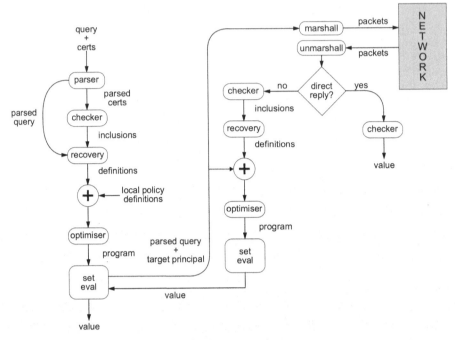

Fig. 6. QCM Engine

be located and retrieved as needed during authorization evaluation, credentials in QCM must be stored with their issuers. Figure 6 [16] shows the stages by which queries and credentials are processed in the evaluator and how the evaluation process interleaves and cooperates with the credential retrieval process.

6.2   Trust Management and Reputation Systems

Since the term Trust Management was first introduced by Blaze et al. in [10], TM became an important and popular research area. However, in many cases the work having TM in the title has often very little in common with TM as understood by its originators. Most of these cases come from the field of *Reputation Systems* [28,34,33,30,21] – also referred in the literature as *Reputation Based Trust Management*. In this paper we do not deal with reputation systems, however, as reputation systems are undoubtedly related to TM, below we provide some background information and we mark the most evident differences with TM.

Reputation systems is now a well researched area [35]. The interest in reputation systems comes from e.g. expert and auction systems [28], like *AllExperts* (http://www.allexperts.com), where everyone can ask an expert volunteer a question from the selected area. The user can then rate the expert so that other users be informed on the quality of advice given by different experts. An example of an auction system is *eBay* (http://www.ebay.com). In eBay, every user is welcome to leave a positive, negative or neutral feedback after each transaction. Sellers and buyers in eBay can rate each others and by this they can discourage (or encourage) prospective users to enter into business with another eBay user.

It has been observed that reputation is an important factor which naturally supports the process of building trust among people [18,28]. The role of a reputation system is then to collect, distribute, and aggregate feedbacks (reputations) concerning participants' past behavior [28]. The past behavior is usually expressed using a so called *trust metric*, which describes the agent's trust in another agent - most often within some well defined context [1]. In defining trust and reputation, authors often refer to social sciences [1,27] or economy and politics [28,13]. In most of the formal approaches to reputation based trust management there is a clear distinction between a so called *direct* and *recommendation* trust [35,20,1,34].

It is clear that the areas that both Trust Management and Reputation Systems cover overlap. There are, however, important differences. Most reputation systems are numeric [11], and do not incorporate language facilities. Reputation systems are also in general highly dynamic and deal mostly with the trust metric definition or recommendation exchange protocols. Reputation systems answer the question how to build trust values from the local history and the information provided by other peers. Most importantly, the trust gained in reputation systems is rather fuzzy in nature as it depends on an often obscure algorithm and on sometimes highly subjective feedback. In Trust Management, on the other hand, trust is obtained as a result of a formal evaluation of a set of credentials with respect to the user policy. Each user is also allowed to have different policy, which is usually not allowed in the existing reputation systems.

References

1. Abdul-Rahman, A., Hailes, S.: Supporting Trust in Virtual Communities. In: Proc. 33rd Hawaii International Conference on System Sciences, vol. 6, p. 6007. IEEE Computer Society Press, Los Alamitos (2000)
2. ANSI: American National Standard for Information Technology – Role Based Access Control. ANSI INCITS 359-2004 (February 2004)
3. Appel, A.W., Felten, E.W.: Proof-Carrying Authentication. In: CCS '99: Proc. 6th ACM Conference on Computer and Communications Security, pp. 52–62. ACM Press, New York (1999)
4. Bauer, L., Schneider, M.A., Felten, E.W.: A General and Flexible Access-Control System for the Web. In: Proc. 11th USENIX Security Symposium, USENIX Association, pp. 93–108 (2002)
5. Bauer, L.: Access Control for the Web via Proof-Carrying Authorization. PhD thesis, Adviser-Andrew W. Appel. (2003)
6. Becker, M.Y., Sewell, P.: Cassandra: Distributed Access Control Policies with Tunable Expressiveness. In: Proc. 5th IEEE International Workshop on Policies for Distributed Systems and Networks (POLICY 2004), pp. 159–168. IEEE Computer Society Press, Los Alamitos (2004)
7. Becker, M.Y., Sewell, P.: Cassandra: Flexible Trust Management, Applied to Electronic Health Records. In: CSFW, pp. 139–154. IEEE Computer Society Press, Los Alamitos (2004)
8. Blaze, M., Feigenbaum, J., Ioannidis, J., Keromytis, A.: The KeyNote Trust-Management System, Version 2. IETF RFC 2704 (1999)

9. Blaze, M., Feigenbaum, J., Ioannidis, J., Keromytis, A.: The Role of Trust Management in Distributed Systems Security. In: Vitek, J., Jensen, C. (eds.) Secure Internet Programming. LNCS, vol. 1603, pp. 185–210. Springer, Heidelberg (1999)

10. Blaze, M., Feigenbaum, J., Lacy, J.: Decentralized Trust Management. In: Proc. 17th IEEE Symposium on Security and Privacy, pp. 164–173. IEEE Computer Society Press, Los Alamitos (1996)

11. Bonatti, P., Duma, C., Olemdilla, D., Shahmehri, N.: An Integration of Reputation-based and Policy-based Trust Management. In: Proc. Semantic Web and Policy Workshop (2005)

12. Clarke, D., Elien, J.E., Ellison, C., Fredette, M., Morcos, A., Rivest, R.L.: Certificate Chain Discovery in SPKI/SDSI. Journal of Computer Security 9(4), 285–322 (2001)

13. Dellarocas, C.: Analyzing the Economic Efficiency of eBay-like Online Reputation Reporting Mechanisms. In: Proc. 3rd ACM conference on Electronic Commerce, pp. 171–179. ACM Press, New York (2001)

14. Ellison, C., Frantz, B., Lampson, B., Rivest, R., Thomas, B., Ylonen, T.: SPKI Certificate Theory. IETF RFC 2693 (September 1999)

15. Etalle, S., Winsborough, W.H.: A Posteriori Compliance Control. In: Proc. 12th ACM Symposium on Access Control Models and Technologies, ACM Press, New York (2007)

16. Gunter, C., Jim, T.: Policy-directed Certificate Retrieval. Software: Practice & Experience 30(15), 1609–1640 (2000)

17. Herzberg, A., Mass, Y., Michaeli, J., Ravid, Y., Naor, D.: Access Control Meets Public Key Infrastructure, Or: Assigning Roles to Strangers. In: Proc. IEEE Symposium on Security and Privacy, pp. 2–14. IEEE Computer Society Press, Los Alamitos (2000)

18. Jarvenpaa, S.L., Tractinsky, N., Vitale, M.: Consumer Trust in an Internet Store. Inf. Tech. and Management 1(1-2), 45–71 (2000)

19. Jim, T.: SD3: A Trust Management System with Certified Evaluation. In: Proc. IEEE Symposium on Security and Privacy, pp. 106–115. IEEE Computer Society Press, Los Alamitos (2001)

20. Jøsang, A.: The Right Type of Trust for Distributed Systems. In: NSPW '96: Proc. Workshop on New Security Paradigms, pp. 119–131. ACM Press, New York (1996)

21. Kamvar, S.D., Schlosser, M.T., Garcia-Molina, H.: The Eigentrust Algorithm for Reputation Management in P2P Networks. In: Proc. 12th International Conference on World Wide Web, pp. 640–651. ACM Press, New York (2003)

22. Li, N., Feigenbaum, J., Grosof, B.N.: A Logic-based Knowledge Representation for Authorization with Delegation (Extended Abstract). In: Proc. 1999 IEEE Computer Security Foundations Workshop, pp. 162–174. IEEE Computer Society Press, Los Alamitos (1999)

23. Li, N., Mitchell, J.: RT: A Role-based Trust-management Framework. In: Proc. 3rd DARPA Information Survivability Conference and Exposition (DISCEX III), pp. 201–212. IEEE Computer Society Press, Los Alamitos (2003)

24. Li, N., Mitchell, J., Winsborough, W.: Design of a Role-based Trust-management Framework. In: Proc. IEEE Symposium on Security and Privacy, pp. 114–130. IEEE Computer Society Press, Los Alamitos (2002)

25. Li, N., Winsborough, W., Mitchell, J.: Distributed Credential Chain Discovery in Trust Management. Journal of Computer Security 11(1), 35–86 (2003)

26. Czenko, M., Tran, H., Doumen, J., Etalle, S., Hartel, P., den Hartog, J.: Nonmonotonic Trust Management for P2P Applications. In: Proc. 1st International Workshop on Security and Trust Management, pp. 101–116. Elsevier, Amsterdam (2005)

27. Mui, L., Mohtashemi, M., Halberstadt, A.: A Computational Model of Trust and Reputation for E-businesses. Hicss 07, 188 (2002)

28. Resnick, P., Kuwabara, K., Zeckhauser, R., Friedman, E.: Reputation systems. Commun. ACM 43(12), 45–48 (2000)

29. Rivest, R., Lampson, B.: SDSI – A Simple Distributed Security Infrastructure (October 1996), Available at
    `http://theory.lcs.mit.edu/~rivest/sdsi11.html`
30. Shmatikov, V., Talcott, C.L.: Reputation-based Trust Management. Journal of Computer Security 13(1), 167–190 (2005)
31. Weeks, S.: Understanding Trust Management Systems. In: Proc. IEEE Symposium on Security and Privacy, pp. 94–105. IEEE Computer Society Press, Los Alamitos (2001)
32. Winsborough, W.H., Li, N.: Towards Practical Automated Trust Negotiation. In: POLICY, pp. 92–103. IEEE Computer Society Press, Los Alamitos (2002)
33. Xiong, L., Liu, L.: A Reputation-based Trust Model for Peer-to-Peer eCommerce Communities. In: ACM Conference on Electronic Commerce, pp. 228–229. ACM, New York (2003)
34. Xiong, L., Liu, L.: PeerTrust: Supporting Reputation-Based Trust for Peer-to-Peer Electronic Communities. IEEE Trans. Knowl. Data Eng. 16(7), 843–857 (2004)
35. Yahalom, R., Klein, B., Beth, T.: Trust Relationships in Secure Systems – A Distributed Authentication Perspective. In: RSP: IEEE Computer Society Symposium on Research in Security and Privacy, IEEE Computer Society, Los Alamitos (1993)

Trusted Mobile Platforms

E. Gallery and C.J. Mitchell*

Royal Holloway, University of London, Egham,
Surrey, TW20 0EX, United Kingdom
{e.m.gallery,c.mitchell}@rhul.ac.uk

Abstract. This article addresses two main topics. Firstly, we review the
operation of trusted computing technology, which now appears likely
to be implemented in future mobile devices (including mobile phones,
PDAs, etc.). Secondly, we consider the possible applications of this technology in mobile devices, and how these applications can be supported
using trusted computing technology. We focus in particular on three mobile applications, namely OMA DRM, SIMLock, and software download.

1   Introduction

Trusted Computing (TC) technology, which is already present in many recently
manufactured PCs, has the potential to revolutionise many aspects of the secure
management of IT, particularly in a corporate environment. In recent years,
attention has been directed at how this technology might be deployed more
broadly, including in a mobile and ubiquitous computing environment.

In this article we aim to do two main things. Firstly, we review the operation of trusted computing technology; we not only describe the main functional
components of this technology, but also summarise the main motivations for its
introduction. Secondly, we consider possible applications of this technology in
mobile devices, since it appears likely that the technology will be implemented
in a wide range of future such devices (including mobile phones, PDAs, etc.). In
particular we consider how three possible applications, i.e. Open Mobile Alliance
Digital Rights Management (OMA DRM), SIMLock, and software download, can
be supported using trusted computing technology.

The remainder of the article is divided into two parts, as follows. The first
main part commences in section 2, where we describe what trusted computing
is intended to achieve and why it has been developed. This is followed in section 3 by a brief history of the development of trusted computing technology.
Section 4 summarises the main technical concepts underlying trusted computing. This leads naturally to an overview of the trusted platform subsystem in
section 5, followed in section 6 by a more detailed description of trusted computing functionality. The second main part of the article, which is concerned
with the application of trusted computing technology to mobile devices, starts

---

* The development of this article was sponsored by the Open Trusted Computing
project of the European Commission Framework 6 Programme.

A. Aldini and R. Gorrieri (Eds.): FOSAD 2006/2007, LNCS 4677, pp. 282–323, 2007.

with a review of the trusted mobile platform in section 7. This is followed by an analysis of three mobile use cases of trusted computing, namely OMA DRM v2, SIMLock and software download, given in sections 8, 9 and 10, respectively. The paper concludes in section 11.

2   Computer Security and Trusted Computing

2.1   Trust

The word *trust* means many different things to different people and in different contexts. Like the word *security*, it has become so over-used that it is almost meaningless unless a definition is provided. This is certainly the case for the term 'trusted computing', and so one thing that we try to do here is define what trust means in this particular context. This theme is returned to in many subsequent parts of this article.

So what does trust mean for our purposes? Well, perhaps the simplest definition would be that *trusted computing* refers to a computer system for which an entity has some level of assurance that (part or all) of the computer system is behaving as expected (or, to quote [1], a platform is trusted if it 'behaves in an expected manner for an intended purpose'). The entity may be various things, including the human user of the PC or a program running on a remote machine. The degree of coverage of this assurance, i.e. whether it covers all aspects of the system or just some part, and the nature of the entity to which assurance is provided, vary depending on the system and the environment within which it is used. Of course, just because the behaviour of a system is as expected, does not necessarily imply that a trusted platform is a secure platform. For example, if an entity can determine that a platform is infected with a virus, whose effects are known, the platform can be trusted by that entity to behave in an expected but malicious manner [2].

It has also been said that 'trusted platforms were so-called because they provide a technological implementation and interpretation of the factors that permit us, in everyday life, to trust others' [3], i.e.

- either first hand experience of consistent behaviour, or trust in someone who vouches for consistent behaviour;
- unambiguous identification; and
- unhindered operation.

In order to implement a platform of this nature, a trusted component, which is usually in the form of built-in hardware, is integrated into a computing platform [4]. This trusted component is then used to create a foundation of trust for software processes running on the platform [4]. Bodies such as the Trusted Computing Group (TCG) (discussed in section 3) standardise specific functionality to be incorporated into end systems which are known as 'trusted platforms'. Depending on how the specified functionality is implemented, such a platform is then able to provide a degree of assurance about some aspect of its operation.

2.2   Computer Security

Computer security is a long-established subject, with a considerable literature dating back to the 1960s. There are many books on the subject of secure computing (see, for example, Gollmann [5] and Pfleeger [6]). Trusted computing, with the meaning applied here, is a much more recent phenomenon, and is essentially one specialised part of the larger subject of computer security. One reason that the notion has emerged is because of the changing nature of computer systems, and their increasing ubiquity.

Historically, computer security has provided a theory to understand and reason about fundamentally important security functionality within operating systems. This functionality covers issues such as access control to resources within the context of multi-user operation. Most of computer security is thus concerned with security aspects of software, and pays relatively little attention to hardware security issues.

The reason for this is clear. Until the advent of the PC, computers were relatively large and expensive devices, typically with a number of users. The hardware was often kept in a physically secure location, to which access was only granted to authorised staff. Hence the main security issue was to design the file system software such that one user could not access data and resources to which he or she was not entitled, including other users' data. The security of the hardware was not something directly addressed — it was essentially a prerequisite for the correct operation of the software.

This resulted in a large and well-developed theory of computer security, covering such topics as multi-level system security and a host of models for access control systems. This theory remains very important; however despite overlapping terminology, this is not the main subject of this article. Terminological confusion is a particular problem, not just because of the overuse of the word *trust*, but because the term *Trusted Computing Base (TCB)* has become widely used to mean something somewhat different to the recent use of *trusted computing*.

As defined in the Orange Book [7] (see also Gollmann [5]) the TCB is the totality of protection mechanisms within a computer system, including hardware, firmware and software. Whilst this is by no means unrelated to trusted computing, as discussed here, the meaning is definitely not the same.

Of course, it is true that physically secure subsystems have always had a place in the spectrum of secure computing, but they have mainly been used in specialist applications. For example, many secure subsystems have been designed and used in applications requiring physical security for stored keying material — examples of such systems include the IBM 4758 [8] (see also Chapter 15 of [9] for a discussion of interfaces to such subsystems).

2.3   Computer Security and PCs

The traditional assumptions regarding the physical security of important computer systems are clearly completely inappropriate for the vast majority of PCs in use today. Most such PCs have only a single user, and no physical security is provided for the PC hardware. Short term access to the PC can easily result in unauthorised copying of information and/or modifications to software and data; this is easy to achieve regardless of what software protections exist, simply by temporarily removing a hard disk and attaching it to a different system. That is, regardless of how 'secure' the operating system is in the traditional sense, the lack of guarantees about physical security means that the correctness of software or information stored on the PC cannot be trusted; neither can the confidentiality of any such information. The situation is made worse by the fact that modern PC operating systems and application software are enormously complex, and removing all software vulnerabilities is an almost impossible task. Hence for a combination of reasons today's systems are very vulnerable to a range of attacks.

Trusted computing as we mean it here is an idea which has arisen from the need to address these problems. Trusted computing refers to the addition of hardware functionality to a computer system to enable entities with which the computer interacts to have some level of trust in what the system is doing. Pearson [10] defines a related notion, namely that of a *trusted platform*, as follows.

A trusted platform is a computing platform that has a trusted component, probably in the form of built-in hardware, which it uses to create
a foundation of trust for software processes.

The exact nature of a trusted platform is an issue that is explored below. An interesting discussion of trust and trusted computing can be found in [11]. A useful high level introduction to trusted computing has also been given by Felten [12].

2.4   Goals of Trusted Computing

The main goals of trusted computing are to add some (modest) set of hardware enhancements to a computer system to enable (a) the state of the system to be checked, both locally and remotely, and (b) data to be protected so that it will be available only when the system is in a specified state. Achieving these apparently limited goals requires adding a significant amount of functionality to a PC, although most of the necessary functionality can be incorporated into a special-purpose chip, the *Trusted Platform Module (TPM)*.

Achieving the first of these goals is perhaps the most fundamental, and much of the functionality of the TPM is necessary simply to meet this goal. For example, it is clear that, unless there is some way of providing assurance about the correct functioning of the operating system, then there is no way of providing any assurance about the correct operation of applications. This means that it is necessary to monitor the process of booting the operating system, in such a way that the integrity of the system after the boot process has been completed can be verified. This is by no means a simple requirement, since booting a platform such as a PC is a highly complex process.

Essentially, it requires the first piece of software that executes to be fixed (unchangeable), and also for each piece of software that runs subsequently to be checked (measured) by its predecessor. This process of measurement involves applying a cryptographic hash function to the software, storing the result, and later reporting the result in a reliable way. As we will see below, this means that the 'roots of trust' for measurement, storage and reporting are essential to meet the first goal.

This notion of monitoring the booting of an operating system also highlights the limitations of hardware-based trusted computing. That is, since modern operating systems are large and complex, it is clear that determining whether a measured version of the operational state of a PC can be trusted or not is essentially a hopeless task. This is because there will be a very large number of different possible 'valid' states for such a system, each of which will generate a measurement. As a result, trying to decide whether a measurement represents a valid or invalid software state becomes infeasible.

Thus, whilst the TPM can measure the initial stages of the booting of a PC, this process cannot be extended indefinitely to the entire system. As a result, at some point the software must be trusted to 'look after itself'. That is, at least for complex multi-purpose systems such as PCs, the use of hardware-based measurements of software state must be combined with some other means of providing ongoing protection for a system.

This is achieved by introducing the notion of a isolation layer (discussed in more detail below). That is, the trusted computing hardware can be used to provide assurance that a particular isolation layer has been booted; after that the isolation layer must itself guarantee the integrity of the system. An isolation layer will typically be booted immediately prior to starting up one or more 'guest' operating systems. The isolation layer must be trusted to provide ongoing security for the operating systems which it hosts. In particular, it must be trusted to isolate the different operating systems (and applications running on operating systems) so that data cannot pass between them in unauthorised ways, and so that even if malicious code is introduced into one environment it cannot damage other environments.

Of course, this analysis does not necessarily apply to all trusted platforms. For single use, simple platforms, e.g. as might be the case for embedded or mobile systems, ongoing hardware-based measurement and verification of the complete software environment may be possible, because the number of possible valid states may not be very large.

Finally, note that the functionality provided by the TPM can be used for a host of purposes, many quite distinct from the fundamental goals discussed above. Indeed, the addition of a TPM to a computer system is somewhat akin to equipping every PC with a physically secure 'hardware security module'. The presence of such hardware is likely to give rise to a host of new applications, which we cannot begin to envisage today.

3   A Brief History of Trusted Computing

The concept of trusted computing, as described throughout this article, was initially defined by the Trusted Computing Platform Alliance (TCPA). The TCPA, an industry working group which focussed on the development and standardisation of trusted computing technology, was formed in January 1999 by Compaq, HP, IBM, Intel and Microsoft. Some of the earliest papers introducing this paradigm were published by HP in 2000 [13,14]. In early 2001, following the expansion of the group, the TCPA published the first specification for a TPM, a fundamental component of a trusted platform. Following this, a PC-specific specification, detailing the additional changes required in order to produce a TCPA-compliant trusted PC, was published. The TCPA TPM and PC specifications are described in [4].

In April 2003 the TCPA was superseded by the TCG. The TCG have continued to develop and expand the TPM specifications, the current version of which is v1.2 [15,16,17]. The TPM specifications are supported by a standard set of TPM APIs which provide an abstraction of the TPM to software developers/vendors [18]. The TCG has defined how a TPM may be utilised on a variety of platform types such as a PC client, server, hard copy device, and storage device. A trusted mobile platform is also being specified (see also section 7). In conjunction with this, work is ongoing on specifications designed to aid the seamless adoption, integration and inter-operability of trusted computing platforms.

Microsoft's proposals for a trusted computing architecture were initially released under the name Palladium, and subsequently under the title Next Generation Secure Computing Base (NGSCB). The fundamental component of the most recently described version of the Microsoft architecture is an isolation layer designed to support the execution of isolated runtime environments for sensitive applications. This architecture assumes the presence of TPM functionality, as defined by the TCG, in conjunction with processor enhancements and chipset extensions which enable the implementation of the high-assurance isolation layer. For further information see [19,20,21,22].

The Terra system architecture [23], the Perseus framework [24,25], the Open Trusted Computing architecture [26] and the European Multilaterally Secure Computing Base (EMSCB) [27] have some similarities to the current version of NGSCB. At the heart of each architecture is an isolation layer, which has been designed to support the isolated execution of software. Terra is based on the notion of a Trusted Virtual Machine Monitor (TVMM), that partitions a computing platform into multiple, isolated virtual machines. The Perseus framework and the Open Trusted Computing architecture have been designed to use either a virtual machine monitor such as XEN [28] or a microkernel in order to provide isolated execution environments. EMSCB incorporates an L4 microkernel-based isolation layer. Each architecture also assumes a hardware platform which includes a TPM. The presence of chipset and processor enhancements are also acknowledged within all architectures as pivotal in order to ensure a high-assurance isolation layer implementation.

Hardware manufacturers such as Intel and AMD have specified the required processor enhancements and chipset extensions under the names of LaGrande [29] and Presidio respectively.

As this technology has evolved and matured, a growing body of work has emerged on the potential applications of trusted computing. Both Balacheff et al.

[30] and Spalka, Cremers and Langweg [31] describe how trusted computing functionality may be utilised in order to enhance the security of the digital signature process. Schechter et al. [32], Kinateder and Pearson [33] and Balfe, Lakhani and Paterson [34] discuss the application of trusted computing to peer-to-peer networks. The deployment of trusted computing functionality has also been proposed in order to enable secure software download [35], support secure single sign-on solutions [36], improve the security and privacy of a biometric user authentication process [37] and to facilitate identity management [38,39]. A number of authors have also considered trusting computing's applicability to the agent paradigm [40,41,42,43] and online gaming [44]. Further application scenarios are described in [4,23,26,45].

While the benefits of trusted computing functionality have become apparent, this new technology has also been criticised. Anderson [46] expresses the view that trusted computing may be used to support censorship, stifle competition between software vendors, and hinder the deployment and use of open source software. The issues of software 'lock in' and interoperability, the contentious issue of TC-enabled DRM, and, more generally, remote control of the software on a platform, are also highlighted by members of the Electronic Frontier Foundation, namely Scheon [47] and von Lohmann [48]. Privacy concerns relating to trusted platforms have also been widely discussed [49], and will be revisited in section 6. A high level account of these criticisms is provided by Arbaugh [50].

In parallel to the development of the trusted computing technologies described above, closely related concepts such as secure boot have been widely discussed, and a number of alternative architectures have been developed with the goal of providing more secure and trustworthy computing platforms. The concept of a secure boot has been repeatedly discussed in the literature, most notably by Tygar and Yee [51], Clark [52], Arbaugh, Farber and Smith [53] and Itoi et al. [54]. While the eXecute-Only Memory (XOM) architecture [55,56] and the architecture for tamper evident and tamper resistant processing (AEGIS) [57] are not strictly examples of trusted computing platforms, like trusted computing they provide strong process isolation through the development of hardened processors.

4   Trusted Computing Concepts

Trusted computing, as defined by the TCG, is synonymous with four fundamental concepts: integrity measurement, authenticated boot, sealing and platform attestation. A platform incorporating these concepts constitutes what we refer to here as a *Trusted Platform (TP)*. Note that, since the original description was published, the definition of what constitutes trusted computing functionality has been revised and extended to incorporate the concept of software isolation.

4.1   Integrity Measurement

An integrity measurement is defined in [22] as the cryptographic digest or hash of a platform component (i.e. a piece of software executing on the platform).

For example, the integrity measurement of a program could be calculated by computing the cryptographic digest or hash of its instruction sequence, its initial state (i.e. the executable file) and its input.

An integrity metric is defined as 'a condensed value of integrity measurements' [4]. Integrity metrics indicate the history of the platform.

4.2   Authenticated Boot

An authenticated boot is the process by which a platform's configuration or state is reliably captured and stored. During this process, the integrity of a pre-defined set of platform components is measured, as defined in section 4.1. These measurements are condensed to form a set of integrity metrics which are then stored in a tamper-resistant log. A record of the platform components which have been measured is also stored on the platform. Condensing enables an unbounded number of platform component measurements to be stored. If each measurement was stored separately, an unbounded amount of memory would be required to store them [4].

4.3   Sealing

Sealing is the process by which sensitive data can be associated with a set of integrity metrics representing a particular platform configuration, and encrypted. The protected data can only be decrypted and released for use when the current state of platform matches the integrity metrics sealed with the data.

4.4   Attestation

Attestation is the process by which a platform can reliably report evidence of its identity and its current state (i.e. the integrity metrics which have been stored to the tamper resistant log, and the record of the platform components which have been measured, as described in section 4.2).

4.5   Software Isolation

Isolation enables the unhindered execution of software through the provision of assured memory space separation between processes [58].

5   The Trusted Platform Subsystem

As stated in section 2.1, in order to provide the services described in sections 4.1 to 4.4, a 'trusted component' must be integrated into a computing platform. This 'trusted component' is made up of three roots of trust — the Root of Trust for Measurement (RTM), the Root of Trust for Storage (RTS) and the Root of Trust for Reporting (RTR). In order to provide software isolation, as described in section 4.5, an isolation layer can be deployed on the platform. In conjunction with this, the platform may also incorporate processor enhancements and chipset extensions which have been designed to enable a secure and high assurance isolation layer implementation.

5.1   The RTM

The RTM is a computing engine capable of measuring at least one platform component, and hence providing an integrity measurement, as described in section 4.1. The RTM is typically implemented as the normal platform processor controlled by a particular instruction set (the so-called 'Core Root of Trust for Measurement' (CRTM)). On a PC, the CRTM may be contained within the BIOS or the BIOS Boot Block (BBB), and is executed by the platform when it is acting as the RTM. It is required by the TCG that the CRTM is protected against software attack: the CRTM must be immutable, as defined by the TCG, meaning that its replacement or modification must be under the control of the host platform manufacturer alone [59]. It is also preferable that the CRTM be physically tamper-evident [4].

5.2   The RTS and RTR

The RTS is a collection of capabilities which must be trusted if storage of data inside a platform is to be trusted [4]. The RTS is capable of maintaining an accurate summary of integrity measurements made by the RTM, i.e. condensing integrity measurements and storing the resulting integrity metrics, as described in section 4.2. The RTS also provides integrity and confidentiality protection to data and enables sealing.

In conjunction with the RTM and RTS, an additional root of trust is necessary for the implementation of platform attestation, namely the RTR. The RTR is a collection of capabilities that must be trusted if reports of integrity metrics are to be trusted (platform attestation) [4].

The RTR and the RTS constitute the minimum functionality that should be provided by a TPM [15,16,17]. A TPM is generally implemented as a chip which must be physically bound to a platform. In order to support RTS and RTR functionality, a TPM incorporates a number of functional components such as: input/output; non-volatile and volatile memory; a minimum of 16 *Platform Configuration Registers (PCRs)*, which are used by the RTS to store the platform's integrity metrics; a random number generator; a HMAC engine; a SHA-1 engine; key generation capabilities; an asymmetric encryption and digital signature engine; and an execution engine, as shown in figure 1. The TPM must be protected completely against software attack, i.e. the RTS and RTR (i.e. the TPM) must be immutable, which implies that the replacement or modification of RTS and RTR code must be under the control of the TPM manufacturer alone. The TPM is required to provide a limited degree of protection against physical attack (tamper-evidence) [4].

5.3   Software Isolation Technology

A number of approaches have been proposed in order to facilitate software isolation. Many of these approaches, however, have associated difficulties with respect to assurance, device support, legacy OS compatibility and performance.

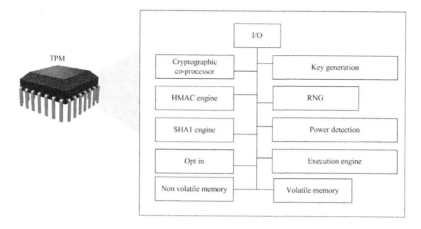

Fig. 1. The TPM chip

OS-Hosted VMM: In the case of an OS-hosted virtual machine monitor, such as VMWare workstation, all guest OSs executing in VMs utilise the host OS device drivers. While this implies that the every guest can utilise drivers developed for the host machine, it also means that the isolation layer essentially incorporates the VMM and the host OS, making assurance problematic [22,60].

Standalone VMM: In a standalone virtual machine monitor, such as Terra [23], all devices are virtualised or emulated by the VMM. This means that the VMM must contain a virtual device driver for every supported device. As the set of devices utilised in consumer systems is often large, and as many virtual device drivers are complex, the size of the VMM quickly grows at the cost of assurance. A standalone VMM exposes the original hardware interface to its guests. While this implies that legacy OSs can be supported, it also means that the VMM size is increased because of the complexity involved in virtualising the x86 CPU instruction set [22].

Para-Virtualisation: Isolation layers using para-virtualisation techniques, such as XEN [28], have been designed for efficiency, and try to alleviate the complexity introduced when devices are virtualised. Two common approaches used in order to para-virtualise I/O are as follows [60]. In the first case, an I/O-type-specific API for each device is integrated into the VMM, in conjunction with the device drivers [60]. This approach requires a guest OS to incorporate para-virtualised drivers which enable communication with the VMM APIs rather than the hardware device interfaces. While this gives performance gains over full virtualisation, the guest OS must be modified to communicate with the I/O-type-specific APIs. Alternatively, a service OS, which incorporates the VMM APIs and the device drivers, may execute in parallel to guest OSs, which are modified to incorporate para-virtualised drivers [60]. To enable this approach, devices are exported to the service OS. While this approach means that device drivers do not have to be implemented within the isolation layer, the isolation layer may become open to attack from a guest in control of a direct memory access device which is, by default, given unrestricted access to the full physical address space of the machine.

An Isolation Layer with Hardware Support: The isolation layer described as part of the NGSCB [21,22] was designed to take advantage of CPU and chipset extensions incorporated in a new generation of processor hardware; such hardware is being provided, for example, by Intel's LaGrande initiative [29]. The isolation kernel has been designed to execute in a CPU mode more privileged than the existing ring 0, effectively in ring -1, which is being introduced in new versions of the x86 processors. This enables the isolation layer to operate in ring -1 and all guest OSs to execute in ring 0. Thus, complexity problems which arise when virtualising the x86 instruction set are avoided [22]. The original hardware interface is exposed to one guest OS [22]. However, rather than necessitating the virtualisation of all devices, as a VMM does, devices are exported to guest OSs which contain drivers for the devices they choose to support. Guest operating systems may then efficiently operate directly on the chosen device.

This does, however, leave the problem of uncontrolled DMA devices, which by default have access to all physical memory. In order to prevent DMA devices circumventing virtual memory-based protections provided by the isolation layer, it is necessary for the chipset manufacturers to provide certain instruction set extensions. These enable a DMA policy to be set by the isolation layer which indicates, given the state of the system, if a particular subject (DMA device) has access (read or write) to a specified resource (physical address), [22]. The DMA policy is then read and enforced by hardware, for example the memory controller or bus bridges.

Hardware extensions required in order to facilitate the implementation of the NGSCB isolation layer have been provided as part of Intel's LaGrande [29] and AMD's Presidio initiatives. Both enable the efficient and secure implementation of an isolation layer, as described by Microsoft, through the implementation of CPU and chipset extensions. Both also support the establishment of trusted channels between the input and output devices and programs running within an isolated environment.

6   The Trusted Platform Subsystem Functionality

6.1   The Authenticated Boot Process

An authenticated boot process enables the state of a platform to be measured and recorded. In order to describe an authenticated boot process we need to introduce some fundamental TPM concepts. A PCR is a 20-byte integrity-protected register present in a TPM; a TPM must contain a minimum of 16 such registers. When a component is 'measured', a 20-byte SHA-1 hash of the component is computed. The output hash value (i.e. the measurement of the component) is then stored in one of the TPM PCRs. In order to ensure that an unlimited number of measurements can be stored in the limited number of PCRs in a TPM, multiple measurements can be stored in a single PCR. This is achieved by concatenating a new measurement with the existing contents of a PCR, hashing the resulting string, and then storing the output hash code in the PCR.

A record of all measured components is stored in the *Stored Measurement Log (SML)*, which is maintained externally to the TPM. The information in the SML is necessary to interpret the PCR values, but does not need to be integrity protected.

A simplified authenticated boot process might proceed as follows, where we assume that the CRTM is part of the BBB. The CRTM measures itself and the rest of the BIOS (i.e. the POST BIOS). The computed measurements are then passed to the RTS, which condenses them and records the resulting integrity metric in the first of the 16 PCRs (PCR-0) within the TPM. Control is then passed to the POST BIOS which measures the host platform configuration, the option ROM code and configuration, and the Operating System (OS) loader. The computed measurements are passed to the RTS, which condenses them and stores the resulting integrity metrics in PCRs 1-5. Control is then passed to the OS loader which measures the OS. At each stage a record of all measurements computed is stored to the SML. This process is illustrated in figure 2.

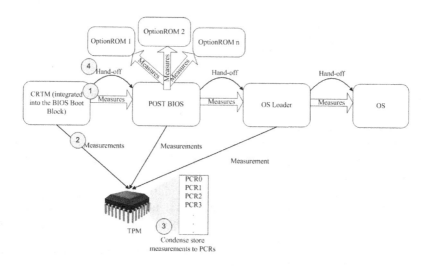

Fig. 2. The authenticated boot process

This process of measuring, condensing, storing, and handing-off, continues until the platform's configuration has been measured and stored. The exact measurement process is dependent on the platform; for example, the TCG specifications detail authenticated boot processes for a platform which has a 32-bit PC architecture BIOS [59] and for an Extensible Firmware Interface (EFI) platform [61].

6.2   TPM Protected Storage

The TPM provides secure ('protected') storage functionality, which incorporates a sealing capability. This functionality was designed so that an unbounded number of secrets/data could be confidentiality and integrity protected on a TP.

Each TPM contains a 2048-bit asymmetric key pair known as a *Storage Root Key (SRK)*. The private key from this key pair is permanently stored inside the TPM. This key pair is the root of the *TPM protected object hierarchy*. A TPM protected object in this hierarchy may be classified as either a *TPM protected key object*, i.e. an asymmetric key pair whose private key is encrypted using a key at a higher layer in the hierarchy, or a *TPM protected data object*, i.e. data (or, indeed, a symmetric key), which has been encrypted using a key at a higher layer of the hierarchy. A simplified TPM protected object hierarchy is illustrated in figure 3.

Asymmetric encryption is used to confidentiality-protect key and data objects. Protected storage also provides implicit integrity protection of TPM protected objects. Data can be associated with a string of 20 bytes of authorisation data before it is encrypted. When data decryption is requested, the authorisation data must be submitted to the TPM. The submitted authorisation data is then compared to the authorisation data in the decrypted string, and the decrypted data object is only released if the values match. If the encrypted object has been tampered with, the authorisation data will most likely have been corrupted (because of the method of encryption employed) and access will not be granted even to an entity which has submitted the correct authorisation data. However, functionality to control how data is used on its release, or to protect data from deletion, is not provided.

The TPM protected storage functionality incorporates an asymmetric key generation capability. This capability enables the generation of key pairs for which the private keys can only be used on the TPM on which they were generated. An additional constraint may also be applied which prevents private key use unless the TPM host platform is in a specified state. Moreover, key pairs can be generated with the property that the private keys from the pairs are never exported from the TPM in unencrypted form.

The TPM enables the encryption of keys or data outside the TPM in such a way that they can only be decrypted on a particular TPM. It also enables the encryption of keys or data so that they can only be decrypted when a particular TPM host platform is in a specified state.

Finally, sealing functionality is provided, i.e. the ability to associate data with a particular platform configuration, and then encrypt the data so that it is bound to this configuration. The configuration is recorded as a pair of sets of integrity metrics, which represent the state of the platform when the data was sealed (*digest at creation*), and the state of the platform required for the data to be unsealed (*digest at release*). The sealed data can only be decrypted by the TPM on which it was encrypted, and will only be released by the TPM of the host platform is in the state specified in the *digest at release*. Once the data has been released the *digest at creation* must be checked in order to ensure that the data was not sealed by rogue software.

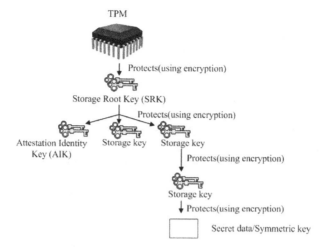

Fig. 3. The TPM protected object hierarchy

6.3   Platform Attestation

Platform attestation enables a TPM to reliably report information about its identity and the current state of the TPM host platform. This is achieved using asymmetric cryptography, as we describe below. However, to achieve this, it uses a set of key pairs and associated credentials (certificates); this somewhat complex process is necessary in order to allow TP anonymity. We describe the key pairs and the credentials before describing the attestation process itself.

Platform Keys and Credentials: Each TPM is associated with a unique asymmetric encryption key pair called an *endorsement key pair*, which is generated at the time of manufacture. The TP incorporating the TPM is further equipped with a set of *credentials*, i.e. signed data structures (certificates), signed by a variety of third parties. It is to be expected that these credentials will all be in place at the time the platform is provided to an end user.

We next briefly enumerate the three key types of credential.

- A entity known as the *trusted platform management entity* (which is likely to be the TPM manufacturer) attests to the fact that the TPM is genuine by digitally signing an *endorsement credential*. This certificate binds the public endorsement key to a TPM description.
- *Conformance credentials* are certificates that attest that, when considered together, a particular type of TPM, associated components such as a CRTM, the connection of a CRTM to a motherboard, and the connection of a TPM to a motherboard, conform to the TCG specifications. Such a certificate might be signed by a third party testing laboratory.
- A *platform entity* (typically the platform manufacturer) offers assurance in the form of a *platform credential* that a particular platform is an instantiation

of a TP. In order to create a platform credential, a platform entity must examine the endorsement credential of the TPM, the conformance credentials relevant to the TP, and the platform to be certified.

Since a TPM can be uniquely identified by the public key from its endorsement key pair, this key pair is not routinely used by a platform, helping to ensure that the activities of a TP cannot be tracked. Instead, an arbitrary number of pseudonyms in the form of *Attestation Identity Key* (AIK) key pairs (see figure 3) can be generated by a TPM and associated with a TP. This can be achieved using a special type of third party known as a *Privacy-Certification Authority* (P-CA). A P-CA associates AIK public keys with TPs by signing certificates known as *AIK credentials*.

When a platform requests an AIK credential from a P-CA, it must supply the three types of TP credential listed above, as issued at the time of manufacture. The P-CA verifies the TP credentials, thereby obtaining assurance that the TP is genuine, and then creates (signs) an AIK credential binding the AIK public key to a generic description of the TP; note that this generic description should capture enough information for a verifier of the credential to have assurance in the trustworthiness of the platform, but not enough information to uniquely identify it. A highlevel description of a TPM endorsement credential, a platform credential, an AIK credential and their relationship is shown in figure 4.

The AIK private key is then used by the TPM during platform attestation. Note that the fact that a platform can generate arbitrary numbers of AIKs (and obtain associated credentials) enables a platform to obtain and use unlinkable pseudonyms, i.e. so that attestations to different third parties (or even to the same party) can be made unlinkable.

Platform Attestation: As stated above, platform attestation is a process by which a platform makes a verifiable claim about its current state, as captured by the current contents of its PCRs. The process starts with the *challenger*, i.e. the party wishing to have assurance about the current platform state, sending a nonce to the platform. The platform then uses one of its AIK private keys to sign this nonce together with integrity metrics reflecting the current state of the platform.

This signed string is returned to the challenger, along with the record of the platform components which are reflected in the integrity metrics ((a portion of) the SML), together with the appropriate AIK credential. The challenger then uses this information to determine whether it is:

- safe to trust the TP from which the statement has originated by verifying the TPM's signature and the AIK credential;
- safe to trust (all or part of) the software environment running on the platform; this is achieved by validating the integrity metrics received from the TP using 'trustworthy' software integrity measurements attested to by trusted third parties such as software vendors.

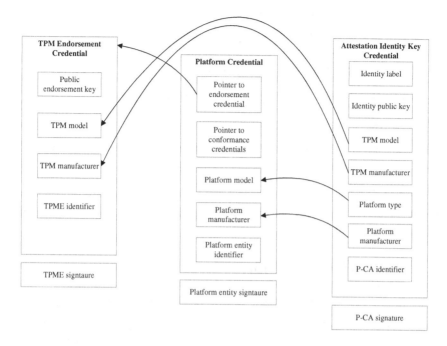

Fig. 4. TP credentials [62]

Anonymity Issues: The above approach has attracted a certain amount of criticism, since it puts the P-CA in a powerful position. That is, because the P-CA generates the AIK credentials, and it also sees all the platform credentials when it does so, a P-CA can link together all the pseudonyms of a particular platform, and hence breach anonymity for that platform.

As a result, v1.2 of the TCG specifications incorporates a new system that allows for trusted platform anonymity/pseudonymity without replying on a third party to keep links between pseudonyms secret. That is, it incorporates a means for an entity to obtain AIK credentials without revealing its 'identity' to the third party generating these credentials. This new technique, known as *Direct Anonymous Attestation* (DAA), is due to Brickell, Camenisch and Chen [63,64,65].

DAA essentially divided the process of obtaining AIK credentials into two phases. In the first phase, a platform obtains a DAA signature from a third party, to which it shows all its credentials. This DAA signature is then used to obtain AIK credentials, in such a way that the issuer of the credentials does not actually get to see the DAA signature, but just receives evidence that the platform possesses such an object. In this way, even the entity which generates the DAA signature cannot link together two or more AIK public keys belonging to the same platform.

Whilst we do not describe the process here (it is, in fact, highly complex) it is important to note that it also possesses a number of other interesting properties. For example, the scheme can be used in such a way that the degree of unlinkability is 'tunable'; this allows the possibility of blacklisting (revoking) credentials for platforms which have been compromised.

6.4   Isolated Execution Environments

An isolated execution environment, independent of how it is implemented, should provide the following services to hosted software [22]:

- protection of the software from external interference;
- observation of the computations and data of a program running within an isolated environment only via controlled inter-process communication;
- secure communication between programs running in independent execution environments; and
- a trusted channel between an input/output device and a program running in an isolated environment.

7   Trusted Mobile Platforms

7.1   The Development of Trusted Mobile Platforms

Whilst trusted computing technology is already becoming commonplace in new PCs, at least as far as the inclusion of TPMs is concerned, the situation is not so advanced for other types of platform. In particular, whilst many potential applications for the technology can be identified for mobile devices (e.g. PDAs, smart phones, etc.), the inclusion of TPMs in such platforms has yet to occur.

Indeed, for a variety of reasons, including cost and complexity, it would appear that trusted computing technology may be implemented in rather different ways in mobile devices. In particular, it would appear that such devices may not include an identifiable separate TPM, but instead the functionality of the TPM could be implemented using a combination of trusted hardware functionality built into a mobile platform and software. How this might be achieved will probably vary widely from manufacturer to manufacturer.

The functionality that must be provided by such a device is in the process of being standardised. This is the role of the TCG Mobile Phone Working Group (MPWG), discussed immediately below.

7.2   The MPWG Activity

The TCG has always had the mission of providing specifications for any type of device that connects to a network. However, the initial standardisation work centred around the specification of the TPM and a standard set of APIs which provide an abstraction of the TPM to software developers/vendors. More recently, the baseline TCG specification set has been expanded by platform-specific working groups to include specifications describing specific platform implementations for PC clients, servers, peripherals and storage systems.

One such working group is the TCG MPWG, the main challenge for which is to determine the 'roots of trust', see section 5, required within a trusted mobile phone. In order to identify the capabilities required of a trusted mobile phone, a number of use cases, whose secure implementation may be aided by the application of trusted platform functionality, have been identified by the MPWG. Among these use cases are SIMLock, device authentication, mobile ticketing, mobile payment and robust DRM implementation [66]. As stated by the MPWG [66], the use cases lay a foundation for the ways in which:

- the MPWG derives requirements that address situations described in the use cases;
- the MPWG specifies an architecture based on the TCG architecture that meet these requirements; and
- the MPWG specifies the functions and interfaces that meet the requirements in the specified architecture.

The MPWG has recently published the TCG Mobile Trusted Module (MTM) Specification [67]. It is assumed that a mobile platform will typically contain multiple MTMs to support multiple mobile device stakeholders. It is envisaged that each MTM will provide a subset of the TPM v1.2 functionality. Some MTMs may also contain additional functionality to ensure that parts of the device boot into a preset state (i.e. secure boot functionality) [68]. More specifically, two types of MTM have been defined.

A *Mobile Local-owner Trusted Module (MLTM)* supports uses (or a subset of uses) similar to those of existing v1.2 TPMs (controlled by an entity with physical access to the platform). Some TPM v1.2 functionality may not be supported because of the restrictions inherent in today's phone technologies [68]. The use cases described by the TCG in [66] have been analysed, along the lines of the analyses given in [69], in order to determine the subset of functionality required within a MTM to enable their secure implementation.

A *Mobile Remote-owner Trusted Module (MLTM)* also supports a subset of uses similar to those of existing v1.2 TPMs. It moreover enables a remote entity (such as the device manufacturer or network operator) to predetermine the state into which some parts of the phone must boot [68].

7.3 Applications

The applications for trusted mobile phones discussed in the current TCG MPWG use case document cover:

- the protection of downloaded content and software;
- the protection of user data and identity information, and device identity information; and
- enabling mobile payment and mobile ticketing.

In this article we focus on three specific use-cases, namely OMA DRM and software download, which involve the protection of downloaded data, and SIMLock, which requires the protection of device identity information. These use cases have been chosen because of their commercial and scientific interest.

In the following sections these three use cases are presented. Also given is an analysis of the trusted computing functionality required of a mobile platform in order to support a secure and robust implementation of each use case.

8   A Robust Implementation of OMA DRM v2

8.1   Use Case Description

DRM: Current 3G systems are already capable of delivering a wide range of digital content to subscribers' mobile telephones, including music, video clips, ring tones, screen savers or java games. As network access becomes ever more ubiquitous and media objects become more easily accessible, providers are exposed to increased risks of illegal consumption and use of their content. DRM facilitates the safe distribution of various forms of digital content in a wide range of computing environments, and gives assurance to the content providers that their media objects cannot be illegally accessed.

A Digital Rights Management system is an umbrella term for mechanisms used to manage the life cycle of digital content of any sort. A DRM agent, i.e. the DRM functionality of a device responsible for enforcing permissions and constraints associated with protected content, must be trusted with respect to its correct behaviour and secure implementation [70]. Stipulation of a trust model, within which robustness rules are defined, is one method of specifying how secure a device implementation of a DRM agent must be, and what actions should be taken against a manufacturer that builds devices that are insufficiently robust [71].

The OMA: The OMA was founded in June 2002. One of the original objectives of the OMA was to define a DRM specification set for use in a mobile environment. OMA DRM v1 was published as a candidate specification in October 2002, and was approved as an OMA enabler specification in 2004 [72], after full interoperability testing had been completed.

Following this, OMA DRM v2 was published as a candidate specification in July 2004 [73]. OMA DRM v2 builds upon the version 1 specifications to provide higher security and a more extensive feature set [71]. Devices other than mobile phones are also supported by OMA DRM v2. The OMA DRM version 2 specification set defines [70]:

- the format and the protection mechanism for protected content;
- the format and the protection mechanism for rights objects;
- the security model for the management of encryption keys; and
- how protected content and rights objects may be transferred to devices using a range of transport mechanisms.

OMA DRM Functional Architecture: The model under consideration is taken from [70] and is summarised in figure 5. A user requests a media object from a content issuer. The requested content, which is packaged in order to prevent unauthorised access, is then sent to the user's device. The packaging of

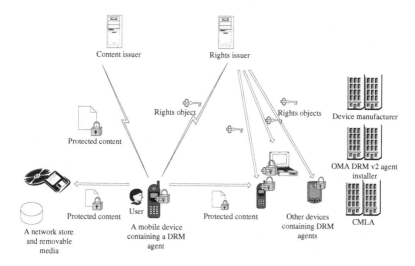

Fig. 5. OMA DRM system model

the content may either be completed by the content issuer or by the content owner, before it is dispatched to the content issuer. The rights object associated with the requested media object is delivered to the user by the rights issuer. In practice, this rights issuer may be the same entity as the content issuer.

OMA DRM v1: Version 1 of the OMA specifications [74,75] represents the OMA's initial attempt to define a DRM solution for a mobile environment. Three main goals were specified for OMA DRM v1 [71]. The solution was required to be timely and inexpensive to deploy. It was also required to be easy to implement on mass market mobile devices. Finally, it was required that the initial OMA DRM solution did not necessitate the roll-out of a costly infrastructure. In the development of OMA DRM v1 a trade-off was made, so that the objectives listed above could be met at the expense of certain security requirements.

Three classes of DRM functionality are specified in OMA DRM v1 [74,75]. The first class of DRM functionality, forward lock, must be supported by an OMA DRM v1 agent on a device. Provision of combined delivery and separate delivery, the second and third classes of DRM functionality, is optional.

1. *Forward lock* prevents unencrypted content being forwarded from the device to which it was initially delivered. The protected content is wrapped inside a DRM message, which indicates to the OMA DRM v1 agent on the receiving device that the content is not to be forwarded. Protection is dependent on the OMA DRM v1 agent acting accordingly.
2. *Combined delivery* involves sending unencrypted content and its associated rights object together within a DRM message.
3. *Separate delivery* involves sending encrypted content and the associated rights object separately. The content is encrypted and sent in a format

known as the DRM Container Format (DCF). Headers, which allow a receiving device to associate the correct rights object with the corresponding DCF object, are also contained in the transmitted file. The associated rights object, which contains the relevant permissions and constraints, and the decryption key for the associated content, is delivered via SMS.

OMA DRM v2: OMA DRM v2 [70,76] builds upon the OMA DRM v1 specifications, with the primary objective of providing a more secure DRM solution. The following security vulnerabilities have been identified in OMA DRM v1 [71].

1. A rights issuer has no way of determining whether the requesting device supports DRM. When using the forward lock and combined delivery features, where the content is not encrypted, this particular security vulnerability enables an attack in which unencrypted content is initially sent to a PC made to look like a compliant phone. On receipt, content is then extracted and illegally distributed.
2. In the separate delivery DRM class, where the content is encrypted, the content encrypting key is not protected. This implies that the attack described above in step 1 is also possible in this case, although it is more complex and more difficult to complete successfully [71].
3. The device has no way of authenticating the rights issuer, and therefore may be sent bogus rights objects from an entity claiming to be the legitimate rights issuer.

OMA DRM v2 addresses the above security weaknesses by using additional security mechanisms.

- Both device authentication and rights issuer authentication are provided.
- Mechanisms are deployed in order to protect the confidentiality of media objects. Content is protected using a Content Encrypting Key (CEK). This CEK is sent in a rights object encrypted using a Rights Object Encrypting Key (REK). The REK itself is sent encrypted using the public key of the device or a pre-established domain key.
- Mechanisms are also deployed so that the OMA DRM v2 agent can determine whether a media object received from a Rights Issuer (RI) has been modified in an unauthorised way.

The OMA DRM v2 specifications are no longer mobile device specific, as was the case with the v1 specifications. It also provides a richer feature set which includes, most notably, support for [71]:

- the automatic preview of protected content;
- subscription services;
- continuous media such as streaming and progressive download of content;
- reward schemes;
- domains, i.e. collections of devices belonging to a single user. A domain can be established by a user. When a device joins a domain, the RI sends

a domain key to the device, encrypted using the device's OMA DRM v2 public key. Following this, content and the associated access rights may be shared among the devices in the domain. Rights objects must be explicitly acquired for the domain rather than a specific device. A RI may control the number of devices allowed in a domain, although the user is entitled to add and remove devices at will, as long as the limit set by the RI is adhered to.
- unconnected devices, i.e. devices not network connected. This feature is supported by the implementation of domains. An unconnected device may be added to a domain, after which content and rights may be copied from a connected domain device to the unconnected device.

In order to support the additional security mechanisms, and, indeed, the expanded feature set described above, a dedicated suite of DRM security protocols, the Rights Object Acquisition Protocol (ROAP) suite, was developed by the OMA. In addition to the ROAP suite, it was agreed that the OMA DRM v2 specification set should be supported by a 'trust model'. Such a trust model enables an RI to obtain assurances about DRM agent behaviour, and the robustness of the DRM agent implementation [70]. It is the responsibility of the Content Management Licensing Administrator for Digital Rights Management (CMLA DRM), or a similar organisation, to provide a trust model, i.e. robustness rules, and to define actions which may be taken against a manufacturer who builds devices which are not sufficiently robust.

The OMA DRM v2 Security-Critical Data: In order to use the ROAP suite, OMA DRM agents must be equipped with the necessary security-critical data.

Every OMA DRM v2 agent is assigned a unique key pair [70]. The private key from this key pair is used by an OMA DRM v2 agent to generate digital signatures, so that a rights issuer can authenticate a particular DRM agent. The public key from this pair is used by rights issuers in order to distribute rights object encryption keys, which are used to protect content encryption keys, that are themselves used to encrypt content.

A certificate, which identifies the DRM agent and binds the agent to the public key described above, is also provided to the DRM agent. The OMA DRM v2 certificate can be specified as part of one or more certificate chains. If so, the OMA DRM v2 certificate comes first in a chain, and each subsequent certificate contains the public key necessary to verify the certificate preceding it [73]. When the rights issuer with whom the OMA DRM v2 agent is communicating, indicates its preferred trust anchor(s), i.e. its trusted root CA(s), the OMA DRM v2 agent must select and send back a device certificate (chain) which points to an appropriate anchor [73], so that the RI can verify the OMA DRM v2 agent certificate.

The *device details* indicate the device manufacturer, model, and version number. Finally, the *trusted RI authorities certificate* is used to indicate which rights issuer trust anchor(s) are recognised by the OMA DRM v2 agent. This trusted RI authorities certificate may either be a single root certificate, as is the case in the CMLA trust model [77] where the trusted RI authorities certificate is a self-signed CMLA root CA certificate, or a collection of self-signed public key certificates representing the preferred trust anchors of the OMA DRM v2 agent.

The ROAP Suite: This dedicated suite of DRM security protocols was developed by the OMA to enhance the security of the DRM process and the functionality of the OMA DRM agent. The ROAP suite consists of five protocols.

The *4-pass registration protocol* is defined by the OMA as a "complete security information exchange and handshake between the RI and a DRM agent in a device" [76]. The protocol enables the negotiation of protocol parameters including protocol version, cryptographic algorithms, certificate preferences, optional exchange of certificates, mutual authentication of the mobile device and RI, integrity protection of protocol messages, and optional device DRM time synchronisation [76]. In this protocol, two messages are sent from the device to the RI, namely the device hello and the registration request, and two messages are sent from the RI to the device, namely the RI hello and the registration response. There are three occasions when the 4-pass registration protocol can be used [76]:

- on first contact between the RI and a mobile device;
- when security information needs to be updated; and
- when the device time source is deemed to be inaccurate by the RI.

On receipt of the registration request message, and before the registration response message is sent, the RI may optionally perform a nonce-based OCSP request for its own certificate, using the device nonce sent in the registration request message [76]. An OCSP request may also be performed if the RI deems the device DRM time source to be inaccurate, or if the device is an unconnected device which does not support DRM time [76]. The device nonce is used to cryptographically bind an OCSP response to the corresponding OCSP request, to prevent replay attacks [78].

The *2-pass* and *1-pass rights acquisition protocols* allow a device to request and acquire a rights object from a RI.

The *2-pass join domain* and *leave domain protocols* are used to manage domains. Once a domain has been established by a user, and after devices have been added to the established domain, protected content and associated rights objects, which have been explicitly created for domain use, may be copied and moved between domain devices. Therefore, rather than requesting a separate rights object for each individual device, only one domain RO need be requested.

8.2   The Robustness Rules

In order to comply with the definition of a 'robust OMA DRM v2 implementation', as defined by the CMLA [77], a number of requirements must be met, as summarised below.

It is required that "an OMA DRM v2 agent can perform self-checking of the integrity of its component parts so that unauthorised modifications will be expected to result in a failure of the implementation to provide the authorised authentication and/or decryption function" [77].

A robust implementation of OMA DRM v2 must confidentiality-protect the OMA DRM v2 agent private key when loaded into and while stored and used on the device.

The OMA DRM v2 agent private key and OMA DRM v2 security critical data such as the OMA DRM v2 agent certificate (chains), the device details and the trusted RI authorities certificate, must be integrity-protected when loaded into, while stored on, and while in use on the device. While it is not necessary to integrity-protect the OMA DRM v2 agent certificate or the OMA DRM v2 agent certificate (chain), as any unauthorised modification will be detected when the certificate(chain)(s) are verified, the trusted authorities certificate, which is defined in the CMLA trust model as a self-signed CMLA root CA certificate, needs to be integrity-protected.

Domain context information, communicated by a rights issuer to a mobile device during a 2-pass join domain protocol, must also be protected:

- the domain ID, the expiry time of the domain context and the rights issuer's public key must be integrity-protected while stored and used on the device; and
- the domain key, used to protect domain rights objects, must be confidentiality and integrity-protected while in storage and in use on the device.

Rights issuer context information, established during the 4-pass registration protocol, such as protocol parameters, protocol version, RI certificate preferences, agreed RI identification information, RI certificate information and the context expiry time, must also be integrity-protected.

The secret keys used to protect the integrity and confidentiality of rights objects must be confidentiality and integrity-protected while in storage and in use on the device.

All of the elements mentioned above should only be accessible by authorised entities, namely the correctly functioning OMA DRM v2 agent.

A robust OMA DRM v2 implementation must incorporate a DRM time source synchronisation mechanism which is reasonably accurate and resistant to malicious modifications by the end user.

Finally, nonces generated on the OMA DRM v2 device and used in the 4-pass registration protocol, the 2-pass RO acquisition protocol or the join domain protocol must be both non-repeating and unpredictable in order to mitigate the threats of both replay and preplay attacks against the protocol suite.

8.3   A Robust Implementation of OMA DRM Using Trusted Computing

In this section, we consider how trusted computing functionality can be used to help meet the requirements in the CMLA client adopter agreement [77] and summarised in section 8.2, thereby enabling a robust implementation of OMA DRM v2.

While TC functionality cannot guarantee the integrity of the OMA DRM v2 agent while it is being stored, TC mechanisms can be used to help detect malicious or accidental modifications or removal. Secure boot functionality can be used to ensure that a set of security-critical platform components boot into a predetermined state. Secure boot is not currently enabled by the TCG TPM main specifications. However, much work on secure boot has been conducted independently of the TCG, including by Tygar and Yee [51], Clark [52], Arbaugh, Farber and Smith [50] and Itoi et al. [54]. Each of these papers describe a similar process, in which the integrity of a pre-defined set of system components is measured, as described in section 4.2, and these measurements are then compared against a set of expected measurements which must be securely stored and accessed by the platform during the boot process. If, at any stage during the boot process, the removal or modification of a platform component, such as the OMA DRM v2 agent, is detected, the boot process is aborted. While a secure boot process is not specified in the TPM specification set, the TCG mobile phone working group has recently released a specification for a Mobile TPM which enables a secure boot process [67].

Security-critical data associated with the OMA DRM v2 agent, such as the device details and the trusted RI authorities certificate, which require integrity protection while in storage, can also be verified as part of a secure boot process.

Alternatively, sealed storage functionality may be used in order to detect the malicious or accidental modification or removal of the OMA DRM v2 agent while in storage, and, indeed, to store data which needs to be confidentiality and/or integrity-protected. It can also ensure that sensitive data is only accessible by authorised entities when the mobile device is in a predefined state, for example, when a legitimate OMA DRM v2 agent is executing in an isolated execution environment.

The security-critical data and any domain and RI context information to be protected is first associated with a 'digest at creation' and a 'digest at release', and then encrypted by the TPM, as described in section 6.2. While integrity-protection is not explicitly provided by the TPM, 20 bytes of authorisation data can be associated with the data to be sealed prior to its encryption, as described in section 6.2, thereby ensuring that the data is integrity-protected while in storage. The sealed data is asymmetrically encrypted and the corresponding private decryption key is securely stored within the TPM, thereby ensuring that the data is confidentiality-protected while in storage. The inclusion of the 20 bytes of authorisation data and the digest at release with the sealed data prior to encryption ensures that only an authorised entity can access the data, and that access can only take place when the platform is in the required software state. Finally, sealing the data to a specified platform configuration also ensures that any unauthorised modification and/or removal of security-critical software (e.g. the OMA DRM v2 agent) reflected in the digest at release will be detected, and access to the sealed data denied.

Rather than using the TPM merely to confidentiality and integrity-protect the OMA DRM v2 private key, the TPM can also be used to generate the required

OMA DRM v2 agent asymmetric key pair as well as to protect the private key while in storage and in use on the device.

TC functionality also enables the isolation of security-critical software and data in a secure execution environment so that it cannot be observed and/or modified in an unauthorised manner by software executing in parallel execution environments.

A good quality random number generator is provided by a TPM, enabling the generation of non-repeating unpredictable nonces for use in the ROAP suite protocols, thereby mitigating replay and preplay attacks. The TPM may also be used to provide accurate time source synchronisation, as described in [15].

9 SIMLock

9.1 Use Case Description

Mobile device personalisation, or SIMLocking, is the process by which the device can be constrained to operate only with certain (U)SIMs. In earlier discussions of the GSM and DCS1800 technical specifications, the fundamental property of SIM mobility was praised as highly advantageous [79]. Over the years, however, the disadvantages associated with SIM mobility have also become apparent. Phone operators, for example, who subsidise the cost of mobile equipment, with the intention of recovering this initial loss from future profits from network or service subscriptions, may suffer a loss if mobile device users can, without authorisation from their current operator, move their phone to another network before the original subscription contract has been upheld. SIM mobility may also encourage handset theft for re-use or re-sale. These issues have led to the need for SIMLock functionality.

SIMLock has five personalisation categories:

- *Network*, where a network operator personalises a mobile device so that it can only be used with (U)SIMs from that particular network operator;
- *Network subset*, where a network operator personalises a mobile device so that it can only be used with a subset of (U)SIMs from that particular network operator;
- *Service provider*, where a service provider personalises a mobile device so that it can only be used with (U)SIMs from that particular service provider;
- *Corporate*, where a corporate customer personalises an employee's or customer's mobile device so that it can only be used with (U)SIMs belonging to that particular company; and
- *SIM/USIM*, where an end user personalises a mobile device so that it can only be used with a particular (U)SIM.

SIMLock Security-Critical Data: A personalisation indicator and a personalisation code or code group are associated with each personalisation category.

- A personalisation indicator is used to show whether a particular personalisation category is active (set to 'on') or deactivated (set to 'off'). Each

category has an independent personalisation indicator. If an indicator is active it shows that the SIM has been locked to a network(s), network subset(s), service provider(s), corporate entity/entities or SIM/(U)SIM(s).
- A personalisation code or code group is used to personalise a device to a particular entity. An independent personalisation code or code group is defined for each category — see [80].

SIMLock-Related Processes: In order to personalise a device the required personalisation code or code group must be entered into the device and the appropriate personalisation indicator set to 'on'. The relevant control key, used for device de-personalisation, must be also be stored within the device.

When a (U)SIM is inserted into the device, or when the device is powered on, the mobile device checks which personalisation indicators are set to 'on'. The personalisation agent reads the (U)SIM, and extracts the required code(s)/code group(s). The code(s)/code group(s) are then verified against the list of values stored on the mobile device. The mobile device then responds accordingly, displaying a message of success or failure to the device user. Should this checking process fail, the device enters 'limited service state' in which only emergency calls can be made [80]. This process is shown in figure 6.

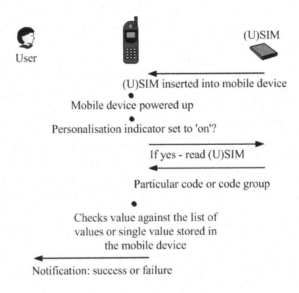

Fig. 6. SIMLock

In order to de-personalise a device, the control key for the particular personalisation category must first be entered into the device. This is then compared against the control key stored by the device. If the entered control key matches the stored value, then the personalisation indicator for the category in question is set to 'off'.

9.2   Threat Analysis

The fundamental threats to the SIMLock process include the following:

- Unauthorised modification or removal of the device personalisation agent software while in storage on or while executing on the device.
- Unauthorised reading/copying of a control key while in storage or in use on the device.
- Unauthorised modification or deletion of a personalisation code/code group, control key or personalisation indicator while in storage or in use on the device.

9.3   Secure SIMLock Using Trusted Computing

The unauthorised modification or removal of the device personalisation agent cannot be prevented using trusted computing technology. However, while the software is in storage, secure boot functionality can be deployed so that, at start-up, a measurement of the device personalisation agent software is verified against an expected value. This enables any unauthorised modification and/or removal to be detected. That security critical data requiring integrity protection, such as network, network subset, corporate and service provider codes or code groups and indicators, can also be incorporated into the secure boot process. TC isolation mechanisms can be used to ensure the integrity of the personalisation agent, and that any security-critical data is protected while in use on the device.

Alternatively, personalisation code/code groups, personalisation indicators and control keys could simply be sealed to an isolated execution environment which hosts a device personalisation agent. In this way, security-critical data can be both integrity and confidentiality-protected while in storage. If the personalisation agent, and/or the supporting environment to which the data is sealed, is modified, then the security-critical data will be inaccessible. While sealing ensures that data is released into a predefined execution environment, isolation technologies are necessary to ensure that both the device personalisation agent and the security related data remain confidentiality and integrity-protected while in use on the platform.

10   Software Download

10.1   Use Case Description

Two distinct types of software can be downloaded to a mobile device, namely *application software* (e.g. games) and *core software* (e.g. operating system software/updates/patches) [81]. For the purpose of this use case, we will focus on the secure download of core software, including updates or patches to the device's native OS, such as DRM agents or browsers, or firmware updates or patches. Core software download enables efficient device management, and can also be used to support applications such as Software Defined Radio (SDR) and Digital Video Broadcast (DVB) in a mobile environment.

Device Management: Core software not only enhances device management, but can also be used to enhance the end user experience. As devices become more complex, it is increasingly likely that they have to be recalled because of core software bugs [82]. The ability to download core software, however, enables more efficient bug fixing. It is also desirable that users are able to upgrade core software on their devices, e.g. to give added functionality or enhanced security or performance [82]. As devices become more open, it is also likely that users will wish to extend the capabilities of their devices through the addition of new software, including, for example, device drivers.

SDR: A *software defined radio* is a communications device "whose operational modes and parameters can be changed or augmented, post manufacturing via software" [83]. This implies that the device can be reconfigured to communicate using multiple frequency bands and protocols, or upgraded in a low cost and efficient manner. Software defined radio is an important innovation for the communications industry, providing many advantages over purely hardware-based wireless networking infrastructures and terminals. Importantly, cost reductions may result from the deployment of a generic hardware platform which can be customised using software [81]. The value of terminals is increased as public/private sector radio system sharing becomes possible, and as terminals can be upgraded to comply with evolving communications standards.

SDR also enables operation and maintenance cost reductions, as bugs can be fixed by software download rather than terminal recall. Re-configurable radios can also be adapted to meet evolving user and/or operator preferences. A terminal can moreover be reconfigured to efficiently cope with changing network conditions such as utilization, interference or radio channel quality, thereby offering an enhanced user experience [82]. Efficient roaming is also enabled, as air interface and frequency bands can be reconfigured as required.

However, while there are many advantages associated with the introduction of SDR terminals, there are also some significant security and safety issues. If SDR is to be accepted, then the security threats introduced by reconfigurable terminals and core software download must be analysed, and measures taken to mitigate these threats.

DVB: It is expected that the next generation of mobile communications systems will be able to interwork with broadcast networks to provide wireless access to video content from a wide range of mobile devices [84]. For a service like this to achieve its full commercial potential, the owners of the content will require assurance that their material is not illegally accessed. Current broadcast systems accomplish this by using conditional access systems to ensure that only bona fide subscribers have access to the content. The DVB organisation has developed several standards defining a common interface to conditional access systems at both the transmission site and at the receiver, while allowing the systems themselves to remain proprietary [85,86,87].

Services broadcast today are protected by a range of proprietary access control systems. The DVB common interface solution requires receiving devices to have a pc-card interface and the user to possess a number of modules, each of which implements a different conditional access system. The cost of adding such an interface to a small mobile device, as well as the practical design issues, could make this an infeasible solution for the mobile environment. The cost of the modules may also deter some subscribers. The alternative solution, Simulcrypt, involves broadcasting each service under the control of as many conditional access systems as possible; this is likely to prove prohibitively complex and expensive for many broadcasters, especially small 'niche' providers. Both current solutions therefore have potential difficulties when applied in a mobile environment, which is likely to significantly restrict the content available to mobile receivers.

In order to overcome these limitations, the mobile platform could be reconfigured to be compatible with the appropriate conditional access system, if the proprietary system is implemented entirely in software. Such software could be delivered to the mobile device on demand. Of course, such a solution presents major security challenges.

Core Software Download — State of the Art: The model under consideration is illustrated in figure 7, and involves three parties: the user, a mobile device, and the software provider.

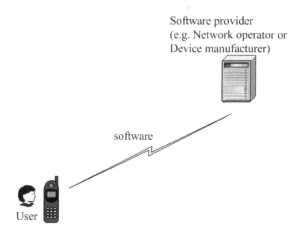

Fig. 7. Core software download model

Core software download, as defined by the OMA Device Management Working Group (DMWG) [82], consists of five stages, as shown in figure 8.

1. *Core software download initiation.* The software download process may be either network initiated or user initiated. The software provider may initiate a data connection with a device in order to:
   - request an inventory of the core software installed on the device so that the necessary software can be updated/patched/installed; or
   - inform the user of available upgrades and/or additional core software.

Alternatively, a user may initiate a data connection with a software provider in order to request additional software over the default configuration. This initiation results in an open data connection between the device and the software provider.

2. *Device information exchange* enables a device to inform the software provider about its current configuration. In this way the software provider can ensure that the appropriate software/updates/patches are delivered to the device. This exchange may require user authorisation.

3. *Core software download* is the process by which the core software is downloaded from the software provider to the mobile device.

4. *Core software installation* is the method by which the software download is processed on the device.

5. Finally, the software provider and/or the end user may be notified of the result of the download.

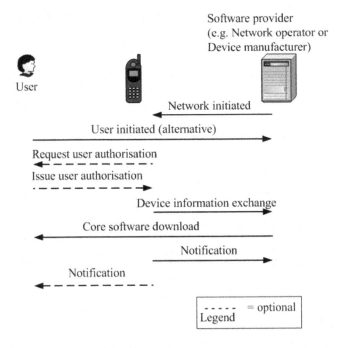

Fig. 8. Core software download

Two mechanisms have been proposed to secure non-application software download. We now briefly review these two approaches.

Firstly, the software provider could digitally sign the core software before it is downloaded to the device, thereby providing software origin authentication and software integrity protection (so that any unauthorised modification to, or addition of, incoming software can be detected by the mobile device) [81]. On receipt of the software, the digital signature of the software provider must be verified by the mobile device. Depending on the outcome of this check and the policy of the mobile device, the software is either executed or discarded. This approach, as described in [81], is, however, susceptible to a replay attack. The mobile device has no way to determine whether the incoming signed software is fresh. An attacker could therefore replay an older version of the software, which will then be installed on the device.

It has therefore been recommended [81] that, in order to mitigate the risk of a replay attack against downloaded software, either timestamps or nonces should used so that freshness of the software can be checked. Either the mobile device generates and transmits a nonce to the software provider, which is then concatenated with the download, digitally signed by the software provider, and returned to the mobile device, or the download is concatenated with a timestamp, digitally signed by the software provider, and delivered to the mobile device. On receipt of the software, the digital signature of the software provider and the freshness mechanism must be verified by the mobile device. Depending on the outcome of the checks and the policy of the mobile device, the software is then either executed/installed or discarded.

A second approach to securing non-application software download is the use of HTTPS, i.e. HTTP carried over one of the following protocols: Transport Layer Security 1.0 (TLS 1.0); Secure Sockets Layer v3 (SSL v3); or Wireless Transport Layer Security (WTLS).

SSL, TLS and WTLS involve two protocol layers. The *record protocol* takes messages to be transmitted, optionally compresses the data, computes a Message Authentication Code (MAC), encrypts, and then transmits the result [88]. Received data is decrypted, the MAC verified, decompressed and passed to higher level clients such as HTTP for processing. The record protocol has been designed to provide: software origin authentication; confidentiality and integrity protection; and freshness, so that the replay of messages can be detected by the mobile device.

The second layer of protocols, the *record protocol clients*, includes the *handshake protocol*, the *change cipher suite protocol* and the *alert protocol*. The handshake protocol enables a client and a server to authenticate each other and to negotiate the security parameters for a client/server session, i.e. an association between a client and a server [89]. Sessions are used so that the expensive process of security parameter negotiation does not have to be completed for each connection between the client and the server [89]. Security parameters include: a session identifier, peer certificate, compression method, cipher suite and a master secret. The cipher suite specifies the MAC and encryption algorithms which will be used to protect data transmitted in an SSL/TLS/WTLS record. The handshake protocol also enables the agreement of a pre-master secret which is used by both the client and the server in order to generate a master secret for an SSL/TLS/WTLS session. This shared master secret is in turn used by the client and the server in order to generate shared MAC and encryption keys for each

SSL/TLS/WTLS connection (i.e. a transient peer to peer relationship between a client and a server [89]).

The change cipher suite protocol consists of only one message. This message is sent either by the client or the server at the end of the handshake protocol to notify the other party that the newly negotiated ciphersuite and master secret will be utilised in the protection of all subsequent records. The alert protocol is used to convey alerts to the peer entity [89].

10.2 Threat Analysis

The threats which impact upon a reconfigurable mobile device can divided into:

- those which impinge on the security of the downloaded reconfiguration software; and
- those which impinge on host security.

The fundamental threat to the security of the downloaded reconfiguration software is unauthorised reading of software while in transit between the software provider and the end host, or while in storage or executing on the end host. This threat could result in an infringement of the intellectual property rights associated with the downloaded reconfiguration software. It might also result in unauthorised access to, and execution of, software.

Fundamental threats to end host security include:

- malicious or accidental modification or removal of security-critical software and data when incorporated into, while in storage on, or when executing on, the end host;
- the download of inappropriate reconfiguration software which does not meet the capability requirements of the mobile device; and
- malicious or accidental modification, addition or removal of downloaded software in development, in transit or while in storage or executing on the end host.

As a result of these threats, a device might be rendered inoperable (a denial of service attack), or user applications and/or data could be compromised by malicious software.

More specifically, in the case of SDR these threats could result in the following.

- An inoperable device. If, for example, a device used software modulation, an improper change of the modulation format could render it inoperable [90].
- Violation of Radio Frequency (RF) spectrum rights. This could, for example, result in RF interference. If a device can be programmed to transmit on a frequency for which it is not authorised, signals from nodes which are authorised to use this frequency might be jammed [90]. Also, spurious emissions resulting from unauthorised radio spectrum use could violate user safety [91].
- Increased output power. If, for example, a device operated at maximum power, its performance may be increased at the expense of other users in the communications network [90]. This in turn may force other users to

use increased power. As a result, the device battery life would be severely shortened; moreover, if the radiated power is sufficiently high, user safety may also be put at risk [91].

10.3 Secure Software Download Using Trusted Computing

We now investigate some of the ways in which trusted computing functionality can be used to address the threats outlined above or, failing that, to limit the level to which a threat may be exploited.

Protecting the Reconfiguration Software: TC mechanisms can be used to confidentiality-protect the reconfiguration software while in transit between the software provider and the end host, while in storage or executing on the end host, and to ensure that only the intended recipient device can access the software. For example, a software download protocol which exploits trusted computing functionality is described in [35,92]. This protocol builds upon sealed storage, platform attestation, and isolation techniques. This protocol is now summarised.

Before the required reconfiguration software can be downloaded to a TP, the TPM is used to generate an asymmetric key pair. This key pair is bound to a set of integrity metrics, so that the private key can only be used by the TPM on which it was generated, and only when the platform is in the specified state. The public key from this pair, and the integrity metrics with which its private key are associated, are then certified by the TPM using a TP AIK, as described in section 6.3, so that the state to which the private key is bound can be shown to the software provider. The certified public key and the corresponding AIK credential are then sent to the software provider.

On receipt of the certified key and the AIK credential, the software provider verifies the TP's AIK credential and the signature of the TPM on the public key and the associated integrity metrics. If these two elements can be verified, and if the software provider considers the platform software state to which the key is bound to be trustworthy, the provider computes a MAC on and encrypts the reconfiguration software, encrypts the secret MACing and encryption keys using the public key received from the TP, signs the encrypted keys using its private signature key, and transmits this data to the TP. The secret keys received by the TP, and therefore the reconfiguration software, can only be accessed when the TP is in the state deemed trustworthy by the software provider. The software provider may require that the integrity metrics to which the private key is bound, represent an isolated execution environment executing on a specified isolation layer, which is turn is supported by a TP which incorporates hardware extensions that enable efficient and secure isolation, as described in section 6.4.

The confidentiality of the reconfiguration software can thus be protected while it is in transit between the software provider and the TP, in storage, and executing on the device. The software provider is also given assurance that only a specified TP in a particular state can access the software.

Alternatively, if a more traditional mechanism such as SSL/TLS/WTLS is used in order to secure the download of the reconfiguration software, TC functionality can be used in order to 'harden' the SSL/TLS/WTLS implementation.

In this case, prior to the completion of any SSL/TLS/WTLS protocol, the TPM is used in order to generate the client-side (the mobile device) asymmetric key pair for authentication, which is bound to a set of integrity metrics so that the private key can only be utilised by the TPM on which it was generated, and only when the platform is in the required state. This key is then certified using a TP AIK. Evidence that this SSL/TLS/WTLS key pair has been generated on, and certified by, a TPM is then provided by a Certification Authority (CA) in an extension of the mobile device's X.509 SSL/TLS/WTLS certificate.

During an SSL/TLS/WTLS protocol run between a software provider and the mobile device, the information provided in the extension of the mobile device's X.509 SSL/TLS/WTLS public key certificate enables a software provider to trust that the mobile device's private SSL/TLS/WTLS key is held within a TPM, and that the key can only be used when the platform is in a particular state. As above, the software provider may require that the integrity metrics to which the private key is bound, represent an isolated execution environment into which the software will be downloaded and executed. This hardened implementation of SSL/TLS/WTLSS gives the software provider assurance that the mobile device's SSL/TLS/WTLS private key is stored securely and cannot been stolen. Evidence of the device's ability to provide an isolated execution environment for the downloaded software can also be demonstrated. This process is described in [93].

Protecting the Host's Security-Critical Software: While the integrity of security-critical software while in storage cannot be ensured using TC functionality, TC mechanisms can be used to help detect its malicious or accidental modification or removal, through the deployment of secure boot functionality. Security-critical data, such as device private keys, the public key certificate store and the core software download policy, can also be verified during a secure boot process.

Alternatively, sealed storage functionality can be used to ensure that security-critical data is stored in encrypted form and only accessible when the mobile platform is in a predefined state. As described above, the TPM can also be used to generate asymmetric key pairs, as well as protect any private keys while in storage and in use on the device.

TC functionality also enables the isolation of security-critical software and data in a secure execution environment so that it cannot be observed or modified when in use by software executing in parallel insecure execution environments.

Protecting the Host from Reconfiguration Software: A capability exchange could be performed by the network and the mobile device prior to software download, to ensure that the appropriate software entities and parameter sets are selected for a particular mobile device. The use of platform attestation, as described in section 6.3, could be used to ensure that the reports sent by the device are accurate.

TC cannot prevent denial of service attacks resulting from the removal/ deletion of the downloaded reconfiguration software, either in development, or in transit between the software provider and the host or in storage on the host. However, standard cryptographic mechanisms, such as digital signatures and/or MACs, can be used in combination with freshness mechanisms to mitigate these threats. TC functionality can be used to make such mechanisms more robust. A good quality random number generator is provided by a TPM, thereby enabling the generation of non-repeating unpredictable nonces which may then be sent to a software provider and returned from to a trusted mobile platform in conjunction with the requested software, thereby mitigating replay and preplay attacks against the exchange. If timestamps are used in order to guarantee the freshness of the downloaded software, the TPM could be used to provide an accurate and trusted time source, as described in [15].

In the advent of malicious or buggy software being downloaded to and executed on a device, there are a number of ways in which TC can lessen the impact of this threat. If the downloaded software is isolated in its own execution environment, as described in section 6.4, then any malicious behaviour can be controlled and its effects limited. If sealed storage is used to protect private user data (e.g., credit card numbers), then the impact of malicious software is lessened, as it cannot gain access to security sensitive data which has been protected. On connection/reconnection to a service provider, a trusted mobile platform could be required to attest to its state so that a decision can be made as to whether the device should be considered trusted for a particular purpose.

11   Conclusions

In this article we have reviewed the main functional components of a trusted platform. We have also considered why such functionality is necessary, and how the technology might be used. We have then considered possible applications of this technology to mobile devices, and have considered in detail three specific applications. In each case we have discussed how the security functionality necessary for the application could be supported using the trusted computing capabilities.

References

1. TCG: TCG Specification Architecture Overview. TCG Specification Version 1.2, The Trusted Computing Group (TCG), Portland, Oregon, USA (April 2003)
2. Grawrock, D.: The Intel Safer Computing Initiative. Intel Press, Oregon (2006)
3. Proudler, G.: Concepts of trusted computing. In: Mitchell, C.J. (ed.) Trusted Computing. IEE Professional Applications of Computing Series 6. The Institute of Electrical Engineers (IEE), London, UK, pp. 11–27 (April 2005)
4. Pearson, S. (ed.): Trusted Computing Platforms: TCPA Technology in Context. Prentice Hall, Upper Saddle River, New Jersey (2003)
5. Gollmann, D.: Computer Security, 2nd edn. John Wiley and Sons Ltd., Chichester (2005)

6. Pfleeger, C.P.: Security in Computing, 2nd edn. Prentice Hall PTR, Upper Saddle River, NJ (1997)
7. Department of Defense: DoD 5200.28-STD: Department of Defense Trusted Computer System Evaluation Criteria (1985)
8. IBM: PCI Cryptographic Processor: CCA Basic Services Reference and Guide, Release 2.41 (September 2003)
9. Dent, A.W., Mitchell, C.J.: User's Guide to Cryptography and Standards. Artech House, Boston, MA (2005)
10. Pearson, S.: Trusted computing platforms, the next security solution. Technical Report HPL-2002-221, Hewlett-Packard Laboratories (November 2002), Available at http://www.hpl.hp.com/techreports/
11. Varadharajan, V.: Trustworthy computing. In: Zhou, X., Su, S., Papazoglou, M.M.P., Orlowska, M.E., Jeffery, K.G. (eds.) WISE 2004. LNCS, vol. 3306, pp. 13–16. Springer, Heidelberg (2004)
12. Felten, E.W.: Understanding trusted computing: Will its benefits outweigh its drawbacks? IEEE Security & Privacy 1(3), 60–62 (2003)
13. Balacheff, B., Chen, L., Pearson, S., Proudler, G., Chan, D.: Computing platform security in cyberspace. Information Security Technical Report 5(1), 54–63 (2000)
14. Chen, L., Pearson, S., Proudler, G., Chan, D., Balacheff, B.: How can you trust a computing platform? In: Proceedings of Information Security Solutions Europe (ISSE 2000) (2000)
15. TCG: TPM Main, Part 1: Design Principles. TCG Specification Version 1.2 Revision 94, The Trusted Computing Group (TCG), Portland, Oregon, USA (March 2006)
16. TCG: TPM Main, Part 2: TPM Data Structures. TCG Specification Version 1.2 Revision 94, The Trusted Computing Group (TCG), Portland, Oregon, USA (March 2006)
17. TCG: TPM Main, Part 3: Commands. TCG Specification Version 1.2 Revision 94, The Trusted Computing Group (TCG), Portland, Oregon, USA (March 2006)
18. TCG: TCG Software Stack (TSS) Specification. TCG Specification Version 1.2 Level 1, The Trusted Computing Group (TCG), Portland, Oregon, USA (January 2006)
19. Chen, Y., England, P., Peinado, M., Willman, B.: High assurance computing on open hardware architectures. Microsoft Technical Report MSRTR–2003–20, Microsoft Corporation (March 2003)
20. England, P., Lampson, B., Manferdelli, J., Peinado, M., Willman, B.: A trusted open platform. IEEE Computer 36(7), 55–62 (2003)
21. Peinado, M., Chen, Y., England, P., Manferdelli, J.: NGSCB: A trusted open system. In: Wang, H., Pieprzyk, J., Varadharajan, V. (eds.) ACISP 2004. LNCS, vol. 3108, pp. 86–97. Springer, Heidelberg (2004)
22. Peinado, M., England, P., Chen, Y.: An overview of NGSCB. In: Mitchell, C.J. (ed.) Trusted Computing. IEE Professional Applications of Computing Series 6. The Institute of Electrical Engineers (IEE), London, UK, pp. 115–141 (April, 2005)
23. Garfinkel, T., Rosenblum, M., Boneh, D.: Flexible OS support and applications for trusted computing. In: Proceedings of the 9th USENIX Workshop on Hot Topics on Operating Systems (HotOS-IX), Kauai, Hawaii, USA, USENIX, The Advanced Computing Systems Association, pp. 145–150 (May 18-21, 2003)
24. Pfitzmann, B., Riordan, J., Stuble, C., Waidner, M., Weber, A.: The PERSEUS system architecture. Technical Report RZ 3335 (#93381), IBM Research Division, Zurich Laboratory (April 2001)

25. Sadeghi, A., Stuble, C.: Taming Trusted Platforms by operating system design. In: Chae, K., Yung, M. (eds.) Information Security Applications. LNCS, vol. 2908, Springer, Heidelberg (2004)

26. Kuhlmann, D., Landfermann, R., Ramasamy, H., Schunter, M., Ramunno, G., Vernizzi, D.: An open trusted computing architecture — secure virtual machines enabling user-defined policy enforcement (June 2006), www.opentc.net

27. Sadeghi, A.R., Stueble, C., Pohlmann, N.: European multilateral secure computing base — open trusted computing for you and me. White paper (2004)

28. Barham, P., Dragovic, B., Fraser, K., Hand, S., Harris, T., Ho, A., Neugebauery, R., Pratt, I., Warfield, A.: XEN and the art of virtualization. In: Proceedings of the 19th ACM Symposium on Operating Systems Principles (SOSP 2003), Bolton Landing, New York, USA, October 19-22, 2003, pp. 164–177. ACM Press, New York (2003)

29. Intel: LaGrande technology architectural overview. Technical Report 252491-001, Intel Corporation (September 2003)

30. Balacheff, B., Chen, L., Plaquin, D., Proudler, G.: A trusted process to digitally sign a document. In: Raskin, V., Hempelmann, C.F. (eds.) Proceedings of the 2001 New Security Paradigms Workshop, pp. 79–86. ACM Press, New York (2001)

31. Spalka, A., Cremers, A.B., Langweg, H.: Protecting the creation of digital signatures with trusted computing platform technology against attacks by Trojan Horse programs. In: Dupuy, M., Paradinas, P. (eds.) Trusted Information: The New Decade Challenge, IFIP TC11 Sixteenth Annual Working Conference on Information Security (IFIP/Sec'01). IFIP Conference Proceedings, Paris, France, June 11-13, 2001, vol. 193, pp. 403–419. Kluwer Academic Publishers, Boston (2001)

32. Schechter, S.E., Greenstadt, R.A., Smith, M.D.: Trusted computing, peer-to-peer distribution, and the economics of pirated entertainment. In: Proceedings of The Second Annual Workshop on Economics and Information Security (2003) College Park, Maryland (May 29-30, 2003)

33. Kinateder, M., Pearson, S.: A privacy-enhanced peer-to-peer reputation system. In: Bauknecht, K., Min Tjoa, A., Quirchmayr, G. (eds.) E-Commerce and Web Technologies. LNCS, vol. 2738, pp. 206–216. Springer, Heidelberg (2003)

34. Balfe, S., Lakhani, A.D., Paterson, K.G.: Securing peer-to-peer networks using trusted computing. In: Mitchell, C.J. (ed.) Trusted Computing. The Institute of Electrical Engineers (IEE), London, UK, pp. 271–298 (2005)

35. Gallery, E., Tomlinson, A.: Secure delivery of conditional access applications to mobile receivers. In: Mitchell, C.J. (ed.) Trusted Computing. IEE Professional Applications of Computing Series 6. The Institute of Electrical Engineers (IEE), London, UK, pp. 195–238 (2005)

36. Pashalidis, A., Mitchell, C.J.: Single sign-on using trusted platforms. In: Boyd, C., Mao, W. (eds.) ISC 2003. LNCS, vol. 2851, pp. 54–68. Springer, Heidelberg (2003)

37. Chen, L., Pearson, S., Vamvakas, A.: On enhancing biometric authentication with data protection. In: Howlett, R.J., Jain, L.C. (eds.) Proceedings of the Fourth International Conference on Knowledge-Based Intelligent Engineering Systems and Allied Technologies, vol. 1, pp. 249–252. IEEE, Los Alamitos (2000)

38. Mont, M.C., Pearson, S., Bramhall, P.: Towards accountable management of identity and privacy: Sticky policies and enforceable tracing services. In: DEXA 2003, pp. 377–382. IEEE Computer Society, Los Alamitos (2003)

39. Mont, M.C., Pearson, S., Bramhall, P.: Towards accountable management of privacy and identity information. In: Snekkenes, E., Gollmann, D. (eds.) ESORICS 2003. LNCS, vol. 2808, pp. 146–161. Springer, Heidelberg (2003)

40. Pridgen, A., Julien, C.: A secure modular mobile agent system. In: Proceedings of the 2006 international workshop on Software engineering for large-scale multi-agent systems (SELMAS '06), Shanghai, China, pp. 67–74. ACM Press, New York (2006)

41. Pearson, S.: How trusted computers can enhance for privacy preserving mobile applications. In: Proceedings of the 1st International IEEE WoWMoM Workshop on Trust, Security and Privacy for Ubiquitous Computing (WOWMOM '05), Taormina, Sicily, Italy, pp. 609–613. IEEE Computer Society, Washington, DC (2005)

42. Pearson, S.: Trusted agents that enhance user privacy by self-profiling. Technical Report HPL-2002-196, HP Labs, Bristol, UK (July 15, 2002)

43. Crane, S.: Privacy preserving trust agents. Technical Report HPL-2004-197, HP Labs, Bristol, UK (November 11, 2004)

44. Balfe, S., Mohammed, A.: Final fantasy — securing on-line gaming with trusted computing. In: Proceedings of the 4th International Conference on Autonomic and Trusted Computing (ATC-07), Hong Kong (July 2007)

45. Yan, Z., Cofta, Z.: A method for trust sustainability among trusted computing platforms. In: Katsikas, S.K., Lopez, J., Pernul, G. (eds.) TrustBus 2004. LNCS, vol. 3184, pp. 11–19. Springer, Heidelberg (2004)

46. Anderson, R.: Cryptography and competition policy — Issues with trusted computing. In: Proceedings of PODC '03, Boston, Massachsetts, USA, July 13-16, 2003, pp. 3–10. ACM, New York (2003)

47. Schoen, S.: Trusted computing: Promise and risk. Electronic Frontier Foundation Article (October 2003)

48. von Lohmann, F.: Meditations on trusted computing. Electronic Frontier Foundation Article (2003)

49. Reid, J., Gonzalez Nieto, J.M., Dawson, E.: Privacy and trusted computing. In: DEXA 2003, pp. 383–388. IEEE Computer Society, Los Alamitos (2003)

50. Arbaugh, B.: Improving the TCPA specification. IEEE Computer 35(8), 77–79 (2002)

51. Tygar, J., Yee, B.: Dyad: A system for using physically secure coprocessors. Technical Report CMU-CS-91-140R, Carnigie Mellon University, Pittsburgh, Pennsylvania, USA (May 1991)

52. Clark, P., Hoffman, L.: BITS: a smartcard protected operating system. Communications of the ACM 37, 66–94 (1994)

53. Arbaugh, W., Farber, D., Smith, J.: A secure and reliable bootstrap architecture. In: Proceedings of the 1997 IEEE Symposium on Security and Privacy (S&P 1997), Oakland, California, USA, pp. 65–71. IEEE Computer Society Press, Los Alamitos, California (1997)

54. Itoi, N., Arbaugh, W., Pollack, S., Reeves, D.: Personal secure booting. In: Varadharajan, V., Mu, Y. (eds.) ACISP 2001. LNCS, vol. 2119, pp. 130–141. Springer, Heidelberg (2001)

55. Lie, D.: Architectural Support for Copy and Tamper Resistant Software. PhD thesis, Department of Electrical Engineering, Stanford University, Stanford, California, USA (December 2003)

56. Lie, D., Thekkath, C., Mitchell, M., Lincoln, P., Boneh, D., Mitchell, J., Horowitz, M.: Architectural support for copy and tamper resistant software. In: Proceedings of the 9th International Conference on Architectural Support for Programming Languages and Operating Systems (ASPLOS-IX), Cambridge, Massachusetts, USA, pp. 169–177. ACM Press, New York (2000)
57. Suh, E., Clarke, D., Gassend, B., van Dyke, M., Devadas, S.: The AEGIS processor architecture for tamper–evident and tamper-resistant processing. In: 17th Annual ACM International Conference on Supercomputing (ICS'03), San Francisco, California, USA, pp. 160–171. ACM Press, New York (2003)
58. Barrett, M.F.: Towards an open trusted computing framework. Masters thesis, Department of Computer Science, The University of Auckland, New Zealand (February 2005)
59. TCG: TCG PC client specific implementation specification for conventional BIOS. TCG specification Version 1.2 Final, The Trusted Computing Group (TCG), Portland, Oregon, USA (July 2005)
60. Abraham, D., Jackson, J., Muthrasanallur, S., Neiger, G., Regnier, G., Sankaran, R., Schionas, I., Uhlig, R., Vembu, B., Wiegert, J.: Intel virtualization technology for directed i/o. Intel Technology Journal 10(3), 179–192 (2006)
61. TCG: TCG EFI platform — for TPM family 1.1 or 1.2. TCG specification Version 1.2 Final, The Trusted Computing Group (TCG), Portland, Oregon, USA (June 2006)
62. TCG: TCG Credential Profiles. TCG Specification Version 1.1 Revision 1.014 For TPM Family 1,2; Level 2, The Trusted Computing Group (TCG), Portland, Oregon, USA (May 2007)
63. Brickell, E., Camenisch, J., Chen, L.: Direct anonymous attestation. Technical Report HPL-2004-93, Hewlett-Packard Laboratories (June 2004), Available at http://www.hpl.hp.com/techreports/
64. Brickell, E., Camenisch, J., Chen, L.: Direct anonymous attestation. In: Pfitzmann, B., Liu, P. (eds.) Proceedings of CCS '04, ACM Press, pp. 132–145. ACM Press, New York (2004)
65. Brickell, E., Camenisch, J., Chen, L.: The DAA scheme in context. In: Mitchell, C.J. (ed.) Trusted Computing. IEE Professional Applications of Computing Series 6. The Institute of Electrical Engineers (IEE), London, UK, pp. 143–174 (2005)
66. TCG MPWG: Use Case Scenarios. TCG Specification Version 2.7, The Trusted Computing Group, Mobile Phone Working Group, Portland, Oregon, USA (September 2005)
67. TCG MPWG: The TCG mobile trusted module specification. TCG specification version 0.9 revision 1, The Trusted Computing Group (TCG), Portland, Oregon, USA (September 2006)
68. TCG MPWG: Mobile trusted module specification overview document. Mobile trusted module specification support documents, The Trusted Computing Group (TCG), Beaverton, Oregon, USA (2006)
69. Gallery, E.: Authorisation issues for mobile code in mobile systems. Technical Report RHUL-MA-2007-3, Department of Mathematics, Royal Holloway, University of London (2007)
70. OMA: DRM architecture v2.0. Technical Specification OMA-DRM-ARCH-V2.0-2004071515-C, The Open Mobile Alliance (OMA) (July 2004)
71. Irwin, J., Wright, T.: Digital rights management. Vodafone internal newsletter, Vodafone, Newbury, England, UK (August 2004)
72. OMA: OMA DRM V1.0 approved enabler specification. Technical Specification OMA-DRM-V1.0-20040625-A, The Open Mobile Alliance (OMA) (June 2004)

73. OMA: OMA DRM V2.0 approved enabler specification. Technical Specification OMA-ERP-DRM-V2_0-20060303-A, The Open Mobile Alliance (OMA) (July 2004)
74. OMA: Digital Rights Management v1.0. Technical Specification OMA-Download-DRM-V1_0-20040615-A, The Open Mobile Alliance (OMA) (June 2004)
75. OMA: DRM architecture specification v1.0. Technical Specification OMA-Download-ARCH-V1_0-20040625-A, The Open Mobile Alliance (OMA) (June 2004)
76. OMA: DRM specification v2.0. Technical Specification OMA-DRM-DRM-V2_0-20040716-C, The Open Mobile Alliance (OMA) (July 2004)
77. CMLA: Client adopter agreement. Technical Report Revision 1.00-050708, The Content Management License Administrator Limited Liability Company (CMLA, LLC) (August 2005)
78. Myers, M., Ankney, R., Malpani, A., Galperin, S., Adams, C.: X.509 internet public key infrastructure: Online certificate status protocol — OCSP. RFC 2560, Internet Engineering Task Force (IETF) (June 1999)
79. Mouley, M., Pautet, M.: The GSM System for Mobile Communications. Cell & Sys. Correspondence, Palaiseau, France (1992)
80. 3GPP GSM TSGS: Personalisation of mobile equipment (ME), Mobile functionality specification (release 5). Technical specification TS 22.022 v5.0.0, 3rd Generation Partnership Project (3GPP), Global System for Mobile Communications (GSM) — Technical Specification Group Services and System Aspects, Sophia Antipolis, France (2002)
81. NTT DoCoMo, IBM, Intel Corporation: Trusted Mobile Platform (May 2004)
82. OMA: Device management requirements candidate version 1.2. Technical Specification OMA-RD-DM-V1_2-20060424-C, The Open Mobile Alliance (OMA) (April 2006)
83. SDRF: Overview and definition of software download for rf reconfiguration. SDRF Archived Approved Document DL-DFN Document SDRF-02-A-0002-V.0.0, The Software Defined Radio Forum (SDRF) (August 2002)
84. Tuttlebee, W., Babb, D., Irvine, J., Martinez, G., Worrall, K.: Broadcasting and Mobile Telecommunications: Interworking — Not Convergence. EBU Technical Review 293, 1–11 (2003)
85. European Committee for Electrotechnical Standardization (CENELEC) Brussels, Belgium: Common Interface Specification for Conditional Access and other Digital Video Broadcasting Decoder Applications (February 1997)
86. European Telecommunications Standards Institute (ETSI) Sophia-Antipolis, France: Digital Video Broadcasting (DVB): Head-End Implementation of DVB Simulcrypt (January 2003)
87. European Telecommunications Standards Institute (ETSI) Sophia-Antipolis, France: Digital Video Broadcasting (DVB); Support for use of Scrambling and Conditional Access (CA) within Digital Broadcasting Systems (October 1996)
88. WAPF: Wireless transport layer security version 06. Technical Specification WAP-2610WTLS-20010406-a, The Wireless Application Protocol Forum (WAPF) (April 2001)
89. Stallings, W.: Cryptography and Network Security, Principles and Practices, 2nd edn. Prentice Hall, Upper Saddle River, New Jersey (1999)
90. Hill, R., Myagmar, S., Campbell, R.: Threat analysis of GNU software radio. In: Proceedings of the World Wireless Congress (WWC 2005), Palo Alto, California, USA (May 24-27, 2005)

91. SDRF: Security considerations for operational software defined radio devices in a commercial wireless domain. SDRF working document, The Software Defined Radio Forum (SDRF) (October 2004)

92. Gallery, E., Tomlinson, A.: Protection of downloadable software on SDR devices. In: Proceedings of the 4th Software Defined Radio Forum Technical Conference (SDR 2005), Orange County, California, USA, Software Defined Radio Forum (SDRF) (November 14-18, 2005)

93. TCG: Subject key attestation evidence extension. TCG specification version 1.0 revision 7, The Trusted Computing Group (TCG), Portland, Oregon, USA (June 2005)

Author Index

Lecture Notes in Computer Science

Sublibrary 4: Security and Cryptology

Vol. 4064: R. Büschkes, P. Laskov (Eds.), Detection of Intrusions and Malware & Vulnerability Assessment. X, 195 pages. 2006.

Vol. 4058: L.M. Batten, R. Safavi-Naini (Eds.), Information Security and Privacy. XII, 446 pages. 2006.

Vol. 4047: M. Robshaw (Ed.), Fast Software Encryption. XI, 434 pages. 2006.

Vol. 4043: A.S. Atzeni, A. Lioy (Eds.), Public Key Infrastructure. XI, 261 pages. 2006.

Vol. 4004: S. Vaudenay (Ed.), Advances in Cryptology - EUROCRYPT 2006. XIV, 613 pages. 2006.

Vol. 3995: G. Müller (Ed.), Emerging Trends in Information and Communication Security. XX, 524 pages. 2006.

Vol. 3989: J. Zhou, M. Yung, F. Bao (Eds.), Applied Cryptography and Network Security. XIV, 488 pages. 2006.

Vol. 3969: Ø. Ytrehus (Ed.), Coding and Cryptography. XI, 443 pages. 2006.

Vol. 3958: M. Yung, Y. Dodis, A. Kiayias, T.G. Malkin (Eds.), Public Key Cryptography - PKC 2006. XIV, 543 pages. 2006.

Vol. 3957: B. Christianson, B. Crispo, J.A. Malcolm, M. Roe (Eds.), Security Protocols. IX, 325 pages. 2006.

Vol. 3956: G. Barthe, B. Grégoire, M. Huisman, J.-L. Lanet (Eds.), Construction and Analysis of Safe, Secure, and Interoperable Smart Devices. IX, 175 pages. 2006.

Vol. 3935: D.H. Won, S. Kim (Eds.), Information Security and Cryptology - ICISC 2005. XIV, 458 pages. 2006.

Vol. 3934: J.A. Clark, R.F. Paige, F.A.C. Polack, P.J. Brooke (Eds.), Security in Pervasive Computing. X, 243 pages. 2006.

Vol. 3928: J. Domingo-Ferrer, J. Posegga, D. Schreckling (Eds.), Smart Card Research and Advanced Applications. XI, 359 pages. 2006.

Vol. 3919: R. Safavi-Naini, M. Yung (Eds.), Digital Rights Management. XI, 357 pages. 2006.

Vol. 3903: K. Chen, R. Deng, X. Lai, J. Zhou (Eds.), Information Security Practice and Experience. XIV, 392 pages. 2006.

Vol. 3897: B. Preneel, S. Tavares (Eds.), Selected Areas in Cryptography. XI, 371 pages. 2006.

Vol. 3876: S. Halevi, T. Rabin (Eds.), Theory of Cryptography. XI, 617 pages. 2006.

Vol. 3866: T. Dimitrakos, F. Martinelli, P.Y A Ryan, S. Schneider (Eds.), Formal Aspects in Security and Trust. X, 259 pages. 2006.

Vol. 3860: D. Pointcheval (Ed.), Topics in Cryptology – CT-RSA 2006. XI, 365 pages. 2006.

Vol. 3858: A. Valdes, D. Zamboni (Eds.), Recent Advances in Intrusion Detection. X, 351 pages. 2006.

Vol. 3856: G. Danezis, D. Martin (Eds.), Privacy Enhancing Technologies. VIII, 273 pages. 2006.

Vol. 3786: J.-S. Song, T. Kwon, M. Yung (Eds.), Information Security Applications. XI, 378 pages. 2006.

Vol. 3108: H. Wang, J. Pieprzyk, V. Varadharajan (Eds.), Information Security and Privacy. XII, 494 pages. 2004.

Vol. 2951: M. Naor (Ed.), Theory of Cryptography. XI, 523 pages. 2004.

Vol. 2742: R.N. Wright (Ed.), Financial Cryptography. VIII, 321 pages. 2003.